EARLY ENGLISH
CLASSICAL TRAGEDIES

EDITED WITH INTRODUCTION AND NOTES

BY

JOHN W. CUNLIFFE, M.A., D.Lit.

PROFESSOR OF ENGLISH IN COLUMBIA UNIVERSITY
IN THE CITY OF NEW YORK
AND ASSOCIATE DIRECTOR OF THE SCHOOL OF JOURNALISM

OXFORD
AT THE CLARENDON PRESS

1912

Republished, 1970
Scholarly Press, 22929 Industrial Drive East
St. Clair Shores, Michigan 48080

57986

Library of Congress Catalog Card Number: 71-144960
Standard Book Number 403-00913-8

HENRY FROWDE, M.A.

PUBLISHER TO THE UNIVERSITY OF OXFORD

LONDON, EDINBURGH, NEW YORK

TORONTO AND MELBOURNE

This edition is printed on a high-quality,
acid-free paper that meets specification
requirements for fine book paper referred
to as "300-year" paper

PREFACE

THIS little book includes the results of studies I began
as Shakespeare Scholar and Berkeley Fellow at the
Owens College, Manchester, resumed in the comparative
leisure of a lectureship at McGill University, Montreal,
continued in a busy quinquennium as Chairman of the
Department of English in the University of Wisconsin,
and completed as Professor of English at Columbia
University in the City of New York. In the meantime
I have printed some of my conclusions in the Publications of the Modern Language Association and elsewhere,
and the writing of the Introduction was encouraged by
an invitation to give a course of lectures on Renascence
Tragedy at Johns Hopkins University, Baltimore. For
courtesies from gentlemen connected with all the organi-
zations mentioned I am too extensively indebted for
it to be possible to mention each by name; but my
obligations to a former colleague and fellow student,
Dr. H. A. Watt, who has kindly contributed the notes
on *Gorboduc*—a play of which he has made a very
thorough study—are so considerable that I cannot let
them pass without due acknowledgement. I wish also
to thank the Earl of Ellesmere and his Librarian,
Mr. Strachan Holme, for giving me access to the unique
Bridgewater copy of *Gorboduc* (1565).

CONTENTS

INTRODUCTION

THIS is not the place to recount the glories of classical
tragedy in its original home at Athens—so ethereally brilliant,
and so soon over—

> Brief as the lightning in the collied night,
> That, in a spleen, unfolds both heaven and earth,
> And ere a man hath power to say 'Behold!'
> The jaws of darkness do devour it up.
> So quick bright things come to confusion.

Between the last great tragedy of Euripides and the advent of
Marlowe and Shakespeare to the Elizabethan stage, there seems
to be the dismal 'reign of Chaos and old Night'. But the
darkness is not really so black as it appears at first sight, and
the burst of splendour in Periclean Athens is not completely
separated from the renewed glories of Elizabethan England.
Between the two we may discern a line of dimly-glowing sparks,
never entirely disconnected from the original source of light and
heat. Seneca, who pillaged all the great masters of Greek
tragedy, may be compared to a damp and crackling torch which
gave off more smoke and sputter than warmth and brightness,
but he still served as a conveyer of the sacred fire. Born in
Cordova about 4 B.C., the son of a famous orator, he was himself rather a rhetorician than a dramatist, and the age in which
he lived was in no way favourable to dramatic production. One
does not see how the ten tragedies which pass under his name
could have been acted, for they are singularly ill-suited to stage
representation; but their hard metallic verse, brilliant antithetical dialogue, sententious commonplaces, and highly polished
lyrics no doubt commended them to the decadent literary circles
to which they were originally recited, no less than their sensa-

tional situations, keen psychological character-analysis, and sceptical philosophy allured the critics of the Renascence. Inferior in every point of art to the great Greek dramatists, of which they appear almost a Brummagem imitation, they were, in spite of these defects, and in part, indeed, because of them, better suited to the modern world, which has tried in vain to take up classical tragedy where Euripides left it and to breathe new life into the ancient form. Where Milton and Matthew Arnold failed, one need not wonder that the Renascence dramatists did not succeed, though it may be natural ground for surprise that so few of them tried to imitate the Greek model. The main reason for the common adoption of the Senecan tragedies as the standard by Renascence critics and dramatists was, no doubt, the very simple fact that they were much more familiar with Latin than with Greek ; but from an early date in the history of Renascence tragedy the Greek masters were accessible in Latin translations, and even when the humanists knew both languages, their judgement was not always in favour of Athens as against Rome. Julius Caesar Scaliger writes : ' Quatuor supersunt maximi poetae . . . quorum Seneca seorsum suas tuetur partes, quem nullo Graecorum maiestate inferiorem existimo : cultu uero ac nitore etiam Euripide maiorem.' [1] The reasons for a preference which appears to us no less extraordinary than it would have done to the Athenians at the age of Pericles are various. The very fact that Senecan tragedy was not a truly national drama gave it greater universality of appeal, and its strongly marked characteristics made it easier to imitate, even if those characteristics were defects and exaggerations. The Renascence conception of tragedy, moreover, was influenced by the ideas which had been inherited from the Middle Ages, and these it must be our first task to trace. For the present, then, we content ourselves with the general observation (of which ample proof will be given hereafter in detail), that Senecan tragedy gave the Renascence a point of departure for a new form of art, widely divergent from

[1] *Poetices* lib. 6, c. 6, p. 323 (ed. 1561).

classical tradition although indebted to it for some important details, and one all-important principle—regularity of structure —which, from all appearances, it would have taken centuries for the mediaeval drama to attain without the stimulus and authority of classical example.

THE MEDIAEVAL CONCEPTION OF TRAGEDY.

It is not surprising that, under the Roman Empire, tragedy very soon began to lose its hold on the public mind, if, indeed, it can be said ever to have had a lodging there. Even in the healthier days of the Republic, comedy, always the more popular form, had maintained its position with difficulty. On this point, the two prologues furnished by Terence to the *Hecyra* are very significant. From there we learn that when the comedy was first presented, the crowd was so uproarious in its expectation of a popular tight-rope dancer that the play could not even be heard. At the second attempt, the first Act was successfully presented ; then a report spread that the gladiators were coming, and in the confusion that ensued, owing to the rush for places, the play was driven from the stage ; it was only at the third presentation that the *Hecyra* got a quiet hearing and gained approval. Horace bears similar testimony as to the state of things in his day :

> Saepe etiam audacem fugat hoc terretque poetam
> quod numero plures, uirtute et honore minores,
> indocti stolidique et depugnare parati
> si discordet eques, media inter carmina poscunt
> aut ursum aut pugiles : his nam plebecula gaudet.[1]

Merivale in his *History of the Romans under the Empire*,[2] translating Bulenger, *De Theatro*, says that the regular drama was unable to withstand the competition of ' crowds of rope dancers, conjurors, boxers, clowns, and posture makers, men who walked on their heads, or let themselves be whirled aloft by machinery, or suspended upon wires, or who danced upon

---

[1] *Epistles*, II. i. 182–6.   [2] ch. xli.

stilts, or exhibited feats of skill with cups and balls'; these performers distracted the audience between the acts of the regular drama, which was ultimately driven to small theatres of wood temporarily erected for the purpose, or to private houses. Under these conditions it is not astonishing that the plays attributed to Seneca remain the only contribution to tragedy which has come down to us from the Roman world, and that of these no manuscript dates back further than the eleventh century,[1] though the intervening period is spanned by a few excerpts and imitations.[2] The seven genuine tragedies of Seneca were imitated after his death in the *Agamemnon*, and these eight in the *Hercules Oetaeus*, which marks a further recession from the conditions of stage representation. A further imitative attempt, the *Octavia*, is dated by Peiper and Richter, in the preface to their edition of the tragedies, as late as the fourth century ; but the ten tragedies emerged from the Middle Ages under one name. Dracontius, an imitator of Seneca who died *c.* 450, has so little notion of the tragic muse that he invites Melpomene to inspire his epic *Orestes*, which is described by him or by his copyist as a tragedy.[3] It is evident that with the lapse of years the very idea of tragedy as a dramatic form of art faded from common knowledge. When plays were no longer acted, information about the drama could be obtained in two ways—from the texts, and from general treatises. As the texts became rarer (though Terence was always read), the treatises became the chief source of knowledge. Of these the most important was one written by Evanthius, who died at Constantinople *c.* 359 ; it was included in many editions of Terence, and was used by the compilers of glosses and encyclopaedias. His knowledge of the drama was extensive and accurate ; but only a part of it was handed on by the compilers

---

[1] Sandys, *A History of Classical Scholarship*, vol. i, p. 628.
[2] R. Peiper, *Rheinisches Museum für Philologie, n. f.* (1877), vol. xxxii, pp. 532-7.
[3] See Cloetta, *Komödie und Tragödie im Mittelalter*. This and Creizenach, *Geschichte des neueren Dramas*, vol. i, are my main authorities for this part of the subject.

who copied from him. The sentence on which they mainly relied was the following :

Inter tragoediam autem et comoediam cum multa tum inprimis hoc distat, quod in comoedia mediocres fortunae hominum, parui impetus periculorum laetique sunt exitus actionum, at in tragoedia omnia contra, ingentes personae, magni timores, exitus funesti habentur ; et illic prima turbulenta, tranquilla ultima, in tragoedia contrario ordine res aguntur ; tum quod in tragoedia fugienda uita, in comoedia capessenda exprimitur ; postremo quod omnis comoedia de fictis est argumentis, tragoedia saepe de historia fide petitur.[1]

This contrast between tragedy and comedy runs through almost all the mediaeval compilations, and has had its influence down to our own day. Another book of very general reference was the *Consolatio Philosophiae* of Boethius (d. 525), who mentions and quotes from Euripides, and also mentions Seneca, whose metres he copies ; he has also the following passage (*Consolatio* II, prose 2, 36–40 Teubner text) :

Quid tragoediarum clamor aliud deflet nisi indiscreto ictu fortunam felicia regna uertentem ? Nonne adulescentulus δοιοὺς πίθους, τὸν μὲν ἕνα κακῶν, τὸν δὲ ἕτερον ἐάων in Iouis limine iacere didicisti ?

Isidore of Seville (d. 636) is still on the right track He says in his *Etymologiae* (XVIII. xlv) :

Tragoedi sunt qui antiqua gesta atque facinora sceleratorum regum luctuoso carmine, spectante populo, concinebant.

But he includes Horace, Persius, and Juvenal among the writers of comedy, and it is not until five centuries later (Honorius of Autun, d. 1140) that we find Lucan cited as the representative of tragedy A Munich gloss of the tenth century, however, gives *Tragoedia luctuosum carmen*—a definition evidently extracted from the passage from Isidore above—and this is expanded by Notker Labeo (d. 1022), in his commentary on the passage from Boethius already quoted, into the statement that tragedies are *luctuosa carmina*, written by Sophocles *apud grecos, de euersionibus regnorum et urbium* ; he says, moreover, that he does

[1] Teubner edition of Donatus, p. 21.

not know whether there were any Latin tragic writers.   From this it is but a step to the ignorance of Johannes Anglicus de Garlandia, who in his *Poetria* (*c.* 1260) says :

Unica uero tragoedia scripta fuit quondam ab Ouidio apud Latinos, que sepulta sub silentio non uenit in usum. hec est secunda tragoedia, cuius proprietates diligenter debent notari.

He proceeds to give this second tragedy of his own composition, first in prose, and then in 126 hexameter lines :

In a besieged city there were sixty soldiers, divided into two companies, each of which had a washerwoman, who served them for other ends beside washing.   One of the washerwomen fell in love with a soldier in the company of her colleague, who resented the invasion of her rights, and a quarrel between the two women resulted.   One night the offended washerwoman found the faithless pair together, and put them both to the sword.   In order to conceal her crime, she secretly admitted the enemy to the besieged city.   All the garrison were slain, including a brother of the revengeful washerwoman.

Upon this Johannes makes the following comment :

Huius tragoediae proprietates sunt tales : graui stilo describitur, pudibunda proferuntur et scelerata, incipit a gaudio et in lacrimis terminatur.

The main point about this conception of tragedy is, of course, the fact that the idea of acting as a necessary element has entirely disappeared.   The same was true of comedy, so that Dante, writing of the Comedy which all men have called divine, in his letter to Can Grande (*c.* 1316–17) says:

Libri Titulus est : Incipit COMOEDIA Dantis Alligherii, Florentini natione, non moribus.   Ad cuius notitiam sciendum est quod *Comoedia* dicitur a *comos* idest *uilla* et *oda* quod est *cantus* unde *Comoedia* quasi *Villanus Cantus*.   Et est Comoedia genus quoddam poeticae narrationis, ab omnibus aliis differens.   Differt ergo a tragoedia in materia per hoc, quod tragoedia in principio est admirabilis et quieta, in fine siue exitu est foetida et horribilis : et dicitur propter hoc a *tragos* quod est *hircus* et *oda* quasi *cantus hircinus* idest foetidus ad modum hirci ut patet per Senecam in suis Tragoediis.[1]

Some of Dante's commentators, Francesco da Buti, for instance, carry their etymological vagaries much further, but it is enough here to remember that Boccaccio uses the word tragedy in the sense of a narrative with a sad ending. So does Chaucer, translating the passage from Boethius, *Consolatio*, thus :

What other thing biwailen the cryinges of tragedies but only the dedes of Fortune, that with an unwar stroke overtorneth realmes of grete nobley ? ... GLOSE. *Tragedie is to seyn, a ditee of a prosperitee for a tyme, that endeth in wrecchednesse* ... Lernedest nat thou *in Greke*, when thou were yonge, that in the entree, *or in the celere*, of Iupiter, ther ben couched two tonnes ; that on is ful of good, that other is ful of harm ?

In the *Canterbury Tales*, the Monk, who has a hundred tragedies in his cell, gives the following definition :

> Tragedie is to seyn a certeyn storie,
> As olde bokes maken us memorie,
> Of him that stood in greet prosperitee
> And is y-fallen out of heigh degree
> Into miserie, and endeth wrecchedly.
> And they ben versifyed comunly
> Of six feet, which men clepe *exametron*.
> In prose eek been endyted many oon,
> And eek in metre, in many a sondry wyse.

He accordingly begins, ' I wol biwale in maner of Tragedie,' and ends his stories of misfortune with the words : *Explicit Tragedia*. The following passage from *Troilus and Criseyde* (Bk. V, st. 256) is even more significant on account of the classical models referred to in the last line :

> Go, litel book, go litel myn tregedie,
> Ther god thy maker yet, er that he dye,

---

[1] Ep. X, sec. 10. Even if the doubts which have been thrown on the authenticity of this letter should be justified, its value as an indication of the current opinion of the time would still hold.

> So sende might to make in som comedie!
> But litel book, no making thou n'envye,
> But subgit be to alle poesye;
> And kis the steppes, wher-as thou seest pace
> Virgile, Ovyde, Omer, Lucan, and Stace.

Through Lydgate this mediaeval tradition passes on to the *Mirror for Magistrates* and the age of Elizabeth.

A Curious Error.

When the information of the mediaeval commentators is more definite, it is not, as a rule, more accurate. John of Salisbury (d. 1180) should be mentioned as an honourable exception, for his chapter *De histrionibus* &c. (*Polycraticus* I. viii) shows a remarkable freedom from the usual misconception as to the way in which classical drama was acted. But from the tenth century onwards there was a growing agreement, even among the commentators of Terence, that a play was recited by a single actor, sometimes identified with the dramatist. This misconception possibly arose, as Creizenach suggests, from a misunderstanding of the passages in Livy (VII. ii) and in Valerius Maximus (II. iv), in which it is stated that the Roman actor, Livius Andronicus, on account of the weakness of his voice, had the *cantica* of comedy sung for him by a boy whom he accompanied with appropriate gestures, and that this came to be a practice on the Roman stage. Livy says clearly enough : *Inde ad manum cantari histrionibus coeptum diuerbiaque tantum ipsorum uoci relicta.* Evanthius, too, is clear on this point : *Deuerbia histriones pronuntiabant.*[1] But the later scribes did not understand Evanthius, as is shown by the readings *de umbia* and *de umbra*, and the definition in Osbern, *Pannormia* : *Deuerbium, canticum quod ante mortuum canitur.* Isidore is less clear than Evanthius, and it was perhaps from a misunderstanding of his statements, rather than from a negligent reading of Livy (for the mediaeval commentators

[1] p. 30, *u. s.*

rarely consulted the classical authorities) that the misconception
arose. He says (XVIII. xliii):

Scaena autem erat locus infra theatrum in modum domus instructa
cum pulpito, qui pulpitus orchestra uocabatur, ubi cantabant comici,
tragici, atque saltabant histriones et mimi.

Another passage (quoted below) makes it clear that Isidore
understood that the *orchestra* or *pulpitum* was a place for
dialogue, but it is significant that this crucial sentence is
omitted by Papias, *Elementarium doctrinae erudimentum* (1053).
Isidore says under *orchestra* (XVIII. xliv):

Orchestra autem pulpitus erat scenae ubi saltator agere
posset, aut duo inter se disputare. Ibi enim poetae comoedi et
tragoedi ad certamen conscendebant, hisque canentibus, alii gestus
edebant.

This last sentence, in which Isidore perhaps had in mind the
cantica only, might easily cause confusion by being referred to
the play as a whole. In any case we find Papias defining
scaena as *umbraculum ubi poetae recitabant*, and *orchestra* as *ubi
cantabant et psallebant histriones et mimi*. We have the misconception evidently well established in the *Catholicon* (1286)
of Johannes Januensis, who defines *scaena* thus ·

Umbraculum, locus obumbratus in theatro et cortinis coopertus
similis tabernis mercennariorum, quae sunt asseribus et cortinis
coopertae . . . In illo umbraculo latebant personae laruatae quae ad
uocem recitatoris exibant ad gestus faciendos.

and *mimus*:

Ioculator et proprie rerum humanarum imitator, sicut olim erant
in recitatione comoediarum, quia quod uerbo recitator dicebat,
mimi motu corporis exprimebant.

The commentators of Terence added to the confusion by an odd
mistake, whereby Calliopius, a copyist who signed his name to
a manuscript of the comedies, was elevated into a personal
friend of the dramatist, and the contemporary exponent of his
plays on the stage. The Vita Oxoniensis so describes him, and
we find him so pictured, in a box with a book in his hand, in
the later Terence manuscripts. The legend thus evolved was

handed down from one compiler to another, and gathered detail in its course. A Terence commentary ascribed to the eleventh century gives the following :

Illud etiam animaduertendum, has fabulas non ab ipso recitatas esse in scena, sed a Calliopio clarissimo uiro satisque erudito, cui ipse praecipue adhaerebat cuiusque ope sustentabatur et auctoritate audiebatur. Modulator autem harum Fabularum fuit Flaccus ; quotiescunque enim recitabantur, erat modulator et alii, qui gestu corporis eosdem affectus agebant.[1]

Nicholas Trivet or Treveth (*c.* 1260–1330) an English Dominican who edited Seneca's tragedies, explains in the introduction to the *Hercules Furens* that in a little house in the theatre, called *scena*, the prologue of the play was read, while a *mimus* with gestures imitated the angry Juno. It is apparently upon this comment that the following passage in the Commentary on Dante's *Divine Comedy* by his son Pietro was based :

Libri titulus est Comoedia Dantis Allegherii, et quare sic uocetur aduerte. Antiquitus in theatro, quod erat area semicircularis, et in eius medio erat domuncula, quae scaena dicebatur, in qua erat pulpitum, et super id ascendebat poeta ut cantor, et sua carmina ut cantiones recitabat. Extra uero erant mimi, id est, ioculatores, carminum pronuntiationem gestu corporis effigiantes per adaptationem ad quemlibet ex cuius persona ipse poeta loquebatur ; unde cum loquebatur, pone de Iunone conquerente de Hercule priuigno suo, mimi, sicut recitabat, ita effigiabant Iunonem inuocare furias infernales ad infestandum ipsum Herculem ; et si tale pulpitum seu domunculam ascendebat poeta qui de more uillico caneret, talis cantus dicebatur comoedia.

Lydgate, in the *Troy Book* (1412–20), set forth the matter with his usual prolixity. The hint upon which he spoke was a remark in the *Historia Trojana* of Guido delle Colonne that tragedies and comedies are said to have been first acted at Troy. Lydgate expands this into the following (II. 842–926) :

> And first also, I rede, þat in Troye
> Wer song and rad lusty fresche comedies,
> And oþer dites, þat called be tragedies.

---

[1] Terence, ed. Westerhovius (1726), vol. i, p. xxxiii.

And to declare, schortly in sentence,
Of boþe two þe final difference :
A comedie hath in his gynnyng,
At prime face, a maner compleynyng,
And afterward endeth in gladnes ;
And it þe dedis only doth expres
Of swiche as ben in pouert plounged lowe ;
But tragidie, who so list to knowe,
It begynneth in prosperite,
And endeth euer in aduersite ;
And it also doth þe conquest trete
Of riche kynges and of lordys grete,
Of myȝty men and olde conquerou[ri]s,
Whiche by fraude of Fortunys schowris
Ben ouercast and whelmed from her glorie

Of a Theatyre stondynge in þe princypale paleys of Troye,
declarenge the falle of Pryncys and othere.

And whilon þus was halwed þe memorie
Of tragedies, as bokis make mynde,
Whan þei wer rad or songyn, as I fynde,
In þe theatre þer was a smal auter
Amyddes set, þat was half circuler,
Whiche in-to þe Est of custom was directe ;
Vp-on þe whiche a pulpet was erecte,
And þer-in stod an aw[n]cien poete,
For to reherse by rethorikes swete
Þe noble dedis, þat wer historial,
Of kynges, princes for a memorial,
And of þes olde, worþi Emperours,
Þe grete emprises eke of conquerours,
And how þei gat in Martis hiȝe honour
Þe laurer grene for fyn of her labour,
Þe palme of knyȝthod disservid by [old] date,
Or Parchas made hem passyn in-to fate.
And after þat, with chere and face pale,
With stile enclyned gan to turne his tale,
And for to synge, after al her loos,
Ful mortally þe stroke of Antropos,
And telle also, for al her worþihede,
Þe sodeyn brekyng of her lives threde :

How pitously þei made her mortal ende
Þoruȝ fals Fortune, þat al þe world wil schende,
And howe þe fyn of al her worþines
Endid in sorwe and [in] hiȝe tristesse,
By compassyng of fraude or fals tresoun,
By sodeyn mordre or vengaunce of poysoun,
Or conspiringe of fretyng fals envye,
How vnwarly [þat] þei dide dye ;
And how her renoun and her hiȝe fame
Was of hatrede sodeynly made lame ;
And how her honour drowe vn-to decline ;
And þe meschef of her vnhappy fyne ;
And how Fortune was to hem vnswete—
Al þis was tolde and rad of þe poete.
And whil þat he in þe pulpit stood,
With dedly face al devoide of blood,
Singinge his dites, with muses al to-rent,
Amydde þe theatre schrowdid in a tent,
Þer cam out men gastful of her cheris,
Disfigurid her facis with viseris,
Pleying by signes in þe peples siȝt,
Þat þe poete songon hath on hiȝt ;
So þat þer was no maner discordaunce
Atwen his dites and her contenaunce :
For lik as he aloft[e] dide expresse
Wordes of Ioye or of heuynes,
Meving and cher, byneþe of hem pleying,
From point to point was alwey answering—
Now trist, now glad, now hevy, and [now] liȝt,
And face chaunged with a sodeyn siȝt,
So craftily þei koude hem transfigure,
Conformyng hem to þe chaunt[e]plure,
Now to synge and sodeinly to wepe,
So wel þei koude her observaunces kepe ;
And þis was doon in April and in May,
Whan blosmys new, boþe on busche and hay,
And flouris fresche gynne for to springe ;
And þe briddis in þe wode synge
With lust supprised of þe somer sonne,
Whan þe[se] pleies in Troye wer begonne,

And in theatre halowed and y-holde.
And þus þe ryyt [of] tragedies olde,
Priamus þe worþi kyng began.
Of þis mater no more telle I can.

It is curious that this misconception should have continued after the miracle plays began to be acted, but Creizenach says that the parallel between classical and mediaeval drama was first suggested in 1204 in connexion with the Riga Prophet Play (*ludus quem Latini comoediam uocant*), and that explanations of passages in the classics by allusions to the religious drama were exceedingly rare. He quotes one such instance from a commentary on the *Ars Poetica* of Horace, dating from the eleventh or twelfth century. The translation into Latin by Hermannus Alemannus in 1267 of the commentary by Averroes on the Poetics of Aristotle did not help matters much. Averroes had as little experience of the drama as the mediaeval monk; he takes tragedy to be the art of inspiring men to good deeds by exhibiting to them examples of virtue, and the illustrations he gives are taken from the Old Testament—the story of Joseph and his brethren, and of the sacrifice of Isaac.

THE SENECA REVIVAL.

So far as tragedy was concerned, the ages we have been discussing were, indeed, dark. Light began to break with the increasing knowledge of the classics, for Seneca was one of the first authors to be studied in the classical revival with which we associate the earlier Renascence. About the middle of the thirteenth century Vincent of Beauvais[1] refers to Seneca's ten tragedies, and gives a long list of quotations from them, though it is doubtful whether the selection was made from a full text, or merely from another compilation. The first step towards a better knowledge of Seneca was taken early in the fourteenth century by the English Dominican already mentioned, Nicholas Treveth, who edited and commented upon the tragedies at the

---

[1] *Speculum maius triplex*, vol. i, bk. 8, chaps. 102 and 113.

instance of Cardinal Niccolò Albertini di Prato, one of the leading figures of the papal court at Avignon.[1] Treveth's commentary became well known in Europe, especially in Italy, some indication of its influence upon the interpreters of Dante having been already given. We have seen too that Seneca's tragedies were known to Dante himself, as they were also to Petrarch and Boccaccio. But it was at Padua that the most notable stimulus was given to Senecan studies. Here Lovato de' Lovati (d. 1309) discussed Seneca's metres, and his friend, Albertino Mussato, wrote, in avowed imitation of Seneca, a Latin tragedy, *Ecerinis*, for which, on December 3, 1315, he was crowned with laurel in the presence of the university and citizens, and given the cognomen Mussatus, 'quasi musis aptus.'[2] The *Ecerinis* has been regarded by all historians of the modern drama as an event of capital importance; it was at once furnished with an elaborate commentary by two of the author's fellow citizens, and in recent times has been honoured by a worthy edition, including a careful study by the poet Carducci. Every commentator brings out what, indeed, the author himself was quick to acknowledge—his indebtedness to Seneca. The imitation is most marked in the metres used and in the copying of particular passages; in the adoption of Senecan structure, Mussato is less successful. He obviously aims at Seneca's division into five acts, each followed by a chorus, but he overlooked Seneca's practice of concentrating the action about some critical event. The tragedy deals with that tyrant of Padua, Ezzelino III, who died the year before Albertino was born; and the action covers a period of at least

---

[1] An interesting correspondence between the cardinal and the scholar on the subject of this literary undertaking is preserved in the Treveth MSS. in the Bibliothèque Nationale and the Vatican Library. It is summarized by Creizenach, i. 488, and given in full by Peiper, *De Senecae tragoediarum lectione vulgata*, Breslau, 1893.

[2] For an account of the honours paid to Mussato on this occasion and on subsequent anniversaries, see Scardeonius, *De Urbis Patavii Antiquitate et Claris Civibus Pataviis*, in Graevius, *Thesaurus*, vol. vi, pt. 3, 259–60. Mussato also refers to them frequently in his epistles. See Tiraboschi, vol. v, bk. 2, chap. 6, par. 28, and Burckhardt (translated by Middlemore), p. 141.

forty-six years. It is significant that the division into acts, which is given in the printed edition, does not occur in any of the manuscripts, and that the contemporary commentators divide the poem into three books. It was read, not acted, and was written with the former purpose in the author's mind, for he has introduced a narrative passage five lines long (86–90) to describe the descent of Ezzelino to the lowest part of the castle for an infernal invocation—the one definite indication of place in the tragedy, for generally the scene is left absolutely uncertain. It is noteworthy, as Carducci points out, that Mussato calls his tragedy *Ecerinis*, and not by the name of the principal character, Ecerinus, and that he compares it to the *Thebais* of Statius, which was also, he believes, recited on the stage. Evidently the author was greatly influenced by some of the mediaeval conceptions of tragedy then current, and it is partly for this reason that, in spite of his close imitation of his chosen model, the tragedy lacks some of the characteristic Senecan features. It has horrors enough and no little rhetoric, but it lacks Seneca's combination of extreme tension of sensational interest with elaborate descriptive passages or brilliant antithetical dialogue; in structure, too, it is deficient, judged by the Senecan, or, indeed, by any other standard.

The tragedy may be outlined as follows :—In the opening scene Adelaide (Adelheita) reveals to her sons, Ecerinus and Albricus, the secret of their infernal origin; far from being terrified at the news, Ecerinus is overjoyed to know that Satan was his father, and hastens to the lowest part of the castle to invoke his help. The chorus moralizes on the evils of ambition. A breathless messenger next informs the chorus of the battles between Azo of Este with Richard, Count Boniface, on one side, and Ecerinus with Salinguerra on the other. Ecerinus has subjected Verona by treachery and Padua by bribery. He now holds the sceptre, and his reign is marked by fire, crucifixion, imprisonment, exile, and the direst tortures. The chorus, addressing Christ sitting on the right hand of his Father on high, elaborates into some fifty lines the much-admired Senecan rhetoric of *Phaedra* 679-680:

Magne regnator deum,
tam lentus audis scelera, tam lentus uides?

Ecerinus sets forth to his brother his ambitious plans: Verona, Vicenza, and Padua have already submitted to him; he has the promise of Lombardy, and he proposes to extend his conquests to the East, even if he has to attack heaven itself, from which his father fell. Albricus has no less ambitious designs in the north, and they agree to profess enmity of each other, the better to carry out their schemes. Ziramons enters to report the execution of Monaldus and the public apathy at his death. Ecerinus exults in the prospect of unrestrained slaughter. Frater Lucas argues that all things are subject to the law of God, and he who would obey God's law should cultivate Faith, Hope, and Charity. ' Does God on high see these things that I am doing?' asks Ecerinus. The brother replies that He does. 'Will He restrain me when He wishes to?'—'He will.' ' Then, why does He delay?' asks Ecerinus, and goes on to argue that he is an instrument in the hand of God, like Nebuchadnezzar, Pharaoh, Alexander, and Nero, a scourge of the nations for their crimes. A messenger comes to announce the loss of Padua, and is rewarded for his evil tidings by having his foot cut off; Ansedisius, the representative of Ecerinus at Padua, who confirms the news of its capture, is punished by horrible tortures. The soldiers of Ecerinus address him and exhort him to undertake the siege of Padua. The chorus describes the siege, and the slaughter by Ecerinus of 11,000 innocent prisoners. Ecerinus announces his abandonment of the siege, and his departure for the East. A messenger describes his defeat and death at a ford of the Adua. The chorus gives thanks to God. A messenger then describes the death of Albricus and his wife and children, and the play ends with an appeal on the part of the chorus to the righteous to observe the everlasting law.

That the *Ecerinis* was widely circulated is proved by the numerous manuscripts that have survived, including four in English libraries—one at Holkham, Norfolk, one in the Bodleian, and two in the British Museum. One of the last was copied, along with the tragedies of Seneca, by Coluccio Salutati (1331–1406), the Florentine Chancellor, who took a keen interest in Senecan study. As early as 1371 he questioned the identity of the philosopher with the tragedian, and pointed out that the *Octavia* cannot be his. This led to a lively discussion of the authorship of the tragedies among the humanists of the time, some record of which will be found in Francesco Novati's notes to the *Epistolario* of Coluccio Salutati (published in *Fonti per la Storia d'Italia*, vol. 1, pp. 150–5). He appears to have stimulated Antonio Loschi of Verona about 1387 to write the second Latin tragedy of the early Renascence, the *Achilleis*, which was influenced by the *Ecerinis* as well as by Seneca, whom Loschi succeeds in imitating more closely. Before 1429 came another imitation, the *Progne* of Gregorio Corraro, a pupil of Vittorino da Feltre at Mantua, the material being taken from Ovid and cast into the mould of Seneca's *Thyestes*, which the author acknowledges as his model. By this time Seneca was being lectured upon and translated, and the way to a knowledge of the plays was made easy. A closer knowledge of the texts, together with the study of classical architecture, removed the misconceptions as to the way in which the drama was acted, though some of them died hard, for we find Erasmus saying in his *Adagia* (2nd ed. 1513), in explanation of the phrase, *Nihil ad uersum*:

Translatum uidetur a scena, ubi histrio saltatu gestuque carminis genus repraesentat. Et haud scio an alius fuerit qui recitaret uersus, alius qui gesticularetur. Apparet enim unum aliquem fuisse recitatorem, cuius est illa uox in calce comoediarum: Calliopius recensui.

The leader in the movement at Rome for the revival of classical culture was Pomponius Laetus (1427–97). His biographer and contemporary, Marcus Antonius Sabellicus, says:

Pari studio ueterem spectandi consuetudinem desuetae ciuitati restituit, primorum antistitum atriis pro theatro usus, in quibus Plauti, Terentii, recentiorum etiam quaedam agerentur fabulae, quas ipse honestos adolescentes et docuit et agentibus praefuit.

The young Inghirami (b. 1470), who took part in these representations, distinguished himself so much in the performance of Seneca's *Phaedra* that the name of Fedra was given him by his admiring companions, and borne by his family long after they had forgotten its origin. One of the patrons who made these classical revivals possible was Cardinal Raffaele Riario, and it was in the court of his palace that the *Phaedra* was acted. Sulpicius Verulanus, in dedicating his edition of Vitruvius to the Cardinal, speaks of the performance as taking place *in media circi cavea*, which seems to imply that the spectators sat in a circle round the performers : he also refers to a *scena picturata*, but as the play was acted under a tent this can hardly mean the introduction of painted scenery. The illustrations to the editions of Terence make it clear that more accurate notions as to the performance of the classical drama now prevailed. Jodocus Badius (1462–1535) in his *Praenotamenta* gives a perfectly clear and reasonable account (Ch. ix) :

Intra igitur theatrum ab una parte opposita spectatoribus erant scenae et proscenia, i.e. loca lusoria ante scenas facta. Scenae autem erant quaedam umbracula seu absconsoria, in quibus abscondebantur lusores, donec exire deberent, ante autem scenas erant quaedam tabulata, in quibus personae quae exierant ludebant.

CAMMELLI'S *Filostrato e Panfila*.

Jacobus Volaterranus in his *Diarium Romanum* (1482) says : *fuerunt* . . . *qui comoedias actitarunt, veterum mores et arte imitantes ;* [1] but the real centre of dramatic activity in Italy, and indeed in Europe, for the next half century was Ferrara. As early as 1444 there had been acted at the Carnival a Latin dialogue in elegiacs—the *Isis* of Francesco Ariosto, which was introduced by the inevitable Calliopius. Politian's *Orfeo* was acted at Mantua in 1471, but it belongs to the history of pastoral rather than to the history of tragedy. The first play in the vernacular to which the latter name can fairly be given—and it calls itself a tragedy—is the *Filostrato e Panfila* of Antonio Cammelli, commonly called il Pistoia, which was acted at Ferrara in 1499. In addition to the important fact that it is the first Italian tragedy, it has the further claim that it represents an important

---

[1] Muratori, xxiii, 162.

class of early plays, called by the historians of Italian literature *drammi mescolati*, in which the method of the *sacre rappresentazioni* is combined with classical influences. Cammelli's play is introduced by the ghost of Seneca, as the ghost of Tantalus opens Seneca's *Thyestes*; we have Seneca's five acts separated by choruses, and a few passages imitated from Seneca; but in the main, it is clear that the author is endeavouring to apply the method he had observed in the religious drama to his own story, which is taken from the first novel of the fourth day of Boccaccio's *Decamerone*. This admirable tragic material is handled by the dramatist with very slight skill, as will be seen from the following outline:

After Seneca has set forth the argument, he introduces Demetrio, King of Thebes, and his daughter, Panfila, widow of the Duke of Athens. Demetrio expatiates on the vanity of all earthly things, and says that if it were not for honour he would resign his crown; she is fortunate in that she has no husband to lord it over her. He invites his daughter to reply to this proposition, which he has made merely to pass the time and to give opportunity for reflection. She excuses herself on account of her youth and lack of experience, but advises him to live in pleasure as long as he can—songs, instrumental music, balls, feasts, and games. Somewhat to our surprise, from the tone of Demetrio's first speech, he commends his daughter's advice and proceeds to eulogize one of his servants, the young Filostrato, who although low born, shows real nobility of character. He ends with a description of the coming of spring and advises his daughter to go to dinner, for he knows that her appetite increases as his diminishes, and it is dinner time. Apparently, however, it is Demetrio who goes off and Panfila who remains to set forth her love for Filostrato; but as marriage is out of the question for her on account of her father's opposition, she concludes that a good lover is really to be preferred. The act closes with the praises of love, sung by the chorus, and acknowledged by Love himself.

Act II is opened by Filostrato in love; at the request of Demetrio he has given Panfila two roses. These she now returns to him and tells him that she has bound them with a golden thread; she asks him to bring two fresh ones bound with the same thread. (This is

the dramatist's substitute for the hollow reed in which Boccaccio's
heroine conceals her first letter.) Filostrato is overjoyed at Panfila's
invitation to visit her ; only two things distress him, he has not
a friend to whom to confide his bliss, and he does not know the cave
by which he is to gain access to her chamber. Both these defects
are supplied by Tindaro, a discontented courtier (added by the
dramatist) ; after reading the letter from Panfila which Filostrato
shows him, Tindaro reveals the secret of the cave, hoping to revenge
himself on the king by the dishonour of his daughter. Four sirens
sing a chorus on the variability of fortune.

In Act III Filostrato recounts the happy issue of his enterprise
to Tindaro, who advises prudence. Demetrio then enters and
explains, in soliloquy, that he has seen with his own eyes the dishonour of his daughter. Pandero, his secretary, is disturbed because
he has seen in a dream two harpies defile the palace and surround
it with blood. Demetrio calls him within to confide to him the cause
of his distress, and Pandero sees that his dream will come true.
Tindaro flees for fear of the revelation of his guilt. The three Fates
elaborate the commonplace : 'Ciascun nasce per morire.'

In Act IV Pandero, having given orders, according to the king's
command, for the capture of Filostrato at the cave, advises Demetrio
to marry the two lovers, but the king is bent upon vengeance.
Filostrato replies briefly to his reproaches, but does not repent.
Panfila repeats (though in sadly mutilated guise) the defiance of
Boccaccio's heroine in the same situation. Demetrio decides on
the death of Filostrato, and Atropos and the chorus lament :
' Ciascun mal sempre è punito.'

Act V begins with the report to Pandero of the execution of
Filostrato, whose heart has been torn out of his body by order of
the king. The heart is delivered by the executioner to Demetrio,
who sends it to his daughter with the same message as we find in
Boccaccio. Panfila, who has foreseen Filostrato's fate in a vision,
makes the same lament over her lover's heart, except that the
dramatist, in turning the prose of the novel into *terza rima*, some-
how robs the words of all dignity and all passion. Panfila sends
for poison, takes it, and dies on the stage, requesting her father
to lay her body beside that of her lover. Demetrio repents of his
rashness, and gives orders accordingly to Pandero, who closes the
play with the traditional request for applause.

La Sofonisba.

Filostrato e Panfila was followed by other dramas of the same type, the most notable being Galeotto del Carretto's *Sofonisba* (wr. 1502, pr. 1546). This follows even more frankly than the older play the method of the mediaeval drama, Livy being substituted for the Holy Scriptures and versified in the measure of the *sacre rappresentazioni* (*ottava rima*) with about the same degree of fidelity to the original. There is, indeed, a chorus, but it is used often in the same way as Shakespeare employed it later in *Henry V*, to set forth changes of scene, which in this *Sofonisba* are many and various. The play begins before the marriage of Sophonisba to Syphax, and omits no detail of Livy's history, to which little is added except commonplace reflections and the elaboration of stock situations. Liguori in his *La Tragedia Italiana* suggests that this *Sofonisba* may have been made known, through Isabella Gonzaga, to whom it was dedicated, to Gian Giorgio Trissino, who in his *Sofonisba* has dealt with the story in a very different way; indeed beyond a comparison of Sophonisba to Helen of Troy, which might have occurred to any one, there is nothing common to the two tragedies which is not to be found in Livy.

Trissino's Sophonisba begins, according to the classical convention, with a long account of past events to her confidante and sister, Erminia. Opening with a reference to the story of Dido, she passes rapidly over the sixteen years that Hannibal has spent in Italy, and comes to her own fortunes and those of her father, Hasdrubal, who, in order to detach Syphax, king of the Numidians, from a threatened league with the Romans, gave her to him to wife, in spite of having previously promised her to Massinissa. The latter thus became the mortal enemy of Hasdrubal and Syphax, and fought a successful campaign against them in Africa with Scipio. They are now at Cirta, and expecting a new attack that very day, which she fears they will be unable to resist, for if the veterans could not stand against Massinissa and the Romans, what can raw recruits do? Moreover, she has been terrified, just before dawn, by a fearful dream. In a dark wood, she appeared to be surrounded by dogs and shepherds who had taken and bound her husband; fearing their impious fury, she turned to a shepherd, and implored his protection ; he opened his arms to her, but in his embrace she heard such a fierce barking that she withdrew from him into a dark cave, to which he pointed her, as a refuge. Erminia advises her to pray to God, and she withdraws for this purpose, while the chorus lament her misfortunes. A messenger brings word of the defeat of the Numidians and the capture of Syphax by Massinissa. A second messenger gives further details of the discomfiture, and upon his heels follows Massinissa, to whom Sophonisba appeals for protection against the Romans. Massinissa, after hearing her plea, swears to her that she shall not pass into the control of the Romans while life is in his body ; she expresses her gratitude, and Massinissa withdraws with her into the palace to consider the means of fulfilling his promise, while the chorus hail the celestial ray of the sun. At the end of the chorus, Laelius enters and asks the women what has happened ; while they are in conversation, a messenger comes out of the palace and reports that Massinissa has just married Sophonisba, in order to save her from falling into the power of the Romans. Massinissa comes out, and is reproached by Laelius for his conduct ; he pleads that Sophonisba was espoused to him before she became the wife of Syphax. Laelius urges him to give her up, and when he refuses, orders his soldiers to seize her ; Massinissa forbids them to enter the palace, and there is danger of a serious conflict when Cato comes in and suggests that the whole matter should be submitted to Scipio. The chorus having expressed the wish that all will yet be well, Scipio enters and asks for the prisoners. In answer to his question, Syphax tells him that the cause of his rebellion was Sophonisba, and his one comfort is that she will ruin Massinissa, as she ruined him. Scipio determines to separate Massinissa from her, and after sending for him warns him of the danger of giving way to passion. Massinissa argues that Helen was restored to Menelaus at the end of the Trojan war, although she had been away from her husband for twenty years, and why should he not have Sophonisba? Scipio replies that Helen was a wife, Sophonisba merely a promised bride, and that Massinissa has acted most improperly in marrying her in the midst of the campaign, without asking the consent of the Roman Senate. Massinissa replies that he will endeavour to keep his promise to Sophonisba without breaking his obligations to the Roman people. After a chorus on the might of Love, a messenger announces that

Massinissa has not been able to save Sophonisba ; a second messenger announces that she has taken poison, which Massinissa sent to her, not being able in any other way to save her from the Romans. Sophonisba then comes in lamenting her fate to Erminia, to whom she commits her little son. Massinissa, who enters immediately after her death, expresses regret for the haste with which he has acted, and sends Erminia away by night in the hope that this will be pleasing to the shade of Sophonisba. The chorus ends the play with moral reflections on the vanity of mortal expectations.

Trissino, it is obvious, adopted the Greek model ; he has not Seneca's division into five acts, and he has endeavoured to imitate particular passages from Sophocles' *Antigone* and Euripides' *Iphigenia in Aulis* and *Alcestis*. But not being a Sophocles or a Racine, he has not the skill to adapt his material to the strict requirements of the Greek form. The opening narrative of Sophonisba is clumsily managed, and the events are crowded, with obvious improbability, within the one day limit ; the device of the messenger is overdone, and when the heroine should touch our hearts, she subsides into commonplaces. But, as the pioneer of the new school, Trissino received praise which was sometimes deserved, and sometimes exaggerated. His principal successor, Giraldi, says of him :

> El Trissino gentil che col suo canto
> Prima d'ognun dal Tebro e da l'Iliso
> Già trasse la Tragedia a l'onde d'Arno.

Niccolò Rossi of Vicenza, discoursing of *Sofonisba* to the Olympic Academy there in 1590, gave it the first place among modern tragedies, and held it superior even to the *Oedipus Tyrannus* of Sophocles. In the use of unrhymed verse (*endecasillabi sciolti*) he was also a pioneer. Galeotto del Carretto, it is true, had used this measure for short passages in his *Sofonisba*, but it was Trissino who employed it for all except the lyrical parts of tragedy and established its usage on the tragic stage. 'Voi foste il primo,' says Palla Rucellai, 'che questo modo di scrivere in versi materni, liberi dalle rime, poneste in luce.' Written in 1515, and printed in 1524, with a dedication to the

reigning Pope, Leo X, it passed through six editions during the
next half century, and must have exercised considerable
influence, both in Italy and in other countries.   It was imitated
in the *Rosmunda* of Rucellai (pr. 1524), the *Tullia* of Martelli
(pr. 1533), and the *Didone in Cartagine* of Pazzi, all of which
follow the Greek model.   It was twice translated into French,
by Mellin de Saint-Gelais in prose (pr. 1559), and by Claude
Mermet in verse (1585); the prose version was acted 'avec
grande pompe et digne appareil' before Henri II and Catherine de' Medici at Blois some time before its publication.   But
in Italian it was not acted till 1562, when it received a magnificent representation, given by the Olympic Academy at Vicenza.
The scenery was designed by Palladio and painted by Fasolo ;
there were eighty actors, marvellous costumes, divine music ; all
the Lombard nobility and the European ambassadors residing
at Venice were present.   But by 1562 Italian tragedy had taken
a different direction under the guidance of Giambattista Giraldi
Cinthio, who had at Ferrara an advantage over all his contemporaries in the patronage of a dynasty interested in the
drama and willing to contribute on the material side towards its
development.

GIRALDI.

Giraldi (1504–73) unquestionably had a great opportunity at
Ferrara, the city where he was born and died ; if he failed to
contribute to the development of tragedy to the same degree as
Ariosto had contributed to the development of comedy, it was
due only in part to the greater popularity of the latter form of
art : the main reason was his own inferior literary skill.   The
interest in the revival of classical drama at Ferrara dates from
at least as far back as 1486, when the *Menoechmi* of Plautus
was acted in the presence of 10,000 people, under the patronage
of Hercules I, who spent 1,000 ducats on the festival.   Under
his successor, Alfonso I, the brother of Isabella and Beatrice
d'Este, Ariosto produced the brilliant series of comedies which
founded the modern European drama, and the first regular

European theatre was built, only to be burnt down just before
Ariosto's death in 1532. Hercules II, the next duke, was no
less intelligent and interested as a patron of the drama than his
predecessors. He was present at the first performance of
Giraldi's *Orbecche* in the author's own house in 1541, and took
a keen interest in the discussion that followed as to the mode of
representation. Giraldi divided the play into five acts, according to the precepts of Horace and the practice of Seneca, both
of which he pleads in his own defence for the separation of the
acts by music or *intermedii*. When the tragedy was repeated
for the delectation of the Cardinals of Salviati and Ravenna, a
Greek in the service of the former found fault with it because
the action was not continuous, but was interrupted by the
pauses between the acts ; and at the request of the cardinals,
the play was presented again in the Greek fashion. The following Sunday, it was performed once more as the author had
originally planned it, and the Cardinals and the Duke expressed
their preference for the Roman as against the Greek manner of
presentation. Hercules II interested himself in other ways in
the composition and performance of Giraldi's tragedies, and
suggested the subject of one of them—the *Cleopatra*[1] After
the performance of the *Orbecche* Hercules made Giraldi his
secretary, and Giraldi held this post until the Duke's death in
1558. Giraldi had had a good education in medicine as well
as letters, and one of the reasons he gives for his delay in pro-
ducing the *Cleopatra* is the burden of his public lectures on
philosophy. His collection of Novels, first published in 1565
after his removal from Ferrara to Mondovi, passed through
many editions, and made his name famous throughout Europe;
Greene borrowed from it the plot of *James IV*, and Whetstone
that of *Promos and Cassandra*, on which Shakespeare founded
Measure for Measure.[2] Giraldi wrote a treatise on the drama

[1] See Appendix to *Didone* and letters from Giraldi to the Duke published
by Campori in *Atti e memorie . . . per le provincie modensi e parmensi*, vol.
viii, fasc. 4 (1876).
[2] I cannot accept Dr. Richard Garnett's conclusion that because there is
a character in the play Giraldi founded on his own story named Angela,

(*Discorso sulle Comedie e sulle Tragedie*), and had indeed
enough, perhaps too much, learning ; he was hampered also by
ill health and domestic affliction, only one of his five sons surviving to publish his tragedies after his death.   But the fact is
that Giraldi had not enough dramatic talent to repeat the
achievement of Ariosto in the adaptation of the classical drama to
the conditions of modern life.   No doubt the task was more
difficult in tragedy than in comedy, for a wider departure from
classical tradition was demanded ; after Aristophanes there had
been the developments of Menander, Plautus, and Terence.
Greek tragedy stayed where Euripides left it during the life-.
time of Aristophanes, and Seneca (to leave Menander out of the
comparison) had less initiative, less vitality, and less dramatic
skill than the two great Roman comic writers, who worked, no
doubt, under more favourable conditions.   Seneca was Giraldi's
model, and when he departs from the Roman practice or from
the precepts of Aristotle, he endeavours to justify himself by
pedantic arguments, founded, not on the needs of the time, or
the demands of his art, but on the interpretation of his authorities.   His justification in the *Discorso* of his practice of allowing
deaths on the stage is a case in point, and one can only plead
in mitigation that the public for which he wrote attached over-
whelming importance to classical tradition.   Giraldi showed
considerable independence in the choice of his subjects, seven
out of his nine tragedies being founded on stories included in
his collection of Novels, the *Ecatomiti* ; the other two, *Cleopatra*
and *Didone*, are, of course, from classical sources.   Of all his
plays the most notable is undoubtedly the *Orbecche*, which was
printed in 1543, two years after its original production at
Ferrara, and undoubtedly exercised widespread influence.   Luigi
Groto, a generation later, in the dedication of his *Dalida*, speaks
of *Orbecche* as the model of all subsequent tragedies, and there

and Shakespeare calls the villain of *Measure for Measure* Angelo, he must
have seen Giraldi's play as well as the novel.   No English dramatist shows
any trace that I can discover of acquaintance with Giraldi's dramatic work
(which in its collected form was not published till 1583), though Shakespeare took the plot of *Othello* from his collection of novels.

can be no question that it was decisive in turning Renascence
tragedy away from the Greek model adopted by Trissino to the
imitation of Seneca. It was frequently acted; the author
mentions a performance at Parma before the Academy, in
addition to those already referred to, and speaks in his *Discorso*
as if the representations were numerous :

> Quelle che ogni volta vi erano venute, non poteano contenere
> i singhiozzi e i pianti ... I giudiziosi non solo non l'hanno biasimata,
> ma trovata degna di tanta lode, che in molti luoghi dell'Italia è
> stata solennemente rappresentata, e già tanto oltre fu grata che ella
> favella in tutte le lingue che hanno cognizione della nostra, e non si
> sdegnò il re Cristianissimo volere che nella sua lingua ella facesse
> di sè avanti sua maestà solenne mostra.[1]

That the *Orbecche* should have aroused so much emotion
cannot but be surprising to a modern reader of the play, for it
is just in the point of dramatic expression, to which Giraldi
refers in introducing the above testimony, that he seems to fall
short. The plot is certainly horrible enough, and these horrors
are treated in characteristic Senecan fashion, the model adopted
being evidently the *Thyestes* :

A prologue apologizes for the novelty of performing a tragedy on
the stage, and explains that the woes to be presented occur in
Susa, an ancient city of Persia. In the first scene of Act I Nemesis
invokes the Furies to fill the court of Sulmone with the horrors which
befell Tantalus and Thyestes. Scene II is taken up with the ghost
of Selina, the wife of Sulmone, clamouring for revenge for her execution by her cruel husband, who found her *in flagrante delicto* with
his son. The discovery was made through her precocious child,
Orbecche, now secretly married to Oronte, and upon them too she
invokes destruction. The chorus of Susan women sing of the power
of Venus.

In Act II Orbecche laments to her nurse that her father wishes
to marry her to King Selino. The nurse advises her to consult
Oronte, and Oronte comes, being in fact sent by the king to urge his
daughter to marry Selino. He advises Orbecche to confide in the

---

[1] Biblioteca Rara pubblicata da G. Daelli, vol. 52, p. 17.

old counsellor Malecche. After a lament by Orbecche, a chorus on mortal infelicity concludes Act II.

In the next act Malecche moralizes on the situation, and is sent for by Sulmone, who has discovered the marriage of his daughter through her chambermaid's overhearing her lamentations in her distress at the prospect of the marriage with Selino. Malecche advises moderation and prudence, pardon for Orbecche and Oronte, but in spite of all his arguments he does not soften the heart of Sulmone, who in soliloquy sets forth his plan of slaying the two children of Oronte and Orbecche along with their father. He feigns a reconciliation, however, for the sake of making his revenge more effective and complete. Oronte, after reviewing the chances of his life, which seem now to have come to a happy end, goes to the king's presence, as he thinks, to be received as successor to the throne, but really to be assassinated. The chorus sings of love.

In Act IV, a Messenger tells the story (elaborately imitated from Seneca's *Thyestes*) of the death of Oronte and his children. The scene was a desolate chamber in the bottom of the old tower, dedicated to the rites of Pluto and Proserpina. There Oronte was conducted, and his hands placed on a block so that Sulmone could cut them off with a knife, with which he then stabbed the eldest son, throwing the dead body at the father's feet. The other son ran for protection to his father's mutilated arms, and Sulmone struck both dead at one blow. He then had the body of Oronte thrown to the dogs, the head and hands put into a silver vessel covered with black taffeta. In two similar vessels the bodies of the children were placed, one with a knife in his breast, the other with a knife in his throat. Chorus on fidelity and the punishment to overtake Sulmone.

The last Act shows the presentation of the horrible gift to Orbecche, who has all along been distrustful of her father, having been warned by a dream in which a dove and two nestlings were destroyed by an eagle. The head of Oronte and the bodies of the children are set in silver vessels on the stage. Orbecche stabs her father in the breast as he attempts to embrace her, and with the other knife cuts his throat. After rather prolonged lamentations over her husband and children, she stabs herself and dies on the stage.

An address to the reader apologizes for the novelty of the subject, the division into acts and scenes, the long-windedness of Malecche (his expostulations with Sulmone extend to some 600 lines), the excessive wisdom of the women of the chorus, the deaths of Sulmone and Orbecche *coram publico*, and the use of the vernacular. This versified apology adds about 200 lines to the tragedy, which was already considerably over 3,000—a marked departure from both the Greek and the Roman model.

Giraldi's other tragedies hardly call for detailed notice. They were apparently all acted except the *Epitia*, for his son mentions this in the dedicatory preface to the Duchess of Ferrara as a virgin play, which had never made its appearance in public. Dependent as Giraldi was upon classical authority, in some ways he showed remarkable freedom and self-reliance. Even before the *Orbecche* was acted, he had written a play with a happy ending, the *Altile*, and one of the tragedies founded on his own novels, the *Arrenopia*, is distinctly romantic in character, as the following argument, as set forth by its author, sufficiently shows :

Arrenopia, daughter of Orgito, king of Scotland, marries Astazio, king of Ireland, against the will of her father. Astazio falls in love with the daughter of Melissa, Lady of the Isle of Man, and in order to marry her, he directs one of his captains to kill Arrenopia. She comes to blows with the captain, is seriously wounded by him, and would have been killed if a knight named Ipolipso had not rescued her from his hands ; Arrenopia, having lost her hair, which had been cut off during sickness just before, is taken by Ipolipso for a knight, as she does not wish to make herself known. Having recovered from her wounds in his house, she innocently excites his jealousy of Semne, his wife, and is accused by him of treachery ; he seeks a duel with her, and in order to conceal her identity, Arrenopia calls herself Agnoristo. Orgito, father of Arrenopia, believing in his daughter's death, wages war against Astazio in revenge for the outrage. Arrenopia in the heat of the conflict reveals her identity to her father and her husband, relieves Ipolipso from his unjust suspicion of his wife, is reconciled to her father, and lives happily with her husband ever after.

The theme lent itself to dramatic treatment after the romantic fashion, and Greene, who took the story from the novel, made it one of his most effective plays. Giraldi's fashion of dealing with it is remarkable by way of contrast; he begins with the jealousy of Ipolipso, which occupies the whole of the first Act; first of all he confides it to the wise man Sofo, then Sofo soliloquizes about it, next Sofo discusses it with Semne, who soliloquizes in turn, a chorus on the same subject closing the Act without any progress being made in the action. Indeed the relations between Arrenopia, Ipolipso, and Semne, which take the first place in our interest, remain unchanged until Arrenopia reveals herself to her husband and father in the last fifty lines of the play. It is evident that Giraldi was unable to deal with a romantic subject in a romantic way. He was able to break away in some respects from classical traditions, but he remained bound to classical devices such as the chorus, the confidant, and the messenger, which the modern stage could hardly tolerate; and he lacked the power to give living force to his characters and probability to his story. If he had had skill equal to his courage he would have filled a much larger place in the history of European drama.

Lodovico Dolce.

Lodovico Dolce (1508–1568) was not endowed with any more dramatic ability than Giraldi, and was even more un-fortunate in the circumstances of his life and the conditions of his work. He was born and died at Venice, where he was employed as hack writer and proof-corrector by the publishing house of the Gioliti. He translated Plautus and Seneca, Horace, Virgil, Ovid, and Cicero; he made versions, too, from Homer and Euripides, but in these he was handicapped by his ignorance of Greek. He dealt very freely with the authors he translated, omitting and adding at his own pleasure. The version of the *Phoenissae* of Euripides which is included in this volume, as translated into English by Gascoigne and Kinwelmersh, may serve as an example of Dolce's method of treating a classical masterpiece. A very slight error indicates that he had before him, not the original text of Euripides, but the Latin translation published at Basel by R. Winter in 1541, in which line 982 reads 'ad solum Thesbrotorum'. The Aldine edition of the Greek text (1503), upon which most subsequent editions were founded, the Basel edition of Hervagius (1537), and all the other printed editions likely to be within Dolce's reach have the reading Θεσπρωτῶν οὖδας; but Dolce, like the Latin translator, spells *Tesbroti* with a *b*. Italian critics of his other translations discover much more serious departures from the original Greek, his version of the *Odyssey* being described as nothing more than a story taken from Homer. Yet he was a dramatist of note in his own time, continuing the work of Giraldi, according to the Senecan tradition. Besides translating Seneca, he adapted three other plays from Euripides in addition to the *Phoenissae*, made a *Didone* out of Virgil, and a *Marianne* out of Josephus. The last was, perhaps, his greatest achievement, for when it was acted at the Duke of Ferrara's palace in Venice, the crowd was so great that the performance could not be carried through. It is a compilation after the manner of Giraldi, whose *Orbecche* is closely imitated. Dolce was less of a scholar and less of an artist than Giraldi, and would hardly merit even so much attention as he is here given if it were not that he was well known in England and exercised some influence on our early drama. The translation of his *Giocasta* and its performance at Gray's Inn in 1566 will call for fuller notice later, and so will the imitation of the prologue of *Gismond of Salerne* (Inner Temple, 1567–8) from Dolce's *Didone* (1547). Some of his sonnets were translated by Lodge, as has been pointed out by Max Th. W. Foerster in *Modern Philology*, and by Sir Sidney Lee in his *Introduction to Elizabethan Sonnets* (*English Garner*).

It would be unprofitable to pursue the history of cinquecento tragedy to its final extinction. It was never more than a flickering spark, but it lasted long enough to communicate the dramatic impulse to France and England, where the conditions for dramatic production were more favourable. The reasons for the failure of tragedy to maintain itself in Italy need not be elaborately explained. It was always either court tragedy or

closet tragedy—never a national form of art, for there was no
Italian nation to appeal to, and it was never popular ; even in
the smaller communities in which the munificence of a royal
patron secured a performance, it seems doubtful whether there
was any real interest beyond that of the few aristocratic patrons
who prided themselves on their share in the revival of a
classical form of art.   The Medicean ambassador, Canigiani,
who saw a tragedy performed at Ferrara in 1568, probably
represents the common opinion of those who were not intimi-
dated by the weight of classical tradition and royal approval ;
he says the performance fulfilled both the ends of tragedy set
forth by Aristotle, viz. anger and compassion, for it made the
spectators angry with the poet and sorry for themselves.   When
we add to the general indifference the fact that there was no
regular theatre, the failure of Italian tragedy is sufficiently
accounted for without taking into consideration the determining
factor—there were no tragic writers of sufficient dramatic power
to hold public attention or to create enduring works of art.
They were, however, able to establish a dramatic tradition, and
to assist in a discussion as to the ends and means of tragedy, to
which we must now turn our attention.

Practice and Theory in Renascence Tragedy.

The influences affecting the development of Renascence
tragedy were by this time somewhat complex.   For the sake of
clearness, they may be set forth in tabular form :

1. *a.* Greek tragedies in the original.
    b. Greek tragedies translated into Latin.
    c. Greek tragedies translated into the vernacular.
    d. Imitations of Greek tragedy.
2. *a.* The tragedies of Seneca.
    b. Translations of Seneca.
    c. Imitations of Seneca.
3. Printed Italian tragedies.
4. Acted Italian tragedies.

5. Critical treatises :
   a. Aristotle's Poetics.
   b. Translations of the Poetics and commentaries on it.
   c. Horace, *Ars Poetica*.
   d. Independent critical treatises.
6. The mediaeval tradition :
   a. As to the idea of tragedy.
   b. As to its mode of representation.

Among all these influences the most potent was that of the acted tragedies, which were nearly always printed either before representation (as in the case of Trissino's *Sofonisba*) or after (as in the case of Giraldi's *Orbecche*). The mode of production was considerably affected by what had already been done in the performance of Renascence comedy, which had the advantage of many years over its graver and older sister in classical art. The *Menoechmi* of Plautus was reproduced at Ferrara as early as 1486, and the performance was repeated in 1491. Two points about the revival of this popular play call for remark. In each case (the first performance was in the open air, the second in the great hall) the staging was that of the *sacre rappresentazioni*, four or five houses or castles being provided, each with a door and a window. In the intervals between the acts, *intermedii* were given, and proved in fact the most popular feature of the performance, consisting mainly of Morris dances with humorous accompaniments. These *intermedii*, which in the end contributed to the decay of Renascence drama and were resented even by the writers of comedy, were introduced also into tragedy. Trissino, as became a pupil of Demetrius Chalkondylas and a reverent imitator of the Greek model, protested against them as unworthy of the dignity of tragedy ; but Giraldi, having adopted the Roman practice of division into acts, defended them as a recreation for the minds of the spectators (Appendix to *Didone*). Dolce acknowledged that there was no justification for them in classical authority or example, but used them to adorn the performance of his *Troiane* (1566). After the first act of the tragedy, there was a discourse between the chorus and Trojan citizens on the misfortunes of their country ; after the second, Pluto appeared with the ghosts of the Trojan slain ; after the third, Neptune and the council of the gods ; after the fourth, other deities, especially Venus and Juno.   The contrivers of the *intermedii* sometimes neglected to relate them to the subject of the tragedy, but this was held to be a fault.   The author of *Il successo dell'Alidoro*, acted at Reggio in 1568, condemns the practice of introducing such diverse figures as Endymion, Temperantia, and Curtius between the acts of the same tragedy. Sometimes the *intermedii* had reference to the act just finished, as in the *Giocasta* presented by the Academy of Viterbo in 1570 : after Act I, the lawless ambition of Eteocles was emphasized by the figure of Empty Fame riding on a Chimaera in the air, while on the stage the evils of Division were illustrated by a figure in black, riding on a camel (the lowest of animals), and holding a chain in which he led Ambition, clad in a white robe with peacock's wings.   De Sommi, the Mantuan Jew, whose suggestions for dramatic performances are still in manuscript in the Turin National Library, and have been summarized in Creizenach vol. ii, recommends that the *intermedii* should give the spectators a hint of impending calamities, e. g. the three Fates to portend a tragic death, or a dance of Furies with torches to foreshadow some dreadful crime.   The practice passed over into French tragedy ; Jean-Antoine de Baïf and Ronsard wrote poems to serve as texts for *intermèdes*, and Garnier suggested their introduction in *Bradamante*, which has no chorus, to mark the division into acts and suggest the lapse of time.   There can be little doubt that we owe to the Italian *intermedii* the English dumb shows, which are of the same general character and serve the same purpose ; Gascoigne, in the third dumb show of *Jocasta*, uses the story of Curtius, one of the stock figures of the Italian *intermedii*, and though it is no doubt possible that the English practice may have arisen independently from the native allegorical pageants, the resemblance of the dumb shows to the *intermedii* seems too close to be set down to mere coincidence.

Still another influence must be mentioned as contributing to the formation of Renascence tragedy by combating the mediaeval tradition and spreading juster notions of how classical tragedy was performed—the study of Vitruvius and of the remains of the ancient theatres. Serlio, in his treatise on architecture (1545), gave sketches of three scenes for tragedy, comedy, and pastoral or satyric drama respectively, and each of the comedies of Ariosto was furnished with a single set scene representing a landscape in perspective—usually a city with churches, houses, and gardens. For tragedy the conventional scene was a palace front with pillars, and it was no doubt such a scene that was painted for Giraldi's tragedies in 1551 and 1561 by Niccolò Roselli and Girolamo Bonaccioli. Pellegrino Prisciano's Latin treatise, *Spectacula*, still in manuscript in the library at Ferrara, shows what care was given to the revival of the classical drama at Ferrara under Hercules I, the Maecenas of the beginning of the sixteenth century. Giraldi's duke was perhaps less generous, and it was to Messer Girolamo Maria Contugo that he appealed to provide for the first performance of the *Orbecche*; the choragus, as he is called by Giraldi, who is nothing if not classical, spared neither trouble nor expense, and the scene had the grandeur and majesty that the nature of the play demanded. The curtain fell at the opening of the play, the usage of Latin comedy having been already adopted by Ariosto, and there was only one scene; but Giraldi did not on this account hold himself restricted to one precise place. The objection made by Bartholomeo Calvalcanti that Giraldi's kings uttered their most secret designs in public seemed to the author of the tragedy altogether foolish:

Ma pouero ch' egli è, non si auede egli, che quantunque la scena rappresenti una Città, non si considera ella nondimeno in tali ragionamenti, altrimente che se essi si facessero nelle più segrete, & più riposte stanze de' Signori? Et perciò s' introducono nella scena, in quello istesso modo, che se fauellassero nelle camere loro. Perche così ricerca la rappresentatione.[1]

[1] Appendix to *Didone*.

This presumption that the scene is what the action suggests and requires is almost Elizabethan in its generosity; but Giraldi justified himself in this instance, as in many others, by the Roman practice, and the convention he seeks to establish is obviously due to the authority of Seneca rather than to the custom of Greek tragedy. Seneca's sensational themes and the morbid introspection and self-analysis of his characters are less suited to the open air than the action of most Greek tragedies, which reflect the Athenian fondness for public life, though Euripides had already shown the tendency to greater individualism and privacy which Seneca accentuated all the more easily because his tragedies were not written for the stage. Giraldi frequently expresses his admiration for Seneca, whom he holds superior to all the Greeks 'nella prudenza, nella gravità, nel decoro, nella maestà, nelle sentenze'. He pleads Seneca's example too for the introduction of deaths on the stage, contrary to the precepts of Aristotle and Horace, about which he argues with great subtlety and erudition. He adopted Seneca's division into five acts, and has much to say in defence of Seneca's practice of bringing the chorus on to the stage only between the acts, except when they were needed as interlocutors. His choruses were not sung, but recited by one member, the others merely standing in view on the stage; but even here Giraldi claims the support of an ancient Greek usage. It is, of course, on the authority of Aristotle that he bases his practice of restricting the action of his tragedies to one, or, at most, two days; for the extension to two days in the *Altile* and *Didone*, he quotes also the examples of the *Heautontimorumenos* of Terence, the *Amphitryon* of Plautus, the *Heracleidae*, *Phoenissae*, *Hecuba* of Euripides. Although not published till 1554, the *Discorso* is dated by its author April 20, 1543, and the appendix to the *Didone* appears to have been written about the same time. The *Discorso* excited a lively controversy, as part of the credit for it was claimed by Giraldi's young pupil, Giambattista Pigna, and it became well known, both in Italy and abroad.

Giraldi holds an important place among the Renascence

critics, not only because of his early date, but because he com-
bines practice with theory. Submissive as he was to the
authority of the ancients, he does, once in a while, in the *Discorso*,
as in the epilogue to *Orbecche*, humbly suggest that as the
Romans departed from the custom of the Greeks, he may be
permitted some innovations, as in the adoption of modern
themes. He is conscious, too, of the difficulty of accommodating
a modern plot to Greek conditions of representation, which
resulted to some extent from the Greek mode of life. The interpreters of Aristotle who preceded and followed Giraldi were
less open-minded and more pedantic, even more submissive to
the weight of authority. So far from relaxing the strictness of
Aristotelean dogma, they were inclined to add to the burden.
Averroes' commentary on the Poetics, translated into Latin by
Hermannus Alemannus, was printed in 1481, but it had departed
so far from the text that its restrictive force on the drama was
slight. A Latin translation by Valla, founded on the original
text, followed in 1498, and the Greek text was printed in 1508;
the first commentary, that of Robortello, appeared in 1548, and
with all three of these Giraldi was acquainted, as he was also, no
doubt, with Segni's Italian translation (finished 1548, pub.
1549). Robortello was the first to argue that the limit set by
Aristotle was an artificial day of twelve hours—from sunrise to
sunset—on the ground that night is the time for repose, not
for action :

Noctu enim homines conquiescunt, indulgentque somno ; neque
quidpiam agunt, aut ulla de re inter se colloquuntur.

Segni favours a natural day of twenty-four hours, because for
many deeds night is a more suitable time than day. But both,
like Giraldi, distinguish between the time of representation and
the time of the events represented ; and neither contends for
the unity of place, there being no mention of any such rule or
custom in Aristotle. Trissino follows the Greek practice of
continuity, and the action seems to take place entirely in the
public square in front of Sophonisba's palace; but this is a
strange setting for the interview between Scipio and Syphax,

and it is noteworthy that it is precisely at this point that the indications of locality, which are frequent in the rest of the play, are altogether lacking. Giraldi, as we have seen, contents himself with a very general indication of a city or neighbourhood ; all his tragedies begin with the direction, ' The scene is in . . . ,' and the name of the city in question is given ; in the *Arrenopia*, it is Limerick, but part of the action represented on the stage takes place in the camp of the hostile army, and part between the two. The identification of the time and place of the representation with the time and place of the action was left to a later critic of European reputation, an Italian, too, although he spent much of his life in France, Julius Caesar Scaliger.

SCALIGER'S *Poetice*.

Scaliger's *Poetice* (1561) is peculiarly significant ; he unites the predominant influences of the past, and gives the controlling direction of the future. He departs from the authority of Aristotle to follow the theories of the later Latin writers upon which the mediaeval tradition had been founded. As M. Gustave Lanson has pointed out,[1] he changes Aristotle's definition into the traditional sense, omitting the purgation of the passions and adding the unhappy ending, translating σπουδαίας by *illustris*,[2] and substituting elevation of style for metre. Equally significant is his adoption of Seneca as a model ; he says of him :

Nullo Graecorum maiestate inferiorem existimo : cultu ueró ac nitore etiam Euripide maiorem. Inuentiones sanè illorum sunt : at maiestas carminis, sonus, spiritus ipsius.[3]

It is in accordance with Seneca's conception of tragedy and with the mediaeval tradition that Scaliger described the proper subjects for tragic treatment :

Res Tragicae grandes, atroces, iussa Regum, caedes, desperationes, suspendia, exilia, orbitates, parricidia, incestus, incendia, ·

---

[1] *L'idée de la tragédie en France avant Jodelle*, in *Revue d'histoire littéraire de la France*, 11⁰ année (1904), p. 583.
[2] In this he followed Robortello.   [3] Lib. VI, c. 6, p. 323.

pugnae, occaecationes, fletus, ululatus, conquestiones, funera, epitaphia, epicedia.[1]

These horrible themes are to be treated after Seneca's sensational manner, and his favourite device of the ghost is especially recommended, as will be seen from the passage quoted below. Entirely Senecan is Scaliger's idea of the importance of rhetorical commonplaces :

Quum autem sententiarum duo sint modi, utrisque tota Tragoedia est fulcienda. Sunt enim quasi columnae, aut pilae quaedam uniuersae fabricae illius.[1]

His chorus, too, is Seneca's chorus, not that of Greek tragedy, nor that prescribed by Aristotle and Horace :

Chorus est pars inter actum et actum. In fine tamen Fabularum etiam Choros uidemus. Quare tutior erit definitio quae dicat : post actum, introducta cum concentu.[2]

Of even greater significance for the future of Renascence tragedy was Scaliger's dislike of incident and his reverence for external probability :

Mendacia maxima pars hominum odit. Itaque nec praelia illa, aut oppugnationes, quae ad Thebas duobus horis conficiuntur, placent mihi, nec prudentis Poetae est efficere ut Delphis Athenas, aut Athenis Thebas, momento temporis quispiam proficiscatur. Sic apud Aeschylum interficitur Agamemnon, ac repentè tumulatur : adeoque citò, uix ut actor respirandi tempus habeat. Neque probatur illud, si Licham in mare iaciat Hercules, non enim sine ueritatis flagitio repraesentari potest. Argumentum ergo breuissimum accipiendum est : idque maxime uarium multiplexque faciundum. Exempli gratia, Hecuba in Thracia, prohibente reditum Achille. Polydorus iam interfectus est. Caedes Polyxenae. Exoculatio Polymestoris. Quoniam uero mortui quidam non possunt introduci, eorum phasmata, siue idola, siue spectra subueniunt : ut Polydori, ut Darii apud Aeschylum quod et supra dicebamus. Sic Ceyx apud Ouidium apparet Halcyone. Ex qua fabula si Tragediam contexes : neutiquam à digressu Ceycis incipito. Quum enim Scaenicum negotium totum sex octoue horis peragatur, haud uerisimile est, et ortam tempestatem, et obrutam nauem eo in maris tractu, unde terrae con-

---

[1] Lib. III, c. 97, p. 144.   [2] Lib. I, c. 9, p. 16.

spectus nullus. Primus actus esto conquestio, hinc chorus detestans
nauigationes. Secundus actus, Sacerdos cum uotis, colloquens cum
Halcyone et nutrice : arae, ignis, piae sententiae. hinc chorus uota
approbans. Tertius actus, Nuncius, de orta tempestate cum ru-
moribus. hinc chorus, exempla adducens naufragiorum : multa
apostrophe ad Neptunum. Quartus actus, turbulentus uera iam
fama : Naufragia ex nautis, mercatoribus. hinc chorus rem, quasi
defunctum sit, deplorans. Quintus actus, Halcyone anxia mare
spectans cadauer procul uidet. hinc mutatio utriusque, quum ipsa
sibi manus consciscere uellet.[1]

The importance of this passage is not so much its restriction
of the action to a few hours, and the prohibition of changes of
scene, but the adoption of a general principle of realism ; the
dramatist is not permitted to call upon the audience to imagine
anything which their eyes have not seen or which might not
have happened in the same period of time ; and he must not
allow his characters to report anything beyond the distance
which they might have covered under the conditions of the
action. The restriction of the action to its shortest possible
limit is a logical consequence which Scaliger does not fail to
perceive : ' Argumentum breuissimum accipiendum est.' Unity
of action is thus no longer ideal, dependent on the nature of
the subject, but is temporal and spatial, dependent on the
events which may be brought within the time of representation,
and the distance that may be travelled from the precise spot
the stage represents. The one rule that Aristotle laid down,
that of unity of action, is subjected to the later unities of time
and place worked out by Renascence critics. The upshot is
that tragedy is still further impoverished of the element of
incident, and the lyric and descriptive passages, the parts of the
messengers and confidants, are enlarged and emphasized. An
analysis of French Renascence tragedy will show how closely it
answers to the model by which Scaliger illustrates his precepts,
but it will be enough here to point out that this restriction of
the action to its narrowest possible limits was characteristic

[1] Lib. III, c. 97, p. 145.

of French classical tragedy in its noblest period. M. Rigal
writes in *Le théâtre français avant la période classique* (p. 278):
'Qu'est-ce que l'unité d'action, telle que la comprenaient nos
classiques? C'est l'obligation de faire de la tragédie une *crise*, de
ne mettre dans une pièce qu'un fait important, qui forme le
dénoûment, et que les préparations de ce fait, qui remplissent
les premiers actes.' He goes on to remark that 'une telle
unité s'accorde admirablement avec celles du lieu et du temps,
dont elle est la conséquence presque nécessaire', and adds in
a note: 'Le mot peut paraître singulier, car logiquement c'est
à l'unité d'action, la seule nécessaire, qu'il appartenait d'être le
principe des autres. Mais je crois bien que l'ordre fut interverti
chez nous. Peut-être pourrait-on le soutenir même pour
Racine: "La simplicité d'action, qu'il considère comme
essentielle à la tragédie, semble être à ses yeux une conséquence
de l'unité de temps."'

OTHER ARISTOTELEAN CRITICS.

Possibly the first hint of the identification of the time of the
action with the time of representation had been given by
previous critics. Robortello (1548) possibly had it in mind in
the passage quoted above, and Madius (1550) comes near to
the principles Scaliger laid down:

Cùm igitur Tragoedia atque Comoedia, (nam utrique eadem est
temporis ratio) propè ueritatem quoad fieri potest, accedere conentur,
si res gestas mensis unius spatio, duabus, tribusue ad summum horis,
quanto nimirum tempore Tragoedia uel Comoedia agitur, factas
audiremus, res prorsus incredibilis efficeretur. Fingamus enim in
aliqua Tragoedia, Comoediaue, nuntium in Aegyptum mitti, ut
rediens aliquid nuntiet. quis profectò spectator, si post horam hunc
redeuntem illinc, in scenam introduci uideat, non exibilabit, explo-
dètque; & rem à poeta omni prorsus ratione carentem, factam
praedicabit? [1]

But it was Castelvetro who, in his *Poetica d'Aristotele vulgariz-
zata et sposta* (1570), first codified these principles and made

---

[1] Particula xxxi.

them absolutely clear. Commenting upon Aristotle's well known distinction between tragedy and epic, he said :

Percioche l'epopea, narrando con parole sole, puo raccontare una attione avenuta in molti anni & in diversi luoghi senza sconvene-volezza niuna, presentando le parole allo 'ntelletto nostro le cose distanti di luogo, & di tempo, la qual cosa non puo far la tragedia, la quale conviene hauere per soggetto un' attione avenuta in picciolo spatio di luogo, & in picciolo spatio di tempo, cio è in quel luogo, & in quel tempo, dove & quando i rappresentatori dimorano occupati in operatione, & non altrove, ne in altro tempo.   Ma, cosi come il luogo stretto è il palco, cosi il tempo stretto è quello che i veditori possono a suo agio dimorare sedendo in theatro.[1]

One does not see how the rule of identification could be more precisely set forth, but it has been argued [2] that Castelvetro only established the unity of time, not that of place.   In another passage, however, Castelvetro says :

Quanto è allo spatio del luogo . . . nella tragedia è ristretto non solamente ad una citta, o villa, o campagna, o simile sito, ma anchora a quella vista, che sola puo apparere a gli occhi d' una persona.[1]

And he sums up :

La mutatione epopeica puo tirare con esso seco molti di, & molti luoghi, & la mutatione tragica non puo tirar con esso seco se non una giornata, & un luogo.[1]

This is almost the very phrase of Jean de La Taille in his preface to *Saul* (1572), for which priority as to the establishment of the third unity has been claimed :

Il faut tousiours representer l'histoire, ou le jeu en un mesme iour, en un mesme temps, et en un mesme lieu.

Why does Jean de La Taille say *en un mesme iour* as well as *en un mesme temps*? Probably, as M. Rigal suggests, La Taille intended to object to the division into *journées* usual in the mysteries and employed in the trilogy of Des Masures, which La Taille had just been criticizing ; this view is borne out by

---

[1] pp. 109, 535, and 534 (ed. of 1576).
[2] By Ebner, *Beitrag zu einer Geschichte der dramatischen Einheiten in Italien* (Münchener Beiträge, xv).

the fact that Castelvetro also discussed the possibility of
presenting a tragedy in three parts on three successive days,
and expressed himself strongly against it.   Castelvetro was
well known in France, and the two years that elapsed between
the publication of his treatise and Jean de La Taille's preface
are ample for communication, in view of the interest then taken
in the subject all over Europe.   In Spain, Scaliger was praised
by Cueba (c. 1580) and Pinciano (1596), and the former also
mentions the learned Giraldi.   Sidney, in his *Apology for
Poetry* (wr. 1580-1), refers to Scaliger (Arber's Reprint, p. 80),
and was doubtless indebted to Castelvetro for his famous
statement of the unities (Arber, p. 63).[1]

FRENCH RENASCENCE TRAGEDY.

French tragedy followed, after a considerable interval, much
the same course as Italian.   As the Latin tragedies of the
fourteenth and fifteenth centuries were succeeded in the first
half of the sixteenth century by Trissino's *Sofonisba* and Giraldi's
Orbecche in the vernacular, so Buchanan's Latin tragedies, in
which Montaigne acted when a student at Bordeaux about 1545,
were succeeded by Jodelle's *Cléopâtre captive* in 1552.   By
this time all the influences noted as affecting the later development of Renascence tragedy were already in existence.   Greek
tragedy was accessible in the original, and in translations, into
either Latin or French ; the Latin versions of the *Hecuba* and
the *Iphigenia at Aulis* by Erasmus were printed at Paris in 1506,
and French translations of the *Electra* of Sophocles and the
Hecuba by Lazare de Baïf appeared in 1537 and 1544
respectively.   Seneca's tragedies were first printed at Paris in
1485, and numerous editions were published during the first
half of the sixteenth century.   But there can be little doubt
that Jodelle's first attempt was prompted by Italian example,
and that the subsequent development of French tragedy was
influenced by the Italian tragedies already in existence.   During

[1] See Harold S. Symmes, *Les débuts de la critique dramatique en
Angleterre*, Paris, 1903.

the formative period of French tragedy, social and political, as well as literary relations with Italy were exceedingly close. François I had been educated by an Italian humanist, Quinziano Stoa, who afterwards became Rector of the University of Paris. The King chose an Italian as tutor for his children, and brought four Italians to Paris as professors in the Collège de France, which he founded. With the aid of his sister Margaret he introduced the culture of the Italian Renascence at Court, and the movement was continued under his son and grandson. 'Pour quarante Italiens qu'on voyait autrefois à la cour, maintenant on y voit une petite Italie,' said Henri Estienne, who in his works, particularly in his *Deux Dialogues du Nouveau Langage François italianizé*, ridiculed the Italian words and phrases adopted by the courtiers of his time; Du Bellay's sonnet on the same subject (*Les Regrets*, No. 86) is well known. Paul Louis Courier has shown that Amyot and Montaigne use many Italianisms, and he adds : C'était la mode et le bel air au temps d'Amyot de parler italien en français.' [1]

International relations more directly connected with the drama were not lacking.   As early as 1548 Bibbiena's *Calandra* was acted at Lyons before Henry II and Catherine de' Medici by Italian actors, 'et estoit accompagnée de force intermedies et faintes, qui contenterent infiniment le roy, la reine et toute leur cour' (Brantôme).   Lord Buckhurst, in a letter to Queen Elizabeth, dated Paris, March 4, 1571,[2] mentions among the entertainments at Court, 'a Comedie of Italians that for the good mirth and handling thereof deserved singular comendacion,' and in the autumn of the same year Charles IX granted them letters patent to play publicly in the city 'tragedies and comedies'.   This led to a conflict with Parliament, which was renewed in 1577 when Henry III granted similar privileges to a company known as I Gelosi, at whose public performances, says l'Estoile in his *Journal*, 'il y avoit tel concours et afluence de

---

[1] J. Demogeot, *Histoire des littératures étrangères considérées dans leurs rapports avec le développement de la littérature française.* Fuller details will be found in two essays in Francesco Flamini's *Studi di Storia Letteraria.*

[2] Calendar of State Papers, Foreign, 1569-71, p. 414.

peuple que les quatre meilleurs prédicateurs de Paris n'en avoient pas tretous ensemble autant quand ils preschoient.' Several Italian companies visited Paris before the end of the century, and it is evident that they offered formidable competition to the French actors. The royal patronage they enjoyed not only made their performances fashionable, and protected them from the interference of too zealous officials, but gave them social advantages. Actors at this time were outcasts at whom honest burghers, clergy, and Parliament alike hurled reproaches. It was because she was an Italian that the actress Isabella Andreini was buried with great solemnity at Lyons in 1604, and we have an amusing letter from Tristano Martinelli, describing the rivalries in the royal family for the honour of being sponsor to one of his children yet unborn.[1]

Most of the plays acted by Italian companies in France were doubtless comedies or farces, for Italian and French tragedy alike belonged in the main to the academic or closet drama; but it is evident that Italian tragedy was not unknown in France. As has been already pointed out, Trissino's *Sofonisba* was twice translated into French, by Mellin de Saint-Gelais in prose (pr. 1559), and by Claude Mermet in verse (1585); the prose version was acted in 1556 at Blois, and it was apparently for this performance that de Baïf wrote his *Entremets de la Tragedie de Sophonisbe*. Tragedies on the same subject were written by Montchrestien (1600), Nicolas de Montreux (1601), and Jean de Mairet (1634), and even Brunetière, who is very sceptical as to the influence of Italian on French tragedy, is willing to admit that Trissino's *Sofonisba* may have counted for something.[2] Giraldi's *Orbecche* was acted in the presence of the French king, but whether this was in France may be doubted, though Professor Francesco Flamini (*Il Cinquecento*, p. 255)

[1] Given in Armand Baschet, *Les comédiens italiens à la cour de France sous Charles IX, Henri III, Henri IV, et Louis XIII*, p. 235, and Eugène Rigal, *Le théâtre français avant la période classique*, p. 150. See also Albéric Cahuet, *La liberté du théâtre*, Paris, 1902, and N. M. Bernardin, *La comédie italienne en France*, Paris, 1902.

[2] *L'évolution d'un genre, la tragédie*, in *La Revue des Deux Mondes*, Nov. 1, 1901.

says it was ; but the play was published in 1543, and must have
been well known. So must Alamanni's *Antigone*, for he resided
in France for some years, and dedicated to François I the
edition of his works (including his version of the Sophoclean
tragedy) printed at Lyons in 1533. Morf[1] states that Le
Breton imitated Lodovico Martelli's *Tullia* (1533), and indebtedness has been suspected, though not proved in Jodelle's
Cléopâtre and *Didon*, which were preceded by Italian dramas
on the same subject. Using the same sources and the same
models, and guided by the same critical authorities, French and
Italian tragedy had a great deal in common which did not
necessarily come from direct imitation.

JODELLE.

The performance of Jodelle's *Cléopâtre* was recognized at the
time as a literary event of national importance. Charles de la
Mothe, in his preface to Jodelle's collected works published in
1574, says that in 1552 Jodelle 'mit en auant, & le premier de
tous les François donna en sa langue la Tragedie, & la Comedie,
en la forme ancienne'. Étienne Pasquier, who was present at
one of the early representations, has the following :

> Ceste Comedie, & la *Cleopatre* furent representees deuant le Roy
> Henry à Paris en l'Hostel de Reims, auec un grand applaudissement
> de toute la compagnie : Et depuis encore au College de Boncour,
> où toutes les fenestres estoient tapissees d'une infinité de person-
> nages d'honneur, & la Cour si pleine d'escoliers que les portes du
> College en regorgeoient. Ie le dis comme celuy qui y estois present,
> auec le grand Tornebus en une mesme chambre. Et les entrepar-
> leurs estoient tous hommes de nom : Car mesme Remy Belleau,
> & Iean de la Peruse, iouoient les principaux roulets. Tant estoit
> lors en reputation Iodelle enuers eux.

It was apparently at the second performance that Pasquier was
present, and the later historians may be right in supposing that
at the first Jodelle himself recited the prologue and played the
part of Cleopatra, another part being taken by Ronsard. After

---

[1] *Die französische Litteratur in der zweiten Hälfte des 16ten Jahrhunderts*,
in *Zeitschrift für französische Sprache und Literatur*, xix. 1 (1897).

the performance, Henry II, to whom the prologue was addressed, gave Jodelle 500 crowns, ' outre luy fit tout plein d'autres graces, d'autant que c'estoit chose nouuelle & tres-belle & rare ' (Brantôme). A compliment which excited more general attention was paid to Jodelle by his young fellow poets, who captured a goat, and led it, crowned with ivy, to the hall where Jodelle, also crowned with ivy, was waiting for the joyous band. There was much merriment, and the story got abroad that the goat was offered up as a heathen sacrifice. De Baïf, Ronsard, and his commentator Claude Garnier are at some pains to contradict this scandalous report, and the incident was the occasion for much versifying. We may be sure that the play was acted in the classical manner, so far as its author understood it, and was able to carry it out ; he regrets indeed that the theatre was not semi-circular, as it should be, and that the music between the acts was not modelled upon antiquity. It appears from another passage in Pasquier that the choruses were sung by ' ieunes gars ou filles ' to an instrumental accompaniment.

The opening speech by the ghost of Antony reminds the audience that the unity of time is to be strictly observed :

> Auant que ce Soleil qui vient ores de naistre,
> Ayant tracé son iour chez sa tante se plonge,
> Cleopatre mourra : ie me suis ore en songe
> A ses yeux presenté, luy commandant de faire
> L'honneur a mon sepulchre, & apres se deffaire,
> Plustost qu'estre dans Romme en triomphe portee.

Cloepatra then recounts her dream to Eras and Charmian, and a chorus of a general character closes the act with a lament over the death of Antony and the approaching suicide of Cleopatra.

In Act II Octavius expresses to Agrippa and Proculeius his regret at Antony's death and his determination to lead Cleopatra in triumph at Rome. Chorus in strophe and antistrophe lamenting the humiliation of Cleopatra, which is thus depicted :

> Ore presque en chemise
> Qu'elle va dechirant,
> Pleurant aux pieds s'est mise
> De son Cesar, tirant
> De l'estomach debile
> Sa requeste inutile.

Act III shows Cleopatra as a suppliant at the feet of Octavius, giving him a list of her treasures in gold and silver.   Her treasurer, Seleucus, hints that the list is far from complete, whereupon the queen flies at him, tears his hair, scratches his face, and regrets that she cannot split his sides 'a coups de pied'. [1]   Seleucus turns to Octavius for help, and is advised to run away:

> Et bien, quoy, Cleopatre?
> Estes vous point ia saoule de le battre!
> Fuy t'en, ami, fuy t'en.

The chorus condemn the treachery of Seleucus, and foretell once more the suicide of Cleopatra.

Act IV contains more laments by Cleopatra, Charmian, and Eras, and the chorus report that Cleopatra has entered the enclosure which contains the tomb of Antony (des sepulchres le clos, Où la mort a caché de son ami les os).   Strophe, antistrophe, and epode, in three sets.

In Act V Proculeius reports the deaths of Cleopatra, Eras, and Charmian to the Chorus, who close the play with the reflection:

> Souuent nos maux font nos morts desirables,
> Vous le voyez en ces trois miserables.

I have chosen Jodelle's *Cléopâtre* for somewhat detailed examination, not merely because it is the first French tragedy, but rather because more is known of the circumstances of its representation.   *Didon se sacrifiant* shows more dignity, if not more art, but the date of its composition and of its production, if it had any, are alike unknown.   Jodelle was evidently acquainted with the Greek model, but he also borrowed from Seneca, both in principles of construction and in particular passages.   Charles de la Mothe claims for him originality in his other poems, but not in the tragedies: 'Ains a tousiours suiui ses propres inuentions, fuyant curieusement les imitations, sinon

---

[1] Only the last detail is Jodelle's own.   The rest is in Plutarch's *Life of Antonius* (c. 106).   The passage is thus translated by Amyot:—'A la fin elle luy bailla un bordereau des bagues et finances qu'elle pouuoit auoir. Mais il se trouua là d'aduenture l'un de ses thresoriers nommé Seleucus, qui la uint deuant Caesar conuaincre, pour faire du bon ualet, qu'elle n'y auoit pas tout mis, et qu'elle en receloit sciemment et retenoit quelques choses: dont elle fut si fort pressee d'impatience de cholere, qu'elle l'alla prendre aux cheveux, et luy donna plusieurs coups du poing sur le uisage.   Caesar s'en prit a rire, et la feit cesser.'

quand expressément il a voulu traduire en quelque Tragedie.'
It need not surprise us then that industrious German scholars[1]
have found in Jodelle echoes of Seneca. Even more striking
is the general resemblance in plan and the use of the traditional
devices—the prologuizing ghost, the vision, the confidant with
her sententious commonplaces, the messenger with his elaborate
descriptions. It was perhaps in obedience to the precept of
Aristotle (*Poetics*, c. 18) that Jodelle emphasized and developed
the part of the chorus ; in his play it is 'an integral part of the
whole and shares in the action'. The result is to give French
Renascence tragedy the predominating lyrical character which
no one who has studied it has failed to notice. M. Faguet says :[2]
'On pourrait presque dire que la tragédie du xvie siècle est
une œuvre lyrique ; car c'est toujours la partie lyrique qui en
est la partie plus soignée et souvent qui en est la meilleure.'
Dr. Böhm, in the six early tragedies that he has examined,
notes a considerable increase in the lyric and a decrease in the
dramatic elements as compared with Seneca ; and a table prepared by Dr. John Ashby Lester shows that this lyric tendency
was continued up to the end of the sixteenth century; in five
of Garnier's tragedies the chorus is from one-sixth to one-fourth
of the play.

In the hands of Jodelle's successors, French tragedy passed
more and more under the influence of Seneca. Dr. Böhm has
subjected to very careful examination four other early French
tragedies in addition to Jodelle's *Cléopâtre* and *Didon*. Of these,
two—La Péruse's *Médée* (1555) and Grévin's *Jules César* (1561)—
are largely translations, the first from Seneca, the second from
the Latin tragedy of Muretus ; both are entirely in the Senecan
manner. Bounin's *La Soltane* (1561) offers more opportunity
for originality, its source being a contemporary account of a

---

[1] Paul Kahnt, *Gedankenkreis der Sentenzen in Jodelle's und Garnier's
Tragödien und Seneca's Einfluss auf denselben*, Marburg, 1887. Karl
Böhm, *Beiträge zur Kenntnis des Einflusses Seneca's auf die in der Zeit
von 1552 bis 1562 erschienenen französischen Tragödien*, Münchener
Beiträge, 1902.

[2] *Histoire de la littérature française*, vol. i, p. 456.

recent crime in Turkey, discovered by Dr. Lester in the Harvard College Library: 'Soltani Solymanni Turcarum Imperatoris horrendum facinus, scelerato in proprium filium, natu maximum, Soltanum Mustapham, parricidio, Anno Domini 1553 patratum : Ante octo menses in carcere apud infideles quidem scriptum, nunc uerò primùm in lucem editum : Autore Nicolao à Moffan Burgundo . . . Anno Salutis humanae M.D.LV. Mense Novembri.'[1] Rivaudeau's *Aman* (acted 1561, pub. 1566) is on a scriptural subject, and here too some independence might be expected; but Dr. Böhm says both these dramas must be described as 'copies of the Seneca tragedies'.

GARNIER.

The predominant influence of Seneca upon the beginnings of French tragedy had an abiding effect upon its subsequent development. Garnier, whose tragedies went through thirty editions and were held equal to the masterpieces of the Greek drama, handed on the Senecan tradition to his successors. The fact has been very clearly established by three investigations—*Étude sur Robert Garnier*, by S. Bernage, Paris, 1880 ; *Gedankenkreis der Sentenzen in Jodelle's und Garnier's Tragödien und Seneca's Einfluss auf denselben*, by Paul Kahnt, Marburg, 1887 ; *Seneca's Influence on Robert Garnier*, by H. M. Schmidt-Wartenberg, Darmstadt, 1888. From different points of view all arrive at the same result. The earliest of the three investigators, M. Bernage, arrived at the main conclusion immediately, and all that was left for his successors was to support it by detailed evidence. 'L'imitation de Sénèque, en France, n'est pas un fait obscur d'érudition ; ce n'est pas seulement un point de départ ; c'est un fait capital, dont presque toute notre littérature dramatique se ressent, et que les qualités déployées par Garnier, dans les aspects divers dont il l'a revêtu, ont fait entrer pour une part considérable dans les habitudes

---

[1] Dr. Lester's thesis, *Connections between the Drama of France and Great Britain, particularly in the Elizabethan period*, is still in manuscript in the Harvard Archives.

de l'esprit français.'   Dr. Schmidt-Wartenberg shows by an
analysis dealing with general characteristics of style and manner
how considerable is the extent of Garnier's indebtedness to his
Roman authority.   'When reading Garnier and Seneca we get
the impression that the former has studied his model so well that
he knows his works partly by heart.   The tragedies of the first
epoch show perhaps more of the peculiarities of Senecan style
than the translations.   He must have known Seneca thoroughly
and must have become imbued with his style before he began
to write.'   Dr. Kahnt points out that this influence extends not
only to general resemblances of style but to particular forms of
thought and expression, and that through these, too, Garnier is
connected with his predecessors and successors in French
tragedy.   Garnier, in fact, acted as a kind of clearing-house for
Senecan commonplaces, which he collected from the original
and from his predecessors and handed down to Montchrestien
and Hardy, sometimes to Corneille and Racine.

The immediate consequence was that the French tragic
writers of the sixteenth century, copying a model not meant for
the stage, produced imitations which satisfied the critics, but
did not please popular audiences.   As one reads these plays,
one wonders what there was in them to hold the attention of
even a courtly or a scholastic audience.   Reflections in dialogue
or chorus, descriptive and sometimes narrative passages succeed
one another in unbroken monotony, without any clash of
characters, and very little variety of incident.   Dr. Lester's table
is proof enough in this respect ; in the *Hippolyte* and *Cornélie*
there is no scene in which there are more than three interlocutors ;   one-half of each play consists of dialogue, and
one-quarter of the *Hippolyte* of monologue ; in not more than one-
fifth of either play are there even three speakers on the stage.
This was from no attempt to adopt the Greek rule of three
actors, for in some of Garnier's other plays there are considerable passages with four or more speakers ; it arises, first, from an
adoption of Seneca's methods of construction in general (he
observed the rule of the three actors) ; and secondly, from the

close imitation of particular plays or passages. There has been a lively discussion recently in the *Revue d'histoire littéraire de la France*, between M. Rigal on the one hand and M. Gustave Lanson and M. Jules Haraszti on the other, as to how French Renascence tragedy was acted, and whether, in general, it was acted at all. M. Lanson gives an imposing list of performances and argues that there must have been many more, especially in the provinces ; anything could be played (*tout est jouable*), and even when a tragedy was not actually performed, it was at least written in the hope of representation. The actors were, it is true, often courtiers or collegians, but these occasional performances had a considerable effect in changing the public taste. M. Rigal, on the other hand, contends that these plays were rarely acted, and that they were not, in fact, suitable for stage representation. Most of those that reached the stage were merely recited, and their authors had not even a notion of what a real stage representation meant. Analysing Garnier's plays one by one, he argues that in *Porcie* (1568) the author paid no attention to scenic possibility or probability, and had in mind only the opportunity for declamation. *Hippolyte* (1573) is hardly more than a free translation from Seneca ; whenever Garnier departs from his original, the play loses its suitability for stage representation. *Cornélie* (1574) has no scenic reality, consisting merely of rhetoric and ill-organized poetry. *Marc-Antoine* (1578) falls under the same condemnation. *La Troade* (1579) borrows from the *Troades* of Seneca and of Euripides, and from the latter's *Hecuba*, without assimilating them for stage representation. The *Antigone* (1580) deals in the same fashion with the *Phoenissae* of Seneca and the *Antigone* of Sophocles. *Bradamante* (1582) attempts to deal dramatically with Ariosto's story, but, strictly considered, the action requires five or six scenes. *Les Juifves* (1583) is an elegy inspired by Seneca, the *Thyestes* being the immediate model. M. Rigal next examines the tragedies of Montchrestien, and he proves up to the hilt that the *mise en scène* conceived by the authors of French Renascence tragedy was by no means as precise as it

would be in the present day.   It is, no doubt, true that Garnier
thought he had provided for the regularity of *Antigone* when he
wrote : ' La representation en est hors les portes de la ville de
Thebes.'   Obviously the French classical dramatists of the
sixteenth century did not plan their scene with the exactness of
a modern craftsman.   M. Rigal is entirely right in his contention that the action takes place ' dans un milieu tout irréel ' ;
the writers were content with a general imitation of classical
regularity, and a vague indication of a city or neighbourhood met
their conception of the requirements, as it met Giraldi's.[1]

CLASSICAL HOSTILITY TO THE POPULAR STAGE.

M. Rigal points out that some of these plays could easily be
accommodated to the multiple scene of the popular stage ; but
there is no proof that this arrangement was ever adopted, and
there is every reason against the supposition.   The attitude of
the classical critics and dramatists towards the popular stage was
one of uncompromising hostility.   Buchanan and Scaliger, Du
Bellay and Jodelle, Grévin and Jean de La Taille all speak with
contempt of the plays in possession of the stage.   La Taille says
in the preface to the *Corrivaux* (1574) : ' Et si on m'allegue
qu'on ioue ordinairement assez de ieus qui ont ce nom de
Comedies et Tragedies, je leur rediray encores que ces beaux
tiltres sont mal assortis à telles sottises, lesquelles ne retiennent
rien de la façon ny du style des anciens.' [2]   The public retaliated
by refusing to listen to elegies and philosophical diatribes which
it thought tiresome.   Even the cultivated audiences to which
French tragedy at first appealed found the choruses little to
their taste.   Grévin says in the *Discours sur le théâtre* prefixed
to his *Mort de César* (1558) : ' En ceste tragédie on trouvera
par adventure estrange, que sans estre advoué d'aucun autheur
ancien, j'ay faict la troupe interlocutoire de gensdarmes de
vieilles bandes de César, et non de quelques chantres, ainsi

[1] M. Rigal has reprinted his side of the discussion in his last volume, *De
Jodelle à Molière* (1911).
[2] See also much more to the same effect in his *Art de la tragédie* (1572).

qu'on a accoustumé . . . J'ay en cecy esgard que je ne parloy pas aux Grecs, ny aux Romains, mais aux François, lesquels ne se plaisent pas beaucoup en ces chantres mal exercitez, ainsi que j'ay souventesfois observé aux autres endroits ou l'on en a mis en jeu.' François Ogier in his preface to Jean de Schelandre's *Tyr et Sidon* (1608) says : 'les chœurs . . . sont tousjours desagreables, en quelque quantité ou qualité qu'ils paroissent.' 'L'impatience françoise ne les peut souffrir,' writes Desmarets in the preface to *Scipion* (1639), and early in the seventeenth century the practice appears to have been adopted of omitting them at the theatre 'comme superflus à la representation', to use Hardy's phrase.[1] When they were no longer recited, the dramatists naturally came to the conclusion after a time that it was no use writing them.

Meanwhile the French tragedians lacked the stimulus of an expectant public and were less intent on creating great dramas than on imitating models and keeping rules. In England and Spain the dramatists yielded, not without reluctance in some cases, to the popular demand. Lope de Vega in his *Arte Nuevo de hacer Comedias* (1609) professes the greatest respect for Aristotle and classical models ; 'but when I have to write a comedy for the popular stage (he continues) I lock the precepts up with six keys and turn Terence and Plautus out of my study for fear of hearing their outcries :

> porque como las paga el vulgo, es justo
> hablarle en necio para darle gusto.'

Webster writes in a similar but more serious strain in the preface to *The White Devil*: 'If it be objected this is no true dramatic poem, I shall easily confess it ; *non potes in nugas dicere plura meas ipse ego quam dixi.* Willingly, and not ignorantly, in this kind have I faulted : for, should a man present to such an auditory the most sententious tragedy that ever was written, observing all the critical laws, as height of

---

[1] Preface to *Didon* (1624). See also preface to Jean de Rossin's *La Persienne ou la Délivrance d'Andromède* (1617), and a valuable note in Édélestand Du Méril, *Du développement de la tragédie en France*, pp. 173-4.

style, and gravity of person, enrich it with the sententious
Chorus, and, as it were, liven death in the passionate and
weighty Nuntius; yet, after all this divine rapture, *O dura
messorum ilia*, the breath that comes from the uncapable
multitude is able to poison it.' Jonson, too, in the preface to
Sejanus apologized for the deficiencies of the tragedy 'in the
strict laws of time . . . as also in the want of a proper chorus';
in *Catiline* these defects were made good, but the public
showed the same lack of appreciation as in France. Leonard
Digges, writing in 1640, contrasts the failure of Jonson's
tragedies with the popularity of Shakespeare's:

> Oh how the Audience
> Were ravish'd, with what wonder they went thence,
> When some new day they would not brooke a line,
> Of tedious (though well laboured) Catiline;
> Sejanus too was irksome, they priz'd more
> Honest Iago or the jealous Moore.

MATERIAL CONDITIONS.

On the surface the tastes and behaviour of a sixteenth-
century audience seem to have been much the same on both
sides of the Channel; but no doubt the different lines of development taken by the drama in England and France rest
upon deep-seated national peculiarities.[1] Each nation experi-
mented with various types of tragedy, and adopted the one
best suited to its genius. Still, the conjecture may be hazarded
that the artificial restrictions of the theatre in France counted
for something as well as the more important conditions which
Symonds held necessary for the creation of great tragedy—an
era of intense activity and a public worthy of the dramatist.
The long monopoly enjoyed by the Confrères de la Passion,

---

[1] Brunetière puts it, almost paradoxically, in *La Revue des Deux
Mondes*, Jan. 1, 1903, p. 213: 'Les différences qui séparent la conception
générale du drame anglais de celle de la tragédie française ne viennent pas
d'une différence de culture ou d'éducation littéraire. Si le drame anglais
est ce qu'il est en dépit de Sénèque, il y a lieu de croire que, sans Sénèque,
la tragédie française n'en serait pas moins ce qu'elle est. Il faut creuser
plus profondément.'

which made the Hôtel de Bourgogne the only regular theatre
in Paris from 1548 to 1629, undoubtedly had a bad effect,
preventing competition, and robbing the actors of their legiti-
mate reward.   They were not only obliged to pay rent for a
miserable hall, and prevented by statutes of Parliament and
police ordinances from charging any but the lowest prices;
they suffered from the additional grievance of a long 'free list',
and it seems to have been the custom for many who had no
claim on the 'entrée gratuite', to force their way in without
paying.   This in part accounts for the very different standing
of the profession in England and France.   The English actors
enjoyed the acquaintance, and in some cases the friendship, of
people of high rank; Burbage, Alleyn, and Shakespeare were
men of substance and repute.   M. Rigal, after giving the
particulars summarized above, says: 'Nos comédiens étaient
donc pauvres; leur moralité n'était pas d'un niveau fort élevé.
Tristan les appelle des débauchés. "C'étaient presque tous
filous, dit Tallemant, et leurs femmes vivaient dans la plus
grande licence du monde".'   The writers for the theatre do
not seem to have been much better off.   According to a well-
known passage in *Segraisiana*, the regular price for a drama
was 'trois écus'.[1]   It is certain that the versatile Hardy lived
and died in poverty, in spite of the popularity of his six or
seven hundred dramas.   After a successful career of thirty
years he writes: 'Ma fortune se peut apparier l'emblème
d'Alciat, où les fers de la pauvreté empêchent l'esprit de voler
vers les cieux'; and three years later he again laments his
'pauvre Muse vagabonde et flottante sur un océan de misères'.
All the surroundings of the theatre told against success, and it
is no wonder that Hardy failed to create a permanent form of
art, as he might have done, according to Guizot and Sainte-
Beuve,[2] 'if he had been a genius.'

---

[1] M. Rigal thinks this figure must have been exceptionally low, but he
admits that even Hardy was 'toujours maigrement payé'. *Théâtre français*,
pp. 95-7.

[2] Guizot, *Corneille et son temps*, p. 132: 'Hardy était aussi irrégulier
qu'il le fallait pour devenir un Shakespeare, s'il eut le génie.' Sainte-Beuve,

It was left to Corneille and Racine, aided and, perhaps, to some extent restricted by Richelieu and the Academy, to give France a drama which answered the demands of logical development and regularity of form, and which has not ceased to delight cultivated audiences. It seems idle to speculate on what might have been the destiny of French tragedy if the material conditions of the stage had been otherwise; and equally idle to wonder what might have happened to English tragedy if Burghley had interested himself in the popular drama, or if Sidney had been able to enforce his ideas with the authority of Richelieu, and his Areopagus had had as much influence as the Academy. The Queen, to whom is ascribed the wish to see Falstaff in love, can hardly be credited with classical tastes co-extensive with her classical knowledge; in spite of her daily studies of Greek, and her translation from Seneca now in the Bodleian Library, it is inconceivable that Elizabeth should have undertaken to regularize English tragedy, and equally inconceivable that the Englishmen of the sixteenth century should have submitted, if she had attempted it. The one serious and concerted effort that was made in this direction proved altogether fruitless. It was in vain that Mary Sidney, Countess of Pembroke, with the assistance of Kyd, Daniel, and others, attempted to win English tragedy from its erring way to the imitation of the French model and the acceptance of the rules her brother, Sir Philip Sidney, had laid down in his *Apology for Poetry*.

EARLY ENGLISH TRAGEDY—THE POPULAR ELEMENT.

The distinguishing features of the English drama during the period that we are now considering are its astonishing vitality, variety, and complexity. I know no better or more rational

---

Tableau de la poésie française au 16ᵉ siècle, pp. 402-3. ' Si Hardy avait eu du génie, . . . il . . . pouvait tout créer; . . . il est à croire alors que, par lui, les destinées de notre théâtre eussent changé à jamais et que des voies tragiques bien autrement larges et non moins glorieuses que celles du *Cid* et des *Horaces* eussent été ouvertes aux hommes de talents et aux grands hommes qui suivirent.'

way of setting forth the facts than the method of Dr. Ward's *History of English Dramatic Literature*, and yet there is danger that the student may come away from its perusal with the erroneous impression of an orderly chronological development—from liturgical drama to miracle plays, from miracles to moral plays, from moralities to interludes and histories, and so on to regular comedy and tragedy, the older types disappearing to make way for the new. Professor Schelling succeeds in giving the right impression of the synchronous development of very different forms of dramatic art in his *Elizabethan Drama 1558–1642*, and Mr. Tucker Brooke's excellent little volume, *The Tudor Drama*, is in this respect particularly effective. For a right understanding of the subject, it is assuredly imperative that we should realize that the older forms continued to exist alongside of the newer developments from them, and that the native drama was not superseded by plays copied from foreign or classical models. Our one detailed description of the way in which the miracle plays were acted is given by Archdeacon Rogers of Chester, who died in 1595; the Chester cycle, we know, was acted as late as 1575, and all five manuscripts date from the period 1591–1607. The titles of the plays acted at court during Christmas and Shrovetide, 1567–8, show the catholicity of the Queen's taste and the variety of the dramatic entertainments arranged for her amusement :

For seven playes, the firste namede as playne as Canne be, The seconde the paynfull pillgrimage,[1] The thirde Iacke and Iyll, The forthe sixe fooles, The fivethe callede witte and will, The sixte callede prodigallitie, The sevoenthe of Orestes and a Tragedie of the kinge of Scottes.

The moralities continued to be acted and to be published, in spite of the competition of the regular theatres, *The Contention between Liberality and Prodigality* [2] being printed in 1602, after a performance before the Queen, apparently on February 4, 1601. Mr. Brooke says :

[1] ? *Everyman*. See Feuillerat, *Documents relating to the Office of the Revels in the Time of Queen Elizabeth*, pp. 448–9.

[2] Possibly a revision of the *Prodigallitie* just mentioned as acted in 1567–8.

The later moralities were usually performed by companies of four or five men and a boy—the boy, of course, taking women's parts. These troupes, once formed, continued themselves in unbroken sequence till the Restoration. There seems no doubt that the strolling players of the Commonwealth who roamed from village to village with their contraband dramatic wares, after the suppression of the theatres in 1642, were the lineal descendants, and the inheritors of many a piece of traditional clownage and stage business from those who in pre-Tudor times performed 'The Castle of Perseverance'.

Beside these professional actors, there were the amateurs of the court and of the country-side, of the schools and colleges, and of the Inns of Court, the last being specially interesting to us as the original home of classical tragedy. Shakespeare, in this as in greater matters, shows 'the very age and body of the time his form and pressure'. He has many references to the miracles and moralities; and in *Love's Labour's Lost*, he travesties the court masque along with the village pageant, just as at the Kenilworth Festivities in 1575 the Coventry Hock Thursday Play was performed for the delectation of Elizabeth in the midst of courtly entertainments, in which, there is reason to believe, Leicester himself took a directing hand.[1] In *Hamlet* Shakespeare deals more sympathetically with his professional comrades and their juvenile competitors, and shows his respect for the earlier forms of tragedy. In *A Midsummer Night's Dream* he overwhelms with good-natured ridicule the amateurs of the city guilds in 'The most lamentable comedy and most cruel death of Pyramus and Thisby'—the interlude described later as—

> 'A tedious brief scene of young Pyramus
> And his love Thisbe; very tragical mirth.'

This may serve to remind us of another characteristic of Elizabethan drama, its intermixture of types. Shakespeare recalls it again in the words of Polonius describing the repertoire of the travelling actors:

---

[1] See *Modern Language Review*, vol. iv, pp. 231–3 and 510–11.

The best actors in the world, either for tragedy, comedy, history, pastoral, pastoral-comical, historical-pastoral, tragical-historical, tragical-comical-historical-pastoral, scene individable, or poem unlimited : Seneca cannot be too heavy, nor Plautus too light. For the law of writ, and the liberty, these are the only men. (II. ii.)

It is for this reason that the Elizabethan drama affords to the young student such a bewildering spectacle and to the trained scholar a problem for endless study. The systems of classification we adopt are mere pigeon-holes, into which we put away this play and that for convenience of reference. The drama itself, when it lived and moved, was as various and complex as life itself, the types intermingling and combining in a way that almost defies analysis. The *mélange des genres*, abhorred by classical critics, was an almost universal custom with Elizabethan dramatists. Sidney, of course, protests (*Apology for Poetry*, Arber, p. 65) that even the distinction between tragedy and comedy was not observed : but he was a voice crying in the wilderness. As Mr. Symmes has pointed out, Elizabethan England, so rich in almost every department of creative literature, was singularly barren on the side of criticism :

Comparée avec la critique dramatique en Italie ou en France pendant la même période, cette critique anglaise est quelque chose d'étrange. Comme dans les pays du continent, elle commence avec les idées fausses du moyen âge et le savoir élémentaire des scoliastes. Mais l'Italie et la France, à l'aube de la Renaissance, renoncent d'une façon relativement facile à ces traditions étroites et acceptent volontiers l'interprétation qu'elles font d'Aristote. L'Angleterre, au contraire, en partie à cause de sa nature morale, continue de tenir, avec ténacité, aux idées médiévales. Les théoriciens dramatiques en France et en Italie au seizième siècle sont nombreux et souvent ingénieux. En Angleterre, ils sont peu nombreux, leurs écrits ne sont pas très profonds, et relativement, Sidney et Jonson exceptés, ils sont presque insignifiants. L'Angleterre ne peut montrer une liste de critiques comme Daniello, Minturno, le Trissino, Cinthio et Castelvetro, ni une collection de livres critiques comme ceux des Sibilet, des Scaliger, des Grévin, des Pelletier, des Jean de La Taille, des Vauquelin et des Pierre de Laudun ... En somme, la critique qui existe en Angleterre est au commencement surtout superficielle et diffuse. L'Anglais du seizième siècle manque le goût véritable pour la théorie critique. Il lui manque les traits nationaux si caractéristiques du Français, la méthode, la précision, la clarté, la logique et la raison qui sont les fondements de la critique.

Whatever disadvantage there was in the weakness of English criticism, it had one great advantage—the unbroken continuance of mediaeval tradition. In all kinds of literature this probably counted for more than was realized by students of the last generation, but in the drama the gains were great and manifest. In England, the classical influence, instead of clashing with mediaeval tradition, as it had done in Italy and France, inter mingled and fused with it almost insensibly. This is more evident in comedy than in tragedy, for English tragedy was a late development—late in the history of the type in Europe, and late in the history of the drama in England. The importance of the native element in *Ralph Roister Doister*, our first Plautine comedy, is not overestimated by Mr. Brooke, who also draws attention to the combination of native realism, classical structure, and Italian romance in *Misogonus*, now convincingly ascribed by Professor Kittredge[1] to Lawrence Johnson, who proceeded M.A. at Christ's College, Cambridge, in 1577. In early English classical tragedy, the native elements, though not so obvious or so important, are still noteworthy. As a detailed analysis will show, Latin tragedy in the original and in translation (possibly Greek tragedy in translation, though of this there is little evidence), and Italian classical tragedy combined with native elements and traditions to bring about the emergence of popular tragedy—'the most eventful movement, probably, in the history of English literature.'[2]

In a combination so complex, in which national events and characteristics are involved, as well as literary types and traditions, it is no easy task to estimate the precise importance and extent of a particular influence and to classify the

---

[1] *Journal of Germanic Philology*, vol. iii, p. 335.
[2] Brooke, p. 204.

contributing causes which lead to the emergence of a new type.
Brunetière well said in *L'Évolution d'un Genre : La Tragédie* :

Ni les genres en particulier ni l'art en général ne se renouvellent
d'eux-mêmes ou de leur fond, et l'intervention du génie, si quelque-
fois, très rarement, elle contrarie l'évolution d'un genre, s'y insère,
le plus souvent, pour la hâter en s'y adaptant. C'est la civilisation
tout entière qui doit être renouvelée dans son principe et dans sa
forme, pour que l'art se renouvelle et que les anciens genres, dans
un milieu nouveau lui-même, recommencent à vivre d'une vie
vraiment féconde.[1]

Brunetière goes on to urge that the mediaeval drama had
nothing to do with the development of tragedy :

Il y a solution de continuité dans la chaîne des temps. Les
auteurs de nos Mystères n'ont rien hérité des Latins et des Grecs,
de Pacuvius ni de Sophocle, et, j'ajoute, sans tarder davantage,
qu'ils n'ont préparé ni le drame de Shakespeare, ni la tragédie de
Racine.

Now as to French tragedy Brunetière spoke with knowledge
and authority ; but as to Shakespearean tragedy he was probably
not so well acquainted with the evidence.   In this case, there is
no 'solution of continuity' between the mediaeval drama and
the new form of art, which sprang from the combination of
native and classical elements.   'Of the several causes pre-
requisite to the growth of English national tragedy, the most
indispensable was the example of the Latin classic model,' so
far we may agree with Mr. Brooke, and this is, indeed, the main
thesis of this volume ; but we must not overlook the importance
of the native and popular elements which contributed most
materially to the vitality of the new form of art and prepared the
way for its acceptance on the public stage.   Plays like *A New
Enterlude of Vice Conteyninge the Historye of Horestes with the
cruell revengment of his Fathers death upon his one natur[a]ll
Mother*, by John Pikeryng (1567), *A lamentable Tragedie,
mixed full of plesant mirth, containing the life of Cambises king
of Percia*, by Thomas Preston (S. R. 1569–70), *The excellent*

[1] *Revue des Deux Mondes*, Nov. 1901, p. 136.

Comedie of two the moste faithfullest Freendes, Damon and Pithias, by Richard Edwards (1571, S. R. 1567–8), and *A new Tragicall Comedie of Apius and Virginia,* by R. B. (1575, S. R. 1567–8), are classical only in subject; in structure and method they go back to the mediaeval tradition. *Horestes* was certainly acted in London, as is proved by the prayer for the Lord Mayor at the end ; it was arranged for performance by the usual six players, and the form of the stage directions is significant :

The Vice, who lends the play some small semblance of unity, opens the action with a conversation, apparently with a soldier who is on the battlements of the city of Mycenae. 'Hear entryth Rusticus and hodge.' An interchange of incivilities ends with the traditional stage quarrel. 'Vp with thy staf, and be readye to smyte ; but hodge smit first ; and let y⁰ vice thwacke them both and run out.' Horestes, Idumeus, and Councell forward the action a little, soon to give way to Haultersycke and Hempstringe, who sing and 'fyght at bofites with fystes'. ' Let yᵉ drum play and enter Horestis with his band ; marche about the stage.' Horestes takes leave of Idumeus.; Egistus and Clytemnestra enter singing, and hear the news of the advance of 'the mightey knight Horestes with a mightey pewsaunt hand'. After a comic scene, in which 'Sodyer' is beaten by a woman whom he has taken prisoner, 'Horestes entrith with his bande and marcheth about the stage... Let yᵉ trumpet go towarde the Citie and blowe ... Let yᵉ trumpet leaue soundyng and let Harrauld speake and Clytemnestra speake ouer y⁰ wal . . . Let yᵉ haraulde go out here. . . . Go and make your liuely battel and let it be longe care you can win yᵉ Citie, and when you haue won it, let Horestes bringe out his mother by the arme, and let yᵉ droum sease playing and the trumpet also, when she is taken ; let her knele downe and speake . . . Let Egistus enter and set hys men in a raye, and let the drom playe tyll Horestes speaketh ... stryke vp your drum and fyght a good whil, and then let sum of Egistus men flye, and then take hym and let Horestes drau him vyolentlye, and let yᵉ drums sease.'

Then follows the hanging of Egistus from the battlements in full view of the audience : ' fling him of yᵉ lader and then let on bringe in his mother Clytemnestra ; but let her loke wher Egistus hangeth.' Clytemnestra goes out weeping to her death, and the army of

Horestes enters the city gate. After another song by the Vice, Menalaus gives his daughter Hermione in marriage to Horestes, who, with the consent of Nobilitye and Cominyalte, is crowned king by Truth and Dewty.

The lack of decorum and dignity, the absence of division into acts and scenes and utter formlessness of the whole production, the absolute disregard of time and place, the constant harking back to the moralities in such characters as Councell, Nature, Provisyon, Truthe, Fame, Dewtey, Revenge, Nobilitye, and Cominyalte indicate the persistence of the mediaeval tradition. There is no art in *Horestes*, and little dramatic skill: but there is a good deal of action, of stage business, and of the marching and countermarching afterward a popular feature of the history plays. M. Feuillerat agrees with Collier that 'such a crude production could never have been performed before any audience but one of the lowest description', and he therefore concludes that it was not identical with the *Orestes* acted at court in 1567–8. A slight indication in support of this view may be mentioned: the Revels Account gives 'Orestioes howse Rome' as the item of expenditure, and it is evident that the scene required for our *Horestes* is the city of Mycenae, furnished with a wall, battlements, and an entrance gate—the usual stage setting of the early theatre.

Cambises and *Apius and Virginia* belong to the same group of plays, dealing with classical subjects, but evidently intended for the public stage; the thirty-eight characters of *Cambises* are arranged for eight actors to play, and the stage direction in *Apius and Virginia*, '*Here let Virginius go about the scaffold,*' recalls the practice of the miracles: in both there are many characters (even more than in *Horestes*) taken over from the tradition of the moralities. Yet in *Cambises* we discern an attempt to establish a connexion with the classical stage: the prologue appeals to the authority of Agathon and Seneca, and imitates a passage from the *Thyestes* (213–17). But the most notable advance in this group of early plays was made by Richard Edwards, who was very highly esteemed by his contemporaries as both poet and playwright. Googe, Turberville, and Twynne eulogize him in verse, and Webbe, Puttenham, and Meres all have complimentary references to him in their treatises on poetry. Anthony à Wood has the following in the *Athenae Oxonienses*:

Richard Edwards, a *Somersetshire* Man born, was admitted Scholar of *Corp. Ch. Coll.* under the tuition of *George Etheridge*, on the eleventh of May 1540, and Probationer Fellow 11 *August* 1544, Student of the upper table of *Christ Church* at its foundation by K. *Hen.* 8 in the beginning of the Year 1547, aged 24, and the same Year took the Degree of M. of Arts. In the beginning of Qu. *Elizabeth*, he was made one of the Gentlemen of her Chapel, and Master of the Children there, being then esteemed not only an excellent Musician, but an exact Poet, as many of his compositions in Music (for he was not only skill'd in the practical but theoretical part) and Poetry do shew, for which he was highly valued by those that knew him, especially his associates in *Lincolns* Inn (of which he was a member, and in some respects an Ornament) and much lamented by them, and all ingenious Men of his time, when he died.

Damon and Pithias.

Damon and Pithias, Wood says, was 'acted at Court and in the University', and Mr. W. Y. Durand has shown[1] that it is the play referred to in the following item in the Revels Accounts for 1564 with the side-note, 'Edwardes tragedy,' in Sir William Cecil's handwriting:

Cristmas Anno Septimo Elizabeth, wages or dieats of the officers and Tayllours payntars workinge diuers Cities and Townes carvars Silkewemen for frenge & tassells mercers ffor Sarsnett & other stuf and Lynen drapars for canvas to couer diuers townes and howsses and other devisses and Clowds ffor a maske and a showe and a play by the childerne of the chaple ffor Rugge bumbayst an cottone ffor hosse and other provicions and necessaries.

The 'Rugge bumbayst an cottone ffor hosse' were required for the great breeches with which Jacke and Wyll were laden:

---

[1] *Modern Language Notes*, vol. xxiii, p. 131.

> *Grimme.* Pretie men (quoth you) nay, you are stronge men, els
> you could not beare these britches.
> *Wyll.* Are these great hose? In faith goodman Colier you see
> with your nose.
> By myne honestie, I haue but for one lining in one hose, but vii els
> of Roug.
> *Grimme.* That is but a little, yet it makes thee seeme a great
> bugge.
> *Jacke.* How say you goodman Colier, can you finde any fault
> here?
> *Grimme.* Nay you should finde faught, mary heres trimme
> geare.
> Alas little knaue, doest not sweat, thou goest with great payne,
> These are no hose, but watter bougets, I tell thee playne.

In the edition of 1571 the play is provided with a prologue
'somewhat altered for the proper use of them that hereafter
shall haue occasion to plaie it, either in Priuate, or open
Audience'. We have, therefore, in this instance a play first
acted at Court, then given at the University of Oxford, and
finally published in a form thought suitable for any public or
private performance. In the prologue the author warns the
audience not to expect the 'toying Playes' to which they are
accustomed ; he intends to observe *decorum* (the italics are his)
according to the precepts of Horace, and he has therefore
taken a serious subject — the historical friendship of Damon
and Pithias :

> Which matter mixt with myrth and care, a iust name to applie,
> As seemes most fit wee haue it termed, a Tragicall Commedie.

He pays no attention to later critics, does not divide his play
into acts, and passes over an interval of two months without
any break except such as could be understood from the
dialogue, even Damon's *exit* being left to be implied from his
farewell speech. About this point, where the serious interest
of the play first culminates, the dialogue follows the manner
and matter of Seneca. We have a long passage of rather
halting stichomythia, in which Eubulus offers to Dionysius the

same counsels of prudence and mercy that Seneca gives to Nero in the *Octavia* (463-9):

Dion. Let Fame talke what she lyst, so I may lyue in safetie.

Eub. The onely meane to that, is to use mercie.

Dion. A milde Prince the people despiseth.

Eub. A cruell kynge the people hateth.

Dion. Let them hate me, so they feare mee.

Eub. That is not the way to lyue in safetie.

Dion. My sword and power shall purchase my quietnesse.

Eub. That is sooner procured by mercy and gentilnesse.

Dion. Dionisius ought to be feared.

Eub. Better for him to be welbeloued.

Dion. Fortune maketh all thinges subiect to my power.

Eub. Beleue her not she is a light Goddesse, she can laugh & lowre.

These maxims, taken directly from Seneca, are marked for special attention according to the practice of early editions, and there is no doubt that the author was proud of them. For two or three hundred lines he continues in this serious vein, unbroken except by the remark of Gronno the hangman to Damon :

> Because your eyes haue made suche a doo,
> I wyl knock down this your Lantern, & shut up your shop
>   window too.

The parting of Damon and Pithias is managed with some pathos, though it only needs a touch of exaggeration to convert it into a travesty like the interlude of Pyramus and Thisbe in *A Midsummer Night's Dream* :

Pith. My Damon, farewell, the Gods haue thee in kepeing.

Dam. Oh my Pithias, my Pleadge farewell, I parte from thee weeping

But ioyfull at my day appoynted I wyll retourne agayne,

When I wyll deliuer thee from all trouble and paine :

Stephano wyll I leaue behinde me to wayte upon thee in prison alone,

And I whom fortune hath reserued to this miserie, wyll walke home,

Ah my Pithias, my Pleadge, my life, my friend, farewell.

Pith. Farewell my Damon.

Dam. Loth I am to departe, sith sobbes my trembling tounge doth stay,

Oh Musicke, sounde my dolefull playntes when I am gone my way.

But once Damon is gone on his two months' reprieve, we return to the beating and boxing and other comic business of the stage—the bombast breeches of Jacke and Wyll, and their shaving of Grimme the Collier, who 'singeth Busse' to the tune of

Too nidden and toodle toodle doo nidden,

and is robbed of his money and 'Debenters'. Then the Muses sing :

Alas what happe hast thou poore Pithias now to die,

Wo worth the which man for his death hath geuen us cause to crie.

Eubulus bears the other part in this odd lament, which is immediately followed by the preparations for the execution of Pithias.   His final speech is not ineffective, protesting his faith in the absent Damon, whom he addresses thus :

Oh my Damon farewell now for euer, a true friend to me most deare :

Whyles lyfe doth laste, my mouth shall styll talke of thee,

And when I am dead my simple ghost true witnes of amitie :

Shall hoouer about the place wheresoeuer thou bee.

Gronno congratulates himself on the excellence of the garments of which he despoils Pithias, and the scene continues :

Gronno. Now Pithias kneele downe, aske me blessyng like a pretie boy,

And with a trise thy head from thy shoulders I will conuay.

Here entreth Damon running & stayes the sword.

Damon. Stay, stay, stay, for the kinges aduantage stay,

Oh mightie kyng, myne appoynted time is not yet fully past,

Within the compasse of myne houre loe, here, I come at last :

A life I owe, a life I wyll you pay :

Oh my Pithias, my noble pledge, my constant friende,

Ah wo is me for Damons sake, how neare were thou to thy ende :

Geue place to me, this rowme is myne, on this stage must I play,

Damon is the man, none ought but he to Dionisius his blood to pay.

After the pardon of the two friends by Dionysius we have 'the last song' with the refrain :

> The Lorde graunt her such frindes most noble Queene Elizabeth.

We are at a loss to understand the enthusiasm of Edwards's contemporaries for his work, because we cannot dismiss from our minds the tragedy of Marlowe and Shakespeare of a generation later ; but, to be just to this early Elizabethan 'tragicall commedie', we should compare it, not with what followed, but with what had gone before. Its superiority is then apparent : the omission of abstract characters is in itself an enormous gain, and gives the play a naturalness and directness impossible so long as the conventions of the moralities were retained. Edwards did not dispense with the comic stage business because he could not do without it. Such dramatic talent as he had was for comedy rather than tragedy, and he had to rely on scenes of rough humour to fill out his play and hold the attention of his audience. The prologue to *Damon and Pithias* shows that he had ambitions for the serious drama. Apparently the 'toyes . . . in commycall wise' he had written before had given offence :

> A soden change is wrought,
> For loe, our Aucthors Muse, that masked in delight,
> Hath forst his Penne agaynst his kinde, no more suche sportes to write.

He hoped to achieve success in the serious drama by skill in characterization, and so far his ambition was well-directed : but he had not the ability to make any considerable progress in the way he had marked out for himself. His serious characters are superficially drawn, and have no vitality ; in critical situations they lack tragic dignity and intensity. Edwards had not sufficient command over the means of emotional expression to give tragic interest to a character or situation, and his pathos, simple to the point of artlessness, trembles dangerously near the edge of the ridiculous. It is, perhaps, to his credit that he made no attempt to introduce the tragic passions and sensational situations of Seneca to the English stage, for it was a task to which his powers were ill-suited. He evidently knew Seneca, and he must have known of *Gorboduc*, which had been twice acted, though not yet printed, at the time when *Damon and Pithias* was performed. It was the other side of Elizabethan tragedy he helped to develop—its popular appeal, and the setting of a serious theme amid scenes of rough humour, lively stage business, and popular ditties to be sung by the Children of the Chapel.

Palamon and Arcite.

It seems likely enough that if we had Edwards's lost play of *Palamon and Arcite*, we should think more highly of his powers as a writer of serious drama. The play attracted considerable attention at its performance before the Queen in Christ Church Hall on September 2nd and 4th, 1566, partly on account of an unfortunate accident on the first day, by which three men were killed and others injured owing to the collapse of a stairway as the audience was crowding in. From Wood's report of the Queen's comments and the Latin accounts of Bereblock and Robinson,[1] we can make up a tolerable version of the plot, which was founded upon Chaucer's *Knight's Tale*, possibly through an intermediate Latin version, though Robinson's statement to this effect may be merely an error on his part.

Apparently the play began with the two knights already in prison, and the Lady Emilia gathering flowers prettily in a garden represented on the stage, and singing sweetly in the time of March [? May]. Both the knights fell in love with her, and contended fiercely with each other in prison. Arcite, who was 'a right marshall knight, having a swart countenance and a manly face', was released through the intervention of Perotheus, and banished ; but heeding not the penalty of death, he returned in a meaner garb, and called himself Philostrate, no task being so vile that it was not made sweet to him by the presence of Emilia. Meanwhile, Palamon escaped by drugging his guard, and hid in the woods, .

---

[1] Printed in *Elizabethan Oxford* by Charles Plummer, and translated with comments by W. Y. Durand, *Journal of Germanic Philology*, vol. iv, and *Publications of the Modern Language Association of America*, vol. xx.

where he met Arcite, and was on the point of fighting with him
when the battle was checked by the intervention of Theseus, who
came upon them as he was hunting. Palamon told who he was,
and at the entreaty of the ladies, his life was spared by Theseus,
who gave the knights fourteen days to prepare for a combat for
Emilia's hand. The first part of the play apparently ended with
this hunting scene, which was much admired. Wood says :—' In
the said Play was acted a cry of Hounds in the quadrant, upon the
train of a Fox in the hunting of Theseus : with which the young
Scholars who stood in the remoter parts of the Stage, and in the
windows, were so much taken and surpriz'd (supposing it had been
real) that they cried out, *there, there,—he's caught, he's caught,—*
All which the Queen merrily beholding, said, *O excellent ! those
Boys in very troth are ready to leap out of the windows to follow
the Hounds.'*

At the second day's performance, a gallant show was made at
the lists, Arcite being supported by Emetrius, King of India, with
a hundred knights, and Palamon by as many under the Thracian
Lycurgus, though the issue was to be decided by single combat
between the two chief contestants. Three altars were set up, and
Emilia prayed to Diana, Arcite to Mars, and Palamon to Venus.
In the duel (of which Bereblock gives a lively description, partly
copied from Livy's account of the contest between the Horatii and
the Curatii, I. xxv) Palamon at last sank under his bloody wounds,
which were visible to every one, and in lofty eloquence reproached
Venus for deserting him. Moved by the tears and entreaties of
Venus, Saturn slew Arcite with subterranean fire as he went in
triumph crowned with laurel. There was a great funeral, at which
the actor of Perethous aroused the Queen's admiration by throwing
St. Edward's rich cloak on to the pyre, and saying with an oath,
' Go, fool,' when a bystander would have stayed his arm. By
common consent, Emilia was betrothed to Palamon, amid the
applause of the spectators, the hall being now densely crowded.
The Queen ' gave Mr. Edwards, the maker thereof, great thanks for
his pains', and rewarded the ' pretty boy' who played Emilia with
eight angels.

Among the other parts commended by the Queen was
Trecatio : ' God's pity, what a knave it is' ; he was evidently
a comic character, perhaps, as Mr. Durand suggests, like the

Stephano of *Damon and Pithias*. The most popular feature
of the play was the hunting scene, as to which Wood has the
following note :

This part being repeated before certain Courtiers in the lodgings
of Mr. *Rog. Marbeck* one of the Canons of *Ch. Ch.* by the players
in their Gowns (for they were all Scholars that acted, among whom
were *Miles Windsore* and *Thom. Twyne* of C. C. C.) before the
Queen came to Oxon, was by them so well liked, that they said it
far surpassed *Damon and Pythias*, than which, they thought,
nothing could be better. Likewise some said that if the Author did
proceed to make more Plays before his Death, he would run mad.
But this it seems was the last, for he lived not to finish others that
he had lying by him.

So far as one can judge from the extant evidence, Edwards
dealt with the story of Palamon and Arcite in much the same
way as he had done with that of *Damon and Pithias*, except
that he had a much richer plot to work on, and was not obliged
to fill in with comic business ; this was accordingly subordinated,
and confined, apparently, to the knave Trecatio.   But Edwards
still relied upon such extraneous attractions as Emilia singing
in the garden, the hunting scene, the tournament, the sacrifices
at the altars of Diana, Mars, and Venus, the intervention of
Saturn, and the funeral pyre on which Arcite's body was burnt.
How far he succeeded in giving distinct characters to Palamon,
Arcite, Theseus, and Emilia, and in expressing the passions
that moved them, we are unable to judge.   He spent two
months at the University completing the play, and supervising
the preparation of the stage setting, which was of unusual
magnificence. The same stage, well furnished with houses
and splendidly lighted, served also for a Latin prose comedy,
Marcus Geminus, and a Latin tragedy by Dr. James Calfhill,
Progne ; the latter opened with a prologue by Diomedes, driven
from the infernal regions by furies, and foretelling dreadful
crimes after the manner of the shade of Tantalus in Seneca's
Thyestes. As the same device had been used by Corraro in
his Latin tragedy,[1] it seems likely that Calfhill was indebted to

[1] See p. xxiii.

him, possibly through the Italian version of Lodovico Do-
menichi (1561). It is noteworthy that even this courtly and
academic audience preferred the native flavour of Edwards's
romantic play, for *Progne* 'did not take half so well as the
much admired play of *Palamon and Arcite*'.

The Classical Impulse.

Renascence tragedy began so late in England that it was subject to all the influences which had affected the development of
the type on the Continent. Greek tragedy was, of course,
accessible in the original and in translations.[1] Ascham says in
The Scholemaster (pr. 1570):

In Tragedies, ... the *Grecians, Sophocles* and *Euripides* far ouer
match our *Seneca* in Latin, namely in οἰκονομίᾳ *et Decoro*, although
Senecaes elocution and verse be verie commendable for his tyme.
And for the matters of *Hercules, Thebes, Hippolytus*, and *Troie*, his
Imitation is to be gathered into the same booke, and to be tryed by
the same touchstone, as is spoken before . . . Whan *M. Watson* in
S. Iohns College at Cambrige wrote his excellent Tragedie of
Absalon, M. Cheke, he and I, for that part of trew Imitation, had
many pleasant talkes togither, in comparing the preceptes of
Aristotle and *Horace de Arte Poetica*, with the examples of
Euripides, Sophocles, and *Seneca*. Few men, in writyng of Tragedies in our dayes, haue shot at this marke. Some in *England*, moe
in *France, Germanie*, and *Italie*, also haue written Tragedies in our
tyme : of the which, not one I am sure is able to abyde the trew
touch of *Aristotles* preceptes, and *Euripides* examples, saue onely two,
that euer I saw, *M. Watsons Absalon*, and *Georgius Buckananus
Iephthe*.

Buchanan's *Jephthes* (pr. 1554) and *Johannes Baptistes*
(pr. 1576) were commended also by Sidney in the *Apology for
Poetry* and by R. Wilmot in the preface to the revised edition of

---

[1] See Churton Collins, *Studies in Shakespeare*, pp. 39–42, as to the
Latin translations of Aeschylus, Sophocles, and Euripides, known in England at the beginning of Elizabeth's reign; and pp. 13–15 as to the teaching
of Greek in Elizabethan schools. Ascham, writing from Cambridge in
1542 to his friend Brandesby, says : 'Sophocles et Euripides sunt hic
familiariores quam olim Plautus fuerat, quum tu hic eras.'

Tancred and Gismund (1592). The *Absalon* Ascham mentions
as withheld by Watson from publication 'bicause, *in locis paribus,
Anapestus* is twice or thrice used in stede of *Iambus*', is perhaps identical with a Latin tragedy in the British Museum, MS. 957. Latin
plays on scriptural subjects were also written by Nicholas Grim-
oald or Grimaldi,—*Christus Redivivus*, acted at Oxford in 1542,
and *Archipropheta*, printed at Cologne in 1548 ; the latter is said
to be an adaptation of a tragedy (also printed at Cologne, 1546) by
Jacob Schoepper of Dortmund. Beza's *Abraham's Sacrifice* and
John Knox's *Christ Triumphant* appeared in English versions
in 1577 and 1578 respectively. Ascham at one time (*Epistle* xv)
proposed to translate all Sophocles into Latin, and he is said to
have done the *Philoctetes*, but his version has not survived.
Gabriel Harvey in a manuscript note in his copy of Gascoigne
(now in the Bodleian Library) commends the Latin translation
by Thomas Watson (not identical with the one mentioned
above) of Sophocles' *Antigone* (pr. 1581) as ' magnifice acta
solenni ritu et uerè tragico apparatu '. Translations of the Greek
plays into English were rare, though a version of the *Iphigenia
at Aulis* by Lady Lumley (d. 1577) has survived in manuscript,
and has been recently printed by the Malone Society. George
Peele, when at Christ Church, Oxford, made a translation of the
Iphigenia, but which *Iphigenia* it was, and whether the translation was in Latin or English does not appear. He was also
associated after he left the University with William Gager,
whose *Meleager* (acted 1581, pr. 1592) and *Dido* (acted 1583,
pr. 1592) excited a lively controversy, lasting to the end
of the century, as to the production of plays by university
students ; but by this time the fate of English tragedy had been
decided by Kyd, Marlowe, and Shakespeare. In any case, the
influence of these classical imitations and translations could only
be exerted in a direction already sufficiently determined by
English tragedies of greater influence and wider circulation.

Gorboduc.

Acted at the Christmas Revels of the Inner Temple in 1561–2 and repeated on January 18, 1562, before the Queen at Whitehall, published first surreptitiously in 1565 and then in an authorized edition in 1570-1, *Gorboduc* has a claim for consideration which has been fully acknowledged. Sidney praised it in a passage of the *Apology* too familiar for repetition, and Pope commended it for ' a propriety in sentiments, a dignity in the sentences, an unaffected perspicuity of style, and an easy flow of numbers ; in a word, that chastity, correctness, and gravity of style which are so essential to tragedy ; and which all the tragic poets who followed, not excepting Shakespeare himself, either little understood or perpetually neglected '. In this appreciation Pope followed Rymer, and was followed by Thomas Warton. Among recent critics Mr. Courthope has shown the clearest conception of the aims and achievements of the authors. Norton and Sackville were both young men who had won some poetical fame as undergraduates at Oxford, and Sackville's contributions to the *Mirror for Magistrates* (1559) must have stood out from the first, by their grave beauty and majesty of style, among the tedious versifying of his fellows in that monumental work. It is natural to ascribe to him the adoption of blank verse and its establishment as the characteristic metre of English tragedy, though Norton is given credit by the printer of the first edition for the first three acts of the play, and Dr. H. A. Watt [1] in a careful examination of metrical characteristics finds reasons in support of this division of authorship. Sackville was the younger man, but it is difficult to believe that his was not the controlling personality, in view of the character of Norton's other literary work. Both were members of Elizabeth's first Parliament and were keenly interested in politics, Norton being apparently Chairman of the Committee of the House of Commons which in January, 1563, drew up a petition ' for

[1] Doctor's thesis, published by the University of Wisconsin, 1910, *Gorboduc ; or, Ferrex and Porrex.*

Limitation of the Succession' to be presented to the Queen.[1] In the text, in the dumb shows, and even in the argument of the tragedy, there are numerous suggestions to Elizabeth that she ought to provide the throne with an heir. So, when *Palamon and Arcite* was acted, and Emilia, in answer to her prayer for a virgin life, received a divine admonition to marry, the spectators doubtless gave the oracle a personal interpretation in accordance with their own desires. The allusions to the contemporary political situation in *Gorboduc* are much more direct, and it is not too much to say that this was one of the main things the dramatists had in mind in writing the play. The political disquisitions which the reader of to-day finds so tedious had a very immediate interest to the courtiers and lawyers who first heard them. It was probably this opportunity for political generalizations with a very direct personal application which determined the choice of the subject rather than the superficial parallel to Seneca's *Thebais*. The form of the drama is, indeed, Senecan, but the parallel passages (which are set forth in detail in Dr. Watt's notes in this volume) are neither numerous nor important. The adoption of a native subject is noteworthy, and was perhaps due to Sackville's interest in the *Mirror for Magistrates*. Even more significant is the wide canvas employed, and the absolute disregard of the unities of time and place, which grieved Sidney 'because it might not remaine as an exact model of all Tragedies'. It was the 'stately speeches and well sounding Phrases, clyming to the height of *Seneca* his stile' that won Sidney's admiration, and it was no doubt in this quality of decorum and dignity that the tragedy exercised the greatest influence, apart from such devices as the dumb show and the chorus, which were taken over by the immediate successors of *Gorboduc* in the precise form devised by Norton and Sackville. In other respects, the authors, especially Sackville, made beginnings—though little more than beginnings—which were to be developed into the peculiar merits of Elizabethan tragedy. Sackville deals freely with the incidents of the plot, so as to

[1] See note on p. 298 (*Arg.* 7–9) and 305–6.

give significance and distinction to his characters.   Ferrex and
Porrex are recognizable personalities, not merely interchangeable
parts, like Edwards's Damon and Pithias.   Marcella, too, is
something more than the messenger of classical tradition.
Lamb's suggestion that 'the murdered prince Porrex and she
had been lovers' is perhaps hardly justified by the text, but
undoubtedly her lament over him has a romantic and personal
flavour very welcome in the midst of so much general reflection,
moral platitude, and political argument.   She recalls 'the
fauour of his comely face', 'his princely chere and countenance',
'his faire and seemely personage',

> His noble limmes in such proportion cast
> As would haue wrapt a sillie womans thought;
>
> .   .   .   .
>
> Ah noble prince, how oft haue I behelde
> Thee mounted on thy fierce and traumpling stede,
> Shining in armour bright before the tilt,
> And with thy mistresse sleue tied on thy helme,
> And charge thy staffe to please thy ladies eye,
> That bowed the head peece of thy frendly foe !
> How oft in armes on horse to bend the mace !
> How oft in armes on foote to breake the sworde,
> Which neuer now these eyes may see againe.

In these lines we have the first promise—slight but clear—of a
new form of art.

Jocasta.

Jocasta, presented by Gascoigne and Kinwelmersh at Gray's
Inn, in 1566, has lost the main title to consideration it claimed
at its first appearance, viz. that it was a translation from
Euripides.   It is only in the present generation that this claim
was shown to be misleading [1]; as a matter of fact *Jocasta*
follows, page by page, and line by line, the *Giocasta* of Lodovico Dolce already noted.[2]   Even Dolce did not translate from
the original Greek, but took a Latin version, and dealt with it

---

[1] By Professor J. P. Mahaffy in *Euripides* (*Classical Writers*), pp. 134–5.
[2] See p. xxxvi.

in his own independent fashion.   The changes he made were, however, not important : for the Euripidean prologue by Jocasta he substituted an expository conversation between Jocasta and an old servant ; the παιδαγωγός of Antigone became the ' Bailo di Polinice '.   ' Bailo ', which is the regular Venetian word for a governor or tutor, is retained in the English version, but the service is transferred in the stage directions to Antigone, though the reference to Polynices remains in the text.[1]   It is odd that this confusion and the Italian word ' Bailo ' did not put the critics of *Jocasta* on the right scent as to its origin. Warton's criticism, just and adequate as it is in other respects, is somewhat ludicrously marred by his supposition that there was no intermediary between Euripides and the translators :

It must, however, be observed, that this is by no means a just or exact translation of the *Jocasta*, that is the *Phoenissae*, of Euripides. It is partly a paraphrase, and partly an abridgement, of the Greek tragedy.   There are many omissions, retrenchments, and transpositions.   The chorus, the characters, and the substance of the story, are entirely retained, and the tenor of the dialogue is often preserved through whole scenes.   Some of the beautiful odes of the Greek chorus are neglected, and others substituted in their places, newly written by the translators.   In the favorite address to Mars, Gascoigne has totally deserted the rich imagery of Euripides, yet has found means to form an original ode, which is by no means destitute of pathos or imagination . . . I am of opinion, that our translators thought the many mythological and historical allusions in the Greek chorus, too remote and unintelligible, perhaps too cumbersome, to be exhibited in English.   In the ode to *Concord*, which finishes the fourth act, translated by Kinwelmershe, there is great elegance of expression and versification.   It is not in Euripides.

The passages which are not in Euripides are, of course, in Dolce, and all that we can credit to Gascoigne and Kinwelmersh is the smoothness of the English rendering.   The translators followed their Italian original as closely as they could ; occasionally they misunderstood a passage, usually where either the

---

[1] See p. 78, line 5, and note thereon.

Latin translator or Dolce had failed to convey the meaning of
Euripides with sufficient clearness.   In some cases we can trace
the steps by which the original Greek has descended into
nonsense or platitude, but such instances (given in detail in the
notes to this edition) are not sufficient, even when combined
with the slight changes introduced by Dolce, to rob the play of
its effectiveness.   The *Phoenissae* is, in Paley's opinion, 'over-
loaded with action,' and this fault (if fault it be) no doubt
helped to commend *Jocasta* to Elizabethan spectators and
readers.   Gabriel Harvey wrote the following judgement in his
own copy : ' An excellent Tragedie : full of many discreet, wise
and deep considerations. *Omne genus scripti gravitate Tragoedia vincit.*'   It was again the philosophical reflections and
the dignity of the dialogue that impressed a public eager for the
introduction of these classical virtues into English literature.
The stir and movement of the action, the sensational situations,
and the romantic sacrifice of Meneceus appealed to dramatic
tastes already firmly established.   These qualities are, of course,
due to Euripides, and not to Dolce, or to his translators.   The
members of Gray's Inn added nothing except the argument
(done by Gascoigne), the Epilogue (by Christopher Yelverton),
and the dumb shows, which, like the blank verse, are undoubtedly due to the example of *Gorboduc*.   Though the play
is divided into acts and scenes, the action, like that of the
Phoenissae, is continuous, the four Gentlewomen who compose
the Chorus remaining on the stage from their entrance in Act I
to the end of the tragedy.   The scene represented a palace front,
with the gates called Electrae on one side, and the gates
Homoloydes on the other, the former leading to the city, and
the latter to the camp of Polynices.   The play was acted on
a scaffold, as *Gorboduc* had been, and there was a grave in it,
from which flames burst forth in the second dumb show ; this
served also, no doubt, for the gulf into which Curtius leapt in
the third dumb show.   Beside these spectacular effects, there
were marches and processions about the stage, both in the dumb
shows and in the tragedy itself.   Jocasta was attended at her

first entry by twelve gentlemen and eight gentlewomen, Antigone by three gentlewomen and her governor, Eteocles by twenty gentlemen in armour and two pages, one bearing his target, the other his helm, Creon by four gentlemen, the Priest by sixteen bacchanals 'and all his rytes and ceremonies'. There was an orchestra consisting of flutes, cornets, trumpets, drums, fifes, stillpipes, 'violles, cythren, bandurion, and such like.' Altogether, the play must have provided a gorgeous and exciting spectacle, and have produced an impression not unworthy of Gray's Inn, 'an House', the Queen said on another occasion, 'she was much beholden unto, for that it did always study for some sports to present unto her'.

Gismond of Salerne.

Gismond of Salerne, acted at the Inner Temple in 1567–8, has come down to us in two manuscripts, as well as in the revised version made by R. Wilmot, and printed in 1591 under the title *Tancred and Gismunda*, in which the dumb shows (presented at the performance but not included in the manuscripts) are described, and the rhyming lines of the original version are recast into blank verse 'according to the decorum of these daies'. From the printed edition we learn that the author of the first act was Rod. Staf.[1]; of the second, Hen[ry] No[el]; of the third, G. Al.; of the fourth, Ch[ristopher] Hat[ton]; of the fifth R[obert] W[ilmot]—all, presumably, members of the Inner Temple. The title of the Lansdowne manuscript, *Gismond of Salerne in Loue*, indicates the special claim of this play upon our notice; indeed, its first editor, Wilmot, drew attention to it with the remark: 'in poetry, there is no argument of more antiquity and elegancy than is the matter of love; for it seems to be as old as the world, and to bear date from the first time that man and woman was.' This is the first English love tragedy that has survived, though it seems likely that it was not the first written. Arthur Brooke, in

---

[1] Probably the 'Master Stafford' who was fined £5 in 1556–7 for refusing to act as Marshal.

the preface to his poem *The Tragicall Historye of Romeus and Juliet*, 1562, said that he had seen the same argument 'lately set foorth on stage', and Dr. Harold de W. Fuller believes that there was an English play on the subject, composed between 1559 and 1562, and now represented by a Dutch version, written about 1630, entitled *Romeo en Juliette*.[1] On Feb. 4, 156½, Brooke was given special admission to the Inner Temple without payment 'in consideration of certain plays and shows in Christmas last, set forth by him'. Was the original *Romeo and Juliet* acted then? If so, it has perished, for though Dr. Fuller's argument is ingenious, his conclusion involves too much hypothesis for us to treat this Dutch version very seriously. *Gismond of Salerne* holds its place as the first English tragedy founded on an Italian novel, and the first with two people in love with each other as hero and heroine.

The story is that of Boccaccio's first novel of the fourth day of the *Decameron*, and had been dramatized as early as 1499 by Cammelli, as already noted; but to this version our authors were in no way indebted. As I have shown elsewhere,[2] they went directly to the Italian of Boccaccio, and did not rely, as was formerly supposed, on the English version of Painter's *Palace of Pleasure*. Boccaccio's Ghismonda would make a magnificent tragic heroine in the hands of a capable dramatist, but the Gentlemen of the Inner Temple were at one in their determination to treat her as a victim not merely of her father's despotic cruelty, but of her own ill-regulated passions. 'Herein they all agree, commending virtue, detesting vice, and lively deciphering their overthrow that suppress not their unruly affections.' Wilmot, who held two livings in Essex between the performance of the tragedy and its publication, was able to dedicate it to two 'Right Worshipful and Virtuous Ladies', and to use it, indeed, as an introduction to their notice, 'persuading myself, there is nothing more welcome to your wisdoms than the knowledge of wise, grave, and worthy matters, tending to

---

[1] See *Modern Philology*, vol. iv, pp. 75–120.
[2] *Publications of the Modern Language Association of America*, vol. xxi, pp. 435–61.

the good instructions of youths, of whom you are mothers.'
The moral purpose of the authors is made sufficiently clear in
the choruses and epilogue, so that even 'her Majesty's right
Honourable maidens', who were present at the first performance,
could hear it without offence. This concession to Elizabethan
morality, no doubt, saved the credit of the authors and gratified
their audience ; but it made the task of dramatizing Boccaccio's
novel far more difficult. They had to omit some passages and
transpose others, and Boccaccio's conception of the character
of his heroine was modified in such a way as to gain in moral
significance, but to lose in artistic effect. The whole of the
first act is given up to setting forth Gismond's disconsolate
widowhood—not a very good beginning for a romantic heroine
—and the change of the hero from 'un giovane valletto' to 'the
Counté Palurine' takes away an artistic contrast and resource.
The magnificent speech of Boccaccio's heroine in defiance of
her father thus loses a good deal of its point and effectiveness.
The gaps made by these omissions from the original story,
however, had the advantage (as the authors no doubt considered
it) of allowing them to fill in with material from more reputable
sources. In Seneca and his Italian imitators romantic heroines
were hard to find, but victims of guilty passion were common.
They accordingly opened the play with a passage translated
from Dolce's *Didone*, and borrowed extensively from the
Phaedra and other tragedies of Seneca. The result is a mosaic
of Boccaccio, Dolce, Seneca, and English moralizing, not very
skilfully fitted together, inferior in solemn eloquence to *Gorboduc*,
and in dramatic effectiveness to *Jocasta*. Yet the play was
regarded at the time as a remarkable achievement, for William
Webbe, who as the author of *A Discourse of English Poetrie*
was entitled to some consideration, says in a letter to Wilmot :

The tragedy was by them [the Inner-Temple gentlemen] most
pithily framed, and no less curiously acted in view of her Majesty,
by whom it was then as princely accepted, as of the whole honourable
audience notably applauded : yea, and of all men generally desired,
as a work, either in stateliness of show, depth of conceit, or true

ornaments of poetical art, inferior to none of the best in that kind :
no, were the Roman Seneca the censurer.

It is hard to see upon what Webbe based his judgement, unless
he regarded as ' true ornaments of the poetical art ' the passages
copied from Seneca.   We have, as in the earlier plays, a chorus
of four, and there was the usual attempt to make up for the
lack of dramatic gift by the provision of spectacles—' stateliness
of show,' as Webbe puts it.   Cupid came down from heaven to
speak the prologue, and Megaera came up from hell to open
Act IV.   The dumb shows offered the usual combination of
gorgeous vesture, elaborate allegory, and appropriate music.
At the opening of the play, according to the stage direction of
the printed edition, 'Cupid cometh out of the heavens in a
cradle of flowers, drawing forth upon the stage, in a blue twist
of silk, from his left hand, Vain Hope, Brittle Joy : and with
a carnation twist of silk from his right hand, Fair Resemblance,
Late Repentence.'   The subsequent dumb shows were more
realistic in character, and set forth the incidents of the following
acts in pantomime, like the dumb show of the play within the
play in *Hamlet*.   The *Introductio in Actum Quintum* will serve
for an example :

> Before this act was a dead march played, during which entered
> on the stage Renuchio, Captain of the Guard, attended upon by the
> guard.   They took up Guiscard from under the stage ; then after
> Guiscard had kindly taken leave of them all, a strangling-cord was
> fastened about his neck, and he haled forth by them.   Renuchio
> bewaileth it ; and then, entering in, bringeth forth a standing cup of
> gold, with a bloody heart reeking hot in it, and then saith, *ut
> sequitur*.

In Senecan sensationalism the authors were certainly not
lacking, and though it seems somewhat perfunctory for the
manuscript versions to inform the audience in the epilogue by
way of parenthesis that Tancred ' now himself hath slayen ',
the final speech in Wilmot's edition, in which Tancred first
puts out his eyes and then kills himself, is not altogether an
improvement.

It seems almost sacrilege to suggest such a pitiful predecessor as this for *Romeo and Juliet*; but there is a good deal of blood-shed (beside much else) in Shakespeare's play, and I am inclined to agree with Mr. Brooke that 'fundamentally it belongs to the progeny of Senecan tragedy'.[1] In the use of the chorus and the concentration of the action, Shakespeare shows a conscious, if inconsiderable, submission to classical convention. So much may be said without forgetting the enormous gulf in poetic and dramatic quality which sunders *Romeo and Juliet* from *Gismond of Salerne*. The earlier attempt to present an Italian love-story in the form of a tragedy leaves Shakespeare's achievement hardly less miraculous than if we regard it as having no predecessor.

The Misfortunes of Arthur.

Elaborate dumb shows, prepared by Francis Bacon and other members of Gray's Inn, formed, if one may judge from the title *Certaine deuises and shewes* &c.[2], the most important feature of *The Misfortunes of Arthur* at its first representation in 1588. For us the main significance of the play consists in the imitation of Seneca's form and the wholesale adoption of his material, the maintenance of the traditional blank verse, and the return to a native subject in what we now call the Arthurian legend, though the dramatist doubtless regarded it as part of the national history. Like the authors of *Gorboduc*, Thomas Hughes used Geoffrey of Monmouth as his main source, but he also consulted Malory's *Morte d'Arthur*, and found there some additional motives such as the incestuous birth of Mordred (who in Geoffrey is Arthur's nephew) and the mutual slaughter of father and son. These sensational situations were doubtless welcomed by Hughes as helping to bring his theme up to the proper pitch of Senecan horror. He chose as his model the most popular and the most gruesome of Seneca's tragedies, the *Thyestes*, and the shade of Tantalus appears once

---

[1] *The Tudor Drama*, p. 221.
[2] See p. 219.

more (this time in the shape of Gorlois) to speak the prologue, half a dozen lines of which are literally translated from the Latin. The general relation of Guenevora to Mordred is modelled upon that of Seneca's Clytemnestra to Aegisthus, but the sayings of other Senecan heroines—Phaedra, Medea, Deianira, and Jocasta—are also taken over, so that in one speech of twenty-eight lines, only one can be put down to the credit of the author, all the rest being translated from Seneca. It seems impossible to carry the borrowing of Senecan material further, and indeed Hughes was hindered in the development of his characters by the fetters he imposed upon his own invention. Not only are Arthur, Mordred, and Guenevora hedged round with confidants and counsellors, but they have apophthegms assigned to them taken from so many and so different Senecan characters that all impression of individuality is in danger of being lost. This is the more to be regretted because Hughes was not without the power of uniting dignity with pathos when the situation demanded the combination towards which English tragedy had so long been groping its way. Mordred and Guenevora are, perhaps, merely Senecan types; but Arthur in the final scenes shows some hint of that mysterious personality, which is indeed implied in Malory, but might easily have escaped the Elizabethan transcriber. The versification of the play, too, shows some advance, especially in the attempt to copy Seneca's stichomythia. The chorus, four in number according to established tradition, recite each a stanza in turn, and this division of the chorus, which occurs also in the dialogue of the fifth act, is the one innovation Hughes has introduced. He was indeed a desperate imitator, and such wholesome borrowing carried its own punishment in the defeat of its purpose unless that purpose were merely to impress a courtly audience with the author's familiarity with Seneca. This excessive devotion to Seneca's text, as well as the late date of the play, probably robbed it of any influence on the popular stage, which had by this time begun to go its own way.

UNION OF THE CLASSICAL AND THE POPULAR IMPULSE.

The building of the Theatre and the Curtain in 1576–7 marked the formal establishment of the drama as a popular amusement, and gave opportunity for the rapid development of new types of art. Elizabethan theatre-goers were apparently omnivorous in their tastes, and willing to tolerate anything except boredom. They demanded, above all, action—rapidly moving incidents, strongly marked passions, vehement rhetoric; and they were not, as a whole, refined or scholarly enough to care about the rules of the critics. This probably counted for as much in the type of tragedy ultimately developed as the classical models which the dramatists strove to imitate, though it was natural enough that the playwrights should not begin something entirely new, but should build upon what was already established in public esteem. Seneca was read at school, and was the accepted model of tragedy as Plautus was of comedy.[1] Mediaeval tradition, Senecan example, and popular taste combined to establish an ideal of tragedy which left enduring marks on the masterpieces of the type—*Romeo and Juliet*, *Hamlet*, *Othello*, *Lear*, and *Macbeth*. We have a curious description of some of its earlier characteristics in the Induction to *A Warning for Faire Women* (1599):

> How some damn'd tyrant to obtaine a crowne,
> Stabs, hangs, impoysons, smothers, cutteth throats,
> And then a Chorus too comes howling in,
> And tells us of the worrying of a cat.
> Then [too] a filthie whining ghost
> Lapt in some fowle sheete, or a leather pilch,
> Comes skreaming like a pigge halfc stickt,
> And cries *Vindicta*, reuenge, reuenge.

Sensational horrors, the revenge motive, the ghost, and the chorus were all found in Seneca, and, reinforced by the other

---

[1] Cf. Meres: 'As *Plautus* and *Seneca* are accounted the best for Comedy and Tragedy among the Latines; so *Shakespeare* among yᵉ English is the most excellent in both kinds for the stage'; and Polonius in *Hamlet* II. ii : ' Seneca cannot be too heavy, nor Plautus too light.'

influences mentioned, all except the chorus became established features of English tragedy. Their adoption was probably facilitated by the publication in 1581 of *Seneca His Tenne Tragedies Translated into Englysh*, though all the plays composing the volume had been previously published except the *Hercules Oetaeus* and the *Thebais*. The *Troas* had been printed in 1559, the *Thyestes* in 1560, the *Hercules Furens* in 1561, all from the pen of Jasper Heywood; the *Oedipus* was translated by Alexander Nevyle in 1560 and published in 1563; the *Octavia* was done by Thomas Nuce in 1562 and printed in 1566, the *Medea* and *Agamemnon* by John Studley appearing in the same year; the *Hippolytus* was licensed to Henry Denham in 1556–7, and was doubtless printed, though no copy of this edition is known; the *Thebais* was added in 1581 by Thomas Newton, the editor of the whole, for the sake of completeness.

The Spanish Tragedie.

It seems probable that Senecan tragedy, modified for production on the public stage, was the first kind of drama to win a conspicuous share of public favour. Jonson, in the Induction to *Bartholomew Fair*, has this sneering reference to the prejudices of the old-fashioned theatre-goer:

He that will swear, Jeronimo or Andronicus are the best plays yet, shall pass unexcepted at here, as a man whose judgment shows it is constant, and hath stood still these five-and-twenty or thirty years.

The Induction was printed in 1614, so that Jonson's twenty-five or thirty years take us back to the period 1585–9, and we have the important information that at this time *The Spanish Tragedie* (obviously referred to under the name of Jeronimo) and *Titus Andronicus* were exceedingly popular plays. Jonson's testimony to the popularity of *The Spanish Tragedie* is borne out by the numerous editions—nine or ten—printed by 1633, the long list of entries in Henslowe's Diary, the additions made to it for revival, and the parodies and quotations in later dramas. The Senecan character of this famous play has been established by a number of investigators, so that I need not stay to labour the point. Sarrazin says that ' *The Spanish Tragedie* shows almost upon every page the influence of Seneca'. In addition to the quotation of lines from the *Agamemnon* and the *Troas* in the original Latin,[1] Sarrazin shows that there are scraps of lines (quoted also in the original) from the *Oedipus* and the *Octavia*. Mr. Boas says Kyd ' had Seneca's dramas at his fingers' ends. In *The Spanish Tragedie* almost every one of them is drawn upon. The beginning of the Induction is modelled upon the opening scene in the *Thyestes*. . . . The opening eleven lines of Act III are a paraphrase of seventeen lines in the *Agamemnon*, and in I. iii. 7, and III. xiii. 72, we have reminiscences of phrases in the *Phaedra* and the *Octavia*.' Mr. Brooke describes *The Spanish Tragedie* as ' in many ways a much truer representative of Seneca than confessed imitations like *Ferrex and Porrex*'. This seems to be putting the case strongly, but it is not an exaggeration in the sense intended. Kyd gave Senecan tragedy currency and carrying power. He adopted all the features suitable to the popular stage—the horrors and sensationalism, ghosts and furies, madmen and desperate villains, stirring rhetoric, poetical description, and philosophical reflection—so far as he could, and so far as the public would tolerate them. Andrea's ghost and Revenge, which he substituted for the Chorus, are, in a sense, also taken from Seneca, but it is obvious that they are far more effective than the Chorus as a dramatic device. Kyd saw, too, the necessity of allowing the audience to see the action with their own eyes instead of having it described by messengers, though he retained the messenger to report events that could not very well be represented, such as the battle described in the opening scene.[2] He elaborated and diversified the incidents, sometimes, as at the end of the play, to an extravagant extent; he added the popular motive

---

[1] Noted in the Appendix to my essay, *The Influence of Seneca on Elizabethan Tragedy*.

[2] ' The speeches of the Senecan messenger are here Kyd's general model, but many details are borrowed from Garnier's description of the battle of Thapsus.'—Boas, Introduction, p. xxxii.

of romantic passion, and showed some gift for its expression ;
above all, as Mr. Boas rightly insists, he had a real dramatic
faculty, an eye for striking situations and stage effects.   He had
no great gift of characterization or psychological analysis, but
he was able to present a series of telling scenes which held the
attention and imprinted themselves on the memory of playgoers
for a whole generation.

NASHE'S ATTACK.

It will be convenient to consider at this point a passage in
Nashe's prefatory epistle to Greene's *Menaphon* (1589), which
has been often discussed, but is too important not to be once
more reproduced.   Nashe's letter is addressed ' to the gentlemen
students of both universities ', and is directed, in the first instance, to stir up their resentment at the pretentions of those
who have not had the advantage of a college education.
' Some deepe read Grammarians ', who have ' no more learning
in their scull, than will serue to take up a commoditie ', are
employed to write for the popular stage, and ' (mounted on the
stage of arrogance) think to outbraue better pens with the swelling bumbast of a bragging blanke verse '.

It is a common practise now a daies amongst a sort of shifting
companions, that runne through euery arte and thriue by none, to
leaue the trade of *Nouerint* whereto they were borne, and busie
themselues with the indeuors of Art, that could scarcelie latinize
their necke-verse if they should haue neede ; yet English *Seneca*
read by candle light yeeldes manie good sentences, as *Bloud is
a begger*, and so foorth : and if you intreate him faire in a frostie
morning, he will affoord you whole *Hamlets*, I should say handfulls
of tragical speaches.   But ô griefe ! *tempus edax rerum*, what's
that will last alwaies ?   The sea exhaled by droppes will in continuance be drie, and *Seneca* let bloud line by line and page by page,
at length must needes die to our stage : which makes his famisht
followers to imitate the Kidde in *Æsop*, who enamored with the
Foxes newfangles, forsooke all hopes of life to leape into a new
occupation ; and these men renowncing all possibilities of credit or
estimation, to intermeddle with Italian translations : wherein how
poorelie they haue plodded, (as those that are neither prouenzall

men, nor are able to distinguish of Articles,) let all indifferent
Gentlemen that haue trauailed in that tongue, discerne by their
twopenie pamphelts : & no meruaile though their home-born
mediocritie. be such in this matter ; for what can be hoped of
those, that thrust *Elisium* into hell, and haue not learned so long as
they haue liued in the spheares, the iust measure of the Horizon
without an hexameter.   Sufficeth them to bodge vp a blanke
verse with ifs and ands, & other while for recreation after their
candle stuffe, hauing starched their beardes most curiouslie, to
make a peripateticall path into the inner parts of the Citie,
& spend two or three howers in turning ouer French *Doudie*,
where they attract more infection in one minute, than they can do
eloquence all dayes of their life, by conuersing with anie Authors
of like argument.

There has been a wealth of learning expended on this passage,
most of which will be found summarized in Mr. R. B. McKer-
row's edition of Nashe's works ; but it cannot be said that the
allusions have been altogether cleared up.   The main points
advanced in support of the view that Kyd is the person or one
of the persons against whom the attack is directed may, however, be indicated :

(1) Kyd was not, so far as is known, a university man.   He
attended the Merchant Taylors' School, and might therefore be
included among the ' deepe read Grammarians . . . that neuer
ware gowne in the Universitie '.

(2) His father was a scrivener.

(3) He wrote blank verse for the popular stage and imitated
Seneca.   There is nothing to prove that he used the English
translation, but he might have done so, if he had needed it.

(4) *The Spanish Tragedie* was an exceedingly popular play
at the time of Nashe's attack.

(5) In *The Spanish Tragedie* I. i. 73 ' the faire Elizian greene '
is associated with ' the deepest hell '.

(6) In *The Spanish Tragedie* II. i. 120–3, there are four
consecutive lines beginning with ' and ', and in III. xiii. 99–101,
three beginning with ' if '.   In II. i. 77 Lorenzo exclaims ' what,
Villaine, ifs and ands ' ?

(7) Kyd is identified by Mr. Boas as the T.K. who in 1588 published a slim pamphlet translating Tasso's *Padre di Famiglia* with many mistakes.

(8) The allusion to 'the Kidde in *Æsop*' is paralleled by Jonson's reference to 'sporting Kyd'.

It is, of course, not necessary for the identification that Nashe's taunts should be well founded, but merely that they should be as near the truth as this unscrupulous pamphleteer was in the habit of sailing. One important fact we glean from the passage quoted is that there was in 1589 a play on the subject of *Hamlet* containing many 'tragical speaches' imitated from Seneca. The most likely way of access to the story of Hamlet would be through Belleforest's *Histoires tragiques* (1571), and this is possibly what is meant by the reference to 'French *Doudie*', who is evidently an author, and not, as some have supposed, a woman, of ill-fame. But we must not allow ourselves to be drawn aside into a discussion of the *Ur-Hamlet* problem. It is enough to say that the play upon which presumably Shakespeare's masterpiece was founded was obviously a drama of *The Spanish Tragedie* type with Kyd's sensational incidents — murders, plots, madness, real and assumed—and Kyd's favourite devices—the ghost and the play within the play.

Titus Andronicus AND THE HISTORY PLAYS.

Andronicus, which Jonson mentions as the other popular success of 1585–9, must have been either a play on which Shakespeare's *Titus Andronicus* was founded, or a competing tragedy on the same subject. It seems unnecessary to our purpose to discuss Shakespeare's share in the *Titus Andronicus* published in 1594, or the relation of this to the German and Dutch dramas which have been so carefully analysed by Dr. Fuller.[1] Those who deny the Shakespearean authorship seem to lose sight of the popularity of this type of play at the beginning of Shakespeare's career, and to disregard its excellence

[1] *Modern Language Association Publications*, vol. xvi, pp. 1–65.

in its kind, because they do not like the kind. The inclusion
of *Titus Andronicus* in the list of Meres as well as in the first
folio would be in any case hard to get over, and Professor
G. P. Baker's appreciation of its dramatic qualities [1] should
carry conviction to any one who has made himself familiar with
the literary and dramatic conditions of the time. I should be
inclined to give to this play rather than to *The Spanish
Tragedie* the attainment of perfection in the Senecan style.
Mr. Boas (Introduction, lxxxi) makes a series of very careful
distinctions between the characteristics of the two dramas, and
some of his points are surely well taken. In general the two
dramas belong to the same Senecan school : there are quotations from Seneca's Latin text in *Titus Andronicus*, as there
are in *The Spanish Tragedie*, and there are also passages
imitated from Seneca. There are in both plays sensational
horrors ; but Kyd 'never glances at the grosser side of sexual
relationships'. *Titus Andronicus* deals largely with this theme,
and so does Seneca : the source of the horrible banquet of
v. iii is obviously the *Thyestes*. The highly polished versification, the lively touches of natural description, and the weight
and beauty of the reflective passages—the redeeming qualities
of *Titus Andronicus* which are absent from Kyd's work—are
Senecan characteristics. Churton Collins, commenting upon
the passages imitated from Seneca in *Titus Andronicus*,[2] pointed
out that the resemblance in tone and style was no less striking
than the identity of content. 'In his earlier plays, where the
influence of Seneca is most perceptible, Shakespeare's style is
often as near a counterpart in English of Seneca's style in
Latin as can be.'[3]

The most important advance in *Titus Andronicus* and the
group of early history plays with which it is naturally associated
is in characterization. Aaron and Richard of Gloucester may
well have owed something to Seneca's Atreus, but the main

[1] *The Development of Shakespeare as a Dramatist.*
[2] As noted in my essay *u. s.*
[3] *Studies in Shakespeare*, p. 26.

impulse to the development of these tremendous villains was doubtless due to the master hand of Marlowe. Professor Schelling in *The English Chronicle Play* points out that *The True Tragedie of Richard III* (1594) is 'tinged with a colour of Senecan influence whereby the play becomes alike a history and a tragedy of revenge. . . . The influence of Seneca traditions and models is clear'. The same influence is to be discerned more distinctly in Thomas Legge's Latin play *Richardus Tertius* (acted at St. John's College, Cambridge, in 1573, and apparently repeated in 1579 and 1582) and to a less extent in Shakespeare's *Richard III*. This is not surprising if we accept the view of Professor Churchill[1] that *Richardus Tertius* affected *The True Tragedie of Richard III*, and that this in turn was imitated by Shakespeare ; but he seems to push his conclusions too far when he says that 'to Legge was due the turning of the drama in England in an entirely new direction'. The distinction he makes between 'mythical' and 'actual' English history was probably not recognized by Elizabethan dramatists, and *Gorboduc* can hardly be barred out on this plea. Meres classes *Richard II, Richard III, King John*, and even *Henry IV* among Shakespeare's tragedies, and it is hard to believe that the Elizabethans saw any difference in kind between *The True Tragedie of Richard Duke of Yorke* and *The Lamentable Tragedie of Locrine*, both published in 1595. It would be tempting to build a theory on the difference between 'true' and 'lamentable', but in 1605 we have *The True Chronicle History of King Leir*. All these plays have marks of Senecan influence, especially *Locrine*, which brought on the popular stage the dumb shows of academic tragedy, with Até as chorus, two ghosts, and a duplicated revenge motive ; there are numerous transcripts from Seneca, and the opening scene is imitated from *Gorboduc*. In its present shape, *Locrine* must be later than 1591,[2] but it is likely enough that the printed edition represents a revision of an older play. In any case it

---

[1] *Richard the Third up to Shakespeare, Palaestra*, vol. x.
[2] *The Cambridge History of English Literature*, vol. v, pp. 94–8.

is sufficiently remarkable to find these classical features retained at so late a date along with the rough humour and stirring battle scenes derived from the older histories, which applied to the chronicles the methods of the miracle plays.   In plays of this type, as in the tragedies founded upon other sources, we must recognize the combination of two very different streams of influence—that of the native drama with its vigorous hold on popular taste and tradition, and that of Senecan tragedy, which the amateur dramatists of the Inns of Court and the Universities introduced into England, and which the professional playwrights succeeded in adapting to the public stage.

I

GORBODVC

OR FERREX AND PORREX

BY

THOMAS NORTON AND THOMAS SACKVILLE

B

The text is that of 1570–1 (Q₂) the title-page of which is reproduced in facsimile opposite. All departures from this are enclosed in square brackets except corrections of obvious misprints and minor changes in punctuation, which are noted below. In the variants of Q_1 and Q_3 from Q_2, mere differences in spelling are not included.

$Q_1 =$ The TRAGEDIE OF GORBODVC, Where of three Actes were wrytten by Thomas Nortone, and the two laste by Thomas Sackuyle. Sett forthe as the same was shewed before the QVENES most excellent Maiestie, in her highnes Court of Whitehall, the .xviij. day of Ianuary, Anno Domini. 1561. By the Gentlemen of Thynner Temple in London.

    IMPRYNTED AT LONDON in Fletestrete, at the Signe of the Faucon by William Griffith: And are to be sold at his Shop in Saincte Dunstones Churchyarde in the West of London. Anno. 1565. Septemb. 22.

$Q_3 =$ The Serpent of Deuision. Wherein is conteined the true History or Mappe of Romes ouerthrowe. . . . Whereunto is annexed the Tragedye of Gorboduc, sometime King of this Land, and of his two Sonnes, Ferrex and Porrex. E. Allde for I. Perrin: London, 1590.

    Pt. II: (separate title) The Tragedie of Gorboduc, whereof three Actes were written by Thomas Norton, and the two last by Thomas Sackuyle. Set forth as the same was shewed before the Queenes most excellent maiesty, in her highnes Court of Whitehall, by the Gentlemen of the Inner Temple.

    AT LONDON, Printed by Edward Allde for Iohn Perrin, and are to be sold in Paules Churchyard, at the signe of the Angell. 1590.

¶ The Tragidie of Ferrex
and Porrex,

ſet forth without addition or alteration but altogether as the ſame was ſhewed
on ſtage before the Queenes Maieſtie,
about nine yeares paſt, *vz.* the
xviij. day of Ianuarie. 1561.
by the gentlemen of the
Inner Temple.

Seen and allowed. &c.

Imprinted at London by
Iohn Daye, dwelling ouer
Alderſgate.

❧ The argument of the
Tragedie.

Gorboduc king of Brittaine, diuided his realme in his life time
to his sonnes, *Ferrex* and *Porrex*.   The sonnes fell to discention.
The yonger killed the elder.   The mother that more dearely
loued the elder, for reuenge killed the yonger.   The people
moued with the crueltie of the fact, rose in rebellion and slew 5
both father and mother.   The nobilitie assembled and most
terribly destroyed the rebels.   And afterwardes for want of issue
of the prince whereby the succession of the crowne became
vncertaine, they fell to ciuill warre, in which both they and
many of their issues were slaine, and the land for a long time 10
almost desolate and miserably wasted.

2 discention] dyuision and discention Q_1 : deuision and dissention Q_3

¶ The P. to the Reader.

WHere this Tragedie was for furniture of part of the grand
Christmasse in the Inner Temple first written about
nine yeares agoe by the right honourable Thomas now Lorde
Buckherst, and by T. Norton, and after shewed before her
Maiestie, and neuer intended by the authors therof to be pub- 5
lished : yet one W. G. getting a copie therof at some yongmans
hand that lacked a litle money and much discretion, in the last
great plage. an. 1565. about v. yeares past, while the said Lord
was out of England, and T. Norton farre out of London, and
neither of them both made priuie, put it forth excedingly 10
corrupted : euen as if by meanes of a broker for hire, he should
haue entised into his house a faire maide and done her villanie,
and after all to bescratched her face, torne her apparell, berayed
and disfigured her, and then thrust her out of dores dishonested.
In such plight after long wandring she came at length home to 15
the sight of her frendes who scant knew her but by a few tokens
and markes remayning. They, the authors I meane, though
they were very much displeased that she so ranne abroad without leaue, whereby she caught her shame, as many wantons do, yet
seing the case as it is remedilesse, haue for common honestie 20
and shamefastnesse now apparelled, trimmed, and attired her
in such forme as she was before.   In which better forme since
she hath come to me, I haue harbored her for her frendes sake
and her owne, and I do not dout her parentes the authors
will not now be discontent that she goe abroad among you 25
good readers, so it be in honest companie.   For she is by my
encouragement and others somewhat lesse ashamed of the dis-
honestie done to her because it was by fraude and force.   If
she be welcome among you and gently enterteined, in fauor
of the house from whense she is descended, and of her owne 30
nature courteously disposed to offend no man, her frendes will
thanke you for it.   If not, but that she shall be still reproched
with her former missehap, or quarelled at by enuious persons,
she poore gentlewomã wil surely play Lucreces part, & of her
self die for shame, and I shall wishe that she had taried still 35
at home with me, where she was welcome : for she did neuer
put me to more charge, but this one poore blacke gowne lined
with white that I haue now geuen her to goe abroad among you
withall.

❡ The names of the speakers.

Gorboduc, King of great Brittaine.
Videna, Queene and wife to king *Gorboduc.*
Ferrex, elder sonne to king *Gorboduc.*
Porrex, yonger sonne to king *Gorboduc.*
Cloyton, Duke of Cornewall.   5
Fergus, Duke of Albanye.
Mandud, Duke of Loegris.
Gwenard, Duke of Cumberland.
Eubulus, Secretarie to the king.
Arostus, a counsellor to the king.   10
Dordan, a counsellor assigned by the king to his eldest sonne
              Ferrex.
Philander, a counsellor assigned by the king to his yongest
              sonne *Porrex.*
              { Both being of the olde   15
              { kinges counsell before.
Hermon, a parasite remaining with *Ferrex.*
Tyndar, a parasite remaining with *Porrex.*
Nuntius, a messenger of the elder brothers death.
Nuntius, a messenger of Duke *Fergus* rising in armes.   20
Marcella, a lady of the Queenes priuie chamber.
Chorus, foure auncient and sage men of Brittaine.

5 *Cloyton*] Clotyn $Q_1 Q_3$ 7 Loegris] Leagre $Q_1 Q_3$ 8 Q_2 *comma at end of line*   9 king] king Gorboduc $Q_1 Q_3$ 10 to the king] of king Gorboduc $Q_1 Q_3$ 13 yongest] yonger $Q_1 Q_3$

❡ The order of the domme shew
before the first act, and the
signification therof.

❡ First the Musicke of Violenze began to play, during which came
in vpon the stage sixe wilde men clothed in leaues. Of whom
the first bare in his necke a fagot of small stickes, which they all
both seuerally and together assayed with all their strengthes to
breake, but it could not be broken by them. At the length one 5
of them plucked out one of the stickes and brake it : And the
rest plucking out all the other stickes one after an other did
easely breake them, the same being seuered: which being
conioyned they had before attempted in vaine. After they had
this done, they departed the stage, and the Musicke ceased. 10
Hereby was signified, that a state knit in vnitie doth continue
strong against all force. But being diuided, is easely destroyed.
As befell vpon Duke Gorboduc diuiding his land to his two
sonnes which he before held in Monarchie. And vpon the dis
cention of the brethren to whom it was diuided.   15

Actus primus.   Scena prima.

Viden.   Forrex.

V Iden. The silent night, that bringes the quiet pawse,
     From painefull trauailes of the wearie day,
Prolonges my carefull thoughtes, and makes me blame
The slowe *Aurore,* that so for loue or shame
Doth long delay to shewe her blushing face,   5

   Title sig- signification Q_2 3 in] on Q_3 6 plucked] pulled Q_3
8 them] *om.* Q_1 Q_3

And now the day renewes my griefull plaint.

Ferrex. My gracious lady and my mother deare,
Pardon my griefe for your so grieued minde,
To aske what cause tormenteth so your hart.

Viden. So great a wrong, and so vniust despite,   10
Without all cause, against all course of kinde!

Ferrex. Such causelesse wrong and so vniust despite,
May haue redresse, or at the least, reuenge.

Viden. Neither, my sonne: such is the froward will,
The person such, such my missehappe and thine.   15

Ferrex. Mine know I none, but grief for your distresse.

Viden. Yes: mine for thine my sonne: A father? no:
In kinde a father, not in kindlinesse.

Ferrex. My father? why? I know nothing at all,
Wherein I haue misdone vnto his grace.   20

Viden. Therefore, the more vnkinde to thee and mee.
For, knowing well (my sonne) the tender loue
That I haue euer borne and beare to thee,
He greued thereat, is not content alone,
To spoile thee of my sight my chiefest ioye,   25
But thee, of thy birthright and heritage
Causelesse, vnkindly, and in wrongfull wise,
Against all lawe and right, he will bereaue:
Halfe of his kingdome he will geue away.

Ferrex. To whom?

Viden.   Euen to *Porrex* his yonger sonne,   30
Whose growing pride I do so sore suspect,
That being raised to equall rule with thee,
Mee thinkes I see his enuious hart to swell,
Filled with disdaine and with ambicious hope,
The end the Goddes do know, whose altars I   35
Full oft haue made in vaine, of cattell slaine
To send the sacred smoke to heauens throne,
For thee my sonne, if thinges do so succede,

7 **my]** *om. Q₁ Q₃*   18 not] but not *Q₁ Q₃*   34 hope] pride *Q₁ Q₃*
38 do] *om. Q₁ Q₃*

As now my ielous minde misdemeth sore.

 Ferrex. Madame, leaue care & carefull plaint for me, 40
Iust hath my father bene to euery wight :
His first vniustice he will not extend
To me I trust, that geue no cause therof :
My brothers pride shall hurt him selfe, not me.

 Viden. So graunt the Goddes : But yet thy father so 45
Hath firmely fixed his vnmoued minde,
That plaintes and prayers can no whit auaile,
For those haue I assaied, but euen this day,
He will endeuour to procure assent
Of all his counsell to his fonde deuise. 50

 Ferrex. Their ancestors from race to race haue borne
True fayth to my forefathers and their seede :
I trust they eke will beare the like to me.

 Viden. There resteth all. But if they faile thereof,
And if the end bring forth an ill successe : 55
On them and theirs the mischiefe shall befall,
And so I pray the Goddes requite it them,
And so they will, for so is wont to be.
When lordes, and trusted rulers vnder kinges,
To please the present fancie of the prince, 60
With wrong transpose the course of gouernance,
Murders, mischiefe, or ciuill sword at length,
Or mutuall treason, or a iust reuenge,
When right succeding line returnes againe,
By *Ioues* iust iudgement and deserued wrath, 65
Bringes them to cruell and reprochfull death,
And rootes their names and kindredes from the earth.

 Ferrex. Mother, content you, you shall see the end.

 Viden. The end ? thy end I feare, *Ioue* end me first.

55 ill] euill Q₁ Q₃ 66 cruell] ciuill Q₁ Q₃

Actus primus.   Scena secunda.

Gorboduc.   Arostus.   Philander.   Eubulus.

*G*orb. My lords, whose graue aduise & faithful aide,
Haue long vpheld my honour and my realme,
And brought me to this age from tender yeres,
Guidyng so great estate with great renowme :
Nowe more importeth mee, than erst, to vse   5
Your fayth and wisedome, whereby yet I reigne :
That when by death my life and rule shall cease,
The kingdome yet may with vnbroken course,
Haue certayne prince, by whose vndoubted right,
Your wealth and peace may stand in quiet stay,   10
And eke that they whome nature hath preparde,
In time to take my place in princely seate,
While in their fathers tyme their pliant youth
Yeldes to the frame of skilfull gouernance,
Maye so be taught and trayned in noble artes,   15
As what their fathers which haue reigned before
Haue with great fame deriued downe to them,
With honour they may leaue vnto their seede :
And not be thought for their vnworthy life,
And for their lawlesse swaruynge out of kinde,   20
Worthy to lose what lawe and kind them gaue :
But that they may preserue the common peace,
The cause that first began and still mainteines
The lyneall course of kinges inheritance.
For me, for myne, for you, and for the state,   25
Whereof both I and you haue charge and care,
Thus do I meane to vse your wonted fayth
To me and myne, and to your natiue lande.

3 to] from $Q_1 Q_3$ from] and Q_8 5 than] the $Q_1 Q_3$ 10 in] at Q_3
19 thought] taught $Q_1 Q_3$

My lordes be playne without all wrie respect
Or poysonous craft to speake in pleasyng wise,   30
Lest as the blame of yll succedyng thinges
Shall light on you, so light the harmes also.

    Arostus. Your good acceptance so (most noble king)
Of suche our faithfulnesse as heretofore
We haue employed in dueties to your grace,   35
And to this realme whose worthy head you are,
Well proues that neyther you mistrust at all,
Nor we shall neede in boasting wise to shewe,
Our trueth to you, nor yet our wakefull care
For you, for yours, and for our natiue lande.   40
Wherefore (O kyng) I speake as one for all,
Sithe all as one do beare you egall faith :
Doubt not to vse our counsells and our aides,
Whose honours, goods and lyues are whole auowed
To serue, to ayde, and to defende your grace.   45

    Gorb. My lordes, I thanke you all.   This is the case.
Ye know, the Gods, who haue the soueraigne care
For kings, for kingdomes, and for common weales,
Gaue me two sonnes in my more lusty age,
Who nowe in my decayeng yeres are growen   50
Well towardes ryper state of minde and strength,
To take in hande some greater princely charge.
As yet they lyue and spende hopefull daies,
With me and with their mother here in courte.
Their age nowe asketh other place and trade,   55
And myne also doth aske an other chaunge :
Theirs to more trauaile, myne to greater ease.
Whan fatall death shall ende my mortall life,
My purpose is to leaue vnto them twaine
The realme diuided into two sondry partes :   60
The one *Ferrex* myne elder sonne shall haue,

30 poysonous] poysons Q_3 34 our] your $Q_1 Q_3$ 38 in] no $Q_1 Q_3$
41 as one for] for one as $Q_1 Q_3$ 43 our ... our] their ... their $Q_1 Q_3$
50 decayeng] deceyuynge Q_1 : deceiuing Q_3 53 spende] spende their Q_1 :
spend their Q_3 59 vnto] betweene Q_3

The other shall the yonger *Porrex* rule.
That both my purpose may more firmely stande,
And eke that they may better rule their charge,
I meane forthwith to place them in the same :   65
That in my life they may both learne to rule,
And I may ioy to see their ruling well.
This is in summé, what I woulde haue ye wey :
First whether ye allowe my whole deuise,
And thinke it good for me, for them, for you,   70
And for our countrey, mother of vs all :
And if ye lyke it, and allowe it well,
Then for their guydinge and their gouernaunce,
Shew forth such meanes of circumstance,
As ye thinke meete to be both knowne and kept.   75
Loe, this is all, now tell me your aduise.
     Aros. And this is much, and asketh great aduise,
But for my part, my soueraigne lord and kyng,
This do I thinke.   Your maiestie doth know,
How vnder you in iustice and in peace,   80
Great wealth and honour, long we haue enioyed,
So as we can not seeme with gredie mindes
To wisshe for change of Prince or gouernaunce :
But if we lyke your purpose and deuise,
Our lyking must be deemed to proceede   85
Of rightfull reason, and of heedefull care,
Not for our selues, but for the common state,
Sithe our owne state doth neede no better change :
I thinke in all as erst your Grace hath saide.
Firste when you shall vnlode your aged mynde   90
Of heuye care and troubles manifolde,
And laye the same vpon my Lordes your sonnes,
Whose growing yeres may beare the burden long,
And long I pray the Goddes to graunt it so,
And in your life while you shall so beholde   95

62 yonger] other $Q_1 Q_3$ 63 firmely] framelie Q_1 68 ye] you Q_3
84 we] ye $Q_1 Q_3$ 87 the] our Q_1

Their rule, their vertues, and their noble deedes,
Suche as their kinde behighteth to vs all,
Great be the profites that shall growe therof,
Your age in quiet shall the longer last.
Your lasting age shalbe their longer stay,   100
For cares of kynges, that rule as you haue ruled,
For publique wealth and not for priuate ioye,
Do wast mannes lyfe, and hasten crooked age,
With furrowed face and with enfeebled lymmes,
To draw on creepyng death a swifter pace.   105
They two yet yong shall beare the parted reigne
With greater ease, than one, nowe olde, alone,
Can welde the whole, for whom muche harder is
With lessened strength the double weight to beare.
Your eye, your counsell, and the graue regarde   110
Of Father, yea of such a fathers name,
Nowe at beginning of their sondred reigne,
When is the hazarde of their whole successe,
Shall bridle so their force of youthfull heates,
And so restreine the rage of insolence,   115
Whiche most assailes the yonge and noble mindo,
And so shall guide and traine in tempred stay
Their yet greene bending wittes with reuerent awe,
As now inured with vertues at the first,
Custome (O king) shall bring delightfulnesse.   120
By vse of vertue, vice shall growe in hate,
But if you so dispose it, that the daye,
Which endes your life, shall first begin their reigne,
Great is the perill what will be the ende,
When such beginning of such liberties   125
Voide of suche stayes as in your life do lye,
Shall leaue them free to randon of their will,
An open praie to traiterous flatterie,

106 parted] partie $Q_1 Q_3$ 111 Father] fathers $Q_1 Q_3$ 113 is the]
it is $Q_1 Q_3$ 119 As] And $Q_1 Q_3$ 123 their] the Q_3 124 will]
shall Q_3 127 free to] to free $Q_1 Q_3$

The greatest pestilence of noble youthe.
Whiche perill shalbe past, if in your life,   130
Their tempred youthe with aged fathers awe,
Be brought in vre of skilfull stayednesse.
And in your life their liues disposed so,
Shall length your noble life in ioyfulnesse.
Thus thinke I that your grace hath wisely thought,   135
And that your tender care of common weale,
Hath bred this thought, so to diuide your lande,
And plant your sonnes to beare the present rule,
While you yet liue to see their rulinge well,
That you may longer lyue by ioye therein.   140
What furder meanes behouefull are and meete
At greater leisure may your grace deuise,
When all haue said, and when we be agreed
If this be best to part the realme in twaine,
And place your sonnes in present gouernement.   145
Whereof as I haue plainely said my mynde,
So woulde I here the rest of all my Lordes.
    Philand. In part I thinke as hath bene said before,
In parte agayne my minde is otherwise.
As for diuiding of this realme in twaine,   150
And lotting out the same in egall partes,
To either of my lordes your graces sonnes,
That thinke I best for this your realmes behofe,
For profite and aduauncement of your sonnes,
And for your comforte and your honour eke.   155
But so to place them, while your life do last,
To yelde to them your royall gouernaunce,
To be aboue them onely in the name
Of father, not in kingly state also,
I thinke not good for you, for them, nor vs.   160
This kingdome since the bloudie ciuill fielde
Where *Morgan* slaine did yeld his conquered parte

142 greater] great Q_1 156 do] doth Q_3

Vnto his cosins sworde in *Camberland*,
Conteineth all that whilome did suffice
Three noble sonnes of your forefather *Brute*.   165
So your two sonnes, it maye suffice also.
The moe, the stronger, if they gree in one.
The smaller compasse that the realme doth holde,
The easier is the swey thereof to welde,
The nearer Iustice to the wronged poore,   170
The smaller charge, and yet ynoughe for one.
And whan the region is diuided so,
That brethren be the lordes of either parte,
Such strength doth nature knit betwene them both,
In sondrie bodies by conioyned loue,   ⌄ 175
That not as two, but one of doubled force,
Eche is to other as a sure defence.
The noblenesse and glory of the one
Doth sharpe the courage of the others mynde,
With vertuous enuie to contende for praise.   180
And suche an egalnesse hath nature made,
Betwene the brethren of one fathers seede,
As an vnkindly wrong it seemes to bee,
To throwe the brother subiect vnder feete
Of him, whose peere he is by course of kinde,   185
And nature that did make this egalnesse,
Ofte so repineth at so great a wrong,
That ofte she rayseth vp a grudginge griefe,
In yonger brethren at the elders state :
Wherby both townes and kingdomes haue ben rased,   190
And famous stockes of royall bloud destroied :
The brother, that shoulde be the brothers aide,
And haue a wakefull care for his defence,
Gapes for his death, and blames the lyngering yeres
That draw not forth his ende with faster course :   195
And oft impacient of so longe delayes,

163 *Camberland*] Cumberland Q_3 166 suffice also] also suffise $Q_1 Q_3$
174 them] the Q_1 184 brother] other $Q_1 Q_3$ 187 Ofte so] Oft sore
Q_3 195 draw] brings $Q_1 Q_3$

With hatefull slaughter he preuentes the fates,
And heapes a iust rewarde for brothers bloode,
With endlesse vengeaunce on his stocke for aye.
Suche mischiefes here are wisely mette withall,   200
If egall state maye nourishe egall loue,
Where none hath cause to grudge at others good.
But nowe the head to stoupe beneth them bothe,
Ne kinde, ne reason, ne good ordre beares.
And oft it hath ben seene, where natures course   205
Hath ben peruerted in disordered wise,
When fathers cease to know that they should rule,
The children cease to know they should obey.
And often ouerkindly tendernesse
Is mother of vnkindly stubbornenesse.   210
I speake not this in enuie or reproche,
As if I grudged the glorie of your sonnes,
Whose honour I besech the Goddes encrease :
Nor yet as if I thought there did remaine,
So filthie cankers in their noble brestes,   215
Whom I esteeme (which is their greatest praise)
Vndoubted children of so good a kyng.
Onelie I meane to shewe by certeine rules,
Whiche kinde hath graft within the mind of man,
That nature hath her ordre and her course,   220
Which (being broken) doth corrupt the state
Of myndes and thinges, euen in the best of all.
My lordes your sonnes may learne to rule of you.
Your owne example in your noble courte
Is fittest guyder of their youthfull yeares.   225
If you desire to see some present ioye
By sight of their well rulynge in your lyfe,
See them obey, so shall you see them rule,
Who so obeyeth not with humblenesse

197 preuentes] presentes Q_1 : presents Q_3 198 heapes] keepes Q_1 Q_3
205 where natures course] that where Nature Q_1 Q_3 208 The] And
Q_1 Q_3 209 ouerkindly] our vnkindly Q_1 Q_3 213 encrease] to
encrease Q_1 : to increase Q_3 218 by] my Q_1 Q_3 226 see] seeke Q_1 Q.

Will rule with outrage and with insolence.   230
Longe maye they rule I do beseche the Goddes,
But longe may they learne, ere they begyn to rule.
If kinde and fates woulde suffre, I would wisshe
Them aged princes, and immortall kinges.
Wherfore most noble kynge I well assent,   235
Betwene your sonnes that you diuide your realme,
And as in kinde, so match them in degree.
But while the Goddes prolong your royall life,
Prolong your reigne: for therto lyue you here,
And therfore haue the Goddes so long forborne   240
To ioyne you to them selues, that still you might
Be prince and father of our common weale.
They when they see your children ripe to rule,
Will make them roume, and will remoue you hence,
That yours in right ensuynge of your life   245
Maye rightly honour your immortall name.

    Eub. Your wonted true regarde of faithfull hartes,
Makes me (O kinge) the bolder to presume,
To speake what I conceiue within my brest,
Although the same do not agree at all   250
With that which other here my lordes haue said,
Nor which your selfe haue seemed best to lyke.
Pardon I craue, and that my wordes be demed
To flowe from hartie zeale vnto your grace,
And to the safetie of your common weale.   255
To parte your realme vnto my lordes your sonnes,
I thinke not good for you, ne yet for them,
But worste of all for this our natiue lande,
Within one land, one single rule is best:
Diuided reignes do make diuided hartes.   260
But peace preserues the countrey and the prince.
Suche is in man the gredy minde to reigne,
So great is his desire to climbe alofte,

In worldly stage the stateliest partes to beare,
That faith and iustice and all kindly loue,   265
Do yelde vnto desire of soueraignitie,
Where egall state doth raise an egall hope
To winne the thing that either wold attaine.
Your grace remembreth how in passed yeres
The mightie *Brute*, first prince of all this lande,   270
Possessed the same and ruled it well in one,
He thinking that the compasse did suffice,
For his three sonnes three kingdoms eke to make,
Cut it in three, as you would now in twaine.
But how much Brittish bloud hath since bene spilt,   275
To ioyne againe the sondred vnitie?
What princes slaine before their timely houre?
What wast of townes and people in the lande?
What treasons heaped on murders and on spoiles?
Whose iust reuenge euen yet is scarcely ceased,   280
Ruthefull remembraunce is yet rawe in minde.
The Gods forbyd the like to chaunce againe:
And you (O king) geue not the cause therof.
My Lord *Ferrex* your elder sonne, perhappes
Whome kinde and custome geues a rightfull hope   285
To be your heire and to succede your reigne,
Shall thinke that he doth suffre greater wrong
Than he perchaunce will beare, if power serue.
Porrex the younger so. vpraised in state,
Perhappes in courage will be raysed also.   290
If flatterie then, which fayles not to assaile
The tendre mindes of yet vnskilfull youth,
In one shall kindle and encrease disdaine,
And enuie in the others harte enflame,
This fire shall waste their loue, their liues, their land,   295
And ruthefull ruine shall destroy them both.

275 Brittish] Brutish $Q_1 Q_3$ since] sithence $Q_1 Q_3$ 277 houre]
honour $Q_1 Q_3$ 281 rawe] had $Q_1 Q_3$ 289 vpraised] vnpaised
$Q_1 Q_3$ 294 And] In Q_3

I wishe not this (O kyng) so to befall,
But feare the thing, that I do most abhorre.
Geue no beginning to so dreadfull ende.
Kepe them in order and obedience :　　　　　　　　300
And let them both by now obeying you,
Learne such behauiour as beseemes their state,
The elder, myldenesse in his góuernaunce,
The yonger, a yelding contentednesse.
And kepe them neare vnto your presence still,　　305
That they restreyned by the awe of you,
May liue in compasse of well tempred staye,
And passe the perilles of their youthfull yeares.
Your aged life drawes on to febler tyme,
Wherin you shall lesse able be to beare　　　　　310
The trauailes that in youth you haue susteyned,
Both in your persones and your realmes defence.
If planting now your sonnes in furder partes,
You sende them furder from your present reach,
Lesse shall you know how they them selues demeane :　315
Traiterous corrupters of their plyant youth,
Shall haue vnspied a muche more free accesse,
And if ambition and inflamed disdaine
Shall arme the one, the other, or them both,
To ciuill warre, or to vsurping pride,　　　　　320
Late shall you rue, that you ne recked before.
Good is I graunt of all to hope the best,
But not to liue still dreadlesse of the worst.
So truste the one, that the other be forsene.
Arme not vnskilfulnesse with princely power.　　325
But you that long haue wiscly ruled the reignes
Of royaltie within your noble realme,
So holde them, while the Gods for our auayles
Shall stretch the thred of your prolonged daies.
To soone he clambe into the flaming carre,　　　330
Whose want of skill did set the earth on fire.

315 demeane :] demaund $Q_1 Q_3$　　　330 carre] Carte $Q_1 Q_3$

Time and example of your noble grace,
Shall teach your sonnes both to obey and rule,
When time hath taught them, time shal make thē place,
The place that now is full : and so I pray   335
Long it remaine, to comforte of vs all.
   Gorboduc. I take your faithful harts in thankful part.
But sithe I see no cause to draw my minde,
To feare the nature of my louing sonnes,
Or to misdeme that enuie or disdaine,   340
Can there worke hate, where nature planteth loue :
In one selfe purpose do I still abide.
My loue extendeth egally to both,
My lande suffiseth for them both also.
Humber shall parte the marches of theyr realmes :   345
The Sotherne part the elder shall possesse :
The Notherne shall *Porrex* the yonger rule :
In quiet I will passe mine aged dayes,
Free from the trauaile and the painefull cares,
That hasten age vpon the worthiest kinges.   350
But lest the fraude, that ye do seeme to feare,
Of flattering tongues, corrupt their tender youth,
And wrythe them to the wayes of youthfull lust,
To climyng pride, or to reuenging hate,
Or to neglecting of their carefull charge,   355
Lewdely to lyue in wanton recklessnesse,
Or to oppressing of the rightfull cause,
Or not to wreke the wronges done to the poore,
To treade downe truth, or fauour false deceite :
I meane to ioyne to eyther of my sonnes   360
Some one of those, whose long approued faith
And wisdome tryed, may well assure my harte :
That mynyng fraude shall finde no way to crepe
Into their fensed eares with graue aduise.
This is the ende, and so I pray you all   365
To beare my sonnes the loue and loyaltie

        334 place] pace $Q_1 Q_3$

That I haue founde within your faithfull brestes.

    Arostus. You, nor your sonnes, our soueraign lord shal want,
Our faith and seruice while our liues do last.

    Chorus. When settled stay doth holde the royall throne
In stedfast place, by knowen and doubtles right,
And chiefely when discent on one alone
Makes single and vnparted reigne to light :
Eche chaunge of course vnioynts the whole estate,   5
And yeldes it thrall to ruyne by debate.
The strength that knit by faste accorde in one,
Against all forrein power of mightie foes,
Could of it selfe defende it selfe alone,
Disioyned once, the former force doth lose.   10
The stickes, that sondred brake so soone in twaine,
In faggot bounde attempted were in vaine.
Oft tender minde that leades the parciall eye
Of erring parentes in their childrens loue,
Destroyes the wrongly loued childe therby.   15
This doth the proude sonne of *Apollo* proue,
Who rasshely set in chariot of his sire,
Inflamed the parched earth with heauens fire.
And this great king, that doth deuide his land,
And chaunge the course of his discending crowne,   20
And yeldes the reigne into his childrens hande,
From blisfull state of ioye and great renowne,
A myrrour shall become to Princes all,
To learne to shunne the cause of suche a fall.

❡ The order and signification
of the domme shew before the se-
cond acte.

❡ First the Musicke of Cornettes began to playe, during which
came in vpon the stage a King accompanied with a nombre of
his nobilitie and gentlemen. And after he had placed him self
in a chaire of estate prepared for him : there came and kneled
before him a graue and aged gentelman and offred vp a cuppe 5
vnto him of wyne in a glasse, which the King refused. After
him commes a braue and lustie yong gentleman and presentes
the King with a cup of golde filled with poyson, which the King
accepted, and drinking the same, immediatly fell downe dead
vpon the stage, and so was carried thence away by his Lordes 10
and gentelmen, and then the Musicke ceased. Hereby was
signified, that as glasse by nature holdeth no poyson, but is clere
and may easely be seen through, ne boweth by any arte : So
a faythfull counsellour holdeth no treason, but is playne and
open, ne yeldeth to any vndiscrete affection, but geueth holsome 15
counsell, which the yll aduised Prince refuseth. The delightfull
golde filled with poyson betokeneth flattery, which vnder faire
seeming of pleasaunt wordes beareth deadly poyson, which destroyed the Prince that receyueth it. As befell in the two
brethren Ferrex and Porrex, who refusing the holsome aduise of 20
graue counsellours, credited these yong Paracites, and brought to
them selues death and destruction therby.

Actus secundus. Scena prima.

Ferrex. Hermon. Dordan.

F *Errex.* I meruaile much what reason ledde the king
My Father, thus without all my desert,
To reue me halfe the kingdome, which by course
Of law and nature should remayne to me.
    Hermon. If you with stubborne and vntamed pryde   5

6, 10 the] the the Q_2 8 of] *om.* Q_3 15 geueth] giueth any Q_3
21 to] vnto Q_3

Had stood against him in rebelling wise,
Or if with grudging minde you had enuied
So slow a slidyng of his aged yeres,
Or sought before your time to haste the course
Of fatall death vpon his royall head,   10
Or stained your stocke with murder of your kyn :
Some face of reason might perhaps haue seemed,
To yelde some likely cause to spoyle ye thus.
    Ferrex. The wrekeful Gods powre on my cursed head
Eternall plagues and neuer dying woes,   15
The hellish prince, adiudge my dampned ghost
To *Tantales* thirste, or proude *Ixions* wheele,
Or cruell gripe to gnaw my growing harte,
To during tormentes and vnquenched flames,
If euer I conceyued so foule a thought,   20
To wisshe his ende of life, or yet of reigne.
    Dordan. Ne yet your father (O most noble Prince)
Did euer thinke so fowle a thing of you.
For he, with more than fathers tendre loue,
While yet the fates do lende him life to rule,   25
(Who long might lyue to see your ruling well)
To you my Lorde, and to his other sonne :
Lo he resignes his realme and royaltie:
Which neuer would so wise a Prince haue done,
If he had once misdemed that in your harte   30
There euer lodged so vnkinde a thought.
But tendre loue (my Lorde) and setled truste
Of your good nature, and your noble minde,
Made him to place you thus in royall throne,
And now to geue you half his realme to guide,   35
Yea and that halfe which in abounding store
Of things that serue to make a welthy realme,
In stately cities, and in frutefull soyle,
In temperate breathing of the milder heauen,

    6 rebelling] rebellious $Q_1 Q_3$ 18 growing] groaning Q_3 36 which
in] within $Q_1 Q_3$

In thinges of nedefull vse, which frendly sea,   40
Transportes by traffike from the forreine partes,
In flowing wealth, in honour and in force,
Doth passe the double value of the parte,
That *Porrex* hath allotted to his reigne.
Such is your case, such is your fathers loue.   45
    Ferrex. Ah loue, my frendes? loue wrongs not whŏ he loues.
    Dordan. Ne yet he wrongeth you, that geueth you
So large a reigne, ere that the course of time
Bring you to kingdome by discended right,
Which time perhaps might end your time before.   50
    Ferrex. Is this no wrong, say you, to reaue from me
My natiue right of halfe so great a realme?
And thus to matche his yonger sonne with me
In egall power, and in as great degree?
Yea and what sonne? the sonne whose swelling pride   55
Woulde neuer yelde one poinct of reuerence,
Whan I the elder and apparaunt heire
Stoode in the likelihode to possesse the whole,
Yea and that sonne which from his childish age
Enuieth myne honour and doth hate my life.   60
What will he now do, when his pride, his rage,
The mindefull malice of his grudging harte,
Is armed with force, with wealth, and kingly state?
    Hermon. Was this not wrong, yea yll aduised wrong,
To giue so mad a man so sharpe a sworde,   65
To so great perill of so great missehappe,
Wide open thus to set so large a waye?
    Dordan. Alas my Lord, what griefull thing is this,
That of your brother you can thinke so ill?
I neuer saw him vtter likelie signe,   70
Whereby a man might see or once misdeme
Such hate of you, ne such vnyelding pride.
Ill is their counsell, shamefull be their ende,
That raysing such mistrustfull feare in you,

Sowing the seede of such vnkindly hate,　　75
Trauaile by treason to destroy you both.
Wise is your brother, and of noble hope,
Worthie to welde a large and mightie realme.
So much a stronger frende haue you therby,
Whose strength is your strength, if you gree in one.　　80
　　Hermon. If nature and the Goddes had pinched so
Their flowing bountie, and their noble giftes
Of princelie qualities, from you my Lorde,
And powrde them all at ones in wastfull wise
Vpon your fathers yonger sonne alone :　　85
Perhappes there be that in your preiudice
Would say that birth should yeld to worthinesse.
But sithe in eche good gift and princelie arte
Ye are his matche, and in the chiefe of all
In mildenesse and in sobre gouernaunce　　90
Ye farre surmount : And sith there is in you
Sufficing skill and hopefull towardnesse
To weld the whole, and match your elders prayse :
I see no cause why ye should loose the halfe.
Ne would I wisshe you yelde to such a losse :　　95
Lest your milde sufferaunce of so great a wronge,
Be deemed cowardishe and simple dreade :
Which shall geue courage to the fierie head
Of your yonge brother to inuade the whole.
While yet therfore stickes in the peoples minde　　100
The lothed wrong of your disheritaunce,
And ere your brother haue by settled power,
By guile full cloke of an alluring showe,
Got him some force and fauour in the realme,
And while the noble Queene your mother lyues,　　105
To worke and practise all for your auaile,
Attempt redresse by armes, and wreake your self
Vpon his life, that gayneth by your losse,
Who nowe to shame of you, and griefe of vs,

　　76 treason] reason $Q_1 Q_3$　　　104 the] this $Q_1 Q_3$

In your owne kingdome triumphes ouer you.   110
Shew now your courage meete for kingly state,
That they which haue auowed to spend theyr goods,
Their landes, their liues and honours in your cause,
May be the bolder to mainteyne your parte,
When they do see that cowarde feare in you,   115
Shall not betray ne faile their faithfull hartes.
If once the death of *Parrex* ende the strife,
And pay the price of his vsurped reigne,
Your mother shall perswade the angry kyng,
The Lords your frends eke shall appease his rage.   120
For they be wise, and well they can forsee,
That ere longe time your aged fathers death
Will bryng a time when you shall well requite
Their frendlie fauour, or their hatefull spite,
Yea, or their slackenesse to auaunce your cause.   125
„ Wise men do not so hang on passing state
„ Of present Princes, chiefely in their age,
„ But they will further cast their reaching eye,
„ To viewe and weye the times and reignes to come.
Ne is it likely, though the kyng be wrothe,   130
That he yet will, or that the realme will beare,
Extreme reuenge vpon his onely sonne.
Or if he woulde, what one is he that dare
Be minister to such an enterprise?
And here you be now placed in your owne,   135
Amyd your frendes, your vassalles and your strength.
We shall defende and kepe your person safe,
Till either counsell turne his tender minde,
Or age, or sorrow end his werie dayes.
But if the feare of Goddes, and secrete grudge   140
Of natures law, repining at the fact,
Withholde your courage from so great attempt:
Know ye, that lust of kingdomes hath no law.
The Goddes do beare and well allow in kinges,
The thinges they abhorre in rascall routes.   145

, When kinges on slender quarrells runne to warres,
, And then in cruell and vnkindely wise,
, Commaund theftes, rapes, murders of innocentes,
, The spoile of townes, ruines of mighty realmes :
, Thinke you such princes do suppose them selues   150
, Subiect to lawes of kinde, and feare of Gods?
Murders and violent theftes in priuate men,
Are hainous crimes and full of foule reproch,
Yet none offence, but deckt with glorious name
Of noble conquestes, in the handes of kinges.   155
But if you like not yet so hote deuise,
Ne list to take such vauntage of the time,
But though with perill of your owne estate,
You will not be the first that shall inuade :
Assemble yet your force for your defence,   160
And for your safetie stand vpon your garde.
        Doridon. O heauen was there euer heard or knowen,
So wicked counsell to a noble prince?
Let me (my Lorde) disclose vnto your grace
This hainous tale, what mischiefe it containes,   165
Your fathers death, your brothers and your owne,
Your present murder and eternall shame.
Heare me (O king) and suffer not to sinke
So high a treason in your princely brest.
        Ferrex. The mightie Goddes forbid that euer I   170
Should once conceaue such mischiefe in my hart.
Although my brother hath bereft my realme,
And beare perhappes to me an hatefull minde :
Shall I reuenge it, with his death therefore?
Or shall I so destroy my fathers life   175
That gaue me life? the Gods forbid, I say.
Cease you to speake so any more to me.
Ne you my frend with answere once repeate

148 murders] murder $Q_1 Q_3$ 149 The] To $Q_1 Q_3$ ruines] and reignes
$Q_1 Q_3$ 150 suppose] suppresse $Q_1 Q_3$ 154–5 *come before* 152–3 *in* $Q_1 Q_3$
158 with] with great $Q_1 Q_3$ owne estate] state $Q_1 Q_3$ 173 an] and Q_1

So foule a tale.   In silence let it die.
What lord or subiect shall haue hope at all,   180
That vnder me they safely shall enioye
Their goods, their honours, landes and liberties,
With whom, neither one onely brother deare,
Ne father dearer, could enioye their liues ?
But sith, I feare my yonger brothers rage,   185
And sith perhappes some other man may geue
Some like aduise, to moue his grudging head
At mine estate, which counsell may perchaunce
Take greater force with him, than this with me,
I will in secrete so prepare my selfe,   190
As if his malice or his lust to reigne
Breake forth in armes or sodeine violence,
I may withstand his rage and keepe mine owne.
   Dordan. I feare the fatall time now draweth on,
When ciuil hate shall end the noble line   195
Of famous *Brute* and of his royall seede.
Great *Ioue* defend the mischiefes now at hand.
O that the Secretaries wise aduise
Had erst bene heard when he besought the king
Not to diuide his land, nor send his sonnes   200
To further partes from presence of his court,
Ne yet to yelde to them his gouernaunce.
Lo such are they now in the royall throne
As was rashe *Phaeton* in *Phebus* carre.
Ne then the fiery stedes did draw the flame   205
With wilder randon through the kindled skies,
Than traitorous counsell now will whirle about
The youthfull heades of these vnskilfull kinges.
But I hereof their father will enforme.
The reuerence of him perhappes shall stay   210
The growing mischiefes, while they yet are greene.
If this helpe not, then woe vnto them selues,
The prince, the people, the diuided land.

192 in] with $Q_1 Q_3$ 204 rashe] that Q_3

Actus secundus. Scena secunda.

Porrex. Tyndar. Philander.

POrrex. And is it thus? And doth he so prepare,
    Against his brother as his mortall foe?
And now while yet his aged father liues?
Neither regardes he him? nor feares he me?
Warre would he haue? and he shall haue it so.   5

  Tyndar. I saw my selfe the great prepared store
Of horse, of armour, and of weapon there,
Ne bring I to my lorde reported tales
Without the ground of seen and searched trouth.
Loe secrete quarrels runne about his court,   10
To bring the name of you my lorde in hate.
Ech man almost can now debate the cause,
And aske a reason of so great a wrong,
Why he so noble and so wise a prince,
Is as vnworthy reft his heritage?   15
And why the king, misseledde by craftie meanes,
Diuided thus his land from course of right?
The wiser sort holde downe their griefull heades.
Eche man withdrawes from talke and company,
Of those that haue bene knowne to fauour you.   20
To hide the mischiefe of their meaning there,
Rumours are spread of your preparing here.
The rascall numbers of vnskilfull sort
Are filled with monstrous tales of you and yours.
In secrete I was counselled by my frendes,   25
To hast me thence, and brought you as you know
Letters from those, that both can truely tell,
And would not write vnlesse they knew it well.

  Philand. My lord, yet ere you moue vnkindly warre,
Send to your brother to demaund the cause.   30
Perhappes some traitorous tales haue filled his eares

7 armour] Armours $Q_1 Q_3$ 14 Why] While $Q_1 Q_3$ 23 of] of
the Q_3 29 moue] nowe Q_1 : now Q_3

With false reportes against your noble grace :
Which once disclosed, shall end the growing strife,
.That els not stayed with wise foresight in time
Shall hazarde both your kingdomes and your liues.   35
Send to your father eke, he shall appease
Your kindled mindes, and rid you of this feare.
    Porrex. Ridde me of feare ?   I feare him not at all :
Ne will to him, ne to my father send.
If danger were for one to tary there,   40
Thinke ye it safetie to returne againe ?
In mischiefes, such as *Ferrex* now intendes,
The wonted courteous lawes to messengers
Are not obserued, which in iust warre they vse.
Shall I so hazard any one of mine ?   45
Shall I betray my trusty frendes to him,
That haue disclosed his treason vnto me ?
Let him entreate that feares, I feare him not.
Or shall I to the king my father send ?
Yea and send now, while such a mother liues,   50
That loues my brother, and that hateth me ?
Shall I geue leasure, by my fonde delayes,
To *Ferrex* to oppresse me all vnware ?
I will not, but I will inuade his realme,
And seeke the traitour prince within his court.   55
Mischiefe for mischiefe is a due reward.
His wretched head shall pay the worthy price
Of this his treason and his hate to me.
Shall I abide, and treate, and send and pray,
And holde my yelden throate to traitours knife ?   60
While I with valiant minde and conquering force,
Might rid my selfe of foes : and winne a realme ?
Yet rather, when I haue the wretches head,
Then to the king my father will I send.
The bootelesse case may yet appease his wrath :   65

46 frendes] friende Q_1 : frend Q_3 47 haue] hath Q_1 Q_3 53 all]
at Q_1 Q_3 59 and treate] entreate Q_1 : intreat Q_3

If not, I will defend me as I may.

Philand. Lo here the end of these two youthful kings,
The fathers death, the ruine of their realmes.
„ O most vnhappy state of counsellers,
„ That light on so vnhappy lordes and times,   70
„ That neither can their good aduise be heard,
„ Yet must they beare the blames of ill successe.·
But I will to the king their father haste,
Ere this mischiefe come to the likely end,
That if the mindfull wrath of wrekefull Gods,   75
Since mightie *Ilions* fall not yet appeased
With these poore remnantes of the Troian name,
Haue not determined by vnmoued fate
Out of this realme to rase the Brittishe line,
By good aduise, by awe of fathers name,   80
By force of wiser lordes, this kindled hate
May yet be quentched, ere it consume vs all.

Chorus. When youth not bridled with a guiding stay
Is left to randon of their owne delight,
And weldo whole realmes, by force of soueraign sway,
Great is the daunger of vnmaistred might,
Lest skillesse rage throwe downe with headlong fall   5
Their lands, their states, their liues, them selues & al.
When growing pride doth fill the swelling brest,
And gredy lust doth rayse the climbing minde,
Oh hardlie maye the perill be represt,
Ne feare of angrie Goddes, ne lawes kinde.   10
Ne countries care can fiered hartes restrayne,
Whan force hath armed enuie and disdaine.
When kinges of foresette will neglect the rede
Of best aduise, and yelde to pleasing tales,
That do their fansies noysome humour feede,   15

68 ruine of their realmes] reigne of their two realmes $Q_1 Q_3$ 74 the]
that $Q_1 Q_3$ 77 remnantes] remnant $Q_1 Q_3$ Troian] Troians $Q_1 Q_3$
78 determined by] determinedlie Q_1 : determinedly Q_3
   3 sway] fraie Q_1 : fray Q_3 11 countries] Countrie Q_1 : Country Q_3

Ne reason, nor regarde of right auailes.
Succeding heapes of plagues shall teach to late,
To learne the mischiefes of misguided state.
Fowle fall the traitour false, that vndermines
The loue of brethren to destroye them both.   20
Wo to the prince, that pliant eare enclynes,
And yeldes his mind to poysonous tale, that floweth
From flattering mouth.   And woe to wretched land
That wastes it selfe with ciuil sworde in hand.
Loe, thus it is, poyson in golde to take,   25
And holsome drinke in homely cuppe forsake.

❡ The order and signification
of the domme shewe before the thirde act.

❡ Firste the musicke of flutes began to playe, during which came
in vpon the stage a company of mourners all clad in blacke
betokening death and sorowe to ensue vpon the ill aduised mis-
gouernement and discention of bretherne, as befell vpon the
murder of Ferrex by his yonger brother. After the mourners 5
had passed thryse about the stage, they departed, and than the
musicke ceased.

Actus tertius.   Scena prima.

Gorboduc.   Eubulus.   Arostus.   Philander.   Nuntius.

*G*Orb. O cruel fates, O mindful wrath of Goddes,
Whose vengeance neither *Simois* stayned streames
Flowing with bloud of *Troian* princes slaine,
Nor *Phrygian* fieldes made ranck with corpses dead
Of *Asian* kynges and lordes, can yet appease,   5
Ne slaughter of vnhappie *Pryams* race,

    18 misguided] misguydinge Q_1 : misguiding Q_3
    5 murder] murderer Q_2 7 ceased] caused Q_2
    2 stayned] streined Q_1 Q_3

Nor *Ilions* fall made leuell with the soile
Can yet suffice : but still continued rage
Pursues our lyues, and from the farthest seas
Doth chase the issues of destroyed *Troye.*   10
„ Oh no man happie, till his ende be seene.
If any flowing wealth and seemyng ioye
In present yeres might make a happy wight,
Happie was *Hecuba* the wofullest wretch
That euer lyued to make a myrrour of,   15
And happie *Pryam* with his noble sonnes.
And happie I, till nowe alas I see
And feele my most vnhappye wretchednesse.
Beholde my lordes, read ye this letter here.
Loe it conteins the ruine of our realme,   20
If timelie speede prouide not hastie helpe.
Yet (O ye Goddes) if euer wofull kyng
Might moue ye kings of kinges, wreke it on me
And on my sonnes, not on this giltlesse realme.
Send down your wasting flames frō wrathful skies,   25
To reue me and my sonnes the hatefull breath.
Read, read my lordes : this is the matter why
I called ye nowe to haue your good aduyse.

❡The letter from *Dordan* the Coun-
sellour of the elder prince.

Eubulus readeth the letter.

MY soueraigne lord, what I am loth to write,
But lothest am to see, that I am forced   30
By letters nowe to make you vnderstande.
My lord *Ferrex* your eldest sonne misledde
By traitorous fraude of yong vntempred wittes,
Assembleth force agaynst your yonger sonne,
Ne can my counsell yet withdrawe the heate   35

7 *Q₁ period at end of line*   9 Pursues] Pursue $Q_1 Q_3$ lyues] lynes
?? lines Q_3 10 chase] chast $Q_1 Q_3$ 20 our] this Q_3 23 ye]
??? $Q_3 Q_3$ 33 traitorous fraude] traitours framde $Q_1 Q_3$

And furyous panges of hys enflamed head
Disdaine (sayth he) of his disheritance
Armes him to wreke the great pretended wrong,
With ciuyll sword vpon his brothers life.
If present helpe do not restraine this rage,   40
This flame will wast your sonnes, your land, & you.

> Your maiesties faithfull and most
> humble subiect Dordan.

A Rostus. O king, appease your griefe and stay your plaint.
Great is the matter, and a wofull case.
But timely knowledge may bring timely helpe.
Sende for them both vnto your presence here.   45
The reuerence of your honour, age, and state,
Your graue aduice, the awe of fathers name,
Shall quicklie knit agayne this broken peace.
And if in either of my lordes your sonnes,
Be suche vntamed and vnyelding pride,   50
As will not bende vnto your noble hestes:
If *Ferrex* the elder sonne can beare no peere,
Or *Porrex* not content, aspires to more
Than you him gaue aboue his natiue right:
Ioyne with the iuster side, so shall you force   55
Them to agree, and holde the lande in stay.

   Eub. What meaneth this? Loe yonder comes in hast
Philander from my lord your yonger sonne.

   Gorb. The Goddes sende ioyfull newes.

   Phil.   The mightie *Ioue*
Preserue your maiestie, O noble king.   60

   Gorb. Philander, welcome: but how doth my sonne?

   Phil. Your sonne, sir, lyues, and healthie I him left.
But yet (O king) the want of lustfull health
Could not be halfe so griefefull to your grace,
As these most wretched tidynges that I bryng.   65

   Gorb. O heauens, yet more? not ende of woes to me?

44 timely helpe] manly help Q_3 46 honour, age] honourage Q_2
63 the] this $Q_1 Q_3$ 66 not] no $Q_1 Q_3$

Phil. Tyndar, O king, came lately from the court
Of *Ferrex*, to my lord your yonger sonne,
And made reporte of great prepared store
For warre, and sayth that it is wholly ment   70
Agaynst *Porrex*, for high disdayne that he
Lyues now a king and egall in degree
With him, that claimeth to succede the whole,
As by due title of discending right.
Porrex is nowe so set on flaming fire,   75
Partely with kindled rage of cruell wrath,
Partely with hope to gaine a realme thereby,
That he in hast prepareth to inuade
His brothers land, and with vnkindely warre
Threatens the murder of your elder sonne,   80
Ne could I him perswade that first he should
Send to his brother to demaunde the cause,
Nor yet to you to staie this hatefull strife.
Wherfore sithe there no more I can be hearde,
I come my selfe now to enforme your grace,   85
And to beseche you, as you loue the life
And safetie of your children and your realme,
Now to employ your wisdome and your force
To stay this mischiefe ere it be to late.

    Gorb. Are they in armes? would he not sende to me?   90
Is this the honour of a fathers name?
In vaine we trauaile to asswage their mindes,
As if their hartes, whome neither brothers loue,
Nor fathers awe, nor kingdomes cares, can moue,
Our counsels could withdraw from raging heat.   95
Ioue slay them both, and end the cursed line.
For though perhappes feare of such mightie force
As I my lordes, ioyned with your noble aides,
Maye yet raise, shall represse their present heate,
The secret grudge and malice will remayne,   100

The fire not quenched, but kept in close restraint,
Fedde still within, breakes forth with double flame.
Their death and myne must peaze the angrie Gods.

   Phil. Yelde not, O king, so much to weake dispeire.
Your sonnes yet lyue, and long I trust, they shall.   105
If fates had taken you from earthly life,
Before beginning of this ciuyll strife:
Perhaps your sonnes in their vnmaistered youth,
Loose from regarde of any lyuing wight,
Would runne on headlong, with vnbridled race,   110
To their owne death and ruine of this realme.
But sith the Gods, that haue the care for kinges,
Of thinges and times dispose the order so,
That in your life this kindled flame breakes forth,
While yet your lyfe, your wisdome, and your power   115
May stay the growing mischiefe, and represse
The fierie blaze of their inkindled heate:
It seemes, and so ye ought to deeme thereof,
That louyng *Ioue* hath tempred so the time
Of this debate to happen in your dayes,   120
That you yet lyuing may the same appeaze,
And adde it to the glory of your latter age,
And they your sonnes may learne to liue in peace.
Beware (O king) the greatest harme of all,
Lest by your waylefull plaints your hastened death   . 125
Yelde larger roume vnto their growing rage.
Preserue your life, the onely hope of stay.
And if your highnes herein list to vse
Wisdome or force, counsell or knightly aide:
Loe we, our persons, powers and lyues are yours,   130
Vse vs tyll death, O king, we are your owne.

   Eub. Loe here the perill that was erst foresene,
When you, (O king) did first deuide your lande,
And yelde your present reigne vnto your sonnes,

But now (O noble prince) now is no time   135
To waile and plaine, and wast your wofull life.
Now is the time for present good aduise.
Sorow doth darke the iudgement of the wytte.
,, The hart vnbroken and the courage free
,, From feble faintnesse of bootelesse despeire,   140
,, Doth either ryse to safetie or renowme
,, By noble valure of vnuanquisht minde,
,, Or yet doth perishe in more happy sort.
Your grace may send to either of your sonnes
Some one both wise and noble personage,   145
Which with good counsell and with weightie name,
Of father, shall present before their eyes
Your hest, your life, your safetie and their owne,
The present mischiefe of their deadly strife.
And in the while, assemble you the force   150
Which your commaundement and the spedy hast
Of all my lordes here present can preparo.
The terrour of your mightie power shall stay
The rage of both, or yet of one at lest.   154
     Nun. O king the greatest griefe that euer prince dyd heare,
That euer wofull messenger did tell,
That euer wretched lande hath sene before,
I bryng to you. *Porrex* your yonger sonne
With soden force, inuaded hath the lande
That you to *Ferrex* did allotte to rule,   160
And with his owne most bloudy hand he hath
His brother slaine, and doth possesse his realme.
     Gorb. O heauens send down the flames of your reuenge,
Destroy I say with flash of wrekefull fier
The traitour sonne, and then the wretched sire.   165
But let vs go, that yet perhappes I may
Die with reuenge, and peaze the hatefull gods.

     Chor. The lust of kingdome knowes no sacred faith,
No rule of reason, no regarde of right,

No kindely loue, no feare of heauens wrath :
But with contempt of Goddes, and mans despite,
Through blodie slaughter, doth prepare the waies   5
To fatall scepter and accursed reigne.
The sonne so lothes the fathers lingering daies,
Ne dreades his hand in brothers blode to staine.
O wretched prince, ne doest thou yet recorde
The yet fresh murthers done within the lande   10
Of thy forefathers, when the cruell sworde
Bereft *Morgan* his life with cosyns hand ?
Thus fatall plagues pursue the giltie race,
Whose murderous hand imbrued with giltlesse blood
Askes vengeaunce still before the heauens face,   15
With endlesse mischiefes on the cursed broode.
The wicked childe thus bringes to wofull sire
The mournefull plaintes, to wast his very life.
Thus do the cruell flames of ciuyll fier
Destroy the parted reigne with hatefull strife.   20
And hence doth spring the well from which doth flow
The dead black streames of mourning, plaints & woe.

❡The order and signification
of the domme shew before the fourth act.

❡ First the musick of Howboies begã to plaie, during which there
came from vnder the stage, as though out of hell three furies.
Alecto, Megera, and Ctesiphone, clad in black garmentes
sprinkled with bloud and flames, their bodies girt with snakes,
their heds spred with serpentes in stead of heare, the one bearing 5
in her hand a Snake, the other a Whip, and the third a burning
Firebrand : ech driuing before them a king and a queene, which
moued by furies vnnaturally had slaine their owne children.
The names of the kings and queenes were these.   Tantalus,
Medea, Athamas, Ino, Cambises, Althea, after that the furies and 10
these had passed about the stage thrise, they departed and than

15 still] *omit* $Q_1 Q_3$ 17 thus] this $Q_1 Q_3$ 18 very] wery Q_1 :
weary Q_3 2 came] came forth $Q_1 Q_3$

the musicke ceased: hereby was signified the vnnaturall murders
to follow, that is to say. Porrex slaine by his owne mother.
And of king Gorboduc and queene Viden, killed by their owne
subiectes.   15

Actus quartus. Scena prima.

Viden sola.

Id. Why should I lyue, and linger forth my time
     In longer life to double my distresse?
O me most wofull wight, whom no mishappe
Long ere this day could haue bereued hence.
Mought not these handes by fortune, or by fate,   5
Haue perst this brest, and life with iron reft?
Or in this palace here, where I so long
Haue spent my daies, could not that happle houre
Once, once haue hapt in which these hugic frames
With death by fall might haue oppressed me?   10
Or should not this most hard and cruell soile,
So oft where I haue prest my wretched steps,
Sometime had ruthe of myne accursed life,
To rende in twayne swallow me therin?
So had my bones possessed now in peace   15
Their happie graue within the closed grounde,
And greadie wormes had gnawen this pyned hart
Without my feeling payne: so should not now
This lyuing brest remayne the ruthefull tombe,
Wherin my hart yelden to death is graued: 20
Nor driery thoughts with panges of pining griefe
My dolefull minde had not afflicted thus.
O my beloued sonne: O my swete childe,
My deare *Ferrex*, my ioye, my lyues delyght.
Is my beloued sonne, is my sweete childe,   25
My deare *Ferrex*, my ioye, my lyues delight
Murdered with cruell death? O hatefull wretch,

7 long] loug Q_2 22 had] hath Q_3 25 beloued] wel beloued $Q_1 Q_3$
26 Q_2 *period at end of line*

O heynous traitour both to heauen and earth.
Thou *Porrex*, thou this damned dede hast wrought,
Thou *Porrex*, thou shalt dearely bye the same.   30
Traitour to kinne and kinde, to sire and me,
To thine owne fleshe, and traitour to thy selfe.
The Gods on thee in hell shall wreke their wrath,
And here in earth this hand shall take reuenge,
On thee *Porrex*, thou false and caitife wight.   35
If after bloud, so eigre were thy thirst,
And murderous minde had so possessed thee,
If such hard hart of rocke and stonie flint
Liued in thy brest, that nothing els could like
Thy cruell tyrantes thought but death and bloud :   40
Wilde sauage beasts, mought not their slaughter serue
To fede thy gredie will, and in the middest
Of their entrailes to staine thy deadly handes
With bloud deserued, and drinke thereof thy fill ?
Or if nought els but death and bloud of man   45
Mought please thy lust, could none in Brittaine land,
Whose hart betorne out of his panting brest
With thine owne hand, or worke what death thou wouldest,
Suffice to make a sacrifice to peaze
That deadly minde and murderous thought in thee ?   50
But he who in the selfe same wombe was wrapped,
Where thou in dismall hower receiuedst life ?
Or if nedes, nedes, thy hand must slaughter make,
Moughtest thou not haue reached a mortall wound,
And with thy sword haue pearsed this cursed wombe,   55
That the accursed *Porrex* brought to light,
And geuen me a iust reward therefore ?
So *Ferrex* yet sweete life mought haue enioyed,
And to his aged father comfort brought,
With some yong sonne in whom they both might liue.   60

30 bye] abye $Q_1 Q_3$ 41 their] the $Q_1 Q_3$ 47 panting] louyng Q_1 :
louing Q_3 49 peaze] appeaze Q_1 : appease Q_3 53 thy] thie Q_1 :
this Q_3 must] might Q_3 58 yet] if $Q_1 Q_3$

But whereunto waste I this ruthfull speche,
To thee that hast thy brothers bloud thus shed?
Shall I still thinke that frõ this wombe thou sprong?
That I thee bare? or take thee for my sonne?
No traitour, no: I thee refuse for mine,   65
Murderer I thee renounce, thou art not mine.
Neuer, O wretch, this wombe conceiued thee,
Nor neuer bode I painfull throwes for thee.
Changeling to me thou art, and not my childe,
Nor to no wight, that sparke of pitie knew.   70
Ruthelesse, vnkinde, monster of natures worke,
Thou neuer suckt the milke of womans brest,
But from thy birth the cruell Tigers teates
Haue nursed thee, nor yet of fleshe and bloud
Formde is thy hart, but of hard iron wrought,   75
And wilde and desert woods bredde thee to life.
But canst thou hope to scape my iust reuenge?
Or that these handes will not be wrooke on thee?
Doest thou not know that *Ferrex* mother liues
That loued him more dearly than her selfe?   80
And doth she liue, and is not venged on thee?

Actus quartus.   Scena secunda.

Gorbodue.   Arostus.   Eubulus.   Porrex.   Marcella.

Orb. We maruell much wherto this lingring stay
Falles out so long: *Porrex* vnto our court
By order of our letters is returned,
And *Eubulus* receaued from vs by hest
At his arriuall here to geue him charge   5
Before our presence straight to make repaire,
And yet we haue no worde whereof he stayes.
    Arostus. Lo where he commes & *Eubulus* with him.
    Eubulus. According to your highnesse hest to me,

62 hast] hath Q_3 74 thee] *om.* $Q_1 Q_3$ 78 wrooke] wrekte Q_3
7 haue] heare Q_3

Here haue I *Porrex* brought euen in such sort   10
As from his weried horse he did alight,
For that your grace did will such hast therein.
   Gorboduc. We like and praise this spedy will in you,
To worke the thing that to your charge we gaue.
Porrex, if we so farre should swarue from kinde,   15
And from those boundes which lawe of nature sets,
As thou hast done by vile and wretched deede,
In cruell murder of thy brothers life,
Our present hand could stay no longer time,
But straight should bathe this blade in bloud of thee   20
As iust reuenge of thy detested crime.
No: we should not offend the lawe of kinde,
If now this sworde of ours did slay thee here:
For thou hast murdered him, whose heinous death
Euen natures force doth moue vs to reuenge   25
By bloud againe: and iustice forceth vs   .
To measure death for death, thy due desert.
Yet sithens thou art our childe, and sith as yet
In this hard case what worde thou canst alledge
For thy defence, by vs hath not bene heard,   30
We are content to staye our will for that
Which iustice biddes vs presently to worke,
And geue thee leaue to vse thy speche at full
If ought thou haue to lay for thine excuse.
   Porrex. Neither O king, I can or will denie   35
But that this hand from *Ferrex* life hath reft:
Which fact how much my dolefull hart doth waile,
Oh would it mought as full appeare to sight
As inward griefe doth poure it forth to me.
So yet perhappes if euer ruthefull hart   40
Melting in teares within a manly brest,
Through depe repentance of his bloudy fact,
If euer griefe, if euer wofull man
Might moue regreite with sorrowe of his fault,

16 those] these $Q_1 Q_3$ lawe] lawes $Q_1 Q_3$ 26 and] But $Q_1 Q_3$
43 man] men Q_3

I thinke the torment of my mournefull case   45
Knowen to your grace, as I do feele the same,
Would force euen wrath her selfe to pitie me.
But as the water troubled with the mudde
Shewes not the face which els the eye should see.
Euen so your irefull minde with stirred thought,   50
Can not so perfectly discerne my cause.
But this vnhappe, amongest so many heapes,
I must content me with, most wretched man,
That to my selfe I must reserue my woe
In pining thoughtes of mine accursed fact,   55
Since I may not shewe here my smallest griefe
Such as it is, and as my brest endures,
Which I esteeme the greatest miserie
Of all missehappes that fortune now can send.
Not that I rest in hope with plaint and teares   60
To purchase life: for to the Goddes I clepe
For true recorde of this my faithfull speche,
Neuer this hart shall haue the thoughtfull dread
To die the death that by your graces dome
By iust desert, shall be pronounced to me: 65
Nor neuer shall this tongue once spend the speche
Pardon to craue, or seeke by sute to liue.
I meane not this, as though I were not touchde
With care of dreadfull death, or that I helde
Life in contempt: but that I know, the minde   70
Stoupes to no dread, although the fleshe be fraile,
And for my gilt, I yelde the same so great
As in my selfe I finde a feare to sue,
For graunt of life.
    Gorboduc.   In vaine, O wretch, thou shewest
A wofull hart, *Ferrex* now lies in graue,   75
Slaine by thy hand.
    Porrex.   Yet this, O father, heare:

54 reserue] referre Q_1 Q_3 56 Since] Sithens Q_1: Sithence Q_3 59
Q_2 *comma at end of line*   61 To] Should Q_1 Q_3 66 the] this Q_1 Q_3

And then I end.   Your maiestie well knowes,
That when my brother *Ferrex* and my selfe
By your owne hest were ioyned in gouernance
Of this your graces realme of Brittaine land,   80
I neuer sought nor trauailled for the same,
Nor by my selfe, nor by no frend I wrought,
But from your highnesse will alone it sprong,
Of your most gracious goodnesse bent to me.
But how my brothers hart euen then repined   85
With swollen disdaine against mine egall rule,
Seing that realme, which by discent should grow
Wholly to him, allotted halfe to me?
Euen in your highnesse court he now remaines,
And with my brother then in nearest place,   90
Who can recorde, what proofe thereof was shewde,
And how my brothers enuious hart appearde.
Yet I that iudged it my part to seeke
His fauour and good will, and loth to make
Your highnesse know, the thing which should haue brought 95
Grief to your grace, & your offence to him,
Hoping my earnest sute should soone haue wonne
A louing hart within a brothers brest,
Wrought in that sort that for a pledge of loue
And faithfull hart, he gaue to me his hand.   100
This made me thinke, that he had banisht qnite
All rancour from his thought and bare to me
Such hartie loue, as I did owe to him.
But after once we left your graces court,
And from your highnesse presence liued apart,   105
This egall rule still, still, did grudge him so
That now those enuious sparkes which erst lay raked
In liuing cinders of dissembling brest,
Kindled so farre within his hart disdaine,
That longer could he not refraine from proofe   110

82 nor] or Q_3 97 my] by $Q_1 Q_3$ '109 hart] hartes $Q_1 Q_3$

Of secrete practise to depriue me life
By poysons force, and had bereft me so,
If mine owne seruant hired to this fact
And moued by trouth with hate to worke the same,
In time had not bewrayed it vnto me.   115
Whan thus I sawe the knot of loue vnknitte,
All honest league and faithfull promise broke,
The law of kinde and trouth thus rent in twaine,
His hart on mischiefe set, and in his brest
Blacke treason hid, then, then did I despeire   120
That euer time could winne him frend to me.
Then saw I how he smiled with slaying knife
Wrapped vnder cloke, then saw I depe deceite
Lurke in his face and death prepared for me :
Euen nature moued me than to holde my life   125
More deare to me than his, and bad this hand,
Since by his life my death must nedes ensue,
And by his death my life to be preserued,
To shed his bloud, and seeke my safetie so.
And wisedome willed me without protract   130
In spedie wise to put the same in vre.
Thus haue I tolde the cause that moued me
To worke my brothers death and so I yeld
My life, my death, to iudgement of your grace.

   Gorb. Oh cruell wight, should any cause preuaile   135
To make thee staine thy hands with brothers bloud ?
But what of thee we will resolue to doe,
Shall yet remaine vnknowen : Thou in the meane
Shalt from our royall presence banisht be,
Vntill our princely pleasure furder shall   140
To thee be shewed.   Depart therefore our sight
Accursed childe.   What cruell destenie,
What froward fate hath sorted vs this chaunce,
That euen in those where we should comfort find,
Where our delight now in our aged dayes   145

     111 me] my *Q₃*   115 In] If *Q₃*

Sould rest and be, euen there our onely griefe
And depest sorrowes to abridge our life,
Most pyning cares and deadly thoughts do grow?

   Aros. Your grace should now in these graue yeres of yours
Haue found ere this y͏ͤ price of mortall ioyes,   150
How short they be, how fading here in earth,
How full of chaunge, how brittle our estate,
Of nothing sure, saue onely of the death,
To whom both man and all the world doth owe
Their end at last, neither should natures power   155
In other sort against your hart preuaile,
Than as the naked hand whose stroke assayes
The armed brest where force doth light in vaine.

   Gorbod. Many can yelde right sage and graue aduise
Of pacient sprite to others wrapped in woe,   160
And can in speche both rule and conquere kinde,
Who if by proofe they might feele natures force,
Would shew them selues men as they are in dede,
Which now wil nedes be gods.   But what doth meane
The sory chere of her that here doth come?   165

   Marcella. Oh where is ruth? or where is pitie now?
Whether is gentle hart and mercy fled?
Are they exiled out of our stony brestes,
Neuer to make returne? is all the world
Drowned in bloud, and soncke in crueltie?   170
If not in women mercy may be found,
If not (alas) within the mothers brest,
To her owne childe, to her owne fleshe and bloud,
If ruthe be banished thence, if pitie there
May haue no place, if there no gentle hart   175
Do liue and dwell, where should we seeke it then?

   Gorb. Madame (alas) what meanes your woful tale?

   Marcella. O sillie woman I, why to this houre
Haue kinde and fortune thus deferred my breath,
That I should liue to see this dolefull day?   180

148 grow] graue $Q_1 Q_2$ 155 should] shall $Q_1 Q_2$ 165 of her] *om.* Q_2

Will euer wight beleue that such hard hart
Could rest within the cruell mothers brest,
With her owne hand to slay her onely sonne?
But out (alas) these eyes behelde the same,
They saw the driery sight, and are become　　　185
Most ruthfull recordes of the bloudy fact.
Porrex (alas) is by his mother slaine,
And with her hand, a wofull thing to tell,
While slumbring on his carefull bed he restes
His hart stabde in with knife is reft of life.　　　190
　　Gorboduc. O *Eubulus,* oh draw this sword of ours,
And pearce this hart with speed.　O hatefull light,
O lothsome life, O sweete and welcome death.
Deare *Eubulus* worke this we thee besech.
　　Eubulus. Pacient your grace, perhappes he liueth yet,　　195
With wound receaued, but not of certaine death.
　　Gorboduc. O let vs then repayre vnto the place,
And see if *Porrex* liue, or thus be slaine.
　　Marcella. Alas he liueth not, it is to true,
That with these eyes of him a perelesse prince,　　　200
Sonne to a king, and in the flower of youth,
Euen with a twinke a senselesse stocke I saw.
　　Arostus. O damned deede.
　　Marcella.　　　　　　　But heare hys ruthefull end.
The noble prince, pearst with the sodeine wound,
Out of his wretched slumber hastely start,　　　205
Whose strength now fayling straight he ouerthrew,
When in the fall his eyes euen new vnclosed
Behelde the Queene, and cryed to her for helpe.
We then, alas, the ladies which that time
Did there attend, seing that heynous deede,　　　210
And hearing him oft call the wretched name
Of mother, and to crye to her for aide,
Whose direfull hand gaue him the mortall wound,

190 stabde] stalde $Q_1 Q_3$　　198 if] if that $Q_1 Q_3$　　liue] *om.* $Q_1 Q_3$
203 hys] this $Q_1 Q_3$　　204 wound] wounde Q_1 : wounds Q_3

Pitying (alas) for nought els could we do)
His ruthefull end, ranne to the wofull bedde,   215
Dispoyled straight his brest, and all we might
Wiped in vaine with napkins next at hand,
The sodeine streames of bloud that flushed fast
Out of the gaping wound.   O what a looke,
O what a ruthefull stedfast eye me thought   220
He fixt vpon my face, which to my death
Will neuer part fro me, when with a braide
A deepe fet sigh he gaue, and therewithall
Clasping his handes, to heauen he cast his sight.
And straight pale death pressing within his face   225
The flying ghost his mortall corpes forsooke.

    Arostus. Neuer did age bring forth so vile a fact.

    Marcella. O hard and cruell happe, that thus assigned
Vnto so worthy a wight so wretched end :
But most hard cruell hart, that could consent   230
To lend the hatefull destenies that hand,
By which, alas, so heynous crime was wrought.
O Queene of adamant, O marble brest,
If not the fauour of his comely face,
If not his princely chere and countenance,   235
His valiant actiue armes, his manly brest,
If not his faire and seemely personage,
His noble limmes in such proportion cast
As would haue wrapt a sillie womans thought,
If this mought not haue moued thy bloudy hart   240
And that most cruell hand the wretched weapon
Euen to let fall, and kiste him in the face,
With teares for ruthe to reaue such one by death :
Should nature yet consent to slay her sonne ?
O mother, thou to murder thus thy childe ?   245
Euen *Ioue* with iustice must with lightning flames
Frō heauen send downe some strange reuenge on thee.

    214 *Q*₁ *Q*₃ *no bracket after* alas: *Q*₁ *bracket before* alas : *Q*₃ *before* for
215 ruthefull] rufull *Q*₃   233, 240 *Q*₂ *period at end of line*   238
proportion] preparacion *Q*₁

Ah noble prince, how oft haue I behelde
Thee mounted on thy fierce and traumpling stede,
Shining in armour bright before the tilt,   250
And with thy mistresse sleue tied on thy helme,
And charge thy staffe to please thy ladies eye,
That bowed the head peece of thy frendly foe?
How oft in armes on horse to bend the mace?
How oft in armes on foote to breake the sworde,   255
Which neuer now these eyes may see againe.

    Arostus. Madame, alas, in vaine these plaints are shed,
Rather with me depart, and helpe to swage,
The thoughtfull griefes that in the aged king
Must needes by nature growe, by death of this   260
His onely sonne, whom he did holde so deare.

    Marcella. What wight is that which saw y^t I did see,
And could refraine to waile with plaint and teares?
Not I, alas, that hart is not in me.
But let vs goe, for I am greued anew,   265
To call to minde the wretched fathers woe.

    Chorus. Whan greedy lust in royall seate to reigne
Hath reft all care of Goddes and eke of men,
And cruell hart, wrath, treason, and disdaine
Within ambicious brest are lodged, then
Beholde how mischiefe wide her selfe displayes,   5
And with the brothers hand the brother slayes.
When bloud thus shed, doth staine the heauens face,
Crying to *Ioue* for vengeance of the deede,
The mightie God euen moueth from his place,
With wrath to wreke: then sendes he forth with spede   10
The dreadfull furies, daughters of the night,
With Serpentes girt, carying the whip of ire,
With heare of stinging Snakes, and shining bright
With flames and bloud, and with a brand of fire.
These for reuenge of wretched murder done,   15

257 *Q₄ comma after* Arostus   4 Within] Within the *Q₁ Q₃*   7 the]
this *Q₁ Q₃*   .10 sendes] send *Q₃*

Do make the mother kill her onely sonne.
Blood asketh blood, and death must death requite.
Ioue by his iust and euerlasting dome
Iustly hath euer so requited it.
The times before recorde, and times to come　　　　20
Shall finde it true, and so doth present proofe
Present before our eyes for our behoofe.
O happy wight that suffres not the snare
Of murderous minde to tangle him in blood.
And happy he that can in time beware　　　　25
By others harmes and turne it to his good.
But wo to him that fearing not to·offend
Doth serue his lust, and will not see the end.

❡ The order and signification
of the domme shew before the fifth act.

❡ First the drommes & fluites, began to sound, during which there
came forth vpon the stage a company of·Hargabusiers and of
Armed men all in order of battaile. These after their peeces
discharged, and that the armed men had three times marched
about the stage, departed, and then the drommes and fluits did 5
cease. Hereby was signified tumults, rebellions, armes and
ciuill warres to follow, as fell in the realme of great Brittayne,
which by the space of fiftie yeares & more continued in ciuill
warre betwene the nobilitie after the death of king Gorboduc,
and of his issues, for want of certayne limitacion in succession of 10
the crowne, till the time of Dunwallo Molmutius, who reduced
the land to monarchie.

Actus quintus.   Scena prima.
Clotyn.   Mandud.   Gwenard.   Fergus.   Eubulus.

Clot. Did euer age bring forth such tirants harts?
　The brother hath bereft the brothers life,
The mother she hath died her cruell handes

16 Do make] Dooth cause Q_3　　20 The] These $Q_1 Q_3$　　28 Q_3
comma at end of line　　10 in] in the $Q_1 Q_3$

In bloud of her owne sonne, and now at last
The people loe forgetting trouth and loue,   5
Contemning quite both law and loyall hart,
Euen they haue slaine their soueraigne lord & queene.

   Mand. Shall this their traitorous crime vnpunished rest?
Euen yet they cease not, caryed on with rage,
In their rebellious routes, to threaten still   10
A new bloud shed vnto the princes kinne,
To slay them all, and to vproote the race
Both of the king and queene, so are they moued
With *Porrex* death, wherin they falsely charge
The giltlesse king without desert at all,   15
And traitorously haue murdered him therfore,
And eke the queene.

   Gwena.   Shall subiectes dare with force
To worke reuenge vpon their princes fact?
Admit the worst that may, as sure in this
The deede was fowle, the queene to slay her sonne,   20
Shall yet the subiect-seeke to take the sworde,
Arise agaynst his lord, and slay his king?
O wretched state, where those rebellious hartes
Are not rent out euen from their liuing breastes,
And with the body throwen vnto the foules   25
As carrion foode, for terrour of the rest.

   Ferg. There can no punishment be thought to great
For this so greuous cryme: let spede therfore
Be vsed therin for it behoueth so.

   Eubulus. Ye all my lordes, I see, consent in one   30
And I as one consent with ye in all.
I holde it more than neede with sharpest law
To punish this tumultuous bloudy rage.
For nothing more may shake the common state,
Than sufferance of vproares without redresse,   35
Wherby how some kingdomes of mightie power

9 on] out $Q_1 Q_3$ 32 with] with the $Q_1 Q_3$ 33 this] the $Q_1 Q_3$

After great conquestes made, and florishing
In fame and wealth, haue ben to ruine brought,
I pray to *Ioue* that we may rather wayle
Such happe in them than witnesse in our selues.   40
Eke fully with the duke my minde agrees,
Though kinges forget to gouerne as they ought,
Yet subiectes must obey as they are bounde.
But now my lordes, before ye farder wade,
Or spend your speach, what sharpe reuenge shall fall   45
By iustice plague on these rebellious wightes,
Me thinkes ye rather should first search the way,
By which in time the rage of this vproare
Mought be repressed, and these great tumults ceased.
Euen yet the life of *Brittayne* land doth hang   50
In traitours balaunce of vnegall weight.
Thinke not my lordes the death of *Gorboduc,*
Nor yet *Videnaes* bloud will cease their rage :
Euen our owne lyues, our wiues and children deare,
Our countrey dearest of all, in daunger standes,   55
Now to be spoiled, now, now made desolate,
And by our selues a conquest to ensue.
For geue once swey vnto the peoples lustes,
To rush forth on, and stay them not in time,
And as the streame that rowleth downe the hyll,   60
So will they headlong ronne with raging thoughtes
From bloud to bloud, from mischiefe vnto moe,
To ruine of the realme, them selues and all,

41 *After this line* Q₁ *has the following:*
         That no cause serues, wherby the Subiect maye
         Call to accompt the doynges of his Prince,
         Muche lesse in bloode by sworde to worke reuenge,
         No more then maye the hande cut of the heade,
         In Acte nor speache, no ; not in secrete thoughte
         The Subiect maye rebell against his Lorde,
         Or Judge of him that sittes in *Ceasars* Seate.
         With grudging mind ⟨to⟩ damne those He mislikes.
     Instead of to *in the last line,* Q₁ *has* do, *and* Q₃ *doo.*   Q₁ *and* Q₃ *agree*
in *this passage except for differences of spelling.   See explanatory notes for*
reasons of the omission in Q₂   54 deare] *om.* Q₁ Q₃

So giddy are the common peoples mindes,
So glad of chaunge, more wauering than the sea.   65
Ye see (my lordes) what strength these rebelles haue,
What hugie nombre is assembled still,
For though the traiterous fact, for which they rose
Be wrought and done, yet lodge they still in field
So that how farre their furies yet will stretch   70
Great cause we haue to dreade.   That we may seeke
By present battaile to represse their power,
Speede must we vse to leuie force therfore.
For either they forthwith will mischiefe worke,
Or their rebellious roares forthwith will cease.   75
These violent thinges may haue no lasting long.
Let vs therfore vse this for present helpe,
Perswade by gentle speach, and offre grace
With gift of pardon saue vnto the chiefe
And that vpon condicion that forthwith   80
They yelde the captaines of their enterprise,
To beare such guerdon of their traiterous fact,
As may be both due vengeance to them selues,
And holsome terrour to posteritie.
This shall, I thinke, scatter the greatest part,   85
That now are holden with desire of home,
Weried in field with cold of winters nightes,
And some (no doubt) striken with dread of law.
Whan this is once proclamed, it shall make
The captaines to mistrust the multitude,   90
Whose safetie biddes them to betray their heads,
And so much more bycause the rascall routes,
In thinges of great and perillous attemptes,
Are neuer trustie to the noble race.
And while we treate and stand on termes of grace,   95
We shall both stay their furies rage the while,
And eke gaine time, whose onely helpe sufficeth

75 will] must Q_3 85 scatter] flatter $Q_1 Q_3$

Withouten warre to vanquish rebelles power.
In the meane while, make you in redynes
Such band of horsemen as ye may prepare.   100
Horsemen (you know) are not the commons strength,
But are the force and store of noble men,
Wherby the vnchosen and vnarmed sort
Of skillesse rebelles, whome none other power
But nombre makes to be of dreadfull force,   105
With sodeyne brunt may quickely be opprest.
And if this gentle meane of proffered grace,
With stubborne hartes cannot so farre auayle,
As to asswage their desperate courages,
Then do I wish such slaughter to be made,   110
As present age and eke posteritie
May be adrad with horrour of reuenge,
That iustly then shall on these rebelles fall.
This is my lordes the summe of mine aduise.

    Clotyn. Neither this case admittes debate at large,   115
And though it did, this speach that hath ben sayd
Hath well abridged the tale I would haue tolde.
Fully with *Eubulus* do I consent
In all that he hath sayd : and if the same
To you my lordes, may seeme for best aduise,   120
I wish that it should streight be put in vre.

    Mandud. My lordes than let vs presently depart,
And follow this that liketh vs so well.

    Fergus. If euer time to gaine a kingdome here
Were offred man, now it is offred mee.   125
The realme is reft both of their king and queene,
The ofspring of the prince is slaine and dead,
No issue now remaines, the heire vnknowen,
The people are in armes and mutynies,
The nobles they are busied how to cease   130
These great rebellious tumultes and vproares,

And *Brittayne* land now desert left alone
Amyd these broyles vncertayne where to rest,
Offers her selfe vnto that noble hart
That will or dare pursue to beare her crowne.   135
Shall I that am the duke of *Albanye*
Discended from that line of noble bloud,
Which hath so long florished in worthy fame,
Of valiaunt hartes, such as in noble brestes
Of right should rest aboue the baser sort,   140
Refuse to venture life to winne a crowne?
Whom shall I finde enmies that will withstand
My fact herein, if I attempt by armes
To seeke the same now in these times of broyle?
These dukes power can hardly well appease   145
The people that already are in armes.
But if perhappes my force be once in field,
Is not my strength in power aboue the best
Of all these lordes now left in *Brittayne* land?
And though they should match me with power of mē,   150
Yet doubtfull is the chaunce of battailles ioyned.
If victors of the field we may depart,
Ours is the scepter then of great Brittayne.
If slayne amid the playne this body lye,
Mine enemies yet shall not deny me this,   155
But that I dyed geuing the noble charge
To hazarde life for conquest of a crowne.
Forthwith therefore will I in post depart
To *Albanye*, and raise in armour there
All power I can: and here my secret friendes,   160
By secret practise shall sollicite still,
To seeke to wynne to me the peoples hartes.

140 the] the the Q_2 141 venture] aduenture $Q_1 Q_3$ 144 same]
Fame $Q_1 Q_3$ 154 lye] be $Q_1 Q_3$

Actus quintus.   Scena secunda.

Eubulus. Clotyn. Mandud. Gwenard. Arostus. Nuntius.

Evb. O *Ioue*, how are these peoples harts abusde ?
What blind fury, thus headlong caries them ?
That though so many bookes, so many rolles
Of auncient time recorde, what greuous plagues
Light on these rebelles aye, and though so oft   5
Their eares haue heard their aged fathers tell,
What iuste reward these traitours still receyue,
Yea though them selues haue sene depe death & bloud,
By strangling cord and slaughter of the sword,
To such assigned, yet can they not beware,   10
Yet can not stay their lewde rebellious handes,
But suffring loe fowle treason to distaine
Their wretched myndes, forget their loyall hart,
Reiect all truth and rise against their prince.
A ruthefull case, that those, whom duties bond,   15
Whom grafted law by nature, truth, and faith,
Bound to preserue their countrey and their king,
Borne to defend their common wealth and prince,
Euen they should geue consent thus to subuert
Thee Brittaine land, & from thy wombe should spring   20
(O natiue soile) those, that will needs destroy
And ruyne thee and eke them selues in fine.
For lo, when once the dukes had offred grace
Of pardon sweete, the multitude missledde
By traitorous fraude of their vngracious heades,   25
One sort that saw the dangerous successe
Of stubborne standing in rebellious warre,
And knew the difference of princes power
From headlesse nombre of tumultuous routes,
Whom common countreies care, and priuate feare,   ·   30

4 time] time of Q_3 11 can] can they $Q_1 Q_3$ lewde] *om.* $Q_1 Q_3$
12 loe] to Q_1: too Q_3 15 bond] bounde Q_1: bound Q_3 20 thy]
the $Q_1 Q_3$ spring] bring $Q_1 Q_3$

Taught to repent the errour of their rage,
Layde handes vpon the captaines of their band,
And brought them bound vnto the mightie dukes.
And other sort not trusting yet so well
The truth of pardon, or mistrusting more   35
Their owne offence than that they could conceiue
Such hope of pardon for so foule misdede,
Or for that they their captaines could not yeld,
Who fearing to be yelded fled before,
Stale home by silence of the secret night.   40
The thirde vnhappy and enraged sort
Of desperate hartes, who stained in princes bloud
From trayterous furour could not be withdrawen   ˅
By loue, by law, by grace, ne yet by feare,
By proffered life, ne yet by threatned death,   45
With mindes hopelesse of life, dreadlesse of death,
Carelesse of countrey, and awelesse of God,
Stoode bent to fight, as furies did them moue,
With violent death to close their traiterous life.
These all by power of horsemen were opprest,   50
And with reuenging sworde slayne in the field,
Or with the strangling cord hangd on the tree,
Where yet their carryen carcases do preach
The fruites that rebelles reape of their vproares,
And of the murder of their sacred prince.   55
But loe, where do approche the noble dukes,
By whom these tumults haue ben thus appeasde.

    Clotyn. I thinke the world will now at length beware
And feare to put on armes agaynst their prince.

    Mand. If not? those trayterous hartes that dare rebell,   60
Let them beholde the wide and hugie fieldes
With bloud and bodies spread of rebelles slayne,
The lofty trees clothed with the corpses dead

31 errour] terrour Q_1 Q_3 34 And other] An other Q_1: Another Q_3
36 could] should Q_3 40 Q_2 *comma at end of line*   52 tree] trees
Q_1 Q_3 53 their] the Q_1 Q_3 60 dare] doo Q_3 62 bodies] bodie
Q_1 Q_3 of] with Q_1 Q_3 63 lofty] lustie Q_1 Q_3 the] *omit* Q_1 Q_3

That strangled with the corde do hang theron.

    Arostus. A iust rewarde, such as all times before   65
Haue euer lotted to those wretched folkes.

    Gwen. But what meanes he that commeth here so fast?

    Nun. My lordes, as dutie and my trouth doth moue
And of my countrey worke a care in mee,
That if the spending of my breath auailed   70
To do the seruice that my hart desires,
I would not shunne to imbrace a present death :
So haue I now in that wherein I thought
My trauayle mought performe some good effect,
Ventred my life to bring these tydinges here.   75
Fergus the mightie duke of Albanye
Is now in armes and lodgeth in the fielde
With twentie thousand men, hether he bendes
His spedy marche, and mindes to inuade the crowne.
Dayly he gathereth strength, and spreads abrode   80
That to this realme no certeine heire remaines,
That Brittayne land is left without a guide,
That he the scepter seekes, for nothing els
But to preserue the people and the land,
Which now remaine as ship without a sterne.   85
Loe this is that which I haue here to say.

    Cloyton. Is this his fayth? and shall he falsely thus
Abuse the vauntage of vnhappie times?
O wretched land, if his outragious pride,
His cruell and vntempred wilfulnesse,   90
His deepe dissembling shewes of false pretence,
Should once attaine the crowne of Brittaine land.
Let vs my lordes, with timely force resist
The new attempt of this our common foe,
As we would quench the flames of common fire.   95

    Mand. Though we remaine without a certain prince,
To weld the realme or guide the wandring rule,

---

    64 theron] therin Q_1 : therein Q_3 69 a] and $Q_1 Q_3$ 70 auailed]
auaile $Q_1 Q_3$ 86 here to say] hereto saide Q_1 : hereto said Q_3

Yet now the common mother of vs all,
Our natiue land, our countrey, that conteines
Our wiues, children, kindred, our selues and all   100
That euer is or may be deare to man,
Cries vnto vs to helpe our selues and her.
Let vs aduaunce our powers to represse
This growing foe of all our liberties.

    Gwenard. Yea let vs so, my lordes, with hasty speede.   105
And ye (O Goddes) send vs the welcome death,
To shed our bloud in field, and leaue vs not
In lothesome life to lenger out our dayes,
To see the hugie heapes of these vnhappes,
That now roll downe vpon the wretched land,   110
Where emptie place of princely gouernaunce,
No certaine stay now left of doubtlesse heire,
Thus leaue this guidelesse realme an open pray,
To endlesse stormes and waste of ciuill warre.

    Arostus. That ye (my lordes) do so agree in one,   115
To saue your countrey from the violent reigne
And wrongfully vsurped tyrannie
Of him that threatens conquest of you all,
To saue your realme, and in this realme your selues,
From forreine thraldome of so proud a prince,   120
Much do I prayse, and I besech the Goddes,
With happy honour to requite it you.
But (O my lordes) sith now the heauens wrath
Hath reft this land the issue of their prince,
Sith of the body of our late soueraigne lorde   125
Remaines no moe, since the yong kinges be slaine,
And of the title of discended crowne
Vncertainly the diuerse mindes do thinke
Euen of the learned sort, and more vncertainly
Will parciall fancie and affection deeme :   130
But most vncertainly will climbing pride

---

108 dayes] lynes Q_1 : liues Q_3 109 vnhappes] mishaps Q_3 127
of] of the Q_1 Q_3

And hope of reigne withdraw to sundry partes
The doubtfull right and hopefull lust to reigne:
When once this noble seruice is atchieued
For Brittaine land the mother of ye all,   135
When once ye haue with armed force represt
The proude attemptes of this Albanian prince,
That threatens thraldome to your natiue land,
When ye shall vanquishers returne from field,
And finde the princely state an open pray   140
To gredie lust and to vsurping power,
Then, then (my lordes) if euer kindly care
Of auncient honour of your auncesters,
Of present wealth and noblesse of your stockes,
Yea of the liues and safetie yet to come   145
Of your deare wiues, your children, and your selues,
Might moue your noble hartes with gentle ruth,
Then, then, haue pitie on the torne estate,
Then helpe to salue the welneare hopelesse sore
Which ye shall do, if ye your selues withholde   150
The slaying knife from your owne mothers throate.
Her shall you saue, and you, and yours in her,
If ye shall all with one assent forbeare
Once to lay hand or take vnto your selues
The crowne, by colour of pretended right,   155
Or by what other meanes so euer it be,
Till first by common counsell of you all
In Parliament the regall diademe
Be set in certaine place of gouernaunce,
In which your Parliament and in your choise,   160
Preferre the right (my lordes) without respect
Of strength or frendes, or what soeuer cause
That may set forward any others part.
For right will last, and wrong can not endure.
Right meane I his or hers, vpon whose name   165
The people rest by meane of natiue line,

     132 to] from $Q_1 Q_3$ 161 without] with Q_2 162 or] of $Q_1 Q_3$

Or by the vertue of some former lawe,
Already made their title to aduaunce.
Such one (my lordes) let be your chosen king,
Such one so borne within your natiue land,   170
Such one preferre, and in no wise admitte
The heauie yoke of forreine gouernance,
Let forreine titles yelde to publike wealth.
And with that hart wherewith ye now prepare
Thus to withstand the proude inuading foe,   175
With that same hart (my lordes) keepe out also
Vnnaturall thraldome of strangers reigne,
Ne suffer you against the rules of kinde
Your mother land to serue a forreine prince.

Eubulus. Loe here the end of *Brutus* royall line,   180
And loe the entry to the wofull wracke,
And vtter ruine of this noble realme.
The royall king, and eke his sonnes are slaine,
No ruler restes within the regall seate,
The heire, to whom the scepter longes, vnknowen,   185
That to eche force of forreine princes power,
Whom vauntage of our wretched state may moue
By sodeine armes to gaine so riche a realme,
And to the proud and gredie minde at home,
Whom blinded lust to reigne leades to aspire,   190
Loe Brittaine realme is left an open pray,
A present spoyle by conquest to ensue.
Who seeth not now how many rising mindes
Do feede their thoughts, with hope to reach a realme?
And who will not by force attempt to winne   195
So great a gaine, that hope perswades to haue?
A simple colour shall for title serue.
Who winnes the royall crowne will want no right,
Nor such as shall display by long discent
A lineall race to proue him lawfull king.   200

187 our] your $Q_1 Q_3$ may moue] *omit* $Q_1 Q_3$ 200 lawfull] selfe a
$Q_1 Q_3$

In the meane while these ciuil armes shall rage,
And thus a thousand mischiefes shall vnfolde,
And farre and neare spread thee (O Brittaine land)
All right and lawe shall cease, and he that had
Nothing to day, to morrowe shall enioye   205
Great heapes of golde, and he that flowed in wealth,
Loe he shall be bereft of life and all,
And happiest he that then possesseth least,
The wiues shall suffer rape, the maides defloured,
And children fatherlesse shall weepe and waile,   210
With fire and sworde thy natiue folke shall perishe,
One kinsman shall bereaue an others life,
The father shall vnwitting slay the sonne,
The sonne shall slay the sire and know it not,
Women and maides the cruell souldiers sword   215
Shall perse to death, and sillie children loe,
That playinge in the streetes and fieldes are found,
By violent hand shall close their latter day.
Whom shall the fierce and bloudy souldier
Reserue to life? whom shall he spare from death?   220
Euen thou (O wretched mother) halfe aliue,
Thou shalt beholde thy deare and onely childe
Slaine with the sworde while he yet suckes thy brest.
Loe, giltlesse bloud shall thus eche where be shed.
Thus shall the wasted soile yelde forth no fruite,   225
But dearth and famine shall possesse the land.
The townes shall be consumed and burnt with fire,
The peopled cities shall waxe desolate,
And thou, O Brittaine, whilome in renowme,
Whilome in wealth and fame, shalt thus be torne,   230
Dismembred thus, and thus be rent in twaine,
Thus wasted and defaced, spoyled and destroyed,
These be the fruites your ciuil warres will bring.
Hereto it commes when kinges will not consent

    206 golde] good $Q_1 Q_2$ 207 bereft] reft $Q_1 Q_3$ 212 others] other Q_1
217 playinge] play Q_2 229 Brittaine] *Brittaine* Land $Q_1 Q_2$

To graue aduise, but followe wilfull will. 235
This is the end, when in fonde princes hartes
Flattery preuailes, and sage rede hath no place.
These are the plages, when murder is the meane
To make new heires vnto the royall crowne.
Thus wreke the Gods, when that the mothers wrath 240
Nought but the bloud of her owne childe may swage.
These mischiefes spring when rebells will arise,
To worke reuenge and iudge their princes fact.
This, this ensues, when noble men do faile
In loyall trouth, and subiectes will be kinges. 245
And this doth growe when loe vnto the prince,
Whom death or sodeine happe of life bereaues,
No certaine heire remaines, such certaine heire,
As not all onely is the rightfull heire,
But to the realme is so made knowen to be, 250
And trouth therby vested in subiectes hartes,
To owe fayth there where right is knowen to rest.
Alas, in Parliament what hope can be,
When is of Parliament no hope at all?
Which, though it be assembled by consent, 255
Yet is not likely with consent to end,
While eche one for him selfe, or for his frend,
Against his foe, shall trauaile what he may.
While now the state left open to the man,
That shall with greatest force inuade the same, 260
Shall fill ambicious mindes with gaping hope,
When will they once with yelding hartes agree?
Or in the while, how shall the realme be vsed?
No, no: then Parliament should haue bene holden,
And certeine heires appointed to the crowne, 265
To stay the title of established right,
And in the people plant obedience,

236 fonde] yonge Q_1: yong Q_3 242 spring] springs Q_1: springes Q_3
248 such certaine heire] suche certentie Q_1: such certeintie Q_3 250
knowen] vnknowen Q_1: vnknowne Q_3 251 Q_2 *period at end of line*
256 is] is it $Q_1 Q_3$ 266 the] their $Q_1 Q_3$ 267 in the people plant]
plant the people in $Q_1 Q_3$

While yet the prince did liue, whose name and power
By lawfull sommons and authoritie
Might make a Parliament to be of force,   270
And might haue set the state in quiet stay.
But now O happie man, whom spedie death
Depriues of life, ne is enforced to see
These hugie mischiefes and these miseries,
These ciuil warres, these murders & these wronges.   275
Of iustice, yet must God in fine restore
This noble crowne vnto the lawfull heire:
For right will always liue, and rise at length,
But wrong can neuer take deepe roote to last.

271 state] Realme Q_3 272 whom] whome Q_1: what Q_3 276
God] *Ioue* $Q_1 Q_3$ 279 $Q_1 Q_3$ *below*:
       ❡ The ende of the Tragedie of Kynge *Gorboduc.*

II

JOCASTA

BY

GEORGE GASCOIGNE AND FRANCIS
KINWELMERSH

The text is that of 1575 (Q_2).

Q_1=A Hundreth sundrie Flowres bounde vp in one small Poesie. Gathered partely (by translation) in the fyne outlandish Gardins of Euripides, Ouid, Petrarke, Ariosto, and others : and partly by inuention out of our owne fruitefull Orchardes in Englande : Yelding sundrie sweete sauours of Tragical, Comical, and Morall Discourses, bothe pleasaunt and profitable to the well smellyng noses of learned Readers. Meritum petere, graue. At London, Imprinted for Richarde Smith. [1573.]

Q_2=THE POSIES of George Gascoigne Esquire. Corrected, perfected, and augmented by the Authour. 1575. Tam Marti quàm Mercurio. Printed at London for Richard Smith, and are to be solde at the Northweast doore of Paules Church.

Q_3=The pleasauntest workes of George Gascoigne Esquyre : Newlye compyled into one Volume, That is to say : His Flowers, Hearbes, Weedes, the Fruites of warre, the Comedie called Supposes, the Tragedie of Iocasta, the Steele glasse, the Complaint of Phylomene, the Storie of Ferdinando Ieronimi, and the pleasure at Kenelworth Castle. London Imprinted by Abell Ieffes, dwelling in the Fore Streete, without Creeplegate, neere vnto Grub-streete. 1587.

MS.=B.M. Additional MSS. 34063, the title-page of which is reproduced in facsimile opposite.

Jocasta

A tragedie written in Greke
by Euripides translated and
diuested into Acte by George Gascoign
and Framunco Kynwelmershe of Grayes
Inne.   1566

The argument of the Tragedye.

To scourge the cryme of wycked Layus
and wrecke the foule incest of Oedipus
The Angry goddes stirde vp the sonnes by stryfe
wth blade embrewed to reaue eche others lyfe
his wife, his mother, and his concubyne
whose fearefull harte foredrad their fatall fyne
her sonnes thus deade desdaynethe longer lyfe
and slue her self wth self same blody knyfe
The daughter she surprisd wth redlesse dreade
that durst not dye a lothsome lyfe doth leade
yet rather wisht to ende her honest fame
teyth cruell brond then have his desteny
throwgh the kynge, yt type of Tyranny
And Oedipus mirror of mysery

I O C A S T A:
A Tragedie vvritten in
Greeke by *Euripides*, translated
and digested into Acte by George Gas-
coygnc, and Francis Kinvvelmershe
of Grayes Inne,
and there by them presented,
1 5 6 6.

The argument of the Tragedie.

To scourge the cryme of vvicked Laius,
And vvrecke the foule Incest of Oedipus,
The angry Gods styrred vp theyr sonnes, by strife
VVith blades embrevved to reaue eache others life :
The vvife, the mother, and the concubyne,   5
(VVhose fearefull hart foredrad theyr fatall fine,)
Hir sonnes thus dead, disdayneth longer lyfe,
And slayes hirself vvith selfsame bloudy knyfe :
The daughter she, surprisde vvith childish dreade
(That durst not dye) a lothsome lyfe doth leade,   10
Yet rather chose to guide hir banisht sire,
Than cruell Creon should haue his desire.
Creon is King, the * type of Tyranny,   * Fygure.
And Oedipus, myrrour of misery.

Fortunatus Infœlix.   15

Title. 8 1566] An. 1566 *Q*₃
    3 theyr] his *MS.*   4 blades] blade *MS.*   5 The . . . the . . . the]
his . . . his . . . his *MS.*   13 is King, the] the king ys *MS.*   * Fygure]
MS. and *Q*₁ omit this and all subsequent side-notes   15 *Fortunatus
Infœlix*] *MS. omits*

The names of the Interloquutors.

Iocasta, the Queene.
Seruus, a noble man of the Queenes traine.
Bailo, gouernour to the Queenes sonnes.
Antygone, daughter to the Queene.
Chorus, foure *Thebane* dames.   5
Pollynices &⁊ ⎫
Eteocles.   ⎬ sonnes to *Oedipus* & the Queene.
               ⎭
Creon, the Queenes brother.
Meneceus, sonne to *Creon*.
Tyresias, the diuine priest.   10
Manto, the daughter of *Tyresias*.
Sacerdos, the sacrifycing priest.
Nuntij, three messangers from the campe.
Oedipus, the olde King, father to *Eteocles* and *Pollynices*, sonne
    and husbande to *Iocasta* the Queene.   15

The Tragedie presented as it were
in *Thebes*.

16–17 The . . . *Thebes*] The tragedie represented in Thebes *MS. and* Q₁

¶ The order of the dumme shewes
and Musickes before euery Acte.

Irste, before the beginning of the first Acte, did sounde
a dolefull & straunge noyse of violles, Cythren, Bandurion, and such like, during the whiche, there came in vppon
the Stage a king with an Imperial crown vppon his head, very
richely apparelled: a Scepter in his righte hande, a Mounde 5
with a Crosse in his lefte hande, sitting in a Chariote very
richely furnished, drawne in by foure Kinges in their Dublettes
and Hosen, with Crownes also vpon their heades. Representing
vnto vs Ambition, by the hystorie of *Sesostres* king of *Egypt*,
who beeing in his time and reigne a mightie Conquerour, yet 10
not content to haue subdued many princes, and taken from
them their kingdomes and dominions, did in like maner cause
those Kinges whome he had so ouercome, to draw in his
Chariote like Beastes and Oxen, thereby to content his
vnbrideled ambitious desire. After he had beene drawne twyce 15
about the Stage, and retyred, the Musicke ceased, and *Iocasta*
the Queene issued out of hir house, beginning the firste Acte,
as followeth. *Iocasta* the Queene issueth out of hir Pallace,
before hir twelue Gentlemen, following after hir eight Gentlewomen, whereof foure be the *Chorus* that remayne on the Stage 20
after hir departure. At hir entrance the Trumpettes
sounded, and after she had gone once about
the Stage, she turneth to one of hir most
trustie and esteemed seruaunts, and
vnto him she discloseth   25
hir griefe, as
foloweth.

The first Acte.   *The first Scene.*

IOCASTA.   SERVVS.

O Faithfull seruaunt of mine auncient sire,
   Though vnto thee, sufficiently be knowne
The whole discourse of my recurelesse griefe
By seing me from Princes royall state
Thus basely brought into so great cōtempt,   5
As mine own sonnes repine to heare my plaint,
Now of a Queene but barely bearing name,
Seyng this towne, seing my fleshe and bloude,
Against it selfe to leuie threatning armes,
(Whereof to talke my heart it rendes in twaine)   10
Yet once againe, I must to thee recompte
The wailefull thing that is already spred,
Bicause I know, that pitie will compell
Thy tender hart, more than my naturall childe,
With ruthfull teares to mone my mourning case.   15
   Ser. My gracious Queene, as no man might surmount
The constant faith I beare my souraine Lorde,
So doe I thinke, for loue and trustie zeale,
No Sonne you haue, doth owe you more than I :
For hereunto I am by dutie bounde,   20
With seruice meete no lesse to honor you,
Than that renoumed Prince your deere father.
And as my duties be most infinite,
So infinite, must also be my loue :
Then if my life or spending of my bloude   25
May be employde to doe your highnesse good,
Commaunde (O Queene) commaund this carcasse here,
In spite of death to satisfie thy will,
So, though I die, yet shall my willing ghost
Contentedly forsake this withered corps,   30

For ioy to thinke I neuer shewde my selfe
Ingrateful once to such a worthy Queene.
    Ioca. Thou knowst what care my carefull father tooke,
In wedlockes sacred state to settle me
With *Laius*, king of this vnhappie *Thebs*,   35
That most vnhappie now our Citie is :
Thou knowst, how he, desirous still to searche
The hidden secrets of supernall powers,
Vnto Diuines did make his ofte recourse,
Of them to learne when he should haue a sonne,   40
That in his Realme might after him succeede :
Of whom receiuing answere sharpe and sowre,
That his owne sonne should worke his wailfull ende,   ▾
The wretched king (though all in vayne) did sake
For to eschew that could not be eschewed :   45
And so, forgetting lawes of natures loue,
No sooner had this paynfull wombe brought foorth
His eldest sonne to this desired light,
But straight he chargde a trustie man of his
To beare the childe into a desert wood,   50
And leaue it there, for Tigers to deuoure.
    Ser. O lucklesse babe, begot in wofull houre.
    Ioc., His seruant thus obedient to his hest,
Vp by the heeles did hang this faultlesse Impe,
And percing with a knife his tender feete,   55
Through both the wounds did drawe the slender twigs,
Which being bound about his feeble limmes,
Were strong inough to holde the little soule.
Thus did he leaue this infant scarcely borne,
That in short time must needes haue lost his life,   60
If destenie (that for our greater greefes
Decreede before to keepe it still aliue)
Had not vnto this childe sent present helpe :
For so it chaunst, a shepheard passing by,
With pitie moude, did stay his giltlesse death :   65
He tooke him home, and gaue him to his wife,

With homelie fare to feede and foster vp :
Now harken how the heauens haue wrought the way
To *Laius* death, and to mine owne decay.
   „   *Ser.* Experience proues, and daily is it seene,   70
   „In vaine (too vaine) man striues against the heauens.
     Ioca. Not farre fro thence, the mightie *Polibus*,
Of *Corinth* King, did keepe his princely court,
Vnto whose wofull wife (lamenting muche
Shee had no ofspring by hir noble pheere)   75
The curteous shepherd gaue my little sonne :
Which gratefull gift, the Queene did so accept,
As nothing seemde more precious in hir sight :
Partly, for that, his faitures were so fine,
Partly, for that, he was so beautifull,   80
And partly, for bicause his comely grace
Gaue great suspicion of his royall bloude.
The infant grewe, and many yeares was demde
Polibus sonne, till time, that *Oedipus*
(For so he named was) did vnderstande   85
That *Polibus* was not his sire in deede,
Whereby forsaking frendes and countrie there,
He did returne to seeke his natiue stocke :
And being come into *Phocides* lande,
Toke notice of the cursed oracle,   90
How first he shoulde his father doe to death,
And then become his mothers wedded mate.
     Ser. O fierce aspect of cruell planets all,
That can decree such seas of heynous faultes.
     Ioca. Then *Oedipus*, fraight full of chilling feare,   95
By all meanes sought t'auoyde this furious fate,
But whiles he weende to shunne the shameful deede,
Vnluckly guided by his owne mishappe,
He fell into the snare that most he feared :
For loe, in *Phocides* did *Laius* lye,   100
To ende the broyles that ciuill discorde then

Had raysed vp in that vnquiet lande,
By meanes whereof my wofull *Oedipus*,
Affording ayde vnto the other side,
With murdring blade vnwares his father slewe.   105
Thus heauenly doome, thus fate, thus powers diuine,
Thus wicked reade of Prophets tooke effect:
Now onely restes to ende the bitter happe
Of me, of me his miserable mother.
Alas, how colde I feele the quaking bloud   110
Passe too and fro within my trembling brest?
Oedipus, when this bloudy deede was doone,
Forst foorth by fatall doome, to *Thebes* came,
Where as full soone with glory he atchieude
The crowne and scepter of this noble lande,   115
By conquering *Sphinx* that cruell monster loe,
That earst destroyde this goodly flouring soyle :
And thus did I (O hatefull thing to heare)
To my owne sonne become a wretched wife.

    Ser. No meruayle, though the golden Sunne withdrew   120
His glittering beames from suche a sinfull facte.

    Ioca. And so by him that from this belly sprang,
I brought to light (O cursed that I am)
Aswell two sonnes, as daughters also twaine :
But when this monstrous mariage was disclosde,   125
So sore began the rage of boyling wrath
To swell within the furious brest of him,
As he him selfe by stresse of his owne nayles,
Out of his head did teare his griefull cyne,
Vnworthy more to see the shining light.   130

    Ser. How could it be, that knowing he had done
So foule a blot, he would remayne aliue?

,, *Ioca.* So deepely faulteth none, the which vnwares
,,Doth fall into the crime he can not shunne :
And he (alas) vnto his greater greefe,   135
Prolongs the date of his accursed dayes,

117 flouring] flourishing Q_3 118 I] Q_3 *omits*   128 As] That *MS.*

Knowing that life doth more and more increase
The cruell plages of his detested gilte,
„Where stroke of griesly death dothe set an ende
„Vnto the pangs of mans increasing payne.   140

   Ser. Of others all, moste cause haue we to mone
Thy wofull smarte (O miserable Queene)
Such and so many are thy greeuous harmes.

   Ioca. Now to the ende this blinde outrageous sire,
Should reape no ioye of his vnnaturall fruite,   145
His wretched sons, prickt foorth by furious spight,
Adiudge their father to perpetuall prison :
There buried in the depthe of dungeon darke,
(Alas) he leades his discontented life,
Accursing still his stony harted sonnes,   150
And wishing all th'infernall sprites of hell,
To breathe suche poysned hate into their brestes,
As eche with other fall to bloudy warres,
And so with pricking poynt of piercing blade,
To rippe their bowels out, that eche of them   155
With others bloud might strayne his giltie hands,
And bothe at once by stroke of speedie death
Be foorthwith throwne into the *Stigian* lake.

   Ser. The mightie Gods preuent so fowle a deede,
   Ioca. They to auoyde the wicked blasphemies,   160
And sinfull prayer of their angrie sire,
Agreed thus, that of this noble realme,
Vntill the course of one ful yere was runne,
Eteocles should sway the kingly mace,
And *Polynice* as exul should departe,   165
Till time expyrde : and then to *Polynice*
Eteocles should yeelde the scepter vp :
Thus yere by yere the one succeeding other,
This royall crowne should vnto bothe remayne.

   Ser. Oh thunbridled mindes of ambicious men.   170

---

144 outrageous] outraging *MS.*   156 strayne] stain *MS.*: stayne *Q*₁

Ioca. Eteocles thus plast in princely seate,
Drunke with the sugred taste of kingly raigne,
Not onely shut his brother from the crowne,
But also from his natiue country soyle.
Alas poore *Polynice*, what might he doe,   175
Vniustly by his brother thus betrayed?
To *Argos* he, with sad and heauie cheere
Forthwith conuayde him selfe, on whom at length
With fauning face good fortune smyled so,
As with *Adrastus* king of *Argiues* there,   180
He founde such fauour and affinitie,
As (to restore my sonne vnto his raigne,)
He hath besiedge this noble citie *Thebes*,
And hence proceedes my most extreme annoye:
For, of my sonnes, who euer doe preuaile,   185
The victorie will turne vnto my griefe:
Alas, I feare (such is the chaunce of warre)
That one, or both shall purchase death therby.
Wherfore, to shunne the worst that may befall,
Thoughe comfortlesse, yet as a pitifull mother   190
Whom nature binds to loue hir louing sonnes,
And to prouide the best for their auaile,
I haue thought good by prayers to entreate
The two brethren (nay rather cruel foes)
A while to staie their fierce and furious fight,   195
Till I haue tried by meanes for to apease
The swelling wrath of their outraging willes,
And so with much to doe, at my request
They haue forborne vnto this onely houre.

    Ser. Small space God wot, to stint so great a strife.   200
    Ioca. And euen right now, a trustie man of mine,
Returned from the campe, enforming me
That *Polynice* will straight to *Thebes* come,
Thus of my woe, this is the wailefull sûme.

171 *Eteocles*] *Etocles MS. and Q*₂   183 besiedge] beseedgde *MS.*:
besedge *Q*₁: besiegde *Q*₃   200 God wot] god wot *MS. Q*₁ *Q*₃: good wot *Q*₂

And for bycause, in vaine and bootelesse plainte   205
I haue small neede to spend this litle time,
Here will I cease, in wordes more to bewray
The restlesse state of my afflicted minde,
Desiring thee, thou goe to *Eteocles*,
Hartly on my behalfe beseching him,   210
That out of hand according to his promise,
He will vouchsafe to come vnto my courte,
I know he loues thee well, and to thy wordes
I thinke thou knowst he will giue willing eare.

    Ser. (O noble Queene) sith vnto such affayres   215
My spedie diligence is requisite,
I will applie effectually to doe
What so your highnesse hath commaunded me.

    Ioca. I will goe in, and pray the Gods therwhile,
With tender pitie to appease my griefe.   220

        Iocasta goeth off the stage into hir pallace, hir foure
        handmaides follow hir, the foure Chorus also follow
        hir to the gates of hir pallace, after comming on the
        stage, take their place, where they cōtinue to the end
        of the Tragedie.

SERVVS SOLVS.

„THe simple man, whose meruaile is so great
„ At stately courts, and princes regall seate,
„With gasing eye but onely doth regarde
„The golden glosse that outwardly appeares,

The courte „The crownes bedeckt with pearle and precious stones,   225
liuely
painted. „The riche attire imbost with beaten golde,
„The glittering mace, the pompe of swarming traine,
„The mightie halles heapt full of flattering frendes,
„The chambers huge, the goodly gorgeous beddes,
„The gilted roofes embowde with curious worke,   230
„The faces sweete of fine disdayning dames,

    229 chambers huge] huge chambers *MS. Q*₁   231 faces sweete]
sweete faces *MS. Q*₁

„The vaine suppose of wanton raigne at luste :
„But neuer viewes with eye of inward thought,
„The painefull toile, the great and greuous cares,
„The troubles still, the newe increasing feares,   235
„That princes nourish in their iealous brestes :
„He wayeth not the charge that *Ioue* hath laid
„On princes, how for themselues they raigne not :
„He weenes, the law must stoope to princely will,
„But princes frame their noble wills to lawe :   240
„He knoweth not, that as the boystrous winde
„Doth shake the toppes of highest reared towres,
„So doth the force of frowarde fortune strike
„The wight that highest sits in haughtie state.
Lo *Oedipus*, that sometime raigned king   245
Of *Thebane* soyle, that wonted to suppresse
The mightest Prince, and kepe him vnder checke,
That fearefull was vnto his forraine foes,
Now like a poore afflicted prisoner,
In dungeon darke, shut vp from cheerefull light,   250
In euery part so plagued with annoy,
As he abhorrs to leade a longer life,
By meanes wherof, the one against the other
His wrathfull sonnes haue planted all their force,
And *Thebes* here, this auncient worthy towne,   255
With threatning siege girt in on euerie side,
In daunger lyes to be subuerted quite,
If helpe of heuenly *Ioue* vpholde it not,
But as darke night succedes the shining day,
So lowring griefe comes after pleasant ioy.   260
Well now the charge hir highnesse did commaund
I must fulfill, though haply all in vaine.

> *Seruus goeth off the stage by the gates called* Electræ.
> *Antygone attended with .iij. gentlewomen and hir*
> *gouernour commeth out of the Queene hir mothers*
> *Pallace.*

235 The *omitted in* Q_3

⟨*Scena* 2⟩

BAILO.   ANTIGONE.

O Gentle daughter of King *Oedipus*,
  O sister deare to that vnhappie wight
Whom brothers rage hath reaued of his right,
To whom, thou knowst, in yong and tender yeares
I was a friend and faithfull gouenour,   5
Come forth, sith that hir grace hath graunted leaue,
And let me knowe what cause hath moued nowe
So chaste a maide to set hir daintie foote
Ouer the thresholde of hir secrete lodge?
Since that the towne is furnishte euery where   10
With men of armes and warlike instrumentes,
Vnto our eares there cōmes no other noyse,
But sounde of trumpe, and neigh of trampling stedes,
Which running vp and downe from place to place,
With hideous cries betoken bloude and death: 15
The blasing sunne ne shineth halfe so brighte,
As it was wont to doe at dawne of day:
The wretched dames throughout the wofull towne,
Together clustring to the temples goe,
Beseeching *Ioue* by way of humble plainte,   20
With tender ruthe to pitie their distresse.
    An. The loue I beare, to my sweete *Polynice*,
My deare brother, is onelý cause hereof.
    Bai. Why daughter, knowst thou any remedie
How to defend thy fathers citie here   25
From that outrage and fierce repyning wrathe,
Which he against it, iustly hath co⟨n⟩ceiued?
    An. Oh gouernour might this my faultlesse bloude
Suffise to stay my brethrens dyre debate,
With glad content I coulde afford my life
Betwixte them both to plant a perfect peace.

30 content] consent *MS. Q*₁

But since (alas) I cannot as I woulde,
A hote desire enflames my feruent mind
To haue a sight of my sweete *Polynice*.
Wherfore (good guide) vouchsafe to guide me vp   35
Into some tower about this hugie court,
From whence I may behold our enmies campe,
Therby at least to feede my hungry eyes
But with the sight of my beloued brother :
Then if I die, contented shall I die.   40

    Bai. O princely dame, the tender care thou takste
Of thy deare brother, deserueth double praise :
Yet crau'st thou that, which cannot be obtainde,
By reason of the distance from the towne
Vnto the plaine, where tharmie lies incampte :   45
And furthermore, besemeth not a maide
To shew hir selfe in such vnseemly place.
Whereas among such yong and lustie troupes
Of harebrainde souldiers marching to and fro,
Both honest name and honour is empairde :   50
But yet reioyce, sith this thy great desire,
Without long let, or yet without thy paine,
At wishe and will shortly may be fulfillde.
For *Polynice* forthwith will hither come,
Euen I my selfe was lately at the campe,   55
Commaunded by the Queene to bid him come,
Who laboureth still to linke in frendly league,
Hir iarring sonnes (which happe so hoped for,
Eftsones I pray the gracious gods to graunt)
And sure I am, that ere this hour passe,   60
Thou shalt him here in person safely see.

    Anti. O louing frend, doest thou then warrant me,
That *Polynice* will come vnto this court ?

    Bai. Ere thou be ware thou shalt him here beholde.

    Anti. And who (alas) doth warrant his aduenture,   65
That of *Eteocles* he take no harme?

49 harebrainde] herbrayn *MS*.

Bai. For constant pledge, he hath his brothers faith,
He hath also the truce that yet endures.

An. I feare alas, alas I greatly feare,
Some trustlesse snare his cruell brother layes　　　　70
To trappe him in.

Bai. Daughter, god knowes how willing I would be
With sweete reliefe to comforte thy distresse,
But I cannot impart to thee, the good
Which I my selfe doe not as yet enioye.　　　　75
The wailefull cause that moues *Eteocles*
With *Polynice* to enter ciuil warres
Is ouergreat, and for this onely cause
Full many men haue broke the lawes of truth,
And topsieturuie turned many townes,　　　　80
„To gredie (daughter) too too gredie is
„Desire to rule and raigne in kingly state.
Ne can he bide, that swaise a realme alone
To haue another ioynde with him therin :
Yet must we hope for helpe of heauenly powers,　　　　85
Sith they be iuste, their mercy is at hand,
To helpe the weake when worldly force doth faile.

An. As both my brethren be, so both I beare
As much good will as any sister may,
But yet the wrong that vnto *Polynice*　　　　90
This trothlesse tyrant hath vniustlie shewd,
Doth leade me more, to wishe the prosperous life
Of *Polynice*, than of that cruell wretch,
Besides that, *Polynice* whiles he remainde
In *Thebes* here, did euer loue me more,　　　　95
Than did *Eteocles*, whose swelling hate
Is towards me increased more and more :
Wherof I partely may assure my selfe,
Considering he disdaynes to visite me,
Yea, happly he intends to reaue my life,　　　　100

71 To . . . in] *MS. adds* (—) *at the end of this line*　　85 powers]
MS. puts (.) *instead of* (,) *at end of line*

And hauing power he will not sticke to doe it.
This therefore makes me earnestly desire
Oft tymes to see him : yet euer as I thinke
For to discharge the duetie of a sister,
The feare I haue of hurt, doth chaunge as fast   105
My doubtfull loue into disdainefull spight.
    Bai. Yet daughter, must ye trust in mightie *Ioue*,
His will is not, that for thoffence of one
So many suffer vndeserued smarte :
I meane of thee, I meane of *Polynice*,   110
Of *Iocasta* thy wofull aged mother,
And of *Ismena* thy beloued sister.
Who though for this she doth not outwardly
From drearie eyen distill lamenting teares,
Yet do I thinke, no lesse afflicting griefe   115
Doth inwardly torment hir tender brest.
    An. Besides all this, a certaine ielousie,
Lately conceyude (I know not whence it springs)
Of *Creon*, my mothers brother, appaules me much,
Him doubt I more than any danger else.   120
    Bai. Deare daughter, leaue this foolishe ielousie,
And seeing that thou shalt heere shortly finde
Thy brother *Polynice*, go in agayne.
    An. O ioyfull would it be to me therwhile,
To vnderstande the order of the hoste,   125
Whether it be such as haue sufficient powcr
To ouerthrowe this mightie towne of *Thebes*.
What place supplies my brother *Polynice* ?
Where founde ye him ? what answere did he giue ?
And though so great a care perteineth not   130
Vnto a mayde of my vnskill⟨full⟩ yeres,
Yet, forbicause my selfe partaker am
Of good and euill with this my countrey soyle,
I long to heare thee tell those fearefull newes,

---

126 Whether] *Marked 'read* if' *in* '*Faultes escaped correction*' *Q₁, but*
Q₂Q₃ leave it unchanged   131 vnskillfull *MS. Q₁* : vnskill *Q₂Q₃*

Which otherwise I cannot vnderstand.   135
   Bai. So noble a desire (O worthy dame)
I much commende : and briefly as I can,
Will satisfie thy hungry minde herein.
The power of men that *Polynice* hath brought,
(Wherof he, (being *Adrastus* sonne in lawe)   140
Takes chiefest charge) is euen the floure of *Grece*,
Whose hugie traine so mightie seemes to be,
As I see not, how this our drouping towne
Is able to withstand so strong a siege.
Entring the fielde their armie did I finde   145
So orderly in forme of battaile set,
As though they would forthwith haue giuen the charge :
In battailes seauen the host deuided is,
To eche of which, by order of the king,
A valiant knight for captaine is assignde :   150
And as you know this citie hath seuen gates,
So euerie captaine hath his gate prescribde,
With fierce assault to make his entrie at.
And further, passing through our frouning foes
(That gaue me countnaunce of a messanger)   155
Harde by the King I spied *Polynice,*
In golden glistring armes most richely cladde,
Whose person many a stately prince enpalde,
And many a comely crowned head enclosde :
At sight of me his colour straight he chaungde,   160
And like a louing childe, in clasped armes
He caught me vp, and frendly kist my cheke,
Then hearing what his mother did demaunde
With glad consent according to hir hest
Gaue me his hand, to come vnto the court,   165
Of mutuall truce desirous so he seemde,
He askt me of *Antygone* and *Ismena,*
But chiefelie vnto thee aboue the rest
He gaue me charge most heartly to commend him.
   An. The gods giue grace he may at length possesse   170

His kingly right, and I his wished sight.

 Bai. Daughter no more, t'is time ye nowe returne :
It standes not with the honor of your state
Thus to be seene suspiciously abrode :
„For vulgar tongues are armed euermore   175
„With slaunderous brute to bleamishe the renoume
„Of vertues dames, which though at first it spring
„Of slender cause, yet doth it swell so fast,
„As in short space it filleth euerie eare   A glasse
„With swifte reporte of vndeserued blame :   180 for yong
                      women.
„You cannot be to curious of your name :
„Fond shewe of euill (though still the minde be chast)
„Decayes the credite oft, that Ladies had,
„Sometimes the place presumes a wanton mynde :
„Repayre sometymes of some, doth hurt their honor : 185
„Sometimes the light and garishe proude attire
„Persuades a yelding bent of pleasing youthes.
The voyce that goeth of your vnspotted fame,
Is like a tender floure, that with the blast
Of euerie little winde doth fade away.   190
Goe in deere childe, this way will I goe see
If I can meete thy brother *Polynice.*

   Antigone with hir maides returneth into hir mothers
    pallace, hir gouernour goeth out by the gates Homo-
    loydes.

C H O R V S.

IF greedie lust of mans ambitious eye
 (That thristeth so for swaye of earthly things)
Would eke foresee, what mischefes growe therby,
What carefull toyle to quiet state it brings,
What endlesse griefe from such a fountaine springs : 5
Then should he swimme in seas of sweete delight,

173 standes] standith *MS.* 177 vertues] vertuous *MS.* 180 reporte]
reporte *Q₂*

That nowe complaines of fortunes cruell spight.

    For then he would so safely shielde himselfe
With sacred rules of wisdomes sage aduise,
As no alluring trayne of trustles pelfe,   10
To fonde affectes his fancie should entise,
Then warie heede would quickly make him wise:
Where contrary (such is our skillesse kind)
We most doe seeke, that most may hurt the minde.

    Amid the troupe of these vnstable toyes,   15
Some fancies loe to beautie must be bent,
Some hunt for wealth, and some set all their ioyes,
In regall power of princely gouernement,
Yet none of these from care are cleane exempt:
For either they be got with grieuous toyle,   20
Or in the end forgone with shamefull foyle.

    This flitting world doth firmely nought retaine,
Wherin a man may boldly rest his trust,
Such fickle chaunce in fortune doth remaine,
As when she lust, she threatneth whom she lust,   25
From high renoume to throwe him in the dust:
Thus may we see that eche triumphing ioye
By fortunes froune is turned to annoye.

    Those elder heades may well be thought to erre,
The which for easie life and quiet dayes,   30
The vulgar sorte would seeme for to preferre,
If glorious *Phœbe* with-holde his glistring rayes,
From such a peere as crowne and scepter swayes,
No meruaile though he hide his heauenly face,
From vs that come of lesse renoumed race.   35

Argu-
mentũ à   Selde shall you see the ruine of a Prince,
maiore.   But that the people eke like brunt doe beare,
And olde recordes of auncient time long since,
From age to age, yea almost euerie where,
With proofe herof hath glutted euery eare   40

    13 Where] When *MS.*   16 must] most *MS. Q₁*   24 fickle]
ficklie *MS.*

Thus by the follies of the princes hart,
The bounden subiect still receiueth smart.

    Loe, how vnbrideled lust of priuat raigne,
Hath pricked both the brethren vnto warre:
Yet *Polynice*, with signe of lesse disdaine,   45
Against this lande hath brought from countries farre,
A forraine power, to end this cruell iarre,
Forgetting quite the dutie, loue, and zeale,
He ought to beare vnto this common weale.

    But whosoeuer gets the victorie,   50
We wretched dames, and thou O noble towne,
Shall feele therof the wofull miserie,
Thy gorgeous pompe, thy glorious high renoume,
Thy stately towers, and all shal fall a downe,
Sith raging *Mars* will eache of them assist   55
In others brest to bathe his bloudie fist.

    But thou (∗) O sonne of *Semel*, and of *Ioue*,   Bacchus
(That tamde the proude attempt of glaunts strong)
Doe thou defende, euen of thy tender loue,
Thy humble thralls from this afflicting wrong,   60 Bacchus
Whom wast of warre hath now tormented long: was the
So shall we neuer faile ne day ne night   God whom
With reuerence due thy prayses to resight.   they most
                                                   honored in
                                                   Thebes.

                Finis Actus primi.

             Done by F. Kinwelmarshe.

The order of the second dumbe
shevve.

BEfore the beginning of this seconde Acte dyd soũd a very dolefull noise of flutes : during the which there came in vpon the stage two coffines couered with hearclothes, & brought in by .viij. in mourning weed : & accõpanied with .viij. other mourners : & after they had caried the coffins about the stage, 5 there opened & appeared a Graue, wherin they buried yͤ coffins & put fire to them : but the flames did seuer & parte in twaine, signifying discord by the history of two brethrē, whose discord in their life was not onely to be wondred at, but being buried both in one Tombe (as some writers affirme) the flames 10 of their funeralls did yet parte the one frõ the other in like maner, and would in no wise ioyne into one flame.   After the Funerals were ended & the fire cõsumed, the graue was closed vp again, the mourners withdrew thē off the stage, & immediately by yͤ gates *Homoloydes* entred *Pollinyces* accompanied with vj. 15 gentlemen and a page that carried his helmet and Target : he & his men vnarmed sauing their gorgets, for that they were permitted to come into the towne in time of truce, to the end *Iocasta* might bring the two brethrē to a parle : and *Pollinyces* after good regard takē round about him, speake as foloweth.   20

Actus .2.   Scena .1.

POLINICES.   CHORVS.   IOCASTA.
ETEOCLES.

LOe here mine owne citie and natiue soyle,
   Loe here the nest I ought to nestle in,
Yet being thus entrencht with mine owne towres,
And that, from him the safe conduct is giuen

4 weed] weeds *Q₃*   8 two] the two *MS.*

Which doth enioye as much as mine should be,   5
My feete can treade no step without suspect :
For where my brother bides, euen there behoues
More warie scout than in an enmies campe.
Yet while I may within this right hand holde
This (*) bronde, this blade, (vnyeldē euer yet)   10 〈Sworde.〉
My life shall not be lefte without reuenge.
But here beholde the holy sancturie,
Of *Baccus* eke the worthie Image, loe
The aultars where the sacred flames haue shone,
And where of yore these giltlesse hands of mine   15
Full oft haue offered to our mightie gods :
I see also a worthie companie
Of *Thebane* dames, resembling vnto me
The traine of *Iocasta* my deare mother :
Beholde them clad in clothes of griesly blacke,   20
That hellishe hewe that (*) nay for other harmes   〈Neuer.〉
So well besemed wretched wightes to weare :
For why, ere long their selues, themselues shall see
(Gramercy to their princes tyrannie)
Some spoyled of their sweete and sucking babes,   25
Some lese their husband, other some their sire,
And some their friends that were to them full dere.
But now tis time to lay the sworde aside,
And eke of them to knowe where is the Queene :
O woorthie dames, heauie, vnhappie ye,   30
Where resteth now the restlesse queene of *Thebes* ?

    Chor. O woorthie impe sprong out of worthie race,
Renoumed Prince, whom wee haue lookt for long,
And nowe in happie houre arte come to vs,
Some quiet bring to this vnquiet realme.   35
O queene, O queene, come foorth and see thy sonne,
The gentle frute of all thy ioyfull seede.

    9 within] wthin Q_2 10, 21 (*margin*) Sworde. Neuer.] Q_2 *reverses the order of the two side-notes ; the mistake is corrected in* Q_3 28 the] this *MS.* Q_1 30 ye] you *MS.*

Iocast. My faithfull frends, my deare beloued maydes,
I come at call, and at your wordes I moue
My feebled feete with age and agonie :⁣   40
Where is my sonne ?   O tell me where is he,
For whome I sighed haue so often syth,
For whom I spende both nightes and dayes in teares?

Poli. Here noble mother, here, not as the king,
Nor as a Citizen of stately *Thebes*,   45
But as a straunger nowe, I thanke my brother.

Iocast. O sonne, O sweete and my desyred sonne,
These eyes thee see, these handes of myne thee touche,
Yet scarsly can this mynde beleeue the same,
And scarsly can this brused breast susteyne   50
The sodeyne ioye that is inclosde therein :⁣
O gladsome glasse, wherein I see my selfe.

Chor. So graunt the Gods, ⟨that⟩ for our common good,
You frendly may your sonnes both frendes beholde.

Iocast. At thy departe, O louely chylde, thou lefte   55
My house in teares, and mee thy wretched dame,

Lament-
ing. Myrrour of martirdome, (∗) waymenting still
Th'vnworthie exile thy brother to thee gaue :⁣
Ne was there euer sonne or friende farre off,
Of his deare frendes or mother so desyred,   60
As thy returne, in all the towne of *Thebes.*
And of my selfe more than the rest to speake,
I haue as thou mayste ˋsee, cleane cast asyde
My princely roabes, and thus in wofull weede,
Bewrapped haue these lustlesse limmes of myne :⁣   65
Naught else but teares haue trickled from myne eyes,
And eke thy wretched blynde and aged syre,
Since first he hearde what warre tweene you there was,
As one that did his bitter cursse repent,
Or that he prayed to Ioue for your decaye,   70

---

48 thee see] they see *Qq* :⁣ *MS. puts* they *in both cases, but the* y *was afterwards marked out*   53 that *MS. Q₁* :⁣ *Q₂ Q₃ omit*   57 waymenting] lamentyng *MS.*   58 to] *MS. omits*

With stretching string, or else with bloudie knyfe
Hath sought full ofte to ende his loathed lyfe.
Thou this meane whyle my sonne, hast lingred long
In farre and forreyn coastes, and wedded eke,
By whome thou mayste, (when heauens appoyntes it so)   75
Straunge issue haue by one a stranger borne,
Which greeues me sore, and much the more deare chylde,
Bicause I was not present at the same,
There to performe thy louing mothers due.
But for I fynde thy noble matche so meete,   80
And woorthie bothe for thy degree and byrthe,
I seeke to comforte thee by myne aduise,
That thou returne this citie to inhabite,
Whiche best of all may seeme to be the bowre,
Bothe for thy selfe and for thy noble spouse.   85
Forget thou then thy brothers iniuries,
And knowe deare chylde, the harme of all missehap
That happes twixt you, must happe likewise to mee :
Ne can the cruell sworde so slightly touche
Your tender fleshe, but that the selfe same wounde   90
Shall deepely bruse this aged brest of myne.
   Cho. There is no loue may be comparde to that,
  The tender mother beares vnto hir chyld :
  For euen somuche the more it dothe encrease,
  As their griefe growes, or contentations cease.   95
   Poli. I knowe not mother, if I prayse deserue,
(That you to please, whome I ought not displease)
Haue traynde my selfe among my trustlesse foes :
But Nature drawes (whether he will or nill)
Eche man to loue his natiue countrey soyle :   100
And who shoulde say, that otherwise it were,
His toung should neuer with his hearte agree.
This hath me drawne besyde my bounden due,
To set full light this lucklesse lyfe of myne :
For of my brother, what may I else hope,   105

         75 appoyntes] appoint *MS.*

But traynes of treason, force and falshoode bothe?
Yet neyther perill present, nor to come,
Can holde me from my due obedience:
I graunte I can not grieflesse, wel beholde
My fathers pallace, the holie aultars,   110
Ne louely lodge wherein I fostred was:
From whence driuen out, and chaste vnworthily,
I haue to long aboade in forreyn coastes:
And as the growing greene and pleasant plante,
Dothe beare freshe braunches one aboue another   115
Euen so amidde the huge heape of my woes,
Doth growe one grudge more greeuous than the rest,
To see my deare and dolefull mother, cladde
In mourning tyre, to tyre hir mourning minde,
Wretched alonely for my wretchednesse,   120
So lykes that enimie my brother best:
Soone shall you see that in this wandring worlde,
No enmitie is equal vnto that
That darke disdayne (the cause of euery euill)
Dooth breede full ofte in consanguinitie.   125
But Ioue, he knowes what dole I doe endure,
For you and for my fathers wretched woe,
And eke how deepely I desire to knowe
What wearie lyfe my louing sisters leade,
And what anoye myne absence them hath giuen.   130
    Iocast. Alas, alas, howe wrekefull wrath of Gods
Doth still afflicte *Oedipus* progenie:
The fyrste cause was thy fathers wicked bedde,
And then (oh why doe I my plagues recompte?)
My burden borne, and your vnhappie birth: 135
„But needes we must with pacient heartes abyde,
„What so from high the heauens doe prouide.
With thee my chylde, fayne would I question yet
Of certaine things: ne woulde I that my wordes
Might thee anoye, ne yet renewe thy griefe.   140
    Poli. Saye on, deare mother, say what so you please:

What pleaseth you, shall neuer mee disease.

    Iocast. And seemes it not a heauie happe my sonne,
To be depriued of thy countrey coastes?

    Poly. So heauie happe as toung can not expresse.   145

    Iocast. And what may moste molest the mynde of man
That is exiled from his natiue soyle?

    Poli. The libertie hee with his countrey loste,
„And that he lacketh freedome for to speake,
„What seemeth best, without controll or checke.   150

Exile an exceding griefe to an honest mynde.

    Iocast. Why so? eche seruant lacketh libertie
To speake his minde, without his maisters leaue.

    „ *Poli.* In exile, euery man, or bonde or free,
„Of noble race, or meaner parentage,
„Is not in this vnlike vnto the slaue,   155
„That muste of force obey to eche mans will,
„And prayse the peeuishnesse of eche mans pryde.

All exyles are like bondmen.

    Iocast. And seemed this so grieuous vnto thee?

    Poli. What griefe can greater be, than so constraynde
Slauelike to serue gaynst right and reason bothe,   160
Yea muche the more, to him that noble is,
By stately lyne, or yet by vertuous lyfe,
And hath a heart lyke to his noble mynde.

    Iocast. What helpeth moste in suche aduersitie?

    Poli. Hope helpeth moste to comfort miserie.   165

Hope the help in miserye.

    Ioca. Hope to returne from whence he fyrst was driuen?

    Poli. Yea, hope that happeneth oftentymes to late,
And many die before such hap may fall.

    Iocast. And howe didst thou before thy mariage sonne,
Mainteyne thy lyfe, a straunger so bestad?   170

    Poli. Sometyme I founde (though seldome so it were)
Some gentle heart, that coulde for curtesye,
Contente himselfe to succour myne estate.

    Iocast. Thy fathers friends and thyne, did they not helpe
For to releeue that naked neede of thyne?   175

    „ *Poli.* Mother, he hath a foolishe fantasie,

147 That MS. Q₁ Q₃ : This Q₂

Fuw frends „ That thinkes to fynd a frende in miserie.
in miserye.   *Iocast.* Thou mightest haue helpe by thy nobilitie.
        „ *Poli.* Couered alas, in cloake of pouertie?
        „ *Iocast.* Wel ought we then that are but mortall heere,   180
        „ Aboue all treasure counte our countrey deare :
        Yea let me knowe my sonne, what cause thee moued
        To goe to *Grece*?
            Poli. The flying fame that thundred in myne eares
        How King *Adrastus*, gouernour of *Greece*,   185
        Was answered by Oracle, that he
        Shoulde knitte in linkes of lawfull mariage,
        His two faire daughters, and his onely heires,
        One to a Lyon, th'other to a Boare :
        An answere suche as eche man wondred at.   190
            Iocast. And how belongs this answere now to thee?
            Poli. I toke my gesse euen by this ensigne heere,
        A Lyon loe, which I did alwayes beare :
        Yet thinke I not, but Ioue alonely brought
        These handes of myne to suche an high exploite.   195
            Iocast. And howe yet came it to this straunge effect?
            Poli. The shining day had runne his hasted course,
        And deawie night bespread hir mantell darke,
        When I that wandred after wearie toyle,
        To seke some harbrough for myne irked limmes,   200
        Gan fynde at last a little cabbin, close
        Adioyned faste vnto the stately walles,
        Where king *Adrastus* held his royall towres.
        Scarce was I there in quiet well ycoucht,
Smal   But thither came another exile eke,   205
causes may Named *Tydeus*, who straue perforce to driue
moue the
needy to Mee from this sorie seate, and so at laste,
contend. We settled vs to fell and bloudie fight,
        Whereof the rumour grewe so great foorthwith,
        That straight the king enformed was therof,   210
        Who seeing then the ensignes that wee bare,

181 our] your Q_3 204 ycoucht *MS.* Q_1 : ycought $Q_2 Q_3$

To be euen such as were to him foresayde,
Chose eche of vs to be his sonne by lawe,
And sithens did solemnize eke the same.

Iocast. Yet woulde I know, if that thy wyfe be suche   215
As thou canst ioy in hir? or what she is?

Poli. O mother deare, fayrer ne wyser dame
Is none in *Greece*, *Argia* is hir name.

Iocast. Howe couldst thou to this doubtfull enterprise,
So many bring, thus armed all at once?   220

Poli. Adrastus sware, that he woulde soone restore
Vnto our right both *Tydeus*, and me :
And fyrst for mee, that had the greater neede,
Whereby the best and boldest blouds in *Greece*
IIaue followed me vnto this enterpryse.   225
A thing both iust and grieuous vnto me,
Greeuous I saye, for that I doe lament
To be constrayned by such open wrong,
To warre agaynst myne owne deare countrey fecres.
But vnto you (O mother) dothe pertain   230
To stinte this stryfe, and both deliuer mee
From exile now, and eke the towne from siege :
For otherwise, I sweare you here by heauens,
Eteocles, who now doth me disdayne
For brother, shortly shall see me his lorde.   235
I aske the seate, wherof I ought of right
Possesse the halfe, I am *Oedipus* sonne,
And yours, so am I true sonne to you both.
Wherfore I hope that as in my defence,
The worlde will weygh, so Ioue wil me assiste.   240

> *Eteocles commeth in here by the gates Electræ, himself
> armed, and before him .xx. gentlemen in armour, his
> two pages, wherof the one beareth his Target, the other
> his helme.*

Chor. Beholde O queene, beholde O woorthie queene,
Vnwoorthie he, *Eteocles* here cõmes,

So, woulde the Gods, that in this noble realme
Shoulde neuer long vnnoble tyrant reigne,
Or that with wrong the right and doutlesse heire,   245
Shoulde banisht be out of his princely seate.
Yet thou O queene, so fyle thy sugred toung,
And with such counsell decke thy mothers tale,
That peace may both the brothers hartes inflame,
And rancour yelde, that erst possesse the same.   250

    Eteocl. Mother, beholde, your hestes for to obey,
In person nowe am I resorted hither :
In haste therefore, fayne woulde I knowe what cause
With hastie speede, so moued hath your minde
To call me nowe so causelesse out of time,   255
When common wealth moste craues my onely avde :
Fayne woulde I knowe what quent commoditie
Perswades you thus to take a truce for tyme,
And yeld the gates wide open to my foe,
The gates that myght our stately state defende,   260
And now are made the path of our decay.

  ,, *Ioca.* Represse deare son, those raging stormes of wrath,
,,That so bedimme the eyes of thine intent,
,,As when the tongue (a redy Instrument)
,,Would fayne pronounce the meaning of the minde,   265
,,It cannot speake one honest seemely worde.
,,But when disdayne is shrunke, or sette asyde,
,,And mynde of man with leysure can discourse
,,What seemely wordes his tale may best beseeme,
,,And that the toung vnfoldes without affectes   270
,,Then may proceede an answere sage and graue,
,,And euery sentence sawst with sobernesse :
Wherefore vnbende thine angrie browes deare childe,

And caste thy rolling eyes none other waye,
That here doest not *Medusaes* (*a*) face beholde,   275 One of the furies.
But him, euen him, thy bloud and brother deare.
And thou behold, my *Polinices* eke,
Thy brothers face, wherein when thou mayst see
Thine owne image, remember therewithall,
That what offence thou wouldst to him were done   280
The blowes thereof rebounde vnto thy selfe.
And hereof eke, I would you both forewarne,
When frendes or brethren, kinsfolke or allies,
(Whose hastie hearts some angrie moode had moued)
Be face to face by some of pitie brought,   285
Who seekes to ende their discorde and debate :
They onely ought consider well the cause   Rehersall
For which they come, and cast out of their minde   of olde grudges
For euermore the olde offences past :   doth hinder
So shall sweete peace driue pleading out of place.   290 al recon-
Wherfore the first shall *Polinices* be,   ciliation.
To tell what reason first his minde did rule,
That thus our walles with forrein foes enclosde
In sharpe reuenge of causelesse wrongs receiu'd,
As he alledgeth by his brothers doome :   295
And of this wicked woe and dire (*b*) debate,   (*b*) Cruell or vengeable.
Some God of pitie be the equall iudge,
Whome I beseeche, to breath in both your breasts
A yelding heart to deepe desire of peace.
,, *Poli.* My woorthie dame, I finde that tried truthe   300 Truth pleadeth
,,Doth beste beseeme a simple naked tale,   simply
,,Ne needes to be with painted proces prickt,   when falsse
,,That in hir selfe hath no diuersitie,   hood vseth
,,But alwayes shewes one vndisguised face,   eloquence.
,,Where deepe deceipt and lies must seeke the shade,   305
,,And wrap their wordes in guilefull eloquence,
,,As euer fraught with contrarietie :

291 (*margin*) reconciliation] reconcilition Q_2 294 wrongs] wrong
MS. Q_3

So haue I often sayde, and say againe,
That to auoide our fathers foule reproche
And bitter curse, I parted from this lande   310
With right good will, yet thus with him agreed,
That while the whirling wings of flying time
Might roll one yeare aboute the heauenly spheare,
So long alone he might with peace possesse
(c) Crown Our fathers seate in princely (c) Diademe,   315
or sceptre. And when the yeare should eke his course renue,
Might I succeede to rule againe as long.
And that this lawe might still be kept for aye,
He bound him selfe by vowe of solemne othe
By Gods, by men, by heauen, and eke by earth :   320
Yet that forgot, without all reuerence
Vnto the Gods, without respect to right,
Without respect that reason ought to rule,
His faith and troth both troden vnder foote,
He still vsurps most tyrantlike with wrong   325
The right that doth of right to me belong.
But if he can with equall doome consent,
That I retourne into my natiue soyle
To sway with him alike the kingly seate
And euenly beare the bridle both in hand,   330
Deare mother mine I sweare by all the Gods
To raise with speede the siege from these our walles,
And send the souldiers home from whence they came :
Which if he graunt me not, then must I do
(Though loth) as much as right and reason would,   335
To venge my cause that is both good and iust.
Yet this in heauen the Gods my records be,
And here in earth each mortall man may know,
That neuer yet my giltlesse heart did fayle
Brotherly duetie to *Eteocles*,   340
And that causlesse he holdes me from mine owne.
Thus haue I said O mother, euen as much

337 my] may Q_2

As needefull is, wherein I me assure:
That in the iudgement both of good and badde,
My words may seeme of reason to proceede,   345
Constrained thus in my defence to speake.
  Chor. None may denie, O pere of princely race,
But that thy words, are honest, good and iust,
And such as well beseeme that tong of thine.
„ *Eteo.* If what to some seemes honest good and iust,   350
„Could seeme euen so in euery doubtfull mind,
„No darke debate nor quarell could arise:
„But looke, how many men so many minds,
„And that, that one man iudgeth good and iust,
„Some other deemes as deeply to be wrong.   355
To say the truth (mother) this minde of mine
Doth fleete full farre from that farfetch of his,
Ne will I longer couer my conceit:
If I could rule or reigne in heauen aboue,
And eke commaund in depth of darksome hell,   360
No toile ne trauell should my sprites abashe,
To take the way vnto my restlesse will,
To climbe aloft, nor downe for to descend.
Then thinke you not, that I can giue consent
To yeld a part of my possession,   365
Wherin I liue and lead the (*) monarchie.
„A witlesse foole may euery man him gesse,
„That leaues the more and takes him to the lesse.
With this, reproch might to my name redound,
If he, that hath with forren power spoilde   370
Our pleasaunt fields, might reaue from me perforce,
What so he list by force of armes demand.
No lesse reproofe the citizens ensewes,
If I, for dread of Greekish hosts, should graunt
That he might climbe to heigth of his desire.   375
In fine, he ought not thus of me to craue
Accord, or peace, with bloudy sword in hand,

Marginal notes:
Sundrye men sundry minds.
Onely rule.

362 take] make *MS. Q₁*   364 giue] yelde *MS. Q₁*

But with humilitie and prayer both,
For often is it seene, and proofe doth teach,
„Swete words preuaile, where sword and fire do faile.   380
Yet this, if here within these stately walles
He list to liue, the sonne of *Oedipus*,
And not as king of *Thebes*, I stand content.
But let him thinke, since now I can commaunde,
This necke of mine shall neuer yeld to yoke   385
Of seruitude: let bring his banners splayde,
Let speare and shield, sharpe sworde, and cyndring flames
Procure the parte that he so vainely claimes:
As long as life within this brest doth last,

Wil not.   I nill (∗) consent that he should reigne with me.   390
If lawe of right may any way be broke,
„Desire of rule within a climbing brest

Tullyes   „To breake a vow may beare the buckler best.
opinyon.   „ *Cho.* Who once hath past the bounds of honestie
„In ernest deedes, may passe it well in words.   395
     Ioca. O sonne, amongst so many miseries
This benefite hath croked age, I find,
That as the tracke of trustlesse time hath taught,

Youth   „It seeth much, and many things discernes,
seeth not   „Which recklesse youth can neuer rightly iudge,   400
so much
as age.   Oh, cast aside that vaine ambition,
That corosiue, that cruell pestilence,
That most infects the minds of mortall men:

Ambition   „In princely palace and in stately townes
doth
destroyeal: „It crepeth ofte, and close with it conuayes,   405
equalytie   „(To leaue behind it) damage and decayes:
doth
maynteyne   „By it be loue and amitie destroyde,
al things.   „It breakes the lawes and common concord beates,
„Kingdomes and realmes it topsie turuie turnes,
And now, euen thee, hir gall so poisoned hath,   410
That the weake eies of thine affection
Are blinded quite, and see not to them selfe

     380 do faile] *MS. and Q*₁ *omit* do   387 flames] flame *MS.*

But worthy childe, driue from thy doubtfull brest
This monstrous mate, in steade wherof embrace
„Equalitie, which stately states defends   415
„And binds the minde with true and trustie knots
„Of frendly faith which neuer can be broke,
„This man, of right should properly possesse,
And who that other doth the more embrace,
Shall purchase paine to be his iust reward   420
By wrathfull wo, or else by cruell death.
„This, first deuided all by equall bonds
„What so the earth did yeld for our auaile :
„This, did deuide the nightes and dayes alike,
„And that the vaile of darke and dreadfull night   ▾ 425
„(Which shrowds in misty clouds the pleasaunt light,)
„Ne yet the golden beames of *Phœbus* rayes
„(Which cleares the dimmed ayre with gladsome gleams)
„Can yet heape hate in either of them both.
If then the dayes and nightes to serue our turne   430
Content themselues to yeld each other place,
Well oughtest thou with waightie dome to graunt
Thy brothers right to rule the reigne with thee,
Which heauens ordeyned common to you both :
If so thou nill O sonne, O cruell sonne,   435
„In whose high brest may iustice builde hir boure   If the head
„When princes harts wide open lye to wrong?   be euill the
                                            body
Why likes thee so the tipe of tyrannie   cannot be
With others losse to gather greedy gaine?   good.
„Alas how farre he wanders from the truth   440
„That compts a pompe, all other to command,
„Yet can not rule his owne vnbridled will,
„A vaine desire much riches to possesse
„Whereby the brest is brusde and battered still,
„With dread, with daunger, care and cold suspecte.   445
„Who seekes to haue the thing we call inough,   Content is
„Acquainte him first with contentation,   riche.

            426   *Q₂ gives this final parenthesis at end of* 425

„For plenteousness is but a naked name.

„And what suffiseth vse of mortall men,

„Shall best apay the meane and modest hearts. 450

„These hoorded heapes of golde and worldly wealth

„Are not the proper goods of any one,

Riches are „But pawnes which *Ioue* powres out aboundantly
but
borowed „That we likewise might use them equally,
ware.
„And as he seemes to lend them for a time, 455

„Euen so in time he takes them home agayne,

„And would that we acknowledge euery houre,

„That from his handes we did the same receiue:

„There nothing is so firme and stayde to man,

„But whyrles about with wheeles of restlesse time. 460

Now if I should this one thing thee demaunde,

Which of these two thou wouldest chuse to keepe,

The towne quiet or vnquiet tyrannie?

And wouldest thou say I chuse my kingly chayre?

O witlesse answere sent from wicked heart, 465

For if so fall (which mightie God defende)

Thine enimies hand should ouercome thy might,

And thou shouldest see them sacke the towne of *Thebes*,

More care The chastest virgins rauished for wrecke,
to loose
than The worthy children in captiuitie, 470
plesure to
posses. „Then shouldest thou feele that scepter, crowne, & wealth

„Yeelde deeper care to see them tane away,

„Than to possesse them yeldeth deepe content.

Now to conclude my sonne, Ambition

Is it that most offends thy blynded thought, 475

Blame not thy brother, blame ambition

From whome if so thou not redeeme thy selfe,

I feare to see thee buy repentance deare.

　　Cho. Yea deare, too deare when it shal come too late.

　　Ioc. And now to thee my *Polinices* deare, 480

I say that sillie was *Adrastus* reade,

465 sent] sent Q_2　　475 Is it ... thought] Is it that most of all offends
thy thought *MS.*: Is it that most offendes thy thought Q_1

And thou God knowes a simple sillie soule,
He to be ruled by thy heady wil,
And thou, to warre against the *Thebane* walls,
These walls I say whose gates thy selfe should garde :   485
Tell me I pray thee, if the Citie yeelde,
Or thou it take by force in bloudie fight,
(Which neuer graunt the Gods I them beseeke)
What spoyles? what Palmes? what signe of victorie
Canst thou set vp to haue thy countrie woonne?   490
What title worthie of immortall fame,
Shall blased be in honor of thy name?
O sonne, deare sonne, beleeue thy trustie dame,
The name of glorie shall thy name refuse,
And flie full farre from all thy fonde attemptes.   495
But if so fall thou shouldst be ouercome,
Then with what face canst thou returne to *Greece*,
That here hast lefte so many *Greekes* on grounde?
Eache one shall curse and blame thee to thy face,
As him that onely caused their decaye,   500
And eke condemne *Adrastus* simple heade,
That such a pheere had chosen for his childe.
So may it fall, in one accursed houre,
That thou mayst loose thy wife and countrie both,
Both which thou mayst with little toyle attaine,   505
If thou canst leaue high minde and darke disdaine.
    Cho. O mightie Gods of goodnesse, neuer graunt
Vnto these euilles, but set desired peace
Betwene the hearts of these two friendly foes.
    Ete. The question that betwixt vs two is growen,   510
Beleeue me mother, can not ende with words :
You waste your breath, and I but loose my time,
And all your trauell lost and spent in vaine :
For this I sweare, that peace you neuer get
Betweene vs two, but with condition,   515
That whilst I liue, I will be Lord of *Thebes.*
Then set aside these vaine forwasted wordes,

Small glory
for a rebel
to see his
owne
countrey
spoyled.

And yeelde me leaue to go where neede doth presse :
And now good sir, get you out of these walles,
Vnlesse you meane to buy abode with bloude.   520

  Po. And who is he that seekes to haue my bloude,
And shall not shed his owne as fast as myne ?

  Ete. By thee he standes, and thou standst him before :
Loe here the sworde that shall perfourme his worde.

  Po. And this shall eke mainteine my rightfull cause.   525

  Ioc. O sonnes, dear sonnes, away with glittring armes :
And first, before you touch eache others flesh,
With doubled blowes come pierce this brest of mine.

  Po. Ah wretch, thou art both vile and cowarde like,
Thy high estate esteemes thy life to deare.   530

  Ete. If with a wretch or coward shouldst thou fighte,
Oh dastard villaine, what first moued thee
With swarmes of Greekes to take this enterprise ?

  Po. For well I wist, that cankred heart of thine
Coulde safely kepe thy heade within these walles,   535
And flee the fielde when combate should be callde.

  Ete. This truce assureth thee *Polynices,*
And makes thee bolde to giue such bosting wordes :
So be thou sure, that had this truce not bene,
Then long ere this, these handes had bene embrude,   540
And eke this soyle besprinkled with thy bloude.

  Po. Not one small drop of my bloude shalt thou spill,
But buy it deare against thy cankred will.

  Ioc. O sonnes, my sonnes, for pittie yet refrayne.

  Ch. Good Gods, who euer sawe so strange a sight ?   545
True loue and frindship both be put to flight.

  Po. Yelde villein, yelde my right which thou witholdst.

  Ete. Cut of thy hope to reigne in *Thebane* walles,
Nought hast thou here, nor nought shal euer haue,
Away.   *Po.* O aultars of my countrie soyle.   550

  521 And . . . bloude] *MS. adds in margin* they draw theyr swordes
524 worde] wordes *MS.*   526 O sonnes . . . armes] *MS. adds in margin*
thyr mother steppes betwene them   537 assureth] assured *MS.* Q₁
547 witholdst] with-holds Q₁

Ete. Whome thou art come to spoyle and to deface.

Po. O Gods, giue eare vnto my honest cause.

Ete. With forreine power his countrie to inuade.

Po. O holy temples of the heauenly Gods.

Ete. That for thy wicked deedes do hate thy name.   555

Po. Out of my kingdome am I driuen by force.

Ete. Out of the which thou camst me for to driue.

Po. Punish O Gods this wicked tyrant here.

Ete. Pray to the Gods in *Greece* and not in *Thebes.*

Po. No savage beast so cruell nor vniust.   560

Ete. Not cruel to my countrie like to thee.

Po. Since from my right I am with wrong depriued.

Ete. Eke from thy life if long thou tarie here.

Po. O father heare what iniuries I take.

Ete. As though thy diuelishe deedes were hid from him. 565

Po. And you mother.   *Eteo.* Haue done thou not deseruest
With that false tong thy mother once to name.

Po. O deare Citie.   *Eteo.* When thou ariuest in *Greece,*
Chuse out thy dwelling in some mustie Moores.

Po. I must departe, and parting must I prayse   570
Oh deare mother the depth of your good will.

Ioc. O sonne.   *Eteo.* Away I say out of these walls.

Po. I can not chuse but must thy will obey,
Yet graunt me once my father for to see.

Ete. I heare no prayers of my enemie.   575

Po. Where be my sweete sisters?   *Eteo.* And canst thou yet
With shamelesse tong once name thy noble race
That art become a common foe to *Thebes?*
Be sure thou shall them neuer see againe,
Nor other friend that in these walls remaine.   580

Po. Rest you in peace, O worthy mother myne.

Ioc. Howe can that be and thou my ioye in warre?

Po. Henceforth n'am I your ioy ne yet your sonne.

---

557 camst me for to driue] comest me to dryve *MS.* : camest me to driue
Q₁   573 will] voice *MS.*   579 shall] shalt *MS. Q₁ Q₃*   580
remaine] remaynes *MS.*   583 n'am I] ne I *MS., corrected later to* I nam

Ioc. Alas the heauens me whelme with all mishap.

Po. Lo here the cause that stirreth me by wrong.   585

Ete. Much more is that he profereth vnto me.

Po. Well, speake, darest thou come armed to the fielde?

Ete. So dare I come, wherfore dost thou demaunde?

Po. For needs or thou must ende this life of mine,

Or quenche my thirst with pouring out thy bloud.   590

Eteo. Ah wretch, my thirst is all as drie as thine.

Ioc. Alas and welaway, what heare I sonnes?

How can it be? deare children can it be

That brethrens heartes such rancour should enrage?

Eteo. And that right soone the proofe shall playnely shew.

Io. Oh say not so, yet say not so deare sonnes.   596

Po. O royall race of *Thebes* now take thine ende.

Cho. God shield.   *Eteo.* O slow & sluggish heart of mine,

Why do I stay t'embrew these slothfull hands?

But for his greater griefe I will departe,   600

And at returne if here I finde my foe,

This hastie hande shall ende our hote debate.

> *Eteocles here goeth out by the gates Electræ.*

Po. Deare Citizens, and you eternall Gods,

Beare witnesse with me here before the worlde,

How this my fierce and cruell enimie,   605

Whom causelesse now my brother I do call,

With threates of death my lingring steps doth driue .

Both from my right and from my countrey soyle,

Not as beseemes the sonne of *Oedipus*,

But as a slaue, an abiect, or a wretche: 610

And since you be both pitifull and iuste,

Vouchsafe O Gods, that as I part with griefe,

So may I yet returne with ioyfull spoyle

Of this accursed tyraunt and (he slayne)

I may recouer quietly mine owne.   615

> *Polynice goeth out by the gates Homoloides.*

Io. O wretched wretch *Iocasta*, wher is founde

607 lingring] lingriug *Q₂*

The miserie that may compare to thine?
O would I had nor gasing eyes to see,
Nor listning eares to heare that now I dread:
But what remaines, saue onely to entreate   620
That cruell dole wold yet so curteous be
To reaue the breath out of this wofull brest,
Before I harken to some wofull newes.
Rest you here dames, and pray vnto the Gods
For our redresse, and I in that meane while   625
Will shut my selfe from sight of lothsome light.

Iocasta goeth into hir Pallace.

  Cho. O mightie God, the gouernour of *Thebes*
Pitie with speede the payne *Iocasta* bydes,
And eke our needes O mightie *Bacchus* helpe,
Bende willing eare vnto our iust complaint: 630
Leaue them not comfortlesse that trust in thee,
We haue no gold nor siluer thee to giue,
Ne sacrifice to those thine aultars due,
In steede wherof we consecrate our harts
To serue thy will, and hestes for to obey.   635

Whyles the Chorus is thus praying to Bacchus,
Eteocles returneth by the gates called Electræ.

Scena .2.   Actus .2.

ETEOCLES.   CREON.

SInce I haue ridde mine enmie out of sight,
The best shall be for *Creon* now to sende,
(My mothers brother) that with him I may
Reason, consulte, conferre, and counsell bothe,
What shall be best to vse in our defence,   5
Before we venter forth into the fielde.
But of this trauayle, loe, he me acquites
That comes in haste towards these royall towres.

623 wofull] wery *MS.*   632 no] nor *Q₁*   633 those] these *MS.*

*Here Creon attended by foure gentlemen, commeth
in by the gates Homoloydes.*

Cre. O mightie king, not causelesse nowe I come,
To finde, that long haue sought your maistie,   10
So to discharge the duetie that I owe
To you, by comforte and by counsell bothe.

   Ete. No lesse desire this harte of mine did presse, ·
To send for thee *Creon*, since that in vaine
My mother hath hir words and trauayle spent,   15
To reconcile *Polynices* and me :
For he (so dull was his capacitie)
Did thinke, he could by dread of daunger, winne
My princely heart to yeeld to him his realme.

   Cre. I vnderstande, the armie that he brings   20
Agaynst these walles, is such, that I me doubte
Our cities force may scarce the same resist.
Yet true it is, that right and reason both
Are on our side, which bring the victorie
Oftetimes : for we our countrey to defend,   25
They to subdue the same in armes are come.
But what I would vnto your highnesse shewe,
Is of more weight, and more behoues to know.

   Ete. And what is that ? oh quickly tell it me.

   Cre. A Greeke prisner is come vnto my hands.   30

   Ete. And what sayth he that doth so much importe ?

   Cre. That euen alredy be their ranks in raye,
And streight will giue assault to these our walles.

   Ete. Then must I streight prepare our Citizens
In glittring arms to march into the fielde.   35

   Cre. O Prince (and pardon me) thy youthfull yers
Nor see them selfe, ne let thee once discerne,
What best behoueth in this doubtfull case.
,,For Prudence, she that is the mightie queene
,,Of all good workes, growes by experience,   40

  10 *Q₂ period at end of line*   17 capacitie] caparitie *Q₂*   19 hi°
this *MS. Q₁*   32 be] *MS. Q₁ Q₃* : by *Q₂*

„Which is not founde with fewe dayes seeking for.

   Ete. And were not this both sounde and wise aduise,
Boldly to looke our foemen in the face,
Before they spred our fields with hugie hoste,
And all the towne beset by siege at once ?   45

   Cre. We be but few, and they in number great.

   Ete. Our men haue yet more courage farre than they.

   Cre. That know I not, nor am I sure to say.

   Ete. Those eyes of thine in little space shall see
How many I my selfe can bring to grounde.   50

   Cre. That would I like, but harde it is to doe.

   Ete. I nill penne vp our men within the walles.

   Cre. In counsell yet the victorie consistes.

   Ete. And wilt thou then I vse some other reade ?

   Cre. What else ? be still a while, for hast makes wast.   55

   Ete. By night I will the Cammassado giue.

   Cre. So may you do and take the ouerthrowe.

   Ete. The vauntage is to him that doth assaulte.

   Cre. Yet skirmishe giuen by night is perillous.

   Ete. Let set vpon them as they sit at meat.   60

   Cre. Sodayne assaults affray the minde no doubt,
But we had neede to ouercome.   *Ete.* So shall we do.

   Cre. No sure, vnlesse some other counsell helpe.

   Ete. Amid their trenches shall we them inuade ?

   Cre. As who should say, were none to make defence.   65

   Ete. Should I then yeeld the Citie to my foes ?

   Cre. No, but aduise you well if you be wise.

   Ete. That were thy parte, that knowest more than I.

   Cre. Then shall I say that best doth seeme to me ?

   Ete. Yea *Creon* yea, thy counsell holde I deare.   70

   Cre. Seuen men of courage haue they chosen out.

   Ete. A slender number for so great emprise.

   Cre. But they them chose for guides and capitaynes.

   Ete. To such an hoste ? why they may not suffise.

   Cre. Nay, to assault the seuen gates of the citie.   75

59 *Cre.*] *Cre. Q₂*   60 Let] Lets *Q₂*   62 to ouercome] *MS. omits* to

Ete. What then behoueth so bestad to done?
Cre. With equall number see you do them match.
Ete. And then commit our men in charge to them?
Cre. Chusing the best and boldest blouds in *Thebes.*
Ete. And how shall I the Citie then defende?   80
Cre. Well with the rest, for one man sees not all.
Ete. And shall I chuse the boldest or the wisest?
Cre. Nay both, for one without that other fayles.
„ *Ete.* Force without wisedome then is little worth.
Cre. That one must be fast to that other ioynde.   85
Ete. Creon I will thy counsell follow still,
For why, I hold it wise and trusty both,
And out of hand for now I will departe
That I in time the better may prouide
Before occasion slip out of my hands,   90

Kyll.   And that I may this *Polynices* (∗) quell :
For well may I with bloudy knife him slea
That comes in armes my countrie for to spoyle.
But if so please to fortune and to fate
That other ende than I do thinke may fall,   95
To thee my frend it resteth to procure
The mariage twixt my sister *Antygone*
And thy deare sonne *Hæmone*, to whom for dowre
At parting thus I promise to performe

Promisse.   As much as late I did (∗) beheste to thee :   100
My mothers bloude and brother deare thou arte,
Ne neede I craue of thee to gard hir well,
As for my father care I not, for if
So chaunce I dye, it may full well be sayd
His bitter curses brought me to my bane.   105
Cre. The Lord defend, for that vnworthy were.
Ete. Of *Thebes* towne the rule and scepter loe
I neede nor ought it otherwise dispose
Than vnto thee, if I dye without heyre.
Yet longs my lingring mynde to vnderstand,   110
The doubtfull ende of this vnhappie warre :

Wherfore I will thou send thy sonne to seke
Tyresias the deuine, and learne of him,
For at my call I knowe he will not come
That often haue his artes and him reprovde.   115
    Cre. As you commaund, so ought I to performe.
    Ete. And last, I thee and citie both commaund,
If fortune frendly fauour our attemptes,
And make our men triumphant victors all,
That none there be so hardie ne so bolde   120
For *Polynices* bones to giue a graue :
And who presumes to breake my heste herein,
Shall dye the death in penaunce of his paine :
For though I were by bloud to him conioynde
I part it now, and iustice goeth with me   125
To guide my steppes victoriously before.
Pray you to Ioue he deigne for to defende,
Our Citie safe both now and euermore.
    Cre. Gramercie worthie prince, for all thy loue
And faithfull trust thou doest in me repose,   130
And if should hap, that I hope neuer shall,
I promise yet to doe what best behoues,
But chieflie this I sweare and make a vowe,
For *Polynices* nowe our cruell foe,
To holde the hest that thou doest me commaunde.   135
       Creon attendeth Eteocles to the gates Electra he returneth
       and goeth out by the gates called Homoloydes.

CHORVS.

O Fierce and furious *Mars*, whose harmefull harte,
Reioyceth most to shed the giltlesse blood,
Whose headie wil doth all the world subuert,
And doth enuie the pleasant mery moode,
Of our estate that erst in quiet stoode.   5
Why doest thou thus our harmelesse towne annoye,

       1 *Mars*] God *MS. Q*₁

Which mightie *Bacchus* gouerned in ioye ?
    Father of warre and death, that dost remoue
With wrathfull wrecke from wofull mothers breast,
The trustie pledges of their tender loue,   10
So graunt the Gods, that for our finall rest,
Dame Venus pleasant lookes may please thee best,
Wherby when thou shalt all amazed stand,
The sword may fall out of thy trembling hand.

    And thou maist proue some other way full well   15
The bloudie prowesse of thy mightie speare,
Wherwith thou raiseth from the depth of hell,
The wrathfull sprites of all the furies there,
Who when they wake, doe wander euery where,
And neuer rest to range about the coastes,   20
Tenriche that pit with spoile of damned ghostes.

    And when thou hast our fieldes forsaken thus,
Let cruell discorde beare thee companie,
Engirt with snakes and serpents venemous,
Euen she that can with red virmilion dye   25
The gladsome greene that florisht pleasantly,
And make the greedie ground a drinking cup,
To sup the bloud of murdered bodyes vp.

    Yet thou returne O ioye and pleasant peace,
From whence thou didst against our wil depart,   30
Ne let thy worthie minde from trauell cease,
To chase disdaine out of the poysned harte,
That raised warre to all our paynes and smarte,
Euen from the brest of *Oedipus* his sonne,
Whose swelling pride hath all this iarre begonne.   35
    And thou great God, that doest all things decree,
And sitst on highe aboue the starrie skies,
Thou chiefest cause of causes all that bee,
Regard not his offence but heare our cries,
And spedily redresse our miseries,   40

        19 they wake *MS. Q*₁ *Q*₃: the weake *Q*₂

For what can we poore wofull wretches doe
But craue thy aide, and onely cleaue therto?
Finis Actus secundi.

Done by G. Gascoygne.

The order of the thirde dumbe

shevve.

BEfore the beginning of this .iij. Act did sound a very
dolefull noise of cornettes, during the which there opened
and appeared in the stage a great Gulfe. Immediatly came
in .vi. gentlemē in their dublets & hose, bringing vpon their
shulders baskets full of earth and threwe them into the Gulfe to 5
fill it vp, but it would not so close vp nor be filled. Then came
the ladyes and dames that stoode by, throwing in their cheynes
& Iewels, so to cause it stoppe vp and close it selfe: but when
it would not so be filled, came in a knighte with his sword drawen,
armed at all poyntes, who walking twise or thrise about it, & 10
perusing it, seing that it would nether be filled with earth nor
with their Iewells and ornaments, after solempne reuerence
done to the gods, and curteous leaue taken of the Ladyes and
standers by, sodeinly lepte into the Gulfe, the which did close
vp immediatly: betokning vnto vs the loue that euery worthy 15
person oweth vnto his natiue coūtrie, by the historyc of *Curtius*,
who for the lyke cause aduentured the like in Rome. This
done, blinde *Tyresias* the deuine prophete led in by hys
daughter, and conducted by *Meneceus* the son of *Creon*, entreth
by the gates *Electræ*, and sayth as followeth.   20

41 can *MS.* Q_1: cause $Q_2 Q_3$

Actus .iij.   Scena .1.

THou trustie guide of my so trustlesse steppes
   Deer daughter mine go we, lead thou y^e way,
For since the day I first did leese this light
Thou only art the light of these mine eyes :
And for thou knowst I am both old & weake   5
And euer longing after louely rest,
Direct my steppes amyd the playnest pathes,
That so my febled feete may feele lesse paine.
Meneceus thou gentle childe, tell me,
Is it farre hence, the place where we must goe,   10
Where as thy father for my comming stayes?
For like vnto the slouthfull snayle I drawe,
(Deare sonne) with paine these aged legges of mine,
     Creon returneth by the gates Homoloydes.
And though my minde be quicke, scarce can I moue.
   Cre. Comfort thy selfe deuine, *Creon* thy frend   15
Loe standeth here, and came to meete with thee
To ease the paine that thou mightst else sustaine,

Age must be helped by youth. ,,For vnto elde eche trauell yeldes annoy
And thou his daughter and his faithfull guide,
Loe rest him here, and rest thou therewithall   20
Thy virgins hands, that in sustayning him
Doest well acquite the duetie of a childe.
,,For crooked age and hory siluer heares
,,Still craueth helpe of lustie youthfull yeares.
   Tyr. Gramercie Lorde what is your noble will?   25
   Cre. What I would haue of thee *Tyresias*.
Is not a thing so soone for to be sayde.
But rest a whyle thy weake and weary limmes

Creon .·. . Homoloydes] *MS. puts stage-direction after line* 14 *instead of
before it*   18 elde eche] olde age Q_3

And take some breath now after wearie walke,
And tell I pray thee, what this crowne doth meane,   30
That sits so kingly on thy skilfull heade ?

Tyr. Know this, that for I did with graue aduise,
Foretell the Citizens of *Athens* towne,
How they might best with losse of litle bloude,
Haue victories against their enimies,   35
Hath bene the cause why I doe weare this Crowne,
As right rewarde and not vnmeete for me.

Cre. So take I then this thy victorious crowne,
For our auaile in token of good lucke,
That knowest, how the discord and debate   40
Which late is fallen between these brethren twaine,
Hath brought all *Thebes* in daunger and in dreade.
Eteocles our king, with threatning armes,
Is gone against his greekish enimies,
Commaunding me to learne of thee (who arte   45
A true diuine of things that be to come)
What were for vs the safest to be done,
From perill now our countrey to preserue.

Tyr. Long haue I bene within the towne of *Thebes*,
Since that I tyed this trustie toung of mine   50
From telling truth, fearing *Eteocles* :
Yet, since thou doest in so great neede desire
I should reueale things hidden vnto thee,
For common cause of this our common weale,
I stand content to pleasure thee herein.   55
But first (that to this mightie God of yours
There might some worthie sacrifice be made)
Let kill the fairest goate that is in *Thebes*
Within whose bowelles when the Preest shall loke,
And tell to me what he hath there espyed,   60
I trust t'aduise thee what is best to doen.

Cre. Lo here the temple, and ere long I looke
To see the holy preest that hither cŏmes,

35 victories] victory *MS*.   50 trustie] *Q₂ omits*

Bringing with him the pure and faire offrings,
Which thou requirest: for not long since, I sent   65
For him, as one that am not ignorant
Of all your rytes and sacred ceremonyes:
He went to choose amid our herd of goates,
The fattest there: and loke where now he commes.

       Sacerdos accompanyed with. xvj. Bacchanales and all
       his rytes and ceremonies, entreth by the gates Homo-
       loydes.

  Sacer. O famous Citizens, that holde full deare   70
Your quiet country: Loe where I doe come
Most ioyfully, with wonted sacrifice,
So to beseeche the supreme Citizens,
To stay our state that staggringly doth stand,
And plant vs peace where warre and discord growes: 75
Wherfore, with hart deuoute and humble cheere,
Whiles I breake vp the bowels of this beast,
(That oft thy veneyarde *Bacchus* hath destroyed,)
Let euery wight craue pardon for his faults,
With bending knee about his aultars here.   80
  Tyr. Take here the salt, and sprincle therwithall
About the necke: that done, cast all the rest
Into the sacred fire, and then annoynte
The knife prepared for the sacrifice.
O mightie Ioue, preserue the precious gifte   85
That thou me gaue, when first thine angrie Queene,
For deepe disdayne did both mine eyes do out,
Graunt me, I may foretell the truth in this,
For, but by thee, I know that I ne may,
Ne will, ne can, one trustie sentence say.   90
  Sa. This due is done. *Tyr.* With knife then stick y° kid.
  Sac. Thou daughter of deuine *Tyresias,*
With those vnspotted virgins hands of thine
Receiue the bloude within this vessell here,
And then deuoutly it to *Bacchus* yelde.   95

Venus
made him
blynde for
giuing
sentence
against hir.

    76 hart] harty *MS.*   91 done *Q₂ no period*

Man. O holy God of *Thebes*, that doest both praise
Swete peace, and doest in hart also disdayne
The noysome noyse, the furies and the fight
Of bloudie *Mars* and of *Bellona* both :
O thou the giuer both of ioy and health,   100
Receiue in gree and with well willing hand
These holy whole brunt offrings vnto thee :
And as this towne doth wholy thee adore,
So by thy helpe do graunt that it may stand
Safe from the enimies outrage euermore.   105

Sac. Now in thy sacred name I bowell here
This sacrifice.   *Tyre.* And what entralls hath it ?

Sac. Faire and welformed all in euery poynt,
The liuer cleane, the hart is not infect,
Saue loe, I finde but onely one hart string   110
By which I finde something I wote nere what,
That seemes corrupt, and were not onely that,
In all the rest, they are both sound and hole.

Tyr. Now cast at once into the holy flame
The swete incense, and then aduertise mee   115
What hew it beares, and euery other ryte
That ought may helpe the truth for to coniecte.

Sac. I see the flames doe sundrie coulours cast,
Now bloudy sanguine, straight way purple, blew,
Some partes seeme blacke, some gray, and some be greene.

Tyr. Stay there, suffyseth this for to haue seene.   121
Know *Creon*, that these outward seemely signes
(By that the Gods haue let me vnderstand
Who know the truth of euery secrete thing)
Betoken that the Citie great of *Thebes*   125
Shall Victor be against the Greekish host,
If so consent be giuen : but more than this
I lyst not say.   *Cre.* Alas, for curtesie

111 something] somewhat *MS*.   119 purple, blew] purple blew *MS*
124 Who . . . thing] Who understandith all, and seith secret things *MS. Q₁*
know] knoweth *Q₃*   125 Betoken] betokenith *MS. Q₁*   great] *MS*.
omits

Say on *Tyresias*, neuer haue respect
To any liuing man, but tell the truth.   130

> *Sacerdos returneth with the Bacchanales, by the ga-*
> *tes Homoloides.*

Sac. In this meane while I will returne with speede
From whence I came : for lawfull is it not,
That suche as I should heare your secresies.

Tyr. Contrary then to that which I haue sayde,
The incest foule, and childbirth monstruous   135
Of *Iocasta*, so stirres the wrath of Ioue,
This citie shall with bloudy channels swimme,
And angry *Mars* shall ouercome it all
With famine, flame, rape, murther, dole and death :
These lustie towres shall haue a headlong fall,   140
These houses burnde, and all the rest be razde,
And soone be sayde, here whilome *Thebes* stoode.
One onely way I finde for to escape,
Which bothe would thee displease to heare it tolde,
And me to tell percase were perillous.   145
Thee therfore with my trauell I commende
To *Ioue*, and with the rest I will endure,
What so shall chaunce for our aduersitie.

Cre. Yet stay a whyle,   *Tyr. Creon* make me not stay
By force.   *Cre.* Why fleest thou?   *Tyr.* Syr tis not from thee
I flee, but from this fortune foule and fell.   151

Cre. Yet tell me what behoues the citie doe?

Tyr. Thou *Creon* seemest now desirous still
It to preserue : but if as well as I
Thou knewest that which is to thee vnknowne,   155
Then wouldst thou not so soone consent thereto.

Cre. And would not I with eagre minde desire
The thing that may for *Thebes* ought auayle?

Tyr. And dost thou then so instantly request
To know which way thou mayest the same preserue?   160

Cre. For nothing else I sent my sonne of late

133 secresies] secretnesse *Q₁*

To seeke for thee.   *Tyr.* Then will I satisfie
Thy greedie minde in this : but first tell me,
Menetius where is he ?   *Cre.* Not farre from me.

   Tyr. I pray thee sende him out some other where.   165
   Cre. Why wouldest thou that he should not be here ?
   Tyr. I would not haue him heare what I should say.
   Cre. He is my sonne, ne will he it reueale.
   Tyr. And shall I then while he is present speake ?
   Cre. Yea, be thou sure that he no lesse than I,   170
Doth wishe full well vnto this common weale.

   Tyr. Then *Creon* shalt thou knowe : the meane to saue
This Citie, is, that thou shalt slea thy sonne,
And of his bodie make a sacrifice
For his countrey : lo heere is all you seeke   175
So much to knowe, and since you haue me forst
To tell the thing that I would not haue tolde,
If I haue you offended with my words,
Blame then your selfe, and eke your frowarde fate.

   Cre. Oh cruel words, oh, oh, what hast thou sayde,   180
Thou cruell sothsayer ?   *Tyr.* Euen that, that heauen
Hath ordeined once, and needes it must ensue.

   Cre. How many euils hast thou knit vp in one ?
   Tyr. Though euill for thee, yet for thy countrey good.
   Cre. And let my countrey perishe, what care I ?   185
„ *Tyr.* Aboue all things we ought to holde it deare.
   Cre. Cruell were he, that would not loue his childe.
„ *Tyr.* For cōmō weale, were well, that one man waile.
   Cre. To loose mine owne, I liste none other saue.
„ *Tyr.* Best Citizens care least for priuat gayne.   190
   Cre. Depart, for nowe, with all thy prophecies.
„ *Tyr.* Lo, thus the truth doth alwayes hatred get.
   Cre. Yet pray I thee by these thy siluer heares,
„ *Tyr.* The harme that cōmes from heauen can not be scapt.
   Cre. And by thy holy spirite of prophecie,   195
„ *Tyr.* What heauen hath done, that cannot I vndoe.
   Cre. That to no moe this secrete thou reueale.

Tyr. And wouldst thou haue me learne to make a lye?

Cre. I pray thee hold thy peace. *Tyr.* That will I not :

But in thy woe to yeelde thee some reliefe,   200

I tell thee once, thou shalt be Lorde of *Thebes*,

Which happe of thine this string did well declare,

Which from the heart doth out alonely growe.

So did the peece corrupted playnly shewe,

An argument most euident to proue   205

Thy sonne his death. *Cre.* Well, yet be thou content

To keepe full close this secrete hidden griefe.

    Tyr. I neither ought, ne will keepe it so close.

    Cre. Shall I be then the murtherer of mine owne ?

    Tyr. Ne blame not me, but blame the starres for this.   210

    Cre. Can heauens condemne but him alone to dye ?

    Tyr. We ought beleeue the cause is good and iust.

    „ *Cre.* Uniust is he condemnes the innocent.

    „ *Tyr.* A foole is he accuseth heauens of wrongs.

    „ *Cre.* There can no ill thing come from heauẽs aboue.   215

    Tyr. Then this that heauen commaunds can not be ill.

    Cre. I not beleeue that thou hast talkt with God.

    Tyr. Bicause I tell thee that doth thee displease.

    Cre. Out of my sight accursed lying wretch.

    Tyr. Go daughter go, oh what foole is he   220

That puts in vre to publish prophecies ?

„For if he do fore tell a froward fate,

„Though it be true, yet shall he purchase hate :

„And if he silence keepe, or hide the truth,

„The heauy wrath of mightie Gods ensuth.   225

Appollo he might well tell things to come,

That had no dread the angry to offende.

But hye we daughter hence some other way.

    *Tyresias with Manto his daughter, returneth by the gates
    called Electræ.*

Great follye to accuse the gods. *(margin, beside lines 214–216)*

A thankles office to foretell a mischiefe. *(margin, beside lines 220–222)*

203 alonely] all only *MS*.   217 talkt] talk *MS*.   220 what foole]
what a foole *MS*. Q_1

Scena. 2.

CREON.　MENECEVS.

OH my deare childe, well hast thou heard with eare
　These weery newes, or rather wicked tales
That this deuine of thee deuined hath :
Yet will thy father neuer be thy foe,
With cruell doome thy death for to consent.　　　　5

　Me. You rather ought, O father, to consent
Vnto my death, since that my death may bring
Vnto this towne both peace and victorie.
„Ne can I purchase more prayseworthy death
„Than for my countries wealth to lose my breath.　10

　Cre. I cannot prayse this witlesse will of thine.
„ *Me.* You know deare father, that this life of ours
„Is brittle, short, and nothing else in deede
„But tedious toyle and pangs of endlesse payne :
„And death, whose darte to some men seemes so fell,　15
„Brings quiet ende to this vnquiet life.
„Vnto which ende who soonest doth arriue,
„Finds soonest rest of all his restlesse griete.
„And were it so, that here on earth we felte
„No pricke of paine, nor that our flattring dayes　20
„Were neuer dasht by froward fortunes frowne,
„Yet beeing borne (as all men are) to dye,
„Were not this worthy glory and renowne,
„To yeelde the countrey soyle where I was borne,
„For so long time, so shorte a time as mine?　25
I can not thinke that this can be denied.
Then if to shunne this haughtie high behest,
Mine onely cause, O father, doth you moue,
Be sure, you seeke to take from me your sonne,
The greatest honor that I can attayne :　30

No greater honor than to dye for thy countrey.

Death (indeed) yeldeth more pleasure than lyfe.

But if your owne commoditie you moue,
So much the lesse you ought the same allowe :
For looke, how much the more you haue in *Thebes*
So much the more you ought to loue the same :
Here haue you *Hemone*, he that in my steade   35
(O my deare father) may with you remaine,
So that, although you be depriued of me
Yet shall you not be quite depriued of heires.

    Cre. I can not chuse, deare sonne, but disalowe
This thy too hastie, hote desire of death :   40
For if thy life thou settest all so lighte,
Yet oughtest thou thy father me respect,
Who as I drawe the more to lumpishe age,
So much more neede haue I to craue thine ayde :
Ne will I yet, with stubborne tong denye,   45
„That for his common weale to spende his life,
„Doth win the subiect high renoumed name.
„But howe ? in armour to defende the state,
„Not like a beast to bleede in sacrifice :
And therwithal, if any shoulde consent   50
To such a death, then should the same be I,
That haue prolonged life euen long enough,
Ne many dayes haue I nowe to drawe on. ·
And more auaile might to the countrie come,
Deare sonne, to hold that lustie life of thine,   55
That art both yong and`eke of courage stout.
Than may by me that feeble am and olde.
Then liue deare sonne in high prosperitie,
And giue me leaue that worthy am to dye.

    Mene. Yet worthy were not that vnworthy chaunge.   60
    Cre. If such a death bring glorie, giue it me.
    Mene. Not you, but me, the heauens cal to die.
    Cre. We be but one in flesh and body both.
    Mene. I father ought, so ought not you, to die.
    Cre. If thou sonne die, thinke not that I can liue :   65

43 lumpishe] lymping *MS*.   53 Ne *MS. Q₁* : Nay *Q₂* : Not *Q₃*

Then let me die, and so shall he first die,
That ought to die, and yet but one shal die.

  Me. Although I, father, ought t'obey your hestes,
Yet euill it were in this to yelde your will.

    Cre. Thy wit is wylie for to worke thy wo.   70

    Me. Oh, tender pitie moueth me thereto.

,, *Cre.* A beast is he, that kils himselfe with a knife,
,,Of pitie to preserue an others life.

,, *Me.* Yet wise is he, that doth obey the Gods.

    Cre. The Gods will not the death of any wight.   75

,, *Me.* Whose life they take, they giue him life also.

    Cre. But thou dost striue to take thy life thy selfe.

    Me. Nay them to obey, that will I shall not liue.

    Cre. What fault, O sonne, condemneth thee to death?

,, *Me.* Who liueth (father) here without a fault?   80

    Cre. I see no gylte in thee that death deserues.

    Me. But God it seeth that euery secrete seeth.

    Cre. How shoulde we knowe what is the will of God?

    Me. We knowe it then, when he reueales the same.

    Cre. As though he would come doune to tell it vs,   85

    Me. By diuers meanes his secrets he discloseth.

    Cre. Oh fonde is he, who thinkes to vnderstand
The mysteries of *Ioue* his secrete mynde :
And for to ende this controuersie here,
Loe thus I say, I will we both liue yet :   90
Prepare thee then, my (*) hestes to holde and keepe,   Comaunde-
And pull a downe that stubborne heart of thyne.   ments.

    Me. You may of me, as of your selfe dispose,
And since my life doth seeme so deare to you,
I will preserue the same to your auaile,   95
That I may spende it alwayes to your wil.

    Cre. Then, thee behoues out of this towne to flie :

---

69 euill it were] well were not *MS.* : euil were not Q_1 in this to] to this Q_1 70 thy] this Q_1 72 a] *om. in MS. and* Q_1 73 an] some *MS.*   74 Q_2 *no period at end of line*   92 Q_2 *comma at end of line*

Before the bold and blinde *Tyresias*
Doe publish this that is as yet vnknowne.

 Me. And where, or in what place shall I become? 100
 Cre. Where thou mayste be hence furthest out of sight.
 Me. You may commaunde, and I ought to obey.
 Cre. Go to the lande of *Thesbeoita.*
 Me. Where *Dodona* doth sit in sacred chaire?
 Cre. Euen there my childe. 105
 Me. And who shall guide my wandring steps? *Cre.* high *Ioue.*
 Me. Who shall giue sustenance for my reliefe?
 Cre. There will I send thee heapes of glistring golde.
 Me. But when shall I eftesoones my father see?
 Cre. Ere long I hope : but now, for now depart, 110
For euery lingring let or little stay,
May purchase payne and torment both to me.
 Me. First would I take my conge of the Queene,
That since the day my mother lost hir life,
Hath nourisht me as if I were hir owne. 115
 Cre. Oh, tarry not my deare sonne, tarry not.
    ⟨ *Creon goeth out by the gates Homoloydes.* ⟩
 Me. Beholde father, I goe. You dames of *Thebes,*
Pray to almightie *Ioue* for my retourne :
You see how mine vnhappie starres me driue
To go my countrie fro : and if so chaunce, 120
I ende in woe my pryme and lustie yeares
Before the course of Nature do them call,
Honor my death yet with your drery plaints :
And I shall eke, where so this carkas come,
Pray to the Gods that they preserue this towne. 125
   Meneceus departeth by the gates Electrœ.

 103 *Thesbeoita*] *Thesbrotia MS. Q₁* 116 S.D. *Creon . . . Homo-*
loydes] *MS. Qq put this before line* 116

CHORVS.

WHen she that rules the rolling wheele of chaunce,
    Doth turne aside hir angrie frowning face,
On him, who erst she deigned to aduance,
She neuer leaues to gaulde him with disgrace,
To tosse and turne his state in euery place,   5
Till at the last she hurle him from on high
And yeld him subiect vnto miserie :
    And as the braunche that from the roote is reft,
He neuer winnes like leafe to that he lefte :
    Yea though he do, yet can not tast of ioy   10
Compare with pangs that past in his annoy.

    Well did the heauens ordeine for our behoofe
Necessitie, and fates by them alowde,
That when we see our high mishappes aloofe
(As though our eyes were mufled with a cloude)   15
Our froward will doth shrinke it selfe and shrowde
From our auaile wherwith we runne so farre :
As none amends can make that we do marre :
    Then drawes euill happe & striues to shew his stregth,
And such as yeld vnto his might, at length   20
    He leades them by necessitie the way
That destinie preparde for our decay.

    The Mariner amidde the swelling seas
Who seeth his barke with many a billowe beaten,
Now here, now there, as wind and waues best please,   25
When thundring Ioue with tempest list to threaten,
And dreades in depest gulfe for to be eaten,
Yet learnes a meane by mere necessitie
To saue himselfe in such extremitie :
    For when he seeth no man hath witte nor powre   30
To flie from fate when fortune list to lowre,

---

4 gaulde] galde Q_1 : gall Q_3 9 leafe] *So in* Q_1 ' *Faultes escaped*
correction ': lefe *MS.* : life Q_1 (*text*) Q_2 Q_3 10 not] no *MS.* Q_1 17
farre] faree Q_2

His only hope on mightie Ioue doth caste,
Whereby he winnes the wished heauen at last.

How fond is that man in his fantasie,
Who thinks that Ioue the maker of vs al,   35
And he that tempers all in heauen on high,
The sunne, the mone, the starres celestiall,
So that no leafe without his leaue can fall,
Hath not in him omnipotence also
To guide and gouerne all things here below?   40
    O blinded eies, O wretched mortall wights,
O subiect slaues to euery ill that lights,
    To scape such woe, such paine, such shame and scorne,
Happie were he that neuer had bin borne.

Well might duke *Creon* driuen by destinie,   45
(If true it be that olde *Tyresias* saith)
Redeme our citie from this miserie,
By his consent vnto *Meneceus* death,
Who of himselfe wold faine haue lost his breth :
„But euery man is loth for to fulfill   50
„The heauenly hest that pleaseth not his will.
„That publique weale must needes to ruine go
„Where priuate profite is preferred so.
    Yet mightie God, thy only aide we craue,
This towne from siege, and vs from sorowe saue.   55

Finis Actus tertij.   done by G. Gascoygne.

33 heauen] hauen *MS. Q*₁   42 ill] euill *MS. Q*₁   56 *done by*
G. Gascoygne] *Q*₁ *omits*

The order of the fourth dumbe
shevve.

BEfore the beginning of this fourth Acte, the Trumpets, drummes and fifes sounded, and a greate peale of ordinaunce was shot of: in the which ther entered vpon the stage .vj. knights armed at al points: wherof three came in by the Gates *Electræ*, and the other three by the Gates *Homoloides*: either 5 parte beeing accompanied with .vij. other armed men: and after they had marched twice or thrice about the Stage, the one partie menacing the other by their furious lookes and gestures, the .vj. knights caused their other attendants to stand by, and drawing their Swords, fell to cruell and couragious combate, 10 continuing therein, till two on the one side were slayne. The third perceiuing, that he only remayned to withstand the force of .iij. enimies, did politiquely rūne aside: wherewith immediatly one of the .iij. followed after him, and when he had drawen his enimie thus from his companie, hee turned againe and slewe 15 him. Then the seconde also ranne after him, whom he slewe in like māner, and consequently the thirde, and then triumphantly marched aboute the Stage wyth hys sword in his hand. Hereby was noted the incomparable force of concorde betwene brethren, who as long as they holde togither may not easily by any 20 meanes be ouercome, and being once disseuered by any meanes, are easily ouerthrowen. The history of the brethren *Horatij* & *Curiatij*, who agreed to like combate and came to like ende. After that the dead carkasses were caried from the Stage by the armed men on both parties, and that the victor was trium- 25 phantly accompanied out, also came in a messanger armed from the campe, seeking the Queene, and to hir spake as foloweth.

1-2 the Trumpets . . . fifes] the Trompetts sounded, the droomes and fyfes *MS. Q₁*   20 holde] doo holde *Q₂*

Actus .iiij.   Scena .j.

NVNCIVS.   IOCASTA.

Nuncius commeth in by the gates Homoloides.

O Sage and sober dames, O shamefast maids,
   O faithful seruants of our aged Queene,
Come leade hir forth, sith vnto hir I bring
Such secrete newes as are of great importe.
Come forth, O Queene, surceasse thy wofull plaint,   5
And to my words vouchsafe a willing eare.
   The Queene with hir traine commeth out
      of hir Pallace.
   Ioca. My seruant deare, doest thou yet bring me newes
Of more mishappe? ah werie wretch, alas,
How doth *Eteocles*? whom heretofore
In his encreasing yeares, I wonted ay   10
From daungerous happe with fauoure to defend,
Doth he yet liue? or hath vntimely death
In cruell fight berefte his flowring life?
   Nun. He liues (O Queene) hereof haue ye no doubt,
From such suspecte my selfe will quit you soone.   15
   Ioca. The vētrous Greekes haue haply tane the towne?
   Nun. The Gods forbid.
   Ioca. Our souldiers then, perchance,
Dispersed bene and yelden to the sword.
   Nun. Not so, they were at first in daunger sure,
But in the end obteined victorie.   20
   Ioca. Alas, what then becōmes of *Polynice?*
Oh canst thou tell? is he dead or aliue?
   Nun. You haue (O Queene) yet both your sonnes aliue.
   Ioca. Oh, how my harte is eased of his paine.
Well, then proceede, and briefly let me heare,   25

      9 *Eteocles] Eteocles Q₂*   15 you] ye *MS.*   23 *Q₂ no period at end*
of line   24 his] this *MS. Q₁*

How ye repulst your proud presuming foes,
That thereby yet at least I may assuage
The swelling sorrowes in my dolefull brest,
In that the towne is hitherto preserude :
And for the rest, I trust that mightie *Ioue*   30
Will yeld vs aydc.

   Nun. No soner had your worthy valiant sonne,
Seuerde the Dukes into seauen seuerail partes,
And set them to defence of seuerall gates,
And brought in braue arraye his horssemen out,   35
First to encounter with their mightie foen,
And likewise pitcht, the footemen face to face
Against the footemen of their enimies,
But fiercely straight, the armies did approche,
Swarmıng so thick, as couerde cleane the fieldc,   40
When dreadfull blast of braying trumpets sounde,
Of dolefull drummes, and thundring cannon shot,
Gaue hideous signe of horrour of the fight,
Then gan the *Greekes* to giue their sharpe assaulte,
Then from the walls our stout couragious men,   45
With rolling stones, with paisse of hugie beames,
With flying dartes, with flakes of burning fire,
And deadly blowes, did beate them backe againe :
Thus striuing long, with stout and bloudie fighte,
(Whereby full many thousande slaughtered were)   50
The hardie *Greeks* came vnderneath the walls :
Of whome, first *Capaney* (a lustie Knight)
Did scale the walls, and on the top thereof
Did vaunt himselfe, when many hundred moe,
With fierce assaultes did follow him as fast.   55
Then loe, the Captaines seauen bestirrde themselues,
(Whose names ye haue alreadie vnderstoode)
Some here, some there, nought dreading losse of life,
With newe reliefe to feede the fainting breach :

   30 mightie] *so in MS. and* Q_1: might Q_2: mighty Q_3 50 thousande]
thousandes *MS.*

And *Polynice*, he bended all the force   60
Of his whole charge, against the greatest gate,
When sodenly a flashe of lightning flame
From angrie skies strake captaine *Capaney*
That there downe dead he fell : at sight whereof
The gazers on were fraught with soden feare.   65
The rest, that stroue to mount the walles so fast,
From ladders toppe did headlong tumble downe.
Herewith our men encouragde by good happe,
Toke hardy harts, and so repulst the Grekes.
Ther was *Eteocles*, and I with him,   70
Who setting first those souldiers to their charge,
Ranne streight to thother gates : vnto the weake
He manly comforte gaue : vnto the bold
His lusty words encreased courage still :
In so much as th'amased Grecian king   75
When he did heare of *Capaney* his death,
Fearing thereby the Gods became his foen,
Out from the trench withdrewe his wearie host.
But rashe *Eteocles* (presuming too too much
Vppon their flight) did issue out of *Thebes*,   80
And forwarde straight with strength of chiualrie,
His flying foes couragiously pursude.
Too long it were to make recompt of all
That wounded bene, or slaine, or captiue now :
The cloudy ayre was filled round aboute   85
With houling cries and wofull wayling plaints :
So great a slaughter (O renowmed Queene)
Before this day I thinke was neuer seene.
Thus haue we now cut of the fruitlesse hope
The Grecians had, to sacke this noble towne.   90
What ioyfull end will happen herevnto
Yet know I not : the gods tourne all to good.
„To conquere, lo, is doubtlesse worthy praise,
„But wisely for to vse the conquest gotte,
„Hath euer wonne immortall sound of fame.   95

Well, yet therewhile in this we may reioyce,
Sith heauen and heauenly powers are pleasde therewith.
   Ioca. This good successe was luckie sure, and such,
As for my parte I little loked for :
To saue the towne and eke to haue my sonnes   100
(As you report) preserued yet aliue.
But yet proceede, and further let me know
The finall ende that they agreed vpon.
   Nun. No more (O queene) let this for now suffise,
Sith hitherto your state is safe inough.   105
   Ioca. These words of thine, do whelme my iealous mind
With great suspecte of other mischiefes hidde.
   Nun. What would you more, alredy being sure
That both your sonnes in safetie do remaine ?
   Ioca. I long to know the rest, or good or bad.   110
   Nun. O let me now retourne to *Eteocles*,
That of my seruice greatly stands in neede.
   Ioca. Right well I see, thou doest conceale the woorst.
   Nun. Oh force me not, the good now beeing past,
To tell the yll.   115
   Ioca. Tell it I say, on paine of our displeasure.
   Nun. Since thus ye seeke to heare a dolefull tale,
I will no longer stay : witte ye therefore,
Your desperate sonnes togither be agreed
For to attempt a wicked enterprise :   120
To priuate fight they haue betroutht themselues,
Of which conflicte, the ende must needes be this,
That one do liue, that other die the death.
   Ioca. Alas, alas, this did I euer feare.
   Nun. Now, sith in summe I haue reuealed that,   125
Which you haue heard with great remorse of mind,
I will proceede, at large to tell the whole.
When your victorious sonne, with valiant force
Had chast his foes into their ioyning tents.
Euen there he staide, and straight at sound of trumpe   130

106 do] doth *MS*.   108 you] ye *MS*. Q₁

With stretched voice the herault thus proclaimde :
You princely Greekes, that hither be arriued
To spoile the fruite of these our fertile fields,
And vs to driue from this our Natiue soile,
O suffer not so many giltlesse soules   135
By this debate descend in Stygian lake,
For priuate cause of wicked *Polynice*,
But rather let the brethren, hand to hand,
By mutuall blowes appease their furious rage,
And so to cease from sheding further bloud :   140
And, to the end you all might vnderstand
The profite that to euery side may fall,
Thus much my Lord thought good to profer you,
This is his will, if he be ouercome,
Then *Polynice* to rule this kingly realme :   145
If so it happe (as reason would it should)
Our rightfull prince to conquere *Polynice*,
That then no one of you make more adoo,
But straight to *Argos* Ile hast home againe.
This, thus pronounst vnto the noble Greeks,   150
No soner did the sound of trumpet cease,
But *Polynice* stept forth before the host,
And to these words this answere did he make :
O thou, (not brother) but my mortall foe,
Thy profer here hath pleased me so well,   155
As presently, without more long delay,
I yeld my selfe prepared to the field.
Our noble King no soner heard this vaunt,
But forth as fast he prest his princely steppes,
With eger mind, as hoouering falcon woonts   160
To make hir stoope, when pray appeares in sight :
At all assayes they both were brauely armed,
To eithers side his sword fast being girt,
In eithers hand was put a sturdy launce :
About *Eteocles* our souldiers cloong,   165
To comforte him, and put him then in mind,

He fought for safetie of his country soile,
And that in him consisted all their hope.
To *Polynice* the king *Adrastus* swore,
If he escaped victor from the fielde,　　　　　　　170
At his returne he would in *Greece* erecte
A golden Image vnto mightie *Ioue*
In signe of his triumphing victorie.
But all this while seeke you (O noble queene)
To hinder this your furious sonnes attempte :　　·　175
Intreat the Gods it may not take effecte,
Els must you needes ere long depriued be
Of both your sonnes, or of the one at least.

> *Nuncius returneth to the camp by the gates*
> *Homoloydes.*

IOCASTA.　ANTIGONE.

*A*Ntigone my swete daughter, come forth
Out of this house, that nought but woe retaines,　　180
Come forth I say, not for to sing or daunce,
But to preuent (if in our powers it lie)
That thy malicious brethren (swolne with ire)
And I alas, their miserable mother,
Be not destroide by stroke of dreadfull death.　　185

> *Antigone commeth out of hir mothers Pallace.*

Anti. Ah swete mother, ah my beloued mother,
Alas alas, what cause doth moue ye now
From trembling voice to send such carefull cries?
What painefull pang? what griefe doth gripe you now?

Ioca. O deare daughter, thy most vnhappie brethren　　190
That somctimes lodgde within these wretched loynes
Shall die this day, if *Ioue* preuent it not.

Anti. Alas what say you? alas what do you say?
Can I (alas) endure to see him dead,
Whom I thus long haue sought to see aliue?　　　195

178 s.d. *MS. adds* Nuntius exit　　　189 you] ye *MS.*

Ioca. They both haue vowde (I quake alas to tell)
With trenchant blade to spill eche others blood.

   Antig. O cruell *Eteocles*, ah ruthlesse wretch,
Of this outrage thou only art the cause,
Not *Polynice*, whom thou with hatefull spight   200
Hast reaued first of crowne and countrie soyle,
And now doest seeke to reaue him of his life.

   Ioca. Daughter no more delay, lets go, lets go.

   Anti. Ah my sweete mother, whither shall I go?

   Ioca. With me, deere daughter, to the greekish host.   205

   Anti. Alas how can I go? vnles I go
In daunger of my life, or of good name?

   Ioca. Time serues not now (my well beloued childe)
To way the losse of life or honest name,
But rather to preuent (if so we may)   210
That wicked deede, which only but to thinke,
Doth hale my hart out of my heauie brest.

   Anti. Come then, lets go, good mother let vs go,
But what shall we be able for to doe,
You a weake old woman forworne with yeares,   215
And I God knowes a silly simple mayde?

   Ioca. Our woful wordes, our prayers & our plaintes,
Pourde out with streames of ouerflowing teares,
(Where Nature rules) may happen to preuayle,
When reason, power, and force of armes do fayle.   220
But if the glowing heate of boyling wrath
So furious be, as it may not relent,
Then I atwixt them both will throw my selfe,
And this my brest shal beare the deadly blowes,
That otherwise should light vpon my sonnes :   225
So shall they shead my bloud and not their owne.
Well now deere daughter, let vs hasten hence,
For if in time we stay this raging strife,
Then haply may my life prolonged be :
If ere we come the bloudy deede be done,   230

     198 *Antig.*] *Q*₁ *omits*

Then must my ghost forsake this feeble corps :
And thou, deare childe, with dolour shalt bewaile,
Thy brothers death and mothers all at once.

    Iocasta with Antigone, and all hir traine (excepte the
    Chorus) goeth towards the campe, by the gates Homo-
    loydes.

CHORVS.

WHoso hath felt, what faith and ferueut loue
  A mother beares vnto hir tender sonnes,
She and none other sure, can comprehende
The dolefull griefe, the pangs and secret paine,
That presently doth pierce the princely brest   5
Of our afflicted Queene : alas, I thinke
No martyrdome might well compare with hirs.
So ofte as I recorde hir restlesse state,
Alas me thinkes I feele a shiuering feare
Flit to and fro along my flushing vaines.   10
Alas for ruth, that thus two brethren shoulde,
Enforce themselues to shed each others bloud.
Where are the lawes of nature nowe become ?
Can fleshe of fleshe, alas can bloud of bloud,
So far forget it selfe, as slay it selfe ?   15
O lowring starres, O dimme and angrie skies,
O geltie fate, suche mischiefe set aside.
But if supernall powers decreed haue,
That death must be the ende of this debate,
Alas what floudes of teares shall then suffise,   20
To weepe and waile the neere approching death :
I meane the death of sonnes and mother both,
And with their death the ruine and decay,
Of *Oedipus* and his princely race ?

  1 hath felt] hath ever felt *MS.* faith and] *om. in MS. and* Q_1 7
might] may *MS.* 17 geltie] gilty *MS.* $Q_1 Q_3$

But loe, here *Creon* cōmes with carefull cheare :   25
Tis time that now I ende my iust complaint.

> *Creon commeth in by the gates Homoloydes.*

⟨ *Scena* 2 ⟩

CREON.   NVNCIVS.

Lthough I straightly chargde my tender childe
To flee from *Thebes* for safeguarde of him selfe,
And that long since he parted from my sight,
Yet doe I greatly hang in lingring doubt,
Least passing through the gates, the priuie watch   5
Hath stayed him by some suspect of treason.
And so therewhile, the prophets hauing skride
His hidden fate, he purchast haue the death
Which I by all meanes sought he might eschewe :
And this mischaunce so much I feare the more,   10
How much the wished conquest at the first,
Fell happily vnto the towne of *Thebes*,
,,But wise men ought with patience to sustaine
,,The sundrie haps that slipperie fortune frames.

> *Nuncius commeth in by the gates Electræ.*

Nun. Alas, who can direct my hastie steppes   15
Vnto the brother of our wofull Queene ?
But loe where carefully he standeth here.

Cre. If so the minde may dread his owne mishap,
Then dread I much, this man that seekes me thus,
Hath brought the death of my beloued sonne.   20

Nun. My Lorde, the thing you feare is very true,
Your sonne *Meneceus* no longer liues.

Cre. Alas who can withstand the heauenly powers ?
Well, it beseemes not me, ne yet my yeares,
In bootelesse plaint to wast my wailefull teares :   25
Do thou recount to me his lucklesse deathe,

---

1 chargde] chardgde *MS.*: chargde Q_1 : charge $Q_2 Q_3$ 2 flee] flie
MS. Q_1

The order, forme, and manner of the same.

Nun. Your sonne (my Lorde) came to *Eteocles,*
And tolde him this in presence of the rest :
Renoumed King, neither your victorie,   30
Ne yet the safetie of this princely Realme
In armour doth consist, but in the death
Of me, of me, (O most victorious King)
So heauenly dome of mightie Ioue commaunds.
I (knowing what auayle my death should yeeld   35
Vnto your grace, and vnto natiue land)
Might well be deemde a most vngratefull sonne
Vnto this worthy towne, if I would shunne
The sharpest death to do my countrie good :
In mourning weede now let the vestall Nimphes,   40
With fainyng tunes commend my faultlesse ghost
To highest heauens, while I despoyle my selfe,
That afterwarde (sith *Ioue* will haue it so)
To saue your liues, I may receyue my death,
Of you I craue, O curteous Citizens,   45
To shrine my corps in tombe of marble stone :
Whereon graue this : *Meneceus here doth lie,*
For countries cause that was content to die.
This saide, alas, he made no more a doe,
But drewe his sword, and sheathde it in his brest.   50

Cre. No more, I haue inough, returne ye nowe
From whence ye came.

    Nuncius returneth by the gates Electrae.
Well, since the bloud of my beloued sonne,
Must serue to slake the wrath of angrie *Ioue,*
And since his onely death must bring to *Thebes*   55
A quiet ende of hir vnquiet state,
Me thinkes good reason would, that I henceforth
Of *Thebane* soyle should beare the kingly swaye :
Yea sure, and so I will ere it be long,
Either by right, or else by force of armes.   60

36 Vnto] to my *MS.*   41 fainyng] playnyng *MS.* : fauning Q_1 : faining Q_3

Of al mishap loe here the wicked broode,
My sister first espoused hath hir sonne
That slewe his sire, of whose accursed seede
Two brethren sprang, whose raging hatefull hearts,
By force of boyling yre are bolne so sore   65
As each do thyrst to sucke the others bloude:
But why do I sustaine the smart hereof?
Why should my bloud be spilt for others gilte?
Oh welcome were that messenger to me
That brought me word of both my nephewes deathes: 70
Then should it soone be sene in euery eye,
Twixt prince and prince what difference would appeare,
Then should experience shewe what griefe it is
To serue the humours of vnbridled youth.
Now will I goe for to prepare with speede   75
The funerals of my yong giltlesse sonne,
The which perhaps may be accompanyed
With th'obsequies of proude *Eteocles*.

Any
messèger
is welcome
that
bringeth
tydings of
aduance-
ment.

Creon goeth out by the gates Homoloydes.

Finis   Actus. 4.

CHORVS.

O Blisful concord, bredde in sacred brest
  Of him that guides the restlesse rolling sky,
That to the earth for mans assured rest
From heigth of heauens vouchsafest downe to flie,
In thee alone the mightie power doth lie,   5
With swete accorde to kepe the frouning starres
And euery planet else from hurtfull warres.

In thee, in thee such noble vertue bydes,
As may commaund the mightiest Gods to bend,
From thee alone such sugred frendship slydes   10
As mortall wightes can scarcely comprehend,
To greatest strife thou setst delightfull ende,

O holy peace, by thee are onely founde
The passing ioyes that euery where abound.

Thou onely thou, through thy celestiall might,   15
Didst first of al, the heauenly pole deuide
From th'olde confused heape that *Chaos* hight :
Thou madste the Sunne, the Moone, and starres to glide,
With ordred course about this world so wide :
Thou hast ordainde *Dan Tytans* shining light,   20
By dawne of day to chase the darkesome night.

When tract of time returnes the lustie *Ver.*
By thee alone, the buddes and blossomes spring,
The fieldes with floures be garnisht euery where,
The blooming trees, aboundant fruite do bring,   25
The cherefull birds melodiously do sing,
Thou dost appoint, the crop of sommers seede
For mans reliefe, to serue the winters neede.

Thou doest inspire the heartes of princely peeres
By prouidence, proceeding from aboue,   30
In flowring youth to choose their worthie feeres,
With whome they liue in league of lasting loue,
Till fearefull death doth flitting life remoue,
And loke how fast, to death man payes his due,
So fast againe, doste thou his stocke renue.   35

By thee, the basest thing aduaunced is,
Thou euerie where, dost graffe such golden peace,
As filleth man, with more than earthly blisse,
The earth by thee, doth yelde hir swete increase
At becke of thee, all bloudy discords cease,   40
And mightiest Realmes in quiet do remaine,
Wheras thy hand doth holde the royall raine.

But if thou faile, then al things gone to wracke,
The mother then, doth dread hir naturall childe,
Then euery towne is subiect to the sacke,   45

42 raine] raigne *MS.*

Then spotlesse maids, the virgins be defilde,
Then rigor rules, then reason is exilde :
And this, thou wofull *Thebes*, to our great paine,
With present spoile, art likely to sustaine.

Me thinke I heare the wailfull weeping cries   50
Of wretched dames, in euerie coast resound,
Me thinkes I see, how vp to heauenly skies
From battred walls, the thundring clappes rebound,
Me thinke I heare, how all things go to ground,
Me thinke I see, how souldiers wounded lye   55
With gasping breath, and yet they can not dye.

By meanes wherof, oh swete *Meneceus* he,
That giues for countries cause his guiltlesse life,
Of others all, most happy shall he be :
His ghost shall flit from broiles of bloudy strife   60
To heauenly blisse, where pleasing ioyes be rife :
And would to God, that this his fatall ende
From further plagues, our citie might defend.

O sacred God, giue eare vnto thy thrall,
That humbly here vpon thy name doth call,   65
O let not now, our faultlesse bloud be spilt,
For hote reuenge of any others gilt.
                    Finis Actus quarti.

                Done by F. Kinwelmarshe.

46 the] then *Q*₁   50, 54, 55 Me thinke *Qq* : Me thinks *MS*.

The order of the laste dumbe
shevve.

Irst the Stillpipes sounded a very mournful melody, in
which time came vpon the Stage a womã clothed in a
white garment, on hir head a piller, double faced, the formost
face fair & smiling, the other behinde blacke & louring, muffled
with a white laune about hir eyes, hir lap ful of Jewelles, sitting 5
in a charyot, hir legges naked, hir fete set vpŏ a great roũd bal,
& beyng drawẽ in by .iiij. noble personages, she led in a string
on hir right hand .ij. kings crowned, and in hir lefte hand .ij.
poore slaues very meanly attyred.   After she was drawen about
the stage, she stayed a lĭttle, changing the kings vnto the left 10
handc & the slaues vnto the right hand, taking the crownes
from the kings heads she crowned therwith the ij. slaues, &
casting the vyle clothes of the slaues vpon the kings, she
despoyled the kings of their robes, and therwith apparelled thc
slaues.   This done, shc was drawen eftsones about the stage 15
in this order, and then departed, leauing vnto vs a plaine Type
or figure of vnstable fortune, who dothe oftentimos raise to
heigthe of dignitie the vile and vnnoble, and in like manner
throweth downe frõ the place of promotiõ, euen those whŏ
before she hir selfe had thither aduaunced: after hir departure 20
came in Duke *Creon* with foure gentlemen wayting vpon him
and lamented the death of *Meneceus* his sonne in this maner.

Actus .v. Scena .1.
CREON.   CHORVS.

A Las what shall I do? bemone my selfe?
Or rue the ruine of my Natiue lande,
About the which such cloudes I see enclosde.
As darker cannot couer dreadfull hell.

3 on] and on Q_3
Actus .v.] *So in MS. and* Q_1 : *misprinted iii in* Q_2 *and* Q_3

With mine own eyes I saw my own deare sonne   5
All gorde with bloud of his too bloudy brest,
Which he hath shed full like a friend, too deare
To his countrey, and yet a cruell foe
To me, that was his friend and father both.
Thus to him selfe he gaynde a famous name,   10
And glory great, to me redoubled payne :
Whose haplesse death in my afflicted house,
Hath put suche playnt, as I ne can espie
What comfort might acquiet their distresse.
I hither come my sister for to seeke,   15
Iocasta, she that might in wofull wise
Amid hir high and ouerpining cares,
Prepare the baynes for his so wretched corps,
And eke for him that nowe is not in life,
May pay the due that to the dead pertaynes,   20
And for the honor he did well deserue,
To giue some giftes vnto infernall Gods.
    Cho. My Lorde, your sister is gone forth long since,
Into the campe, and with hir *Antigone*,
Hir daughter deare.   25
    Cre. Into the campe? alas and what to do?
    Cho. She vnderstoode, that for this realme foorthwith
Hir sonnes were greed in combate for to ioyne.
    Cre. Alas, the funerals of my deare sonne
Dismayed me so, that I ne did receiue,   30
Ne seeke to knowe these newe vnwelcome newes.
But loe, beholde a playne apparant signe
Of further feares : the furious troubled lookes
Of him that commeth heere so hastilye.

    23 My Lorde, your sister is] Your sister is, my lord *MS*.   24 with
hir *Antigone*] Antigone with her *MS*.

Scena. 2.

NVNCIVS.　CREON.　CHORVS.

ALas, alas, what shall I doe? alas,
What shriching voyce may serue my wofull wordes?
O wretched I, ten thousande times a wretch,
The messanger of dread and cruell death !

Cre. Yet more mishap? and what vnhappie newes :　　　5
Nun. My Lord, your nephues both haue lost their liues.

Cre. Out and alas, to me and to this towne,
Thou doest accompt great ruine and decay,
You royall familie of *Oedipus* :
And heare you this? your liege and soueraigne Lordes　　10
The brethren both are slayne and done to death.

Cho. O cruell newes, most cruell that can come,
O newes that might these stony walles prouoke
For tender ruthe to brust in bitter teares,
And so they would, had they the sense of man.　　　15

Cre. O worthy yong Lordes, that vnworthy were　　Cesers
Of such vnworthy death, O me moste wretch.　　tears.

Nun. More wretched shall ye deeme your selfe, my lord,
When you shall heare of further miserie.

Cre. And can there be more miserie than this?　　20
Nun. With hir deare sonnes the queene hir self is slaine.

Cho. Bewayle ladies, alas good ladies waile,
This harde mischaunce, this cruell common euill,
Ne hencefoorth hope for euer to reioyce.

Cre. Oh *Iocasta*, miserable mother,　　25
What haplesse ende thy life alas hath hent?
Percase the heauens purueyed had the same,
Moued therto by the wicked wedlocke
Of *Oedipus* thy sonne yet might thy scuse
But iustly made, that knewe not of the crime.　　30
But tell me messanger, oh tell me yet

4 *Q₂ no stop at end of line*　　14 brust] burst *MS. Q₁*

We harken
somtimes
willingly
to wofull
news.

The death of these two brethren, driuen therto,

Not thus all onely by their drearie fate,

But by the banning and the bitter cursse

Of their cruell sire, borne for our annoy,   35

And here on earth the onely soursse of euill.

    Nun. Then know my Lorde, the battell that begonne

Vnder the walles, was brought to luckie ende.

Eteocles had made his foemen flee

Within their trenches, to their foule reproche :   40

But herewithall the brethren both straightway

Eche other chalenge foorth into the fielde,

By combate so to stinte their cruell strife,

Who armed thus amid the fielde appeard,

First *Polynice* turning toward Greece   45

His louely lookes, gan *Iuno* thus beseeche :

O heauenly queene, thou seest, that since the day

I first did wedde *Adrastus* daughter deare,

And stayde in Greece, thy seruant haue I bene :

Then (be it not for mine vnworthinesse)   50

Graunt me this grace, the victorie to winne,

Graunt me, that I with high triumphant hande,

May bathe this blade within my brothers brest :

I know I craue vnworthy victorie,

Vnworthy triumphes, and vnworthy spoyles,   55

Lo he the cause, my cruell enimie.

The people wept to heare the wofull wordes

Of *Polynice*, foreseeing eke the ende

Of this outrage and cruell combate tane,

Eche man gan looke vpon his drouping mate,   60

With mindes amazed, and trembling hearts for dread,

Whom pitie perced for these youthfull knightes.

Eteocles with eyes vp cast to heauen,

Thus sayde :

O mightie *Ioue* his daughter graunt to me,   65
That this right hande with this sharpe armed launce
(Passing amid my brothers cankred brest,)
It may eke pierce that cowarde hart of his,
And so him slea that thus vnworthily
Disturbes the quiet of our common weale.   70
So sayde *Eteocles*, and trumpets blowne,
To sende the summons of their bloudy fighte,
That one the other fiercely did encounter,
Like Lions two yfraught with boyling wrath,
Bothe couch their launces full agaynst the face,   75
But heauen it *nolde that there they should them teinte :   *would
Vpon the battred shields the mightie speares   not.
Are bothe yhroke, and in a thousande shiuers
Amid the ayre flowne vp into the heauens :
Beholde agayne, with naked sworde in hande,   80
Eche one the other furiously assaultes.
Here they of *Thebes*, there stoode the *Greekes* in doubt,
Of whom doth eche man feele more chilling dread,
Least any of the twayne should lose his life,
Than any of the twayne did feele in fight.   85
Their angrie lookes, their deadly daunting blowes,
Might witnesse well, that in their heartes remaynde
As cankred hate, disdayne, and furious moode,
As euer bred in beare or tygers brest.
The first that hapt to hurt was *Polinice*,   90
Who smote the righte thighe of *Eteocles* :
But as we deeme, the blow was nothing deepe,
Then cryed the Greekes, and lepte with lightned harts,
But streight agayne they helde their peace, for why?
Eteocles gan thrust his wicked sworde   95
In the lefte arme of vnarmed *Pollinice*,
And let the bloud from bare vnfenced fleshe,

72 sende] sounde Q_3 79 flowne] flewe *MS.*   80 sworde] swords
Q_3 84 Least] Lest Q_3 92 nothing] not too *MS.*   94 why]
he *MS.* Q_1 : (?) *omitted*   97 bare] thinne *MS.* Q_1

With falling drops distill vpon the ground,
Ne long he stayes, but with an other thrust
His brothers belly boweld with his blade,   100
Then wretched he, with bridle left at large,
From of his horsse fell pale vpon the ground,
Ne long it was, but downe our duke dismountes
From of his startling steede, and runnes in hast,
His brothers haplesse helme for to vnlace,   105
And with such hungry minde desired spoyle,
(As one that thought the fielde already woonne)
That at vnwares, his brothers dagger drawne,
And griped fast within the dying hand,
Vnder his side he recklesse doth receiue,   110
That made the way to his wyde open hart.
Thus falles *Eteocles* his brother by,
From both whose breasts the bloud fast bubling, gaue
A sory shewe to Greekes and *Thebanes* both.
   Cho. Oh wretched ende of our vnhappie Lordes.   115
   Cre. Oh *Oedipus*, I must bewaile the death
Of thy deare sonnes, that were my nephewes both,
But of these blowes thou oughtest feele the smarte,
That with thy wonted prayers, thus hast brought
Such noble blouds to this vnnoble end.   120
But now tell on, what followed of the Queene?
   Nun. Whē thus with pierced harts, by their owne hands
The brothers fell and wallowed in their bloud,
(That one still tumbling on the others gore)
Came their afflicted mother, then to late,   125
And eke with hir, chast childe *Antygone*,
Who saw no sooner how their fates had falne,
But with the doubled echo of alas,
She dymmde the ayre with loude complaints and cryes:
Oh sonnes (quod she) too late came all my helpe,   130

106 desired] gan mynde the *MS.*   122 pierced] piecced *Q₂*   123
and] had *Q₁*   124 That one still] Th one *MS. Q₁*   126 hir] her,
her *MS. Q₁*   129 She dymmde] sore dymmed *MS. Q₁*

And all to late haue I my succour sent :
And with these wordes, vpon their carcas colde
She shriched so, as might haue stayed the Sunne
To mourne with hir : the wofull sister eke,
(That both hir chekes did bathe in flowing teares)   135
Out from the depth of hir tormented brest,
With scalding sighes gan draw these weary words,
O my deare brethren, why abandon ye
Our mother deare, when these hir aged yeares,
(That of themselues are weake and growne with griefc,)   140
Stoode most in neede of your sustaining helpe ?
Why doe you leaue hir thus disconsolate ?
At sounde of such hir weeping long lament,
Eteocles our king helde vp his hand,
And sent from bottome of his wofull brest   145
A doubled sighe, deuided with his griefe,
In faithfull token of his feeble will
To recomfort his mother and sister both :
And in (the) steade of sweete contenting words,
The trickling teares raynde downe his paled chekes :   150
Then claspt his hands, and shut his dying eyes.
But *Polynice*, that turned his rolling eyen
Vnto his mother and his sister deare,
With hollow voyce and fumbling toung, thus spake :
Mother, you see how I am now arryued   155
Vnto the hauen of mine vnhappie ende :
Now nothing doth remaine to me, but this,
That I lament my sisters life and yours,
Left thus in euerlasting woe and griefe :
So am I sory for *Eteocles*,   160
Who though he were my cruell enimie,
He was your sonne, and brother yet to me :
But since these ghostes of ours must needes go downe

133 shriched] shriked *MS.*   140 themselues] themselnes *Q₂*   142
you] ye *MS.*   149 the] *only in MS. and Q₁*   156 hauen *MS.*
Q₁ Q₃ : heauen *Q₂*

With staggring steppes into the *Stigian* reigne,
I you besech, mother and sister bothe,   165
Of pitie yet, that you will me procure
A royall tombe within my natiue realme :
And nowe shut vp with those your tender handes,
These grieffull eyes of mine, whose dazeled light
Shadowes of dreadfull death be come to close.   170
Now rest in peace, this sayde, he yeelded vp
His fainting ghost, that ready was to part.
The mother thus beholding both hir sonnes
Ydone to death, and ouercome with dole,
Drewe out the dagger of hir *Pollinice*,   175
From brothers brest, and gorde therewyth her throte.
Falling betweene hir sonnes :
Then with hir feebled armes, she doth enfolde
Their bodies both, as if for company
Hir vncontented corps were yet content   180
To passe with them in *Charons* ferrie boate.
When cruell fate had thus with force bereft
The wofull mother and hir two deare sonnes,
All sodenly allarme, allarme, they crye,
And hote conflict began for to aryse   185
Betwene our armie and our enemyes :
For either part would haue the victorye.
A while they did with equall force maintaine
The bloudy fight, at last the Greekes do flie,
Of whom could hardly any one escape,   190
For in such hugie heapes our men them slew.
The ground was couerde all with carcases :
And of our souldiers, some gan spoyle the dead,
Some other were that parted out the pray,
And some pursuing.   *Antigone* toke vp   195
The Queene *Iocasta*, and the brethren both,
Whom in a chariot hither they will bring

---

175 *Pollinice*] *Pollinices* Q_1 176 therewyth her] their mothers *MS*.
178 enfolde *MS*. Q_1 : vnfolde $Q_2 Q_3$

Ere long : and thus, although we gotten haue
The victory ouer our enemies,
Yet haue we lost much more than we haue wonne.   200

Creon exit.

Cho. O hard mishap, we doe not onely heare
The wearie newes of their vntimely death,
But eke we must with wayling eyes beholde
Their bodies deade, for loke where they be brought.

Scena. 3.

ANTIGONE. CHORVS.

MOst bitter plaint, O ladies, vs behoues
Behoueth eke not onely bitter plainte,
But that our heares dysheuylde from our heades
About our shoulders hang, and that our brests
With bouncing blowes be all bebattered,
Our gastly faces with our nayles defaced :
Behold, your Queene twixt both hir sonnes lyes slayne,
The Queene whom you did loue and honour both,
The Queene that did so tenderly bring vp
And nourishe you, eche one like to hir owne,   10
Now hath she left you all (O cruell hap)
With hir too cruell death in dying dreade,
Pyning with pensifenesse without all helpe.
O weary life, why bydste thou in my breast
And I contented be that these mine eyes   15
Should see hir dye that gaue to me this life,
And I not venge hir death by losse of life ?
Who can me giue a fountaine made of mone,
That I may weepe as muche as is my will,
To sowsse this sorow vp in swelling teares ?   20

Cho. What stony hart could leaue for to lament ?
Anti. O *Polinice*, now hast thou with thy bloud

5 bebattered] to battered *MS.*

L 2

Bought all too deare the title to this realme,
That cruell he *Eteocles* thee refte,
And now also hath reft thee of thy life,   25
Alas, what wicked dede can wrath not doe?
And out alas for mee.
Whyle thou yet liuedst, I had a liuely hope
To haue some noble wight to be my pheere,
By whome I might be crownde a royall Queene :   30
But now, thy hastie death hath done to dye
This dying hope of mine, that hope hencefoorth
None other wedlocke, but tormenting woe,
If so these trembling hands for cowarde dread
Dare not presume to ende this wretched life.   35
     Cho. Alas deare dame, let not thy raging griefe
Heape one mishap vpon anothers head.
     Anti. O dolefull day, wherein my sory sire
Was borne, and yet O more vnhappie houre
When he was crowned king of stately *Thebes*.   40
The *Hymenei* in vnhappie bed,
And wicked wedlocke, wittingly did ioyne,
The giltlesse mother with hir giltie sonne,
Out of which roote we be the braunches borne,
To beare the scourge of their so foule offence :   45
And thou, O father, thou that for this facte,
Haste torne thine eyes from thy tormented head,
Giue eare to this, come foorth, and bende thine eare
To bloudie newes, that canst not them beholde :
Happie in that, for if thine eyes could see   50
Thy sonnes bothe slayne, and euen betweene them bothe
Thy wife and mother dead, bathed and imbrude
All in one bloud, then wouldst thou dye for dole,
And so might ende all our vnluckie stocke.
But most vnhappie nowe, that lacke of sighte   55
Shall linger life within thy lucklesse brest,

     28 liuedst] lived *MS*.   40 *Q₂ no period at end of line*   50 that]
this *MS*. *Q₁*

And still tormented in suche miserie,
Shall alwayes dye, bicause thou canst not dye.

Oedipus entreth.

Scena. 4.

OEDIPVS. ANTIGONE. CHORVS.

WHy dost thou call out of this darkesome denne,
    (The lustlesse lodge of my lamenting yeres,)
(O daughter deare) thy fathers blinded eyes,
Into the light I was not worthy of?
Or what suche sight (O cruell destenie)   5
Without tormenting cares might I beholde,
That image am of deathe and not of man?
  Anti. O father mine, I bring vnluckie newes
Vnto your eares, your sonnes are nowe both slayne
Ne doth your wife (that wonted was to guyde   10
So piteously your staylesse stumbling steppes)
Now see this light, alas and welaway.
  Oed. O heape of infinite calamities,
And canst thou yet encrease when I thought least
That any griefe more great could grow in thee?   15
But tell me yet, what kinde of cruell death
Had these three sory soules?
  Anti. Without offence to speake, deare father mine
The lucklesse lotte, the frowarde frowning fate
That gaue you life to ende your fathers life,   20
Haue ledde your sonnes to reaue eche others life.
  Oed. Of them I thought no lesse, but tell me yet
What causelesse death hath caught from me my deare,
(What shall I call hir) mother or my wife?
  Anti. When as my mother sawe hir deare sonnes dead,   25
As pensiue pangs had prest hir tender heart,
With bloudlesse cheekes and gastly lookes she fell,

58 thou] thon Q_2 s.d. *Oedipus entreth*] *Oedipus intrat MS.*

Drawing the dagger from *Eteocles* side,
She gorde hirselfe with wide recurelesse wounde :
And thus, without mo words, gaue vp the ghost,　　　30
Embracing both hir sonnes with both hir armes.
In these affrightes this frosen heart of mine,
By feare of death maynteines my dying life.

   Cho. This drearie day is cause of many euils,
Poore *Oedipus*, vnto thy progenie,　　　35
The Gods yet graunt it may become the cause
Of better happe to this afflicted realme.

Scena. 5.

CREON.　OEDIPVS.　ANTIGONE.

GOod Ladies leaue your bootelesse vayne complaynt,
  Leaue to lament, cut off your wofull cryes,
High time it is as now for to prouide
The funerals for the renowmed king :
And thou *Oedipus* hearken to my wordes,　　　5
And know thus muche, that for thy daughters dower,
Antigone with *Hemone* shall be wedde.
Thy sonne our king not long before his death
Assigned hath the kingdome should descende
To me, that am his mothers brother borne,　　　10
And so the same might to my sonne succeede.
Now I that am the lorde and king of *Thebes*,
Will not permit that thou abide therein :
Ne maruell yet of this my heady will,
Ne blame thou me, for why, the heauens aboue　　　15
(Which onely rule the rolling life of man,)
Haue so ordeynde, and that my words be true,
Tyresias he that knoweth things to come,
By trustie tokens hath foretolde the towne,
That while thou didst within the walles remayne,　　　20

    37 *MS. adds* S.D. *Creon intrat*
    7 shall be] shall *altered in a later hand to* to be *MS.* : shall Q_1

It should be plagued still with penurie :
Wherfore departe, and thinke not that I speake
These wofull wordes for hate I beare to thee,
But for the weale of this afflicted realme.

Oedipus. O foule accursed fate, that hast me bredde   25
To beare the burthen of the miserie
Of this colde death, which we accompt for life :
Before my birth my father vnderstoode
I should him slea, and scarcely was I borne,
When he me made a pray for sauage beastes.   30
But what ? I slew him yet, then caught the crowne,
And last of all defilde my mothers bedde,
By whom I haue this wicked offspring got :
And to this heinous crime and filthy facte
The heauens haue from highe enforced mo,   35
Agaynst whose doome no counsell can preuayle.
Thus hate I now my life, and last of all,
Lo by the newes of this so cruell death
Of bothe my sonnes and deare beloued wife,
Mine angrie constellation me commaundes   40
Withouten eyes to wander in mine age,
When these my weery, weake, and crooked limmes
Haue greatest neede to craue their quiet rest.
O cruell *Creon*, wilt thou slea me so,
For cruelly thou doste but murther me,   45
Out of my kingdome now to chase me thus :
Yet can I not with humble minde beseeche
Thy curtesie, ne fall before thy feete.
Let fortune take from me these worldly giftes,
She can not conquere this courageous heart,   50
That neuer yet could well be ouercome,
To force me yeelde for feare to villanie :
Do what thou canst I will be *Oedipus*.

Cre. So hast thou reason *Oedipus*, to say,
And for my parte I would thee counsell eke,   55

21 plagued] plagned Q_2 26 of] *altered in MS. to* and

Still to maynteine the high and hawtie minde,
That hath bene euer in thy noble heart :
For this be sure, if thou wouldst kisse these knees,
And practise eke by prayer to preuayle,
No pitie coulde persuade me to consent   60
That thou remayne one onely houre in *Thebes.*
And nowe, prepare you worthie Citizens,
The funeralls that duely doe pertayne
Vnto the Queene, and to *Eteocles,*
And eke for them prouide their stately tombes.   65
But *Pollynice,* as common enimie
Vnto his countrey, carrie foorth his corps
Out of the walles, ne none so hardie be
On peine of death his bodie to engraue,
But in the fieldes let him vnburied lye,   70
Without his honour, and without complaynte,
An open praie for sauage beastes to spoyle.
And thou *Antigone,* drie vp thy teares,
Plucke vp thy sprites, and cheere thy harmelesse hearte
To mariage : for ere these two dayes passe,   75
Thou shalt espouse *Hemone* myne onely heire.
    Antig. Father, I see vs wrapt in endlesse woe,
And nowe much more doe I your state lamente,
Than these that nowe be dead, not that I thinke
Theyr greate missehappes too little to bewayle,   80
But this, that you (you onely) doe surpasse
All wretched wightes that in this worlde remayne.
But you my Lorde, why banishe you with wrong
My father thus out of his owne perforce ?
And why will you denye these guiltlesse bones   85
Of *Polinice,* theyr graue in countrey soyle ?
    Creon. So would not I, so woulde *Eteocles.*
    Anti. He cruel was, you fonde to hold his hestes.
    Creon. Is then a fault to doe a kings cõmaund ?
    Anti. When his cõmaunde is cruell and vniust.   90

57 euer] euen Q_1

Creon. Is it vniust that he vnburied be?

Anti. He not deseru'd so cruel punishment.

Creon. He was his countreys cruell enimie.

Anti. Or else was he that helde him from his right.

Cre. Bare he not armes against his natiue land? 95

Anti. Offendeth he that sekes to winne his owne?

Cre. In spite of thee he shall vnburied be.

Anti. In spite of thee these hands shall burie him.

Cre. And with him eke then will I burie thee.

Anti. So graunt the gods, I get none other graue, 100
Then with my *Polinices* deare to rest.

Cre. Go sirs, lay holde on hir, and take hir in.

Anti. I will not leaue this corps vnburied.

Cre. Canst thou vndoe the thing that is decreed?

Anti. A wicked foule decree to wrong the dead. 105

Cre. The ground ne shall ne ought to couer him.

Anti. *Creon*, yet I beseche thee for the loue,

Cre. Away I say, thy prayers not prcuaile.

Anti. That thou didst beare *Iocasta* in hir life,

Cre. Thou dost but waste thy words amid the wind. 110

Anti. Yet graunt me leaue to washe his wounded corps.

Cre. It can not be that I should graunt thee so.

Anti. O my deare *Polinice*, this tirant yet
With all his wrongfull force can not fordoe,
But I will kisse these colde pale lippes of thine, 115
And washe thy wounds with my waymenting teares.

She
sheweth yᵉ
frutes of
true kyndly
loue.

Cre. O simple wench, O fonde and foolishe girle,
Beware, beware, thy teares do not foretell
Some signe of hard mishap vnto thy mariage.

Anti. No, no, for *Hemone* will I neuer wed. 120

Cre. Dost thou refuse the mariage of my sonne?

Anti. I will nor him, nor any other wed.

Cre. Against thy will then must I thee constraine.

Anti. If thou me force, I sweare thou shalt repent.

Cre. What canst thou cause that I should once repent? 125

97, 98 In spite of] Perforce to *MS. Q*₁   114 wrongfull] worongfull *Q*₂

Anti. With bloudy knife I can this knot vnknit.

Cre. And what a foole were thou to kill thy selfe?

Anti. I will ensue some worthie womans steppes.

Cre. Speake out *Antigone*, that I may heare.

Anti. This hardie hande shall soone dispatch his life.　　130

Cre. O simple foole, and darste thou be so bolde?

Anti. Why should I dread to do so doughtie deed?

Cre. And wherfore dost thou wedlocke so despise?

Anti. In cruel exile for to folow him.　　(*pointing to* Oedipus

Cre. What others might beseeme, beseemes not thee.　　135

Anti. If neede require with him eke will I die.

Cre. Departe, departe, and with thy father die,

Rather than kill my childe with bloudie knife :

Go hellish monster, go out of the towne.

　　　　　　　　　　　　　　Creon exit.

Oed. Daughter, I must commende thy noble heart.　　140

The duty　　*Anti.* Father, I will not liue in companie

of a childe　And you alone wander in wildernesse.

truly per-

fourmed.　　*Oed.* O yes deare daughter, leaue thou me alone

Amid my plagues : be merrie while thou maist.

Anti. And who shal guide these aged feete of yours,　　145

That banisht bene, in blinde necessitie?

Oed. I will endure, as fatal lot me driues :

Resting these crooked sorie sides of mine

Where so the heauens shall lend me harborough.

And in exchange of rich and stately towers,　　150

The woodes, the wildernesse, the darkesome dennes,

Shall be the bowre of mine vnhappie bones.

Anti. O father now where is your glorie gone?

„ *Oed.* One happie day did raise me to renoune,

„One haplesse day hath throwne mine honour doune.　　155

Anti. Yet will I beare a part of your mishappes.

Oed. That sitteth not amid thy pleasant yeares.

　　130 his] my *MS.*　　134 *pointing to* Oedipus] *MS. omits*　　139 S.D.
Creon exit] *MS. omits*　　141 not liue] neuer come *MS. Q₁　(margin)* The
... perfourmed] *Q₃ omits*　　147 *Oed.*] *MS. omits*　　157 sitteth] fitteth *Q₂*

„ *Anti*. Deare father yes, let youth giue place to age.

Oed. Where is thy moother? let me touch hir face, ·

That with these handes I may yet feele the harme   160

That these blinde eyes forbid me to beholde.

    Anti. Here father, here hir corps, here put your hande.

    Oed. O wife, O moother, O both wofull names,

O wofull mother, and O wofull wyfe,

O woulde to God, alas, O woulde to God   165

Thou nere had bene my mother, nor my wyfe.

But where lye nowe the paled bodies two,

Of myne vnluckie sonnes, Oh where be they?

    Anti. Lo here they lye one by an other deade.

    Oedip. Stretch out this hand, dere daughter, stretch this

Vpon their faces.   (hande   170

    Anti. Loe father, here, lo, nowe you touche them both.

    Oedi. O bodies deare, O bodies dearely boughte

Vnto your father, bought with high missehap.

    Anti. O louely name of my deare *Pollinice*,   175

Why can I not of cruell *Creon* craue,

Ne with my death nowe purchase thee a graue?

    Oedi. Nowe commes *Apollos* oracle to passe,

That I in *Athens* towne should end my dayes:

And since thou doest, O daughter myne, desire   180

In this exile to be my wofull mate,

Lende mee thy hande, and let vs goe togither.

    Anti. Loe, here all prest my deare beloued father,

A feeble guyde, and eke a simple scowte,

To passe the perills in a doubtfull waye.   185

    Oedi. Vnto the wretched, be a wretched guyde.

    Anti. In this all onely equall to my father.

    Oedi. And where shall I sette foorth my trembling feete?

O reache mee yet some surer staffe, to steye

My staggryng pace amidde these wayes vnknowne.   190

    Anti. Here father here, and here set forth your feete.   She giueth

    Oedi. Nowe can I blame none other for my harmes   him a

                                                staffe, and

           185 in a] of our *MS*.   187 all onely] alonly *Q*₃

*stayeth
hym hir
self also.*

But secrete spight of foredecreed fate,
Thou arte the cause, that crooked, olde and blynde,
I am exilde farre from my countrey soyle,   195
And suffer dole that I ought not endure.

*Iustice
sleepeth.*

  „ *Anti.* O father, father, Iustice lyes on sleepe,
„Ne doth regarde the wrongs of wretchednesse,
„Ne princes swelling pryde it doth redresse.

*A Glasse
for brittel
Beutie and
for lusty
limmes.*

    Oedi. O carefull caytife, howe am I nowe changd   200
From that I was? I am that *Oedipus*,
That whylome had triumphant victorie
And was bothe dread and honored eke in *Thebes* :
But nowe (so pleaseth you my frowarde starres)
Downe headlong hurlde in depth of myserie,   205
So that remaynes of *Oedipus* no more
As nowe in mee, but euen the naked name,
And lo, this image, that resembles more
Shadowes of death, than shape of *Oedipus.*

    Antig. O father, nowe forgette the pleasaunt dayes   210
And happie lyfe that you did whylom leade,
The muse whereof redoubleth but your griefe :
Susteyne the smarte of these your present paynes
With pacience, that best may you preserue.
Lo where I come, to liue and die with you,   215
Not (as sometymes) the daughter of a king,
But as an abiect nowe in pouertie,
That you, by presence of suche faithfull guide,
May better beare the wrecke of miserie.

    Oedi. O onely comforte of my cruell happe.   220

    Anti. Your daughters pitie is but due to you?
Woulde God I might as well ingraue the corps
Of my deare *Pollinice,* but I ne maye,
And that I can not, doubleth all my dole.

    Oedi. This thy desire, that is both good and iuste,   225
Imparte to some that be thy trustie frendes,

   197 (*margin*) **Iustice sleepeth**] *Q₂ puts this side-note two lines lower*
212 your *MS. Q₁ Q₃* : you *Q₂*

Who movde with pitie, maye procure the same.
„ *Anti.* Beleeue me father, when dame fortune frownes,
„Be fewe that fynde trustie companions.

    Oedi. And of those fewe, yet one of those am **I** :   230
Wherefore, goe we nowe daughter, leade the way :
Into the stonie rockes and highest hilles,
Where fewest trackes of steppings may be spyde.
„Who once hath sit in chaire of dignitie,
„May shame to shewe himself in miserie.   235

    Anti. From thee, O countrey, am I forst to parte,
Despoiled thus in flower of my youth,
And yet I leaue within my enimies rule,
Ismene my infortunate sister.

    Oed. Deare citizens, beholde your Lord and King   240
That *Thebes* set in quiet gouernmont,   A mirrour
                                          for Magi-
Now as you see, neglected of you all,   strates.
And in these ragged ruthfull weedes bewrapt,
Ychased from his natiue countrey soyle,
Betakes himself (for so this tirant will)   245
To euerlasting banishment : but why
Do I lament my lucklesse lot in vaine ?
„Since euery man must beare with quiet minde,
„The fate that heauens haue earst to him assignde.

CHORVS.

EXample here, loe take by *Oedipus,*
   You Kings and Princes in prosperitie,
And euery one that is desirous
To sway the seate of worldlie dignitie,
How fickle tis to trust in Fortunes whele :   5
For him whome now she hoyseth vp on hie,
If so he chaunce on any side to reele,
She hurles him downe in twinkling of an eye :
And him againe, that grovleth nowe on ground,

      5 tis] is *MS. Q*₁

And lieth lowe in dungeon of dispaire,   10
Hir whirling wheele can heaue vp at a bounde,
And place aloft in stay of statelie chaire.
As from the Sunne the Moone withdrawes hir face,
So might of man doth yeelde dame Fortune place.

    Finis Actus quinti.   Done by G. Gascoigne.   15

Epilogus.

LO here the fruit of high-aspiring minde,
    Who weenes to mount aboue the moouing Skies :
Lo here the trap that titles proud do finde,
See, ruine growes, when most we reach to rise :
Sweete is the name, and statelie is the raigne   5
Of kinglie rule, and swey of royall seate,
But bitter is the tast of Princes gaine,
When climbing heades do hunte for to be great.
Who would forecast the banke of restlesse toyle,
Ambitious wightes do freight their brestes withall,   10
The growing cares, the feares of dreadfull foyle,
To yll successe that on such flightes doth fall,
He would not streyne his practize to atchieue
The largest limits of the mightiest states.
But oh, what fansies sweete do still relieue   15
The hungrie humor of these swelling hates ?
What poyson sweet inflameth high desire ?
Howe soone the hautie heart is pufft with pride ?
Howe soone is thirst of sceptre set on fire ?
Howe soone in rising mindes doth mischief slide ?   20
What bloudie sturres doth glut of honor breede ?

    15 Done by G. Gascoigne Q_1 *omits*
    12 To yll] The euill *MS.* Q_1 doth] do *MS.* Q_1 21 breede]
yelde Q_3

Thambitious sonne doth oft surpresse his sire :
Where natures power vnfained loue should spread,
There malice raignes and reacheth to be higher.
O blinde vnbridled search of Souereintie,   25
O tickle traine of euill attayned state,
O fonde desire of princelie dignitie,
Who climbes too soone, he oft repentes too late.
The golden meane, the happie doth suffise,
They leade the posting day in rare delight,   30
They fill (not feede) their vncontented eyes,
They reape such rest as doth beguile the night,
They not enuie the pompe of haughtie traine,
Ne dreade the dinte of proude vsurping swoorde,
But plaste alowe, more sugred ioyes attaine,   35
Than sway of loftie Scepter can afoorde.
Cease to aspire then, ccase to soare so hie,
And shunne the plague that pierceth noble breastes.
To glittring courtes what fondnesse is to flie,
When better state in baser Towers rests?   40

Finis Epilogi.   Done by Chr. Yeluerton.

NOte (Reader) that there vvere in *Thebes* fovvre principall
gates, vvherof the chief and most commonly vsed vvere the
gates called *Electræ* and the gates *Homoloydes*. Thys I haue
thought good to explane : as also certē vvords vvhich are not
cōmon in vse are noted and expounded in the margent.   I did 5
begin those notes at request of a gentlevvoman vvho vnderstode
not poëtycall vvords or termes.   I trust those and the rest of
my notes throughout the booke, shall not be hurtfull to any
Reader.

26 tickle] fickle *MS*.   32 night *MS. Q₃* : might *Q₁ Q₂*   33 traine]
reigne *MS. Q₁*   41 by] hy *Q₂*
    1-9 Note . . . Reader] *Not in MS. or Q₁*   3 called] *Q₃ omits*   haue]
Q₃ omits

III

GISMOND OF SALERNE

BY

THE GENTLEMEN OF THE INNER TEMPLE

M

THERE are two surviving manuscripts of this tragedy, both in the British Museum, Lansdowne 786, pp. 1–70 (*L*) and Hargrave 205, pp. 9–22 (*H*). Our text reproduces the readings of the former, under the same conditions as are already set forth in the case of *Gorboduc*; the foot-notes give the variants in *H*, unless some other source is indicated. Isaac Reed, in a note to his reprint of Wilmot's altered version of the play (*Tancred and Gismunda*, pr. 1592), included in the 1825 edition of Dodsley's *Old Plays*, gave an extract from the conclusion of the tragedy in its original form, of which he says : ' It is here given from the fragment of an ancient MS. taken out of a chest of papers formerly belonging to Mr. Powell, father-in-law to the author of *Paradise Lost*, at Forest Hill, about four miles from Oxford.' In the main, Reed's version (*R*) agrees with *H*; both give the title at the end of the play as *The Tragedie of Gismond* (*H* gismond, *R* Gismonde) *of Salerne*, and in both the three sonnets to the 'Quenes maydes' follow ; both divide the last act into three scenes instead of, as in *L*, into four. *R* yields, however, a few independent variants, which are given in the foot-notes. There is no title-page in *H*, which begins with the heading *Cupido solus* and the side-note *First Acte*, 1. *Scene*. The title in *L* is *Gismond of Salern in Loue* ; the last two words are in later handwriting and ink.

In *H* there are many variants which were afterwards corrected to agree with *L*; the original words were underscored or crossed out, and the corrections written over or in the margin. Underscored words are marked *u.*, those crossed out *c.*, the corrections following in each case. The transcriber of *H* also made many slips of the pen, and where he corrected these immediately himself, it has not seemed worth while to record the errors. All the later corrections are given.

GISMOND
OF
SALERN:·
in Loue

A sonet of the Quenes maydes.

THey which tofore thought that the heuens throne
  is placed aboue the skyes, and there do faine
the goddes and all the heuenly powers to reigne,
they erre, and but deceaue them selues alone.
Heuen (vnlesse yow think moe be than one)   5
is here in earth, and by the pleasant side
of famous Thames at Grenwich court doeth bide.
And as for other heauën is there none.
There ar the goddesses we honor soe :
there Pallas sittes : there shineth Venus face :   10
bright beautie there possesseth all the place :
vertue and honor there do lyue and grow :
there reigneth she such heauen that doeth deserue,
worthy whom so fair goddesses shold serue.

An other to the same

FLowërs of prime, pearles couched in gold,
  sonne of our day that gladdeneth the hart
of them that shall yor shining beames behold,
salue of eche sore, recure of euery smart,
in whome vertue and beautie striueth soe   5·
that neither yeldes : loe here for yow againe

Gismōdes vnlucky loue, her fault, her woe,
and death at last, here fére and father slayen
through her missehap.   And though ye could not see,
yet rede and rue their woefull destinie.   10
So Ioue, as your hye vertues doen deserue,
geue yow such féres as may yor vertues serue
wth like vertues : and blisfull Venus send
vnto your happy loue an happy end.

An other to the same

G Ismond, that whilom liued her fathers ioy,
   and dyed his death, now dead doeth (as she may)
by vs pray yow to pitie her anoye ;
and, to reacquite the same, doeth humbly pray
Ioue sheld yor vertuous loues from like decay.   5
The faithfull earle, byside the like request,
doeth wish those wealfull wightes, whom ye embrace,
the cōstant truthe that liued within his brest ;
his hearty loue, not his vnhappy case
to fall to such as standen in your grace.   10
The King prayes pardon of his cruel hest :
and for amendes desireth it may suffise,
that wth his blood he teacheth now the rest
of fond fathers, that they in kinder wise
entreat the iewelles where their cōfort lyes.   15
And we their messagers beseche ye all
on their behalfes, to pitie all their smartes :
and on our own, although the worth be small,
we pray ye to accept our simple hartes
auowed to serue wth prayer and wth praise   20
your honors, as vnable otherwayes.

7 wish] w^th : *u.* wishe

The argument.

TAncrede king of Naples and prince of Salerne gaue his onely daughter Gismonde (whome he most derely loued) in mariage to a forein Prynce: after whoes death she returned home to her father. Which, hauing felt grete grefe of her absence while her husband liued (so iñeasurably he did esteme 5 her) determined neuer to suffer any second mariage to take her from him. She on the other side, waxing werry of that her fathers purpose, bent her mynde to the secret loue of the Counté Palurine: to whome (he being likewise enflamed with loue of her) by a letter subtilely enclosed in a clouen cane she 10 gaue to vnderstand a conuenient way for their desired meeting, through an old forgotten vaut, one mouth wherof opened directly vnder her chamber floore. Into this vaut when she was one day descended for the conueyance of her louer, her father in the meane season (whoes only ioy was in his daughter) 15 came to her chamber. Not finding her there, and supposing her to haue ben walked abrode for her disporte, he sate him downe at her beddes fete, and couered his head with the cortine, mynding to abide and rest there till her returne. She, nothing knowing of this her fathers vnseasonable coming, 20 brought vp her louer out of the caue into her chamber. There her father, espieng their secret loue, and he not espied of them, was vpon the sight striken with maruellous grefe. But, either for that the sodein despite had amased him and taken from him all vse of speche, or for that he reserued him self to more 25 conuenient reuëge, he then spake nothing, but noted their returne into the vaut and secretely departed. After great bewayling his vnhap, and charging his daughter withall, he cõmaunded the earle to be atached, emprisoned, strangled, debowelled, and his heart in a cup of golde to be presented to 30 Gismonde. She filled vp the cuppe, wherin the hart was brought, with her teares and with certaine poisonous water by

her distilled for that purpose, and drank out this deadly drink
Which her father hearing came to late to comfort his dyeng
daughter: whoe for her last request besought of him, he 35
louer and her self within one tombe to be buryed together, for
perpetuall memorie of their faithfull loue. Which request he
graunted, adding to the buriall himself slayen with his owne
hand, to the reproche of his owne and terror of others crueltie.

Cupide.	god of loue.
Tancred	king of Nap: price of Salern.
Gismonde.	king Tancredes daughter.
Lucrece	king Tācredes sister.
Guishard.	the Counte Palurine.
Claudia.	womā of Gism. priuy chāber.
Renuchio	gentlemā of the priuy chamber.
Iulio.	captain of the gard.
Megæra.	furie of hell.
Chorus .4.	gentlemen of Salern.

33 out] vp
*The contents of pp. 163–6 are given in H at the end of the play, as they
were in R, though Reed thought ' it were useless to transcribe ' them.*

First Acte. .1. Sceue.

Cupide.

Cupide
cometh
downe
from
heauen.

L Oe I, in shape that seme vnto your sight
  a naked boy, not clothed but with wing,
am that great god of loue that with my might
do rule the world, and euerie liuing thing.
This one hand beares vain hope, short ioyfull state,   5
w th faire semblance the louer to allure :
th is other holdes repentance all to late,
warr, fiër, blood, and paines without recure.
On swete ambrosia is not my foode,
nor nectar is my drink, as to the rest   10
of all the Goddes.   I drink the louers blood,
and eate the liuing hart within his brest.
Well hath my power in heuen and earth ben tried.
The depe Auern my percing force hath knowen.
What secret hollow do tho huge seas hide   15
where blasting fame my actes hath not forthblowen ?
To me the mighty Ioue him self hath yeld,
as witnesse can the Grekish mayd, whome I   Iö.
made like a cow goe grasing in the feld,
least ielous Iuno shold the faute espie.   20
The dobled night, the sonnes restrainëd course,   Alcmena.
his secret stealthes the sclander to eschue
in shape transformed me list not to discourse.
All that and more I forcëd him to do.
The bloody Mars himself hath felt my might,   25
I feared not I his furie, nor disdaine.
This can the Goddes record : before whoes sight

1. i. *Cupide*] *Cupido solus*   6 faire] false : *u.* fayer
             16 my] myne

he lay fast wrapped in Vulcanes suttel chaine.
In earth whoe doeth not know my mighty power,
he may behold the fall and cruel spoile   30
of Troÿe town of Asia the floure
so foule defaced and euened with the soile.
Whoe forced Leander with his naked brest
so many nightes to cutt the frotthy waues,
but Heroes loue that lay enclosed in Sest?   35
The stoutest hartes to me do yeld them slaues.

Hercules.   Whoe could haue matched the huge Alcides strĕgth?
Alexander. Great Macedō what force might haue subdued?
Wise Scipio whoe ouercame at length,
but I that am with greater might endued?   40
Whoe could haue wōne the famous golden flece,
but Iason ayded with Medeaes arte?
Whoe durst haue stolen fair Helen out of Grece,
but I with loue that boldened Paris hart?
What Natures bond, or Lawes restraint auailes   45
against my power, I vouch to witnesse truthe
Myrrha.   the Myrrhe tree, that wth shamefast teares bewailes
her fathers loue, still weping yet for ruthe.
But now the world, not seing in these dayes
such present proues of myne almighty power,   50
disdaines my name, and seketh sondry wayes
to conquer and deface me euerie houre.
My name supprest to raise againe therfore,
and in this age myne honor and renome
by mighty act intending to restore,   55
down to the earth in spite now am I come.
And in this place such wonders shall ye here,
as that yor stubborn and rebelling hartes
in piteous teres and humble yelding chere
shall sone be turned, by sight of others smartes.   60
This royall palace will I entre in,

28 lay fast] fast laie: laie *u. and* laye *inserted before* fast.   57, 66
ye] you

and there enflame the faire Gismonda soe,
in creping thorough all her veines within,
that she thereby shall raise much ruthe and woe.
Loe, this before your eyes so will I showe,   65
that ye shall iustly say with one accord,
we must relent and yeld : for now we knowe,
Loue rules the world, Loue onely is the Lorde.

*Cupide
entreth
into King
Tancredes
palace.*

2. *Scene.*

Gismonde.

*Gismond
cometh
out of her
chamber.*

Oh vaine vnstedfast state of mortall thinges !
Who trustes the world doeth leane to brittle stay.
Such fickle frute his flattering blome forth bringes ;
ere it be ripe it falleth to decaye.
The ioy and blisse, that late I did possesse   5
in weale at will wth one I louëd best,
disturnëd now into so depe distresse
hâth taught me plaine to know o^r states vnrest,
sithe neither witt, ne princely force may serue
gainst recklesse death, that slayes w^thout respect   10
the worthy and the wretch, ne doeth reserue
so much as one for worthinesse elect.
Ah my dere Lord, what well of teres may serue
to fede the streames of my fordullëd eyes,
to wepe thy death as doeth such losse deserue,   15
and waile thy lack in full suffising wise ?
O mighty Ioue, ô heuens and heuenly powers,
whearin had he procurëd your disdaine ?

ii. *Gismonde*] *Gismonda sola*   9 sithe] Since   12 elect.]
H inserts the following lines :

       wo wurthe o death the tyme that thow recevde
       such might wherby alas we ar foredone
       what wrong ys this the lief to be bereavde
       er natures course one half be overroone.

He neuer sought wth vast and hugie toures
to preasse aloft to vexe yor royall reigne.   20
Or what offense haue I cōmitt vnwares,
why thus ayenst me yor furie shold be stirred,
to fraught me thus wth woe and heauy cares?
Nay, sure for enuie the heuens this conspired.
The son his bright vertues had in disdaine.   25
The mighty Mars at his manhode repined.
Yea all the goddes ne could they so susteine
eche one to be excellëd in his kinde.
Alas my ioy where art thow now become?
Thy sprite, I know, doth lingre herabout,   30
and lokes that I pore wretch shold after come.

19-36 He neuer . . . a wife] *Wilmot's printed version of this passage is worth giving for purposes of comparison:*

> He neuer sought with vast huge mounting towers
> To reach aloft, and ouer-view your raigne,
> Or what offence of mine was it vnwares,
> That thus your furie should on me be throwen,
> To plague a woman with such endles cares,
> I feare that enuie hath the heauens this showen.
> The Sunne his glorious vertues did disdaine,
> Mars at his manhood mightily repind,
> Yea all the Gods no longer could sustaine,
> Each one to be excelled in his kind.
> For he my Lord surpast them euerie one,
> Such was his honor all the world throughout,
> But now my loue, oh whither art thou gone?
> I know thy ghost doth houer here about,
> Expecting me (thy heart) to follow thee :
> And I (deare loue) would faine dissolue this strife,
> But staie a while, I may perhaps foresee
> Some meanes to be disburdend of this life,
> „ And to discharge the dutie of a wife,
> „ Which is, not onely in this life to loue,
> „ But after death her fancie not remoue.
> Meane while accept of these our daily rites,
> Which with my maidens I shall do to thee,
> Which is, in songs to cheere our dying spirits
> With hymnes of praises of thy memorie.
>   *Cantant*
> *Quae mihi cantio nondum occurrit.*

Either Wilmot expanded considerably or he was working on a different MS.   The frequent rhymes in these lines suggest the latter explanation.
   The text of this passage in H is identical with L with one exception :
23 thus] so : *u.* thus.

I wold (God wote, my lord) if so I mought.
But yet abide : I may perhappes deuise
some way to be vnburdened of my life,
and with my ghost approche thee in some wise,   35
to do therin the dutie of a wife.

3. *Scene.*

Tancred.   Gismonde.

Tancred
cometh
out of his
palace.

Dere daughter stay the furie of your minde,
and stint yor teres, which may not ought auaile.
Such bootelesse plaint as hath no timely end
doeth but heape grefe to geue new cause to waile.
The world doeth know there lacked not of yor part   5
ought that belonged vnto a faithfull wife,
nor ought that mought be had by help of art.
Yet all (yow see) could not prolong his life.
His date that Nature sett was come : lett be
these vain complaintes : small good to him yow doe,   10
mutch hurt vnto yor self, most grefe to me,
greatest wrong to nature to withstand her soe.
    Gism. Oh sir, was this of Natures course the date,
wherof as yet one half he had not past ?
Nay nay (god wote) it was my cruel fate   15
that spited at my pleasant life forepast.
    Tancr. Yea Natures course I say, as profe doeth teache,
that hath no stint but as the heauëns guide.
His lamp of life it could no farther reache,
by foresett fate it might no longer bide.   20
    Gism. Ah cursed be the fate that so foresett.
    Tanc. My louing daughter, sett this grefe apart.
The more yow ar with hard misshappe besett,
the more yor patiëce shewes a constant hart.

iii. Tancred. Gismonde] Tancred & gismond. *W. has :* The song ended,
Tancred the king cometh out of his palace with his guard.   4 but heape]
heap but   9 His] the : *u.* his   15 god wote] alas : *u.* god woot
21 Ah] Ay

Gism. What hap, alas, may counteruaile my drere?   25
or ells what hope thus comfortlesse alone
may I conceiue, now hauing lost my fere?
What may I do, but still his death bemone?
My minde, alas, it wanteth now the stay,
wheron was wont to leane my recklesse thought.   30
My Lord is gone, my ioy is reft away,
that all with cares my hart is ouerfraught.
In him was all my pleasure and delight:
to him gaue I the frutes of my first loue:
he with the cōfort of his only sight   35
all cares out of my brest could sone remoue.
But now, alas, my ioyes forepast to tell
doeth but renew the sorrowes of my hart,
and maketh me with dolor to rebell
against the fates that so haue wrought my smart.   40

Tancr. My daughter, ceasse yoᵣ sorrow and yoᵣ plaint:
nought can yoᵣ grefe this helplesse chaūce recure.
What doeth auaile to make such hard cōplaint?
A noble hart eche happ can well endure.
And though yoᵣ husband death hath reft away;   45
yet life a louing father doeth susteine,
whoe (during life) to yow a doble stay
as father and as husband will remaine,
with dobled loue, to ease yoᵣ grefe for want
of him whoes loue is cause of yoᵣ complaint.   50
Forgett therfore this vain and ruthefull care:
and lett not teres yoᵣ youthfull beautie paire.

Gism. Oh sir, these teres loue chalengeth as due.
Tanc. But reason sayeth they do no whitt auaile.
Gism. Yet can I not my passions so subdue.   55
Tanc. Your fond affections ought not to preuaile.
Gism. Whoe can but plaine the losse of such a one?
Tanc. Of mortall thinges no losse shold seme so strange.
Gism. Such gĕme was he as erst was neuer none.

45 hath] haue

Tanc. Well, let that passe : and suffer so this change,   60
as that therin yor wisdome may appeare.
Let reason work in yow which time doeth bring
to meanest wittes, whome time doeth teache to beare
the greatest illes.   (*Gism.*) So plētuous is the spring
of sorrowes that surmounten in such sort   65
reason in me, and so encreasce my smart,
that neither can your fatherly comfort
nor coūsel ought remoue out of my hart
the swete remēbrance of him, that was here
in earth myne only ioy.   But (as I may)   70
I will bothe serue his sprite that was my fere
with plaint and teres, and eke yor will obey.

Tancred
and
Gismond
depart
into the
palace.

The Chore.

The diuerse happes which allwayes work o^r care,
our ioy so farr, our woe so nere at hand,
haue long ere this and dayly do declare
the fickle fote on which our state doeth stand.
Whoe plantes his pleasures here to gather roote,   5
and hopes his happy life will still endure,
let him behold how death with stealing fote
steppes in when he shall think his ioyes most sure.
No raūsom serues for to redeme our dayes.
If prowesse could preserue, or worthy dedes,   10
he had yet liued whoes twelue labors displayes
his growing fame, and yet his honor spredes.
The great king, that with so small a power
bereft the mighty Persian his crowne,
is witnesse eke our life is but a floure,   15
though it be decked with honor and renoune,
which growes to day in fauor of the heuen,
nursed with the soñe, and with the showers swete,

62 in] that in. *L originally had also* that in, *but* that *is crossed out.*
The Chore.] Chorus :   8 his] o^r   13 that] w^{ch}   18 nursed] nurst :
ϻ. noorisht

plucked wth the hand it withereth yet ere euen.
So passe our dayes euen as the riuers flete.   20
The famous Grekes, that vnto Troÿe gaue
the ten yeres sege, left but their name behind.
And he, that did so long and onely saue
his fathers walles, found there at last his end.
Hye Rome her self, that whilom layed her yoke   25
on the wide world, and vàquished all wth warre,
yet could she not remoue the fatall stroke
of death frō thē that stretched her power so farr.
Loke what the cruël sisters do decree,
the mighty Ioue him self can not remoue :   30
they ar the seruātes of the heuëns hye,
to work benethe what is cōspired aboue.
But happy is he, that endes this mortal life
by spedy death, whoe is not forced to see
the many cares, nor fele the sondry grefe,   35
which we susteine in woe and miserie.
Here fortune rules, whoe, when she list to play,
whirleth her whele and bringes the hye full lowe,
to morrow takes what she hath geuen to day,
to shew she can aduaūce and ouerthrowe.   40
Not Euripus vnquiet flood so oft
ebbes in a day, and floweth to and froe,
as fortunes chāge pluckes down that was aloft,
and minges o^r mortall ioy wth mortall woe.
Whoes case is such, that frō his coate he may   45
behold afarre the chāge that chaūceth here,
how sone they rise, how sone they do decay
that leane their states on fortunes slipper sphere,
whoe liues alôwe, and feleth not the strokes
of stormes wth which the hyëst toures do fall,   50
ne blustring windes wth which the stoutest okes
stoupen full lowe, his life is surest of all.

19 withereth] withers   ere] or   23 *margin*) hector   44 ioy]
eies : *u.* Ioie   45 coate] cote : *u.* howse

For he may scorne fortune, that hath no power
on him that is cōtent with his estate.
He seketh not her swete, ne feares her sower,   55
but liues alône within his bounded rate,
and marking ʼow these worldly thīges do wade,
reioiseth to him self, and laughes to see
the follie of mortal men, how they haue made
Fortune a god, and placed her in the skye.   60

2. *Acte.* .1. *Scene.*

Gismonde. Lucrece.

Dere aunt, when in my secret thought I weye
my present state, and my forepassed dayes,
new heapes of cares afresh beginne t'assay
my pensiue heart, as when the glistering rayes
of bright Phœbus ar sodenly ouerspred   5
wᵗʰ foule black cloudes that dīme their golden light :
namely when I layed in my secret bed
amidde the silence of the quiet night
wᵗʰ curious thought present before myne eyes
of gladsome youth how fleting is the course,   10
how sone the fading floure of beautie dyes,
how time ones past may neuer haue recourse,
no more than may the rūning streames reuert
to climbe the hilles when they ben ones downrolled
amidde the hollow vales.   There is no art,   15
no worldly power, no not the goddes can hold
the swey of flëing time, nor him reuoke
when he is past : all thinges vnto his might
parforce must bend, and yeld vnto the stroke
of time.   This makes me in the silent night   20
oft to record how fast my youth withdrawes

55 feares] fear   56 alône] *Corrected in L from* alôwe : *H* aloofe
2. Acte .1. Scene.] 2 Actus. 1. Scena.   5 ouerspred] orespredd

Gismond
and
Lucrece
coming
out of
Gism.
chāber.

it self away, how swift doeth rūne his race
my pleasant life.   This, this (aunt) is the cause,
when I aduise me saddly on my case
that maketh me in pensiue dumpes to stay.   25
For if I shold my pleasant yeres neglect
of fresh grene youth frutelesse to fade away :
whearto liue I ? whearto hath nature decked
me with so semely shape?   But neither I
can so consent all sole my youth to passe,   30
nor still (I trust) my father will denie
to marry me againe.   My present case
of widowes state hath greuëd me to mutch,
and pleased him to long.   For if he list
remarry me, is my hard fortune sutch   35
(dere aunt) that I so long shold thus persist
makelesse alone in woefull widowes life?
No, no, sutch hap shold not so long forwast
my youthfull dayes; which bringes me greater grefe,
when I somtime record my pleasure past.   40
But what though?   I force not : I will remaine
still at my fathers hest, and driue away
these fansies quite.   But yet my chefest paine
is that I stand at such vncertain stay.
For if my lingring father wold pronounce   45
his final dome, that I must driue fourth still
my life as I do now ; I wold renounce
myne owne free choise, and frame me to his will ;
in widowes state with patiĕce wold I passe
my dayes, and as I might wold beare the grefe,   50
and force my self contented with such case
to liue, alas, a sole forsaken life.
But now his silence dobleth all my smart
while that my doutfull thoughtes twene hope and fere
in cruel wise distraine my carefull hart,   55
and with the waues of woe and depe despeir

56 woe] hope : c. woe

so tosse my grefefull minde, that but yor ayde
I finde no quiet port where to arriue.

   Lucr. Suffiseth this, good niece, that yow haue sayed.
Full well I see how sondry passions striue   60
in your vnquiet brest: for oft ere this
yor coūtenance half cōfused did plainly showe
some clowdy thoughtes ouerwhelmed all yor blisse.
The ground wherof sins I perceiue to growe
on iust respect of this yor sole estate,   65
and skilfull care of fleting youthes decay,
yor wise foresight such sorrowing all to late
t'eschue, much do I praise, and (as I may)
here do I promise yow to break the same
vnto your father, and to work it soe,   70
as bothe to kepe your honor and your fame,
to yeld yow your desire, and ease yor woe.
Be yow no farther greued : but do yow goe
into your chamber.   I shall, as I may,
performe your will, and yow shall shortly know   75
what I haue wrought, and what the king doeth say.
My niece shall not impute the cause to be
in my defaut her will shold want effect.
But in the king is all my dout, least he
my sute for her new mariage will reiect   80
Yet will I proue.   And loe, him self I see
approche : in happy time I trust it be.

75 Gism.
departeth
into her
chamber,
Lucrece
abiding on
the stage.

Tancred
cometh
out of his
palace..

2. *Scene.*

Lucrece.   Tancred.

Sir, as I haue emplied my sclender powers
by faithfull seruice, such as lay in me,
in my best wise to honor yow and youres,
nor neuer sought to hold in priuitie
the thing that in my simple knowledge was,   5
whearby I mought in any part aduaunce
yor royall state (which long in honors race

the goddes might guide and sheld frō all mischaūce)
so now my bounden dutie moueth me
to moue to yow concerning the estate　　　　　　　　10
of my niece yor daughter, which as yow see
the worthy prince her husband now of late
hath buryëd.　But I see and perceiue
that she hath not layed vp wth him in graue
those sparkes of senses, wch she did receiue　　　　15
when kind to her bothe life and body gaue :
· nor with her husbandes death her life doeth ceasse :
but she yet liues, and liuing she doeth fele
such passions hold her tender hart in presse,
as shew the same not to be wrought of stele,　　　　20
or carued out of the hard and stony rock,
that as by course of kinde can nought desire,
nor feleth nought but as a senselesse stock.
Such stern hardnesse ne ought ye to require
in her, whoes gentle hart and tender yeres　　　　25
yet flouring in her chefest lust of youth
is led of force to feele the whote desires
that fall vnto that age, and asketh ruthe
of yor wonted fatherly tendre Loue,
whome nature bindeth by yor graue foresight　　　　30
to care for her of thinges that ar aboue
her feble force, and farr surpasse her might.
And sir, although　(_Tan._) Sister, I yow beseche,
if yow esteme or ought respect my life,
do stint, and wade no farther in this speche.　　　　35
Yo^r wordes do slay my hart, as if the knife
in cruell wise forthwith shold perce the same.
For well I see wherto your tale doeth tend.
This feared I when yow beganne to name
my daughter ones.　Alas, and is the end　　　　4·
of my poore life, that broken is and done,
so long a time to stay? why liue I then?

11 my] mine　　18 she yet] yet she　　23 nought] owght

Why draw I fourth my dayes vnder the sòne?
My later houre approcheth loe : and when
my dere daughter yclosed hath myne eyes,   45
and with her woefull teres bewept my graue,
then is her dutie done in perfect wise :
there is no farther seruice I may craue.
. But while the fates sustein my fainting breath,
her ioyfull presence will I not forgoe.   50
Rather I will consent vnto my death,
than so to spend my dayes in pining woe.
Her late mariage hath taught me, to my grefe,
that in the frutes of her desirèd sight
doeth rest the only côfort and relefe   55
of my vnweldy age.   For what delight,
what ioy, what côfort in this earth haue I,
if my Gismonda shold depart from me?
O daughter, daughter, rather let me dye
some sodein cruel death, than liue to see   60
my house yet ones againe stand desolate
by thine absence.   Oh let such fansies be.
Tell her, I am her father, whoes estate,
wealth, honor, life, and all that is in me
doeth wholly rest on her.   Tell her I must   65
accompt her all my ioy, and my relefe.
Work as she will : but yet she were iniust,
to seke to hast his death that gaue her life.

Tancred
and
Lucrece
depart
into the
palace.

3. Scene.

Gismonde.   Lucrece.

By this I hope myne aunt hath mouèd soe
vnto the King in my behalf, that I
without delay his settled minde shall knowe,
and end at ones all this perplexitie.

Gismond
cometh
out of her
chamber.

44 later] latter   56 my] myn   64 wealth] weale

Lucrece
returneth
from the
palace.

And loe where now she comes.   Lord, how my hart   5
in doutfull thoughtes doeth pant within my brest!
For in her spede recure of all my smart,
and quiet of my trobled minde doeth rest.

   Lucr. Niece, on the point yow lately willed me
to treat of wth the King in your behalf,   10
I brake euen now wth him so farr, till he
in sodein rage of grefe, ere I scarce half
my tale had told, prayed me to stint my sute,
as that frō which his minde abhorrëd most.
And well I see, his fansie to refute   15
is but displesure gained, and labor lost.
So firmely fixed standes his fond delight,
that, till his aged corps be layed in graue,
he will not part frō the desirëd sight
of your presence, which selder he shold haue   20
if he had ones allyëd yow againe
in mariage to any prince or pere.
This is his final sentēce plat and plaine.
And therfore myne aduise shalbe, to stere
no farther in this case : but sins his will   25
is grounded on his fatherly loue to yow,
and that it lieth in yow to saue or spill
his old forwasted age, yow ought t'eschue
to seke the thing that shold so much agreue
his tender hart : and in the state yow stand   30
content yor self : and let this thought releue
all your vnquiet thoughtes, that in yor hand
yor agëd fathers life doeth rest and stay,
sins without yow it may not long endure,
but rūne to ruthefull ruïne and decay.   35

   Gism. Dere aunt, sithe neither can my case procure,
nor your request entreat, nor sage aduise
can ought persuade my fathers fixed minde
to graunt me my desire in willing wise :

   27 lieth] lies   28 yow] ye   36 sithe] since

I can no more, but bend my self to finde   40
meanes as I may to frame my yelden hart
to serue his will, and as I may to driue
the passions from my brest, that brede my smart,
and diuersly distracting me do striue
to hold my minde subdued in dayly paine :   45
whome yet (I fere) I shall resist in vaine.

Gismond
and
Lucrece
depart into
Gismondes
chamber.

The Chore.

Whoe markes our former times, and present yeres,
what we ar now, and lokes what we haue ben,
he can not but lament with many teres
the great decay and change of mortal men.
For as the world wore on and waxed olde,   5
so vertue quailed, and vice beganne to grow :
so that that age, that whilom was of golde,
is worse than brasse, more vile than iron now.
Those times were such, that (if we ought beleue
our stories olde) wemen examples were   10
of hye vertues. Lucrece disdained to liue
longer than chast, and boldly without fere
toke sharp reuenge on her oppressed corps
with her owne hand, for that it not withstode
the wanton will, but yelded to the force   15
of proud Tarquine, and bought her fame wth blood.
Quene Artemise thought not an heape of stones,
though they the worldes wonder were full wide,
a worthy graue wherin to rest the bones
of her dead Lord, for euer to abide :   20
but drank his hart, and made her tender brest
his tombe, and failëd not of wiuely faith,
of promised loue, and of her bound behest,
vntill she ended had her dayes by death.

43 the] thees   brede] bredd
Ch. 10 wemen] ladies : *W* women   20 dead] dere : *W* dear

Penelope.

Vlysses wife (such was her stedfastnesse)   25
abode his slow returne whole twenty yeres,
and spent her youthfull dayes in pensiuenesse,
bathing her widowes bed wth often teres.

Porcia.

The stout daughter of Cato Brutus wife
when she had heard his death, did not desire   30
longer to liue : and lacking vse of knife
(a strange death) ended her life by fire,
and eate hote burning coles. O worthy dame !
O vertues worthy of eternall praise !
The flood of Lethe can not wash out thy fame,   35
to others great reproche, shame, and dispraise.
Rare ar those vertues now in womens minde.
Where shall ye seke a wight so firme and true?
Scarce can yow now among a thowsand finde
one stedfast hart : we all delight in new.   40
The ladie, that so late lamented here
her princes death, and thought to liue alone,
as doeth the turtle true without her feere :
behold how sone that cōstant minde is gone.
I think those good ladies, that liuëd here   45
a mirrour and a glasse to womankinde,
and in their liues their vertues held so dere,
had them to graue, and left them not behinde :
ells in so many yeres we might haue seen
as good and vertuous dames as they haue ben.   50

3. *Acte.* .1. *Scene.*

Cupide.

Cupide returneth out of the palace.

Now shall they know what mighty Loue can do,
that proudely practise to deface his name,
and vainly striuen with so strong a foe.
From sparkes encreasced by blast a blasing flame

28 widowes] widowishe   37 womens] womans   38 ye] you
III. i. Cupide] *Cupido solus*

shall showe, how Loue can kindle hartes wth heate,   5
and wast the oken brest to cinder dust.
Gismond haue I now framed to forgett
her turtles truthe, and burne wth raging lust.
I made her doting father her denie
the wealfull wyuely state to tast againe,   10
and (Iuno thus forclosed) I made to flye
a thrilling shaft that perced her youthfull vaines
with loue of Counté Palurine: and he
docth fele like wound sent frō my deadly bowe.
The meanes to mete, her hauc I taught, and she   15
by clouën cane shall do the carle to know.
So shall they ioy in tasting of the swete,
to make them iudge more tollngly the grefe
that bitter bringes, and, when their ioy shall flete,
endure redobled dole without relefe.   20
Their death shall make the earth to know my might,
and how it is farr better to obey
my gentle hestes, than with rebelling sprite
my wreking wrath and power to assay.
Their ghostes shall do the grisly helles to here   25
what God is Loue: To heauen will I remount:
to Ioue and all the goddes that dwellen there
in throne of triumph now will I recount,
how I by sharp reuenge on earthly wightes
will be reknowen to earth and helly sprites,   30
and hensefourth ceasse vnserued to sitt in vaine
a God whome men vnpunished may disdaine.

*Cupide re-
mounteth
to heauen.*

2. *Scene.*

Claudia.

*Claudia
cometh
out of
Gism:
chāber.*

Pitie, that moueth euerie gentle hart
to rue their grefe wch be distressed in paine,
enforceth me to waile my ladies smart,

6 oken] yren: *W* oaken   12 vaines] vaine

whoes tender brest no long time may susteine
the restlesse toile, that her vnquiet minde   5
doeth cause her feble body to endure.
But why it is alas I can not finde,
nor know no meane her rest how to procure.
Whoes remedie, as I of dutie ought,
in all that to a seruant doeth belong   10
with carefull heart I haue procured and sought,
though small effect be of my trauail sprong.
And oft times, as I durst, I haue assayed
with humble wordes my ladie to require
to tell it me : which she hath so denayed,   15
that it abashed me farther to enquire
or ask from whense those clowdy thoughtes procede,
whoes stormy force, that smoky sighes fourthsend,
is liuely witnesse how that carefull drede
and whote desire within her brest contend.   20
Whoes sharp conflict disquietes her so sore
that heauy slepe can not procure her rest :
but fearfull dreames present her euermore
most hideous sightes her minde for to molest,
that startling oft therwith she doeth awake   25
to muse vpon those fansies which torment
her thoughtfull heart with horror, that doeth make
the sweat all cold brast fourth incontinent
from her weak līmes : and while the quiet night
geues other rest, she turning to and froe   30
doeth wish for day : but when day bringeth light,
she kepeth her bed, there to record her woe :
and when she doeth arise, her flowing teres
streame fourth full fast ymeint wth dedly grones,
whearby her inward sorrow so appeares,   35
that o^r teres eke the cause vnknowen bemones.
And if she be cõstrained t'abide in preasse,

4 brest] hart   17 those] thees   32 kepeth] kepes   33 and] but
37 t'abide] to byde

her trembling voice she scarcely may restraine
from carefull plaintes : wch restraint doeth encreasce
their force, when place geues libertie to plaine.   40
To others talk when as she shold entend,
her heaped cares her wittes doen so oppresse,
that what they speak, or wherto their wordes tend,
she knoweth not, oft her answeres do expresse.
Her chefe delite is aye to be alone.   45
Her pensiue thoughtes within them selues debate.
But wherupon this restlesse life is growen,
sithe I know not, nor how the same t'abate,
I can no more, but Ioue that knowest it best,
thow shortly bring my ladies hart to rest.   50

Claudia departeth to Gism. chāber.

3. *Scene.*

Guisharde.

Guishard cometh out of the palace.

How greuous paine they dure, wch neither may
forgett their loue, nor yet enioy the same,
I know by profe, and dayly make assay.
Though loue hath brought my ladies hart in frame,
my faithfull loue with like loue to repay :   5
that doeth not quench, but rather cause to flame
the creping fire wch spredeth in my brest,
whoes raging heat grauntes me no time of rest.
If they bewaile their cruel destinie,
which spend their loue where they no loue do finde :   10
well may I plaine, sithe fortune guideth me
to this torment of farr more greuous kinde,
wherin I fele as much extremitie,
as may be felt in body or in minde,
by seing her, which shold recure my paine,   15
for my distresse like sorrow to susteine.

41 entend] attend   42 doen] do   44 do] doen
iii. *Guisharde*] *Palurine*   8 grauntes me no time of] at no time
grauntes me

I well perceiue that only I alone
am her beloued, her coūtenāce telleth me soe :
wherfore of right I haue good cause to mone
her heauy plight that pitieth so my woe.   20
Sithe eithers loue is thus in other growen,
I her to serue, she me withouten moe
onely to loue : o Loue, help that we may
enioy our loue, of thee I humbly pray.
For I see plaine that she desireth no lasse,   25
that we shold mete for to aswage our grefe,
than I, if she could bring the same to passe,
that none it wist : as it appereth by prefe
of her gestures, which shewen me, alas,
how she assentes that I shold haue relefe   30
of my distresse, if she could work the same,
keping her self frō danger of defame.
And euën now this cane I did receiue
of her owne hand : wch gift, though it be small,
receiuing it what ioy I did conceiue   35
within my fainting spirit thearwithall,
whoe knoweth loue aright may well perceiue
by like aduentures wch to them befall.
For nedes the louer must esteme that well
wch cometh from her wth whom his hart doth dwell.   40
Assuredly it is not without cause
she gaue me this : somthing she meant thereby :
for therewithall I might perceiue her pause
a while, as though some weighty thing did lye
vpon her hart, wch she cōceled, bycause   45
the bystanders shold not our loue espie.
This clift declares that it hath ben disclosed :
He breakes parhappes herin she hath some thing enclosed.
the cane,
and findes O mighty Ioue ! who wold not ioy to serue
a letter where wit and beautie chosen haue their place ?   50
enclosed.

19 haue good cause to mone] owght for to bemone : *u.* have good cause
to mone   25 lasse] les   28 appereth] apperes

Who could deuise more wisely to cõserue
thinges frõ suspect ? O Venus, for thy grace,
that thus hâst worthyed me for to deserue
so precious loue, how lucky is this case !
This letter sure some ioyfull newes conteines :   55

He redeth
the letter.

Mine owne as I am yo^{rs} : whoes heart (I know)   "
no lesse than myne for lingring help of woe   "
doeth long to long. Loue, tendering yor case   "
and myne, hath taught recure of both o^r paine.   "   60
My chamber floore doeth hide a caue, where was   "
a vautes one mouth : the other in the plaine   "
doeth rise southward a furlong frõ the wall.   "
Descend yow there. This shall suffice. And soe   "
I yeld my self, myne honor, life, and all   "   65
to yow : Vse yow the same, as there may growe   "
yor blisse, and myne (myne earle) and that the same   "
free may abide from danger of defame.   "
Farewell, and fare so well, as that yor ioy,   "
which only can, may cõfort myne anoye.   "   70
           Youres more than her owne. G.   "

O Ioue. O ioyfull houre. O heuenly hap.
O blisfull chaũce, recure of all my woe.
Cõmes this frõ Gismond ? Did she thus enwrap
this letter in the cane ? May it be soe ?
It can not be : it were to swete a ioy.   75
Why ? shall I dout ? did she not geue the same
to me ? did she not smile, and seme to ioy
thearwth ? She smiled : she ioyed : she raught the cane :
and wth her owne swete hand she gaue it me.
O noble Quene, my ioy, my hartës dere.   80
O swete letter : how may I welcome thee ?
I kisse thee : on my knees I honor here
bothe hand, and pëne, wherwth thow written were.

56 bring] bringes   *Between* 56 *and* 57 Gismondas letter enclosed in
the cane and geven to the Counte palurine   80 ioy,] Joy &

Oh, blissed be that caue, and he that taught
thee to descrie the hidden entrie there. 85
Not only through a dark and vggly vaut,
but fire, and sword, or through what euer be,
myne owne dere ladie, will I come to thee.

Guishard
departeth
into the
palace.

The Chore.

Full mighty is thy power, o cruel Loue,
if Ioue himself can not resist thy bowe :
but sendest him down euen frõ the heuens aboue
in sondry shapes here to the earth belówe.
Then how shold mortal men escape thy dart, 5
the feruent flame, and burning of thy fire ?
sins that thy might is such, and sins thow art
both of the seas and land the lord and sire.
But why doeth she that sprang frõ Iouës hed,
and Phœbus sister shene, despise thy power, 10
ne feares thy bowe?   Why haue they allwayes led
a mayden life, and kept vntouched their floure ?
Why doeth Egisthus loue, and, to obteine
his wicked will, cõspire his vncles death ?
Or why doeth Phædra burne, for whom is slayne 15
Theseus chast sonne? or Helen false of faith ?
, For Loue assaultes not but the idle hart :
, and such as liue in pleasure and delight,
, he turneth oft their glad ioyes into smart,
, their play to plaint, their sport into despight. 20
For loe, Diane, that chaceth wth her bowe
the flyeng hart, the gote, and fomy bore,
by hill, by dale, in heate, in frost, in snowe,
ne resteth not, but wandreth euermore,
Loue seeketh not, nor knowes not where to finde : 25
While Paris kept his heard on Ida downe
Cupide ne sought him not : for he is blinde.

84 he] she
. Ch. 23 frost, in] frost &

But when he left the feld to liue in towne,
he fell into his snare, and brought that brand
from Grece to Troy, wch after sett on fire   30
strong Ilium, and all the Phrygës land.
Such ar the frutes of Loue : such is his hire.
Whoe yeldeth vnto him his captiue hart,
ere he resist, and holdes his open brest
withouten warr to take his bloody dart,   35
let him not think to shake of, when him list,
his heauy yoke.   Resist his first assaulte : .
weak is his bowe, his quĕched brand is cold.
Cupide is but a childe, and can not daunte
the minde that beares him on his vertues bold.   40
But he goues poison so to drink in gold,
and hides vnder such pleasant baite his hoke,
but ye beware it will be hard to hold
your gredy minde.   But if yow wisely loke,
what slye snake lurkes vnder those flowers gay,   45
but ye mistrust some cloudy storme, and fere
a wett showër after so fair a day,
ye may repent, and by yor pleasure dere.
For seldome times is Cupide wont to send
vnto a ioyfull loue a ioyfull end.   50

4. *Act.* .1. *Scene.*

Megæra.

Vengeance and blood out of the depest helles
I bring the cursed house where Gismond dwelles,
sent from the grisly god that holdes his reigne
in Tartares vggly realme, where Pelops sire   Tantalus.
(that wth his own sŏnes flesh, whome he had slayen,   5
did feast the goddes) wth famine hath his hire,

29 his] the : *c.* his   42 baite] baites   44 yow] ye   46, 48 ye] you

to gape and catch at flëing frutes in vaine,
and yelding waters with his gasping throte :

Typhon.   where stormy Eöles sŏne with endlesse paine
rolles vp the rock : whe.re Tytius hath his lot   10
to fede the gripe that gnawes his growing hart :
where proud Ixſon whurlëd on the whele
pursues him self : where due deserued smart
the dolefull damned ghostes in flames do fele.

Mercurie. Thense do I mount : thither the wynged god   15
nephew to Atlas, that vpholdes the skie,
of late down frō the earth with golden rod
to Stygian ferrie Salerne soules did guie,
and made report how Loue that blinded boy,
hyely disdaining his renomes decay,   20
slipped down from heuen hath filled wth fickle ioy
Gismondaes hart, and made her throw away
chastnesse of life, to her iṁortal shame :
mynding to shew by profe of woefull end
some terror vnto those that scorne his name.   25
Black Pluto (that had found Cupide his frend

Proserpina. in winning Ceres daughter Quene of helles,
and partly mouëd by the greuëd ghost
of her late prince, that now in Tartar dwelles,
and prayed due paine for her that thus hath lost   30
due care of him) by great and graue aduise
of Minos, Æäc, and of Rhadamant,
hath made me pearce the settled soile, and rise
aboue the earth, with dole and drere to daunt
the present ioyes wherwith Gismonda now   35
fedes her disteinëd hart, and so to make
Cupide Lord of his will.   Loe, I will throwe
into her fathers brest this stinging snake,
and into hers an other will I cast.
So stong wth wrath, and with recurelesse woe,   "   40
eche shalbe others murder at the last.

33 settled] fixed : c. settled   37 his] his c. her : her u. his

Furies must aide, when men will ceasse to know　　"
their Goddes : and Hell shall send reuēging paine
to those, whome Shame frō sinne can not restraine.

Megæra
entreth
the palace.

2. *Scene.*

Tancrede.　　Renuchio.　　Iulio.

Tancred
cometh
out of
Gismondes
chamber.

O great almighty Ioue, whome I haue heard to be
the god, that guides the world as best it liketh thee,
that doest wth thōder throwe out of the flaming skies
the blase of thy reuenge on whom thy wrath doeth rise ;
graunt me, as of thy grace, and as for my relefe,　　5
that wch thow pourest out as plages, vnto the grefe
of such, whoes siñes haue whet thy sharp and deadly ire.
Send down, o Lord, frō heuen thy whot cōsuming fire,
to reue this rutheful soule, whome tormētes to and froe
do tosse in cruel wise wth raging waues of woe.　　10
O earth, that mother art to euerie liuing wight,
receiue the woefull wretch, whom heuen hath in despight.
O hell (if other hell there be, than that I fele)
do ease him wth thy flames, whom frowning fortunes whele
hath throwen in depe distresse of fan more pīching paine,　　15
than hell can heape on those that in his pitt remaine.
O daughter (whome alas most happy had I ben
if liuing on the earth the sōne had neuer seen)
is thys my hoped ioy, my comfort, and my stay,
to glad my grefefull yeres that wast and wear away ?　　20
For happy life, that thow receiuēd hâst by me,
ten thousand cruel deathes shall I receiue by thee ?
For ioy that I haue had, and for my whole delight,
that I accursed wretch did settle in thy sight,
is this my due reward, alas so to beholdē　　25
the thing that makes me wish that erst the gapīg mold

---

ii. *Tancrede. Renuchio. Iulio.*] Tancred the king : Iulio capteine of the
gard　(*margin*) owt of Gismondes chamber alone : Tan. *at the beginning
of line* 1.　*Below, in later handwriting,* s.d. *as in* L　　15 pīching]
hollyshe : *u.* pinching

had swallowed into hell this caytif corps, than I
shold liue to see the cause that dayly I do dye,
and yet by dayly death I can not that atteine
that death doeth dayly bring to some, whom pining paine   30
makes glad to go frõ hense, and ioyfull to embrace
the gentle dame, that cuttes the cruel twisted lace.
Whom shall I first or most accuse in this my woe?
the god, that guideth all, and yet hath guided soe?
That god shall I blaspheme? or curse the cruel fate,   35
that thus on rockes of ruthe hath stered myne estate?
Or rather that vile wretch, that traitor shall I blame,
by whome I haue receiued my sorrow and my shame?
Or her shall I abhorre? and her shall I auowe
to his reuẽging wrath? whom I beseche to bowe   40
his eare to my request, and graunt that I desire;
to burne to cinder dust wth flash of heuenly fire
the naughty traitor first, to fede my boyling ire,
my cursed daughter next, and then the wretched sire.
When I, as is my wont (such is my fond delight   45
to fede my self wth ioy and pleasure of her sight)
my daughter, now my death, wthin her chãber sought,
where I had hoped she was, but there I found her not,
I demed for her disport she and her damselles were
fourth to the garden walked for to refresh thẽ there,   50
and wening thus did minde awhile alone to stay,
and tarry her returne, as loth to let their play.
At her beds fete I sate, and this accursed hed
wth cortine close I wrapped: thát wold I had ben dead,
and shrouded wth my shete a senslesse corps in graue,   55
my last and longest rest to take, as happily haue
those wealfull wightes, whom death wth frẽdly dart hath slayen,
when I in hope of slepe, to rest my thoughtfull braine,
there sate and saw, how by a secret framed dore,
out of a hideous vaut vp through the chamber flore,   60
Gismõd brought by the hand the Counté Palurine:

36 myne] my   52 and] to

and there, vpon the bed, tofore my cursed eyen,
in most vnshamefast wise, this traitor earle and she
(alas, why is it true?) vnweting made me see,
alas, her shame, his treason, and my deadly grefe,   65
her shamelesse body yelded to the traitor thefe.
The hye despite herof, that griped my grefefull brest,
had wellnere forced my hart wth sorrow all distrest
by sodein shreke to shew some parcell of my smart,
and to vnlade wth wordes the burden of my hart.   70
I thought euen in that pang the cortine to vnfolde,
and thonder at them bothe : but grefe did so wthholde
my minde in traunslike maze, that, as a senslesse stone
I neither wit nor tong could vse t'expresse my mone :
but stayed astõned and forced (as aũcient Poëtes tell,   75
how doeth the griphin gnaw great Tytius hart in hell)
forcelesse parforce to yeld my hart to biting paine,
to gnaw theron, as gredy famine doeth cõstraine
the egre empty hauk pecemeale to pluck her pray.
But ah, what shall I do ? how may I seke to stay   80
the furor of my minde ? or how shall I deuise
to work some due reuẽge to fede these wretched eyes,
that haue cõueyed vnto my soule by cursed sight
the paine that pines my life wth dolor and despite ?
Renuchio.
   Ren.   What is your graces will wth me ?   85
   Tanc. Call my daughter. My heart doeth boile till I may see
her present here, for to vnburden all my brest
vnto her self the only cause of myne vnrest.
Shall I destroy them bothe ? and in my glowing rage
embrue wth bothe their bloods these trẽbling hãdes, t'aswage
the thirsting of reuẽge that boileth in my brest ?   91
And shall I send to hell their ghostes that haue opprest
this hart with hellish grefe ? and shall they both be slayen ?

Renuchio
goeth
to call
Gismonde,
but he
cometh
not in
with her.

62 tofore] before   69 shreke] stroke : *u.* shreke   78 doeth] can :
u. doth   85-88 *and margin* Renuchio . . . her *omitted in H and added
in later handwriting in margin*

and shall they bothe by death abye my cruel paine?
Alas, to me that one, that daughter is to dere.   95
She can not dye the death, and leaue me liuing here.
These armes can soner rend out of this woefull chest
th'unhappy liuing hart, the liuer, and the rest,
that yeld vnto the same their liuely power to moue,
than they one cursed ioint can bend, for to remoue   100
her life, that makes my life in deadly smart surpasse
the farr most cruel kind of death that euer was.
But if the feruēt force of present furie might
surmoūt all natures strēgth, and could wᵗʰ kindled spight
vnkindly weld this hād to reue Gismōdaes life: 105
were there the end? or there mought cesse the stormy strife,
that weltreth vp the waues of wrath and sorrow so
to sink my silly soule in gulf of grefe and woe?
No, no: her bloodlesse ghost will still pursue my sight,
and frō the depest helles will moūt her gashfull sprite,   110
to wayt on me, as shadow in the shining day,
in dolefull wise to wreak her murther as she may.
I will do thus therfore.   The traitor shall not liue
to scorne his pained prince: the hart I will bereue
out of his ripped brest, and send it her, to take   115
her last delight of him, for whome she did forsake,
her father and her self, her dutie and her fame.
For him she shall haue grefe, by whom she hath the shame.
His slaughter and her teres, her sorrow and his blood
shall to my rancorous rage supplie delitefull foode.   120
Iulio, Iulio.

   Iul.   What euer please your noble grace,
loe here prest to performe.

   Tanc.   Iulio, this is the case.
If heretofore we haue not trust in vaine
now must we proue: Iulio, now must we vse
your truthe, yoʳ force, yoʳ courage, and yoʳ paine: 125

---

94 my] the: *c.* my   97 chest] brest: *u.* chest   106 mought]
maie: *u.* mowght   112 murther] sorowe: *u.* murder

We must còmaund, and yow may not refuse.
Iul. How by yor graces bountie I am bound,
beyond the còmon bond, wherin eche wight
standes bound vnto his prince ; how I haue found
worship and wealth by fauor in your sight,   130
I do reknowledge wth most thankfull minde.
My truthe, wth other meanes to serue yor grace,
ar still so prest, what euer be assigned,
as if yow shall còmaund euen in this place
my self, euen but to satisfie yor will,   135
yea though vnkindly horror wold gainsay,
wth cruell hand the liuely blood to spill,
that fedes this faithfull hart, I wold not stay,
but streight before yor face wold fercely staine
this blade in blood, that, at your royall hest,   140
shold largely streame euen frō the derest veine
that serues the soule in this obedient brest.
Tanc. Well, to be short : for I am greued to long
by wrath w^thout reuenge.   I think yow know,
that whilom was this palace builded strong   145
for wari, where dredlesse peace hath planted now
a weaker court, where we long time haue reigned,
and ruled in rest.   But of that palace old
against the force of time one vaut remained,
that secret way vnder the doluen mold   150
conueyëth streight vnto the place where lyes
Gismond my daughter.   There the chāber floore
doeth hyde a hugic hole, where doeth arise
one mouth of this depe caue : there was the dore
within the court. there is an other mouth   155
w^thout the wall, that now is ouergrowen
by time : frō hense it lieth directly south
a furlong from this court. it may be knowen
but by a stomp where stode an oken tree
that sins th'old courtes decay beganne to growe.   160
There will we that yow watch : there shall yow see

a traitor mount out of the vaut belówe.
Bring him to vs : it is th'earle Palurine.
What is his fàut, neither shall yow enquire,
nor I can now declare : These cursed eyen   165
haue seen the flame, this hart hath felt the fire,
that can not ells be quĕched, but by his blood.
This must be done : this see yow do in hast.

    Iul. Both this, and ells what yor grace thinketh good,
I shall obey so long as life doeth last.   170

*Iulio
departeth
into the
palace.*

3. *Scene.*

Tancrede. Gismonde.

*Gismond
cometh
out of her
chamber,
called by
Renuchio.*

Gismond, if either I could cast aside
all care of thee, or if thow woldest haue had
some care of me : it shold not thus betide,
that either through thy faut my ioy shold fade,
or by my follie I shold beare the paine,   5
that thow thow hâst deserued. But neither I
can scape the grefe, whome thow hâst more thã slayen :
nor thow canst now recure the wound : for why,
neither thy chast and vndefiled state
of wemlesse life can be restored to thee,   10
nor my cõfort, whoes losse I rue to late,
can till desired death returne to me.
Gismond, it is no mãnes, or mĕnes report,
that hath by likely proues enflamed in me
a light beleuing rage, in fickle sort   15
to vexe my self, and be displeased wth thee.
No, no : there stayed in me so settled trust,
that thy chast life and vncorrupted minde
wold not haue yelded to vnlawfull lust

    163 to vs] *omitted*   th'] the   earle] countie : *u.* earle   168 be done] you do   see] must : *u.* se   170 so] as : *u.* so
    iii. *Tancrede. Gismonde*] Tancred the king: Gismonda the kings dowghter 7 thã] *om.*

of strayeng loue, other than was assigned   20
lefull by law of honest wedlockes band,
that, if these self same eyes had not behold
thy shame, that wrought the woe, wherin I stand,
in vain ten thousand Catoes shold haue told,
that thow didst ones vnhonestly agree   25
with that vile traitor Counté Palurine,
without regard had to thy self, or me,
vnshamefastly to staine thy state and myne.
But I vnhappiest man alyue haue seen,
and hauing seen I fele the passing grefe,   30
that by these eyes hath perced this hart wth tene,
wch neuer ells had entred in belefe.
I fight within my self. For iustices law
enforced wth furie of enkindled ire
my diuersly distraughted minde doeth draw   35
to wreke the wrong, and so to quêch the fire
wth gylty blood, which floods of gyltlesse teres
still flowing frõ my face can not asswage,
but still it growes, and still my life it weares.
My grete therfore bidden me obey my rage.   40
But Nature, that hath locked w^thin thy brest
my life, on th'other side doeth stiffly striue,
being wellnere now by furies force opprest,
in thee to saue thee and my self alyue.
Thus for the traitor neither right can say,   45
nor nature doth entreat. For him therfore
my full determined minde doeth stand in stay.
But what of thee shalbe decreed, before
I yeld to nature, or obey to right,
I am contented of thy self to know,   50
what for thy self alone thow cannest recite,
t'vphold the side that grefe doeth ouerthrow.

---

25 vnhonestly] unlawfullie : *u.* vnhonestlie   32 w^ch] That   33 iustices]
justice   39–40 *These lines are transposed in H, but corrected to the*
right order   43 force] soare : *u.* force

Say why thow sholdest liue, whoes only crime
bringes hourely paine t'abridge thy fathers time.

    Gism. Father, if either I my self could see   55
why I wold liue, considering the case
of him for whome I liue, or yow wold be
as right and vse of the renomed race
of gentle princes, whense yow do descend,
do teache : then neither now shold I haue nede   60
in his or my defense long time to spend,
nor yet my teres or wordes shold want to shede
or say why I shold liue, or he not dye,
whome as I loue on earth, so when it please
in time the Ioue almighty, either by   65
dome of yor cruell hest or otherwayes
to take to heuen frö hense, my fainting breath
this wretched life shall cesse for to susteine
wch shall w^thhold me from the frendly death,
that shold in during ioy conioine vs twaine.   70
But sithe it so hath settled in your minde,
that neither he shall liue, nor yow will be
the father, or the prince, whom we may finde
such, as my falsed hope behight to me,
as his desertes in seruice to your grace   75
do iustly claime, or as my ruthefull teres
do humbly craue : if neither in this case
for him may he, nor I appease the fearce
and cruel rage of grefe that straines yor hart :
alas vain is to ask what I can say   80
why I shold liue : sufficeth for my part
to say I will not liue and there to stay.

69 w^ch] that : *n.* w^ch   70 that] w^ch : *n.* y^t   78 fearce] feares

4. *Scene.*

Iulio.   Tancrede.   Guisharde.

Iulio
bringeth
the earle
prisoner.

If please your highnesse, loe here haue I brought
captiue, as was cōmaunded by your grace,
this gentleman, whom we haue happly caught,
as was foretold, climbing out of the place
where we were willed to watch.   What ells shal please   5
yor highnesse to cōmaund, loe here the hart,
the hand and body prest by land and seas,
through frost and fire, through peril, peine and smart.
Tanc. Iulio, we praise yor truth.   Ah Palurine,
had I deserued that in so traitorous wise   10
thow shold present vnto these woefull eyen
my shame? whearon so deadly grefe doeth rise,
and whelmes my greued hart wth depe distresse,
that neither can I liue content to liue,
nor cesse to liue.   Such paine doeth still oppresse   15
my soule, that still in wrath and woe I striue,
and straine my fainting breath to fede my grefe
wth wordes, and sighes.   But such, such is the smart,
that neither Ioue him self can geue relefe,
nor wayling can suffice t'expresse my hart.   20
Then Palurine, what shall I deme of thee,
that thus thy woefull prince doest dayly slay?
Sithe plaint and teres suffise not, I will see
if death and blood suffise my paine to stay.
Guis. Sir, neither do your trickling teres delight   25
my wretched soule, nor yet myne owne vnhap
doeth greue my hart.   Such is the endlesse might
of loue, that neuer shall the cruel hap,
that did enuie my ioyes, inuade this brest

---

iv. *Guisharde*] Counte pallurine   1 *left margin*) Iulio   12 grefe
doeth] greifes do   25 *Guis.*] Pal.

so farr wth dolor and with dred, that I   30
for her, that wholly hath my heart possessed,
in greatest lust to liue shold fere to dye.
Such is againe my truthe vnto your grace,
that more your grefe assailes my soule wth paine,
than can my bloody slaughter in this case.   35
But greater lord is loue, and larger reigne
he hath vpon eche god and mortal wight,
than yow vpon yor subiectes haue, or I
vpon my self. What then shall most delight
your greued ghost, that I shall liue or dye,   40
to ease yor paine, I am content to beare.
and eke by death I ioy that I shall showe
my self her owne, that hers was liuing here,
and hers will be, where euer my ghost shall goe.
Vse yow my life or death for your relefe,   45
to stay the teres that moist yor grefefull eyen:
and I will vse my life and death for prefe
that hers I liued and dye that liuëd myne.
   Tanc. Thyne, Palurine? and shall I so susteine
such wrong? is she not myne, and only myne? 50
Me leuer were ten thousand times be slayen,
than thow shold iustly claime and vse for thyne
her that is dearer than my self to me.
Iulio, we will that yow informe streightway
Renuchio, how we cõmaund that he   55
and yow this traitor Palurine conuey
vnto the dongeon depe, where whilom was,
the toure that length of time hath made decay.
There shall he stay till farther of the case
yow vnderstand by vs: for wch we will   60
Renuchio shall resort to vs to know
what we entend, and how he shall fullfill

   32 shold] shall : *u.* shuld   44 my ghost] I : *u.* my ghost   45 your]
my : *c.* yor   58 *There is no rhyme to* decay *in either MS., but there
is no other evidence of a missing line. The author was probably led into an
oversight by the* conuey *of 56.*

our pleasure in the rest.　For sorrow soe
doeth boile within my brest, and stilles the brine
out of these flowing eyes, that till they see　　　　65
some sharp reuenge on thee, ô Palurine,
by cruel slaughter, vaine it is for me
to hope the stay of grefe.

　　Guis.　　　　　　　　O mighty Ioue,
that hâst thy self euen frõ thy heuenly throne
stowped down, felt, and cõfessed the force of Loue,　70
bend gentle eare vnto the woefull mone
of me poore wretch, and graunt that I require.
Help to persuade that same great god, that he
so farr remitt his might, and slake his fire
from my dere ladies kindled hart, that she　　　　75
may heare my death w^{th}out her hurt.　And soe
I yeld my self, my silly soule, and all
to him for her, for whom my death shall showe
I liued, and as I liued I dye her thrall.
Graunt this, o greatest god.　This shall suffise　80
my faithfull heart to dye in ioyfull wise.

Tancred hastyly departeth into the palace.

Cupide.

Guishard is led to prison.

The Chore.

The frutes of Paris loue whoe doeth not know,
nor eke what was the end of Helenes ioy,
he may behold the fall and ouerthrowe
of Priames house, and of the town of Troy,
his death at last, and her eternall shame,　　　5
for whom so many a noble knight was slayen,
so many a duke, so many a prince of fame
bereft his life, and left there in the plaine :
Medëaes armed hand, Elisaes sword,
wretched Lëander drenched in the flood,　　　10
Phyllis so long that wayted for her lord,

Dido.

67 by cruel] w^{th} : *u.* by　　68 Guis.] Pa

do shew the end of wicked loue is blood.
But he that doeth in vertue his lady serue,
ne willes but what vnto her honor longes,
he neuer standes in cruel point to sterue :　15
he feleth not the panges, ne raging thronges
of blind Cupide : he liues not in despeir,
as doen his seruãtes all, ne spendes his dayes
twixt ioy and care, betwixt vain hope and fere :
but sekes allway what may his soueraigne please　20
in honor !　He, who so serues, reapes the frute
of his swete seruice ay.　No ielous drede,
nor no suspect of ought to let the sute,
wch causeth oft the louers hart to blede,
doeth frete his minde, or burneth in his brest.　25
He waileth not by day, nor wakes by night,
when euery other liuing thing doeth rest :
nor findes his life or death in her one sight,
as pleaseth her to smile, or ells to frowne,
that holdes his heart : ne writes his woefull laies,　30
to moue to pitie, or to pluck adowne
her stony minde, wch yeldes, as to the seas
the rocky cliue that standeth on the shore.
And many a time the guerdon of their loue
repentance is.　In vertue serue therfore　35
thy chast ladie : nor do thow not so loue,
as whilom Venus did the fair Adone,
but as Diana loued th'Amazons sonne.
Through her request the goddes to him alone
restored new life : the twine, that was vndoen,　40
was by the sistren twisted him againe.
Desire not of thy soueraine the thing
wherof shame may ensue by any meane :
nor wish not ought that may dishonor bring.
Petrarc. So whilom did the learned Tuscane serue　45

17 liues] lyves : hopes *above the line*　28 findes] fynishe : *u.* findes
33 standeth] standen : *c.* standeth　44 may] might

his chast ladie, and glorie was their end.
Such ar the frutes, that louers doen deserue,
whoes seruice doeth to vertue and honor tend.

5. *Act.* .1. *Scene.*

Renuchio.   the Chore.

Renuchio
cometh
out of the
palace.

O cruel fate !   O dolefull destinie !
O heauy hap !   O woe can not be told !
Suffised not, alas, that I shold see
his piteous death, and wth these eyes behold
so foule a dede ? but wth renewing care   5
thus to distreine my hart ? that I shold be
the woefull messager, that must declare
(o me, alas) that sight wch I did see ?
and that eke vnto her ? to whome when I
my drery message shall pronounce, I know   10
it nedes must end her life.   And vnto me,
that am allrudy fraughted full of woe,
how can it but afresh reuiue my paine
to see this ladie take it so to hart ?
In this distresse loe here do I remaine ;   15
ne wote, alas, the sorrowes of whoes smart
first to lament, either thy wailfull end,
o worthy earle, and of thy death the drere,
or ells the hugie heapes of harmes, that bend,
o woefull Quene, now toward thee so nere.   20

   Chor. What newes be these ?
   Renu.   Is this Salerne I see ?
what ? doeth king Tancred gouern here, and guide ?

5. *Act. . . . the Chore.*] Actus Quintus : Scena prima : Rhenuccio the
messenger :   (*margin*) Renuchio . . . palace] Renuccio the messenger
sent by the king Tancred, wth the hart of Countie pallurine in a Cupp
of gold, vnto faier Gismonda : cometh in wth the said cupp of gold in his
hand and the hart therin, and ther telleth the hoole maner of deathe

Is this the place where ciuile people be?
or do the sauage Scythians here abide?

   Chor. What meanes this cruel folk, and eke this king,   25
that thus yow name? Declare how standes the case:
and whatsoëuer dolefull newes yow bring
recompt fourthwith.

   Ren.   Where shall I turne my face?
or whether shall I bend my weryed sight?
What euer way I seke or can deuise,   30
or do I what I can to ease my plight,
the cruel fact is euer in myne eyes.

   Chor. Leaue of this wise to hold vs in such maze
of doutfull drede what newes yow haue to show.
For drede of thinges vnknowen doeth allway cause   35
man drede the worst, till he the better know.
Tell therfore what is chaunced, and wherunto
this bloody cuppe thus in your hand yow bring.

   Ren. Sins so is your request that I shold do,
although my minde so sorrowfull a thing   40
repine to tell, and though my voice eschue
to say what I haue seen: yet, sins your will
so fixed standes to heare wherfore I rue,
your great desire I shall hearin fulfill.
Fast by Salern citie, amidde the plaine,   45
there standes a hill, whoes bottome huge and round
throwen out in breadth a large space doeth conteine,
and gathering vp in heyghth small frõ the ground
still lesse and lesse it mountes. Here somtime was
a goodly tower vprered, that floured in fame   50
while fate and fortune serued. But time doeth passe,
and wth her swey eke passeth all this same.
For now the walles ben euened wth the plaine,
and all the rest so foully lyeth defaced,
as but the only shade doeth there remaine   55
of that wch there was buylt in time forepast.

        41 though] that: *u.* thowghe

Yet doeth that show what worthy work tofore
hath there ben wrought.   One parcell of that tower
euen yet doeth stand, whome time could not forlore,
fortune downthrowe, nor length of yeres deuoure :   60
a strong turrett cōpact of stone and rock,
hugie without, but horrible within :
to passe to which, by force of handy stroke
a croked streight is made, that entres in,
and leadeth yow into this lothely place.   65
Within the which carued into the ground
a depe dungeon there rūnes of narrow space,
dredefull, and dark, where neuer light is found.
Into this vggly caue, by cruel hest
of King Tancred, wero diuerse seruantes sent,   70
to work the horror of his furious brest,
erst nourished in his rage, and now sterne bent
to haue the same performed.   I woefull wight
was chosen eke for one to do the thing,
that to our charge so streightly was behight,   75
in sort as was cōmaunded by the King.
Within which dredfull prison when we came,
the noble Counté Palurine, that there
lay chained in gyues fast fettred in the same,
out of the dark dongeon we did vprere,   80
and haled him thense into a brighter place,
that gaue vs light to work our murder there.
But when I ones beheld his manly face,
and saw his chere no more appalled wᵗʰ fere
of present death, than he whom neuer drede   85
did ones amoue, my heart abhorrëd than
to geue cōsent vnto so foule a dede,
that wretched death shold reue so worthy a man.
On false fortune I cryed with lowd cōplaint,
that in such sort could deme this earle to dye.   90
But he, whome neither grefe ne fere could taint,

wth smiling chere him self oft willeth me
to leaue to plaine his case, or sorrow make
for him : for he was farr more glad apayed
death to embrace thus for his ladies sake,   95
than life, or all the ioyes of life, he sayed.
For losse of life, he sayed, greued him no more
than losse of that which he estemed least.
His ladies grefe, lest she shold rue thearfore,
was all the cause of grefe within his brest.   100
He prayed therfore that they wold make report
to her of these last wordes that he wold say :
that though he neuer could in any sort
her gentlenesse reacquite, nor neuer lay
wthin his power to serue her as he wold :   105
yet had she ay his hart, wth hand and might
to do her all the honor that he could.
This was to him of all the ioyes, that might
reioise his hart, the chefest ioy of all,
that, to declare the faithfull hart that he   110
did beare to her, fortune so well did fall,
that in her loue he mought bothe liue and dye.
After these wordes he stayed, and spake no more,
but ioyfully beholding vs echeone
his wordes and chere ameruailed vs so sore,   115
that still we stode ; when fourthwth therupon,
but why slack yow (quod he) to do the thing
for which yow come ?   Make spede, and stay no more :
performe your maisters will : now tell the King,
he hath his death, for whoes he longed so sore.   120
And with those wordes him self, wth his own hand,
fastens the bandes about his neck.   The rest
wondring at his stout heart astōnied stand
to see him offre him self to death so prest.
What stony brest, or what hard hart of flint   125

121 those] these : those *aboue*   124 him] himself

wold not haue molt to see this drery sight,
so worthy a man, whome death nor fortunes dint
could not disarme, murdred wth such despight,
and in such sort bereft amidde the floures
of his fresh yeres, that ruthefull was to seen?   130
For violent is death when he deuoures   "
yongmen or virgins while their youth is grene.   "
But iniust fortune, that so seld vpheaues
the worthy man, hath blindly turned her whele :
the whurle wherof bothe life and honor reaues   135
from him, on whome she did so lately smile.
Loe now the seruâtes, seing him take the bandes,
and on his neck him self to make them fast,
wthout delay putt to their woefull handes,
and sought to work their fierce entent wth hast.   140
They stretch the bandes, and euën when the breath
began to faile his brest, they slacked againe
(so did their handes repine against his death)
and oft times loosed, alas, vnto his paine.
But date of death that fixed is so fast,   145
beyond his course there may no wight extend,
for strangled is this noble earle at last,
and reft of life, vnworthy such an end.
    Cho. O cruel dede.
    Ren.   Why ? deme ye this to be
the dolefull newes that I haue now to show?   150
Is here (think yow ?) end of the crueltie.
that I haue seen ?
    Cho.   Could worse or crueller woe
be wrought to him, than to bereue him life ?
    Ren. What ? think yow this outrage did end so well?
The horror of the fact, the greatest grefe,   155
the cruëltie, the terror is to tell.
    Cho. Alack : what could be more ?   They threw percase
the dead body to be deuoured and eate

130 ruthefull] rufull

of the cruel wilde beastes.

Ren.   O me, alas,
Wold god it had ben cast a dolefull meate   160
to beastes and birdes.   But loe that dredfull thing,
wch euen the tygre wold not work, but to
fulfill his hongre wth, that hath the King
withouten ruthe cōmaunded to be do,
only to please his cruel hart withall.   165
Oh, happy had ben his chaūce, to happy alas,
if birdes had eate his corps, yea hart and all
which here I bring, and not thus to the face
of his dere loue I to present the same,
wth sight of wch eke to procure her end.   170

Chor. What kind of crueltie is this yow name,
declare fourthwith : and tell whearto doeth tend
this farther plaint.

Ren.   After his breath was gone
bereft thus from his brest by cruell force
streight they despoiled him, and, not alone   175
contented wth his death, on the dead corps,
whom sauage beastes do spare, ginne they to showe
new crueltie, and wth a swerd they pearce
his naked belly, and vnrippe it soe
that out the bowelles gush.   Whoe can rehearse   180
the dolefull sight, wherewth my hart euen bledde ?
The warme entrailes were toren out of his brest
wthin their handes trēbling not fully dead :
his veines smoked : his bowelles all to strest
ruthelesse were rent, and throwen amidde the place :   185
all clottered lay the blood in lompes of gore,
sprent on his corps, and on his palëd face.
His hart panting out from his brest they tore,
and cruelly vpon a swordës point

they fixe the same, and in this woful wise   190
vnto the King this hart do they present,
a sight longed for to fede his irefull eyes.
The King perceiuing eche thing to be wrought
as he had willed, reioysing to behold
vpon the bloody swerdës point ybrought   195
the perced hart, calles for this cuppe of gold,
into the wch the woefull hart he cast,
and reaching me the same, now goe (quod he)
vnto my daughter, and wth spedy hast
present her this, and say to her from me :   200
Thy father hath here in this cup thee sent   '
that thing to ioy and comfort thee withall   "
wch thow loued best, euen as thow weart content   "
to côfort him wth his chefe ioy of all.   "
    Cho. O hatefull fact !   O passing crueltie !   205
O murder wrought wth to much hard despite !
O haynous dede ! wch no posteritie
will ones beleue.
    Ren.   Thus was this worthy wight
strangled vnto the death, yea after death
his hart and blood debowelled frô his brest.   210
But what auaileth plaint? it is but breath
forwasted all in vain.   Why do I rest
here in this place? why go I not, and do
the woefull message to my charge cômitt?
Now were it not that I am forced thearto   215
by a Kinges will, here wold I stay my fete,
ne one whit farther goe in this entent.
But I must yeld me to my princes hest,
and tell, alas, the dolefull message sent.
Yet doeth this somwhat côfort myne vnrest,   220
that I determe her grefe not to behold,
but goe as sone as is my message tolde.

203 loued] lovest : *u.* loved   221 determe] determine : *u.* determe

2. *Scene.*

Renuchio.   Gismonde.

Thy father, o Quene, here in this cup hath sent
that thing, to ioy and comfort thee withall,
wch thow loued best, euen as thow weart cõtent
to comfort him wth his chefe ioy of all.

   Gism. Now, now, alas come is that houre accurst   5
that I poore wight so long haue loked for.
Now hath my father filled his egre thirst
wth gyltlesse blood wch he desired so sóre.
This perced hart it is myne earles, I know.
My fathers wordes do proue the same to well.   10
This bloody cupp his dolefull death doeth show.
This message doeth the same to plainly tell.
Certes vnto so noble a hart could not
a fitter herse ben lotted than of gold.
Discretely therfore hath my father wrought,   15
that thus hath sent it me for to behold.
In all my life to this my latter day
so passing dere ay haue I found to me
my fathers tender loue, that I ne may
deserue the same : but inespecially   20
so much in this, as I requiër ye
these my last thankes to yeld to him therfore :
wch is to me the greatest grefe may be,
that I can not reacquite the same no more.
Ah pleasant harborrow of my hartës thought.   25
Ah swete delight, ioy, cõfort of my life.
Ah cursed be his crueltie that wrought
thee this despite, and vnto me such grefe,
to make me to behold thus wth these eyes

ii. Renuchio. Gismonde] *om.*   (*margin*) Renuchio . . . chamber]
Renuccio : his message from king Tancred to Gismonda   7 thirst] lust :
c. thurst   24 (*margin*) Renuchio departeth] here doth renuccio departe
25 (*margin*) now turnes she to the cupp & sayes

thy woefull hart, and force me here to see   30
this dolefull sight.   Alas, did not suffise
that wth my hartes eyen cõtinually
I did behold the same?   Thow hâst fordone
the course of kinde, dispatched thy life frõ snares
of fortunes venomed bayt; yea thow hâst rõne   35
the mortall race, and left these worldly cares,
and of thy foe, to honor thee withall,
receiued a worthy graue to thy desert.
Nothing doeth want to thy iust funerall,
but euen my teres to wash thy bloody hart   40
thus fouled and defaced, wch to the end
eke thow might haue, Ioue in the mynde putt soe
of my despitefull father for to send
thy hart to me. and thow shalt haue thẽ loe,
though I determed to shede no tere at all,   45
but wth drye eyes and constant face to dye,
yea though I thought to wett thy funerall
only wth blood, and wth no weping eye.
This doen fourthwth my soule shall come to thee,
whome in thy life thow did so derely loue   50
Ah Lord, wth what more sweter companie,
or more content, or safer may I proue
to seke to passe to places all vnknowen,
than thus wth thee?   For I am sure euen here   55
doest thow yet stay, and tarry me thine owne.
Thy soule abideth me to be thy fere,
and lingreth in this place for me, I know.
Why dye I not thearfore? why do I stay?
why do I not this woefull life forgoe?
and with these handes bereue this breath away?   60 She taketh
This venomed water shall abridge my life :   a glasse of
this for the same entent prouided I,   poyson out
                                                                            of her
                                                                            pocket.

31 Alas] ah: *u.* alas   did] did it (it *u.*)   42 might] mightest
59 I not] not I   61 This] this : *c.* my   (*margin*) She . . . pocket]
now goes she to some cupp borde or place wher the vyoll of poison ys &
takes it & sayes :

wch may bothe ease and end my woefull grefe.
Why then ? and shall we thus vnwroken dye?
Shall I not work some iust reuenge on him   65
that thus hath slayen my loue? shall not these hãdes
fiër his gates, and make the flames to clime
vnto his palace toppes, wth burning brandes
his court here to cõsume, and eke therewith
him self and all, and on his cinders wreke   70
my cruel wrath, and gnash thẽ wth my tethe,
and fall amidde the flames my self, to breke
this woefull life in two?   Thus shall not I
reuenge his death, ere I this body slay,

and reue this brest the life?   But let vs dye :   75
for in such sort it likes vs to assay
to passe down to the paled ghostes of hell,
and there enioy my loue, whome thus my sire
wold not permitt in earth wth me to dwell.

Claudia rũneth into the palace to tell the King of Gismond.

He by my death shall haue more woe, than fire   80
or flames wthin his palace gates could bring.
This shall therfore suffise, that I will dye.
My death his blood shall wreke against the King.
This hart and eke myne owne loe now will I
within one tombe engraue, that so may rest   85
my loue, my life, my death within this brest.

3. *Scene.*

Tancrede.   *Gismonde.*

Tancred cometh out of the palace.

Tancred entreth into Gismõdes chãber.

Ay me, doeth my dere daughter take it soe ?
What ? will she slay her self, and be thereby
worker of her own death, causer of woe
vnto her frendes, and meane to make me dye?
Dẽre daughter recomfort your distresse,   5
and suffer not these heapes of grefe t'assaile
your wery mind.

3 *Scene. Tancrede. Gismonde.*] *omitted* : (*left margin*) **Tancred**

Gism. .   O King, seke not to cesse
my grefe wth plaint, whom plaint may not auaile.

Tanc. O my daughter hâst thow receiued thy life
from me ? and wilt thow, to reacquite the same,   10
yeld me my death? yea death, and greater grefe
to see thee dye for him that did defame
thyne honor thus, my kingdome, and my crowne ?

Gism. Yea rather hearfore gauest thow life to me
to haue my death ? So sayest thow my renoune,   15
thy kingdome and thy crowne defamed to be,
when thow my loue wth cruel handes hâst slayen,
and sent his heart to me for to behold?
But in thy brest if any spark remaine
of thy dere loue : if euer yet I could   20
so much of thee deserue : or at the least
if wth my last desire I may obteine
this at thy handes, geue me this one request,
and let me not spend my last breath in vaine.
My life desire I not, wch neither is   25
in thee to geue, nor in my self to saue
although I wold : nor yet I ask not this
as mercie for myne earle in ought to craue,
whome I to well do know how thow hâst slayen.
No, no, father, thy hard and cruel wrong   30
wth pacience, as I may, I will susteine
in woefull life, wch now shall not be long.
But this one sute, father, if vnto me
thow graunt, though I can not the same reacquite,
th'immortal goddes shall render vnto thee   35
thy due reward, and largely guerdon it :
that, sins it pleased thee not thus secretely
I might enioy my loue, his corps and myne
may nathelesse together graued be,

and in one tombe our bodies bothe to shrine.   40
With wch this small request eke do I pray,
that on the same grauen in brasse thow place
this woefull epitaph wch I shall say,
that all louers may rue this mornefull case
Loe here within one tóbe whear harbour twaine,   "   45
Gismóda Quene, and Counte Palurine :   "
she loued him, he for her loue was slayen,   "
for whoes reuenge eke lyes she here in shrine.   "

Gismond dyeth.   *Tanc.* O me, alas, now do the cruel paines
of cursed death my dere daughter bereue.   50
Alas, why bide I here ?   The sight constraines
me woefull man this woefull place to leaue.

4. *Scene.*

Tancred cometh out of Gismondes chamber.   *Tancrede.*

O dolorous happe, ruthefull, and all of woe !
Alas I carefull wretch, what resteth me ?
Shall I now liue, that wth these eyes did soe
behold my daughter dy ?   What ? shall I see
her death before my face that was my life,   5
and I to lyue that was her lyues decay ?
Shall not this hand reache to this hart the knife,
that may bereue bothe sight and life away,
and in the shadoes dark to seke her ghost
and wander there wth her ?   Shall not, alas,   10
this spedy death be wrought, sithe I haue lost
my dearest ioy of all ?   What ? shall I passe
my later dayes in paine, and spend myne age
in teres and plaint ?   Shall I now leade my life
all solitarie, as doeth the bird in cage,   15
and fede my woefull yeres wth wailefull grefe ?

4. *Scene*] Scena 3^a : Scene III *R*   1 ruthefull] rufull *H, R*   2
carefull] caitif *R*   13 later] latter *H, R*

No, no, so will not I my dayes prolong
to seke to liue one houre, sithe she is gone.
This brest so can not bend to such a wrong,
that she shold dye and I to liue alone.   20
No. thus will I. she shall haue her request
and in most royall sort her funerall
will I performe.   Within one tòbe shall rest
her earle and she. her epitaph withall
grauëd thearon shalbe.   This will I do.   25
And when these eyes some aged teres haue shed,
the tomb my self then will I crepe into,
and wth my blood all bayne their bodies dead.
This heart there will I perce, and reue this brest
the irksome life, and wreke my wrathfull ire   30
vpon my self.   She shall haue her request:
and I by death will purchace my desire.

Epilogus.

If now perhappes yow either loke to see
th'unhappy louers, or the cruel siro
here to be buried as sittes their degree,
or as the dyeng ladie did require,
or as the ruthefull king in depe despeir   5
behight of late, whoe now him self hath slayen:
or if perchaunse yow stand in doutfull fere,
sithe mad Megera is not returned againe,
least wandring in the world she so bestow
the snakes that crall about her furious face,   10
as they may raise new ruthes, new kindes of woe,
bothe so, and there, and such as yow parcase
wold be full lothe so great so nere to see:
I am come fourth to do yow all to wete,

17 not I] I not *H, R*   27, 31 my] me : *u.* my   28 all] *inserted
above line.*   29 perce] place *R*   32 *H, R have* finis *below this line*
     Ep. 1, 7 yow] ye *H, R*   11 they] ther : *u.* they   raise] rise : *u.*
raise

through grefe, wherin the lordes of Salern be,   15
the buriall pompe is not prepared yet.
And for the furie yow shall vnderstand,
that neither doeth the litle greatest God
finde such rebelling here in Britain land
against his royall power, as asketh rod   20
of ruthe from hell to wreke his names decay.
Nor Pluto heareth English ghostes cōplaine
our dames disteined lyues.   Therfore ye may
be free frō fere.   Sufficeth to mainteine
the vertues wch we honor in yow all :   25
so as our Britain ghostes, when life is past,
may praise in heuen, not plaine in Plutœs hall
our dames, but hold them vertuous and chast,
worthy to liue where furie neuer came,
where Loue can see, and beares no deadly bowe ;   30
whoes lyues eternall tromp of glorious fame
with ioyfull sound to honest eares shall blow.

---

23 our] o^r *H*, Or *R*   ye] you *H, R*   25 w^{ch}] that : *u.* which   31
eternall] th' eternall *H, R* : th *u. in H*   32 *H, R have below this*
line : finis.

   At the top of the verso comes in H : The Tragedie of gismond of Salerne.
The sonnets, argument, and dramatis personae follow as on pp. 163–6.

IV

THE MISFORTUNES OF ARTHUR

BY

THOMAS HUGHES

The only authority for the text of this play is the quarto edition (*Q*), of which the title-page is reproduced in facsimile opposite. Two copies survive, that known as the Garrick quarto (*GQ*) in the British Museum, and another in the library of the Duke of Devonshire, which formerly belonged to John Philip Kemble (*KQ*). The Kemble copy lacks the title-page and Nicholas Trotte's prologue, which have been supplied in script. Beyond modernized punctuation, capitalization, and spelling, however, the Kemble script yields nothing except *of* for *to* in line 88 (*of Peeres*) and *plague* for *plagues* in line 129. These are apparently slips of the scribe who supplied the missing pages, probably from the Garrick copy, which is complete ; the script is certainly after 1804, as some of the paper used for it bears that date in a watermark. See Grumbine's edition, p. 99.

CERTAINE DE-
uises and shewes presented to
her MAIESTIE by the Gentlemen of
Grayes-Inne at her Highnesse Court in
Greenewich, *the twenty eighth day of*
Februarie in the thirtieth yeare of her
MAIESTIES most happy
Raigne.

AT LONDON
Printed by Robert Robinson.
1587.

AN INTRODVCTI-
on penned by Nicholas Trotte

Gentleman one of the society of Grayes-Inne ; *which*
was pronounced in manner following. *viz.* Three
Muses *came vpon the Stage apparelled accordingly*
bringing fiue Gentlemen Students with them attyred
in their vsuall garments, whom one of the *Muses* presented to her M A I E S T I E *as Captiues : the cause*
whereof she deliuered by speach
as followeth.

O F Conquest (gratious Queene) the signs & fruits,
Atchiu'd gainst such, as wrongfully withheld
The seruice by choice wits to *Muses* due ;
In humbliest wise, these Captiues we present.
And least your highnes might suspect the gift   5
As spoile of Warre, that Iustice might impeach ;
Heare and discerne how iust our quarrell was
Auowed (as you see) by good successe.
A Dame there is, whom men *Astrea* terme,
Shee that pronounceth Oracles of Lawes,   10
Who to prepare fit seruants for her traine
As by Commission takes vp flowring wits,
Whom first she schooleth to forget and scorne
The noble skils of language and of Arts,
The wisedome, which discourse of stories teach,   15
The ornaments which various knowledge yeelds ;
But Poesie she hath in most disdaine,
And Marshals it next Follyes scorned place.
Then, when she hath these worthy Prints defac'd
Out of the mindes that can endure her hand,   20
What doth she then supplie in steede of these ?
Forsooth some olde reports of altered lawes,
Clamors of Courts, and cauils vpon words,
Grounds without ground, supported by conceit,
And reasons of more subtiltie then sense,   25
What shall I say of Moote points straunge, and doubts
Still argued but neuer yet agreed ?

And shee, that doth deride the Poets lawe,
Because he must his words in order place,
Forgets her formes of pleading more precise,   30
More bound to words then is the Poets lore :
And for these fine conceits she fitly chose,
A tongue that Barbarisme it selfe doth vse.
We noting all these wrongs did long expect
There hard condition would haue made them wise,   35
To offer vs their seruise plac'd so ill,
But finding them addicted to their choyce,
And specially desirous to present
Your Maiestie with fruits of Prouince newe,
Now did resolue to double force and skill,   40
And found and vsde the vantage of the time,
Surprisde their fort, and tooke them Captiues all.
So now submisse, as to their state belongs
They gladly yeelde their homage long withdrawne,
And Poetry which they did most contemne   45
They glory now her fauours for to weare.
My sisters laught to see them take the penne,
And lose their wits all in vnwoonted walkes.
But to your highnes that delight we leaue,
To see these Poets newe their Stile aduaunce.   50
Such as they are, or naught or litle worth,
Deigne to accept, and therewith we beseech,
That nouelty giue price to worthlesse things.

¶ *Vnto this speuch one of the Gentlemen answered as followeth.*

GOOD Ladies vnacquaint with cunning reach,
And easly led to glory in your powre,   55
Heare now abasht our late dissembled mindes.
Not now the first time as your selues best knowe,
Ye Muses sought our seruice to commaund,
Oft haue ye wandred from Pernassus hill,
And shewed your selues with sweet & tempting grace,   60
But yet returnd your traine encreasde with fewe.

57 *Q period after* knowe

This resolution doth continue still.
Vnto *Astreas* name we honour beare,
Whose sound perfections we doe more admire,
Then all the vanted store.of Muses guifts.   65
Let this be one (which last you put in vre,
In well deprauing that deserueth praise)
No eloquence, disguising reasons shape,
Nor Poetrie, each vaine affections nurce,
No various historie that doth leade the minde   70
Abroad to auncient tales from instant vse,
Nor these, nor other moe, too long to note,
Can winne *Astreas* seruants to remoue
Their seruice, once deuote to better things.
They with attentiue mindes and serious wits,   75
Reuolue records of deepe Iudiciall Acts,
They waigh with steaddy and indifferent hand
Each word of lawe, each circumstance of right,
They hold the grounds which time & vse hath sooth'd
(Though shallow sense conceiue them as conceits)   80
Presumptuous sense, whose ignorance dare iudge
Of things remou'd by reason from her reach.
One doubt in mootes by argument encreasc'd
Cleares many doubts, experience doth obiect.
The language she first chose, and still retaines,   85
Exhibites naked truth in aptest termes.
Our Industrie maintaineth vnimpeach't
Prerogatiue of Prince, respect to Peeres,
The Commons libertie, and each mans right :
Suppresseth mutin force, and practicke fraude.   90
Things that for worth our studious care deserue.
Yet neuer did we banish nor reiect
Those ornaments of knowledge nor of toungs.
That slander enuious ignorance did raise.
With Muses still we entercourse allowe,   95
T'enrich our state with all there forreine fraight :
But neuer homage nor acknowledgement
Such as of Subiects alleageance doth require.

Now heere the cause of your late Conquest wonne
We had discouered your intent to be   100
(And sure ye Ladies are not secrete all.
Speach and not silence is the Muses grace)
We well perceiu'd (I say) your minde to be
T'imploy such prisoners, as themselues did yeeld
To serue a Queene, for whom her purest gold   105
Nature refind, that she might therein sette
Both priuate and imperiall vertues all.
Thus (Soueraigne Lady of our lawes and vs)
Zeale may transforme vs into any shape.
We, which with trembling hand the penne did guide   110
Neuer well pleasde all for desire to please
For still your rare perfections did occurre
Which are admir'd of Muses and of men,
Oh with howe steddie hand and heart assur'd
Should we take vp the warlicke Lance or Sword   115
With minde resolu'd to spend our loyall blood
Your least commaund with speede to execute.
O that before our time the fleeting shippe,
Ne'r wandred had in watery wildernes,
That we might first that venture vndertake   120
In strange attempt t'approue our loyall hearts.
Be it Souldiers, Seamen, Poets, or what els.
In seruice once inioynd, to ready mindes
Our want of vse should our deuoyer encrease.
Now since in steade of art we bring but zeale,   125
In steade of prayse we humbly pardon craue.
The matter which we purpose to present,
Since streights of time our liberty controwles
In tragike note the plagues of vice recounts.
How sutes a Tragedie for such a time?   130
Thus. For that since your sacred Maiestie
In gratious hands the regall Scepter held
All Tragedies are fled from State, to stadge.

Nicholas Trotte.

101 *Q period after* ye, *none after* all   113 *Q no stop at end of line.*

The misfortunes of Arthur (Vther Pen-

dragons Sonne) *reduced into Tragicall notes by* THOMAS
HVGHES *one of the societie of* Grayes-Inne. *And here set
downe as it past from vnder his handes and as it was presented,
excepting certaine wordes and lines, where some of the Actors
either helped their memories by brief omission: or fitted their* 5
*acting by some alteration. With a note in the ende, of such
speaches as were penned by others in lue of some of these hereafter following.*

The argument of the
Tragedie.

AT a banquet made by *Vther Pendragon* for the solemnising of
his conquest against the *Saxons,* he fell inamoured with *Igerna*
wife to *Gorlois* Duke of *Cornwell.* Who perceiuing the Kings
passion, departed with his wife and prepared warres at *Cornwell,*
where also in a strong holde beyond him hee placed her. Then 5
the King leuied an armye to suppresse him, but waxing impatient
of his desire to *Igerna,* transformed himselfe by *Merlin* his cunning,
into the likenesse of *Gorlois.* And after his acceptance with *Igerna*
he returned to his siedge, where he slew *Gorlois. Igerna* was
deliuered of *Arthur* and *Anne* twins of the same birth. *Vther* 10
Pendragon 15. yeres after pursuing the *Saxons* was by them
poysoned. *Arthur* delighted in his sister *Anne,* who made him
father of *Mordred.* Seuenteene yeres after *Lucius Tiberius* of
Rome demanded a tribute due by the conquest of *Cæsar. Arthur*
gathered the powers of 13. Kinges besides his owne, and leauing 15
his Queene Gueneuora in the tuition of *Mordred,* to whome likewise
he committed the kingdome in his absence, arriued at *Fraunce,*
where after 9. yeares warres, he sent the slaine bodie of *Tiberius*
vnto *Rome* for the tribute. During this absence *Mordred* grew
ambicious, for th'effecting whereof he made loue to *Gueneuora,* who 20
gaue eare vnto him. Then by th'assistance of *Gilla* a *Brittish* Lord
hee vsurped, and for mainteinance entertayned with large promises,

the *Saxons, Irish, Pictes,* & *Normands.* *Gueneuora* hearing that *Arthur* was alreadie embarked for returne, through dispaire pur-posing diuersly, sometimes to kill her husband, sometimes to kill 25 her selfe, at last resolued to enter into religion. *Arthur* at his landing was resisted on the stronds of *Douer,* where he put *Mordred* to flight. The last fielde was fought at *Cornwell,* where after the death of one hundred and tweentie thousand sauing on either side 20, *Mordred* receiued his death, and *Arthur* his deadly wound.   30

❡ *The Argument and manner of th* first dumbe shewe.

SOunding the musicke, there rose three furies from vnder the stage apparelled accordingly with snakes and flames about their blacke haires and garments. The first with a Snake in the right hande and a cup of wine with a Snake athwart the cup in the left hand. The second with a firebrand in the right hande, and a Cupid 5 *in the left: The thirde with a whippe in the right hande and a* Pægasus *in the left. Whiles they went masking about the stage, there came from another place three* Nuns *which walked by them selues. Then after a full sight giuen to the beholders, they all parted, the furies to* Mordreds *house, the* Nuns *to the Cloister. By* 10 *the first furie with the Snake and Cup was signified the Banquet of* Vther Pendragon, *and afterward his death which insued by poysoned cup. The second furie with her firebrande &* Cupid *represented* Vthers *vnlawfull heate and loue conceyued at the banquet, which neuer ceased in his posteritie. By the third with her whip and* 15 Pægasus *was prefigured the crueltie and ambition which thence insued and continued to th'effecting of this tragidie. By the* Nuns *was signified the remorse and dispaire of* Gueneuora, *that wanting other hope tooke a Nunrie for her refuge. After their departure, the fowre which represented the* Chorus *tooke their places.*   20

The argument of the first Act.

1 IN the first scene the spirit of *Gorlois* Duke of Cornwell, the man first & most wronged in this historie being dispoild both of Wife, Dukedome and life craueth reuenge for these iniuries, denouncing the whole misfortune insuing.

2 In the second scene, *Gueneuora* hearing that *Arthur* was on Seas returning, desperately manaceth his death, from which intent she is disswaded by *Fronia*, a Lady of her Court & priuie to her secretes.

3 In the third scene *Gueneuora* perplexedly mindeth her owne death, whence being diswaded by her sister she resolueth to 'enter into Religion.

4 In the fourth scene *Mordred* goeth about to perswade *Gueneuora* to persist in her loue, but misseth thereof: And then is exhorted by *Conan* (a noble mã of *Brytain*) to reconcile himselfe to his Father at his comming, but refuseth so to doe and resolueth to keepe him from landing by battaile.

The names of the speakers.

Gorlois Duke of Cornwalls ghost.
Gueneuora the Queene.
Fronia a Lady of her trayne.
Angharad sister to the Queene.
Mordred the Usurper.
Conan a faithfull counseller.
Nuntius of Arthurs landing.
The Heralt from Arthur.
Gawin King of Albanie.
Gilla : a Brytishe Earle.
Gillamor King of Ireland.

Cheldrich Duke of Saxonie.
The Lorde of the Pictes.
Arthur King of great Brytain.
Cador Duke of Cornwall.
Hoel King of little Brittaine.
The Heralt from Mordred.
Aschillus King of Denmarke.
The King of Norwaye.
A number of Souldiers.
Nuntius of the last battell.
Gildas a noble man of Brytain.

CHORVS.

THE FIRST ACT
and first scene.

Gorlois.

Gorl. Since thus through channells blacke of *Limbo* lake,
And deepe infernall floude of *Stygian* poole,
The gastly *Caron's* boate transported backe
Thy ghost, from *Pluto's* pittes and glowming shades,
To former light once lost by Destnies doome: 5
Where proude *Pendragon* broylde with shamefull lust,
Dispoylde thee erst of wife, of lande, and life:
Nowe (*Gorlois*) worke thy wish, cast here thy gaule,
Glutte on reuenge: thy wrath abhorrs delayes.

   What though (besides *Pendragons* poysoned end)   10
The vile reproch he wrought thee by thy phere,
Through deepe increase of crymes alike is plagude?
And that the shame thou suffiedst for his lusts,
Reboundeth backe, and stifeleth in his stocke?
Yet is not mischiefe's measure all fulfilde,   15
Nor wreake sufficient wrought: Thy murthered corse
And Dukedome reft, for heauier vengeance cries.

   Come therefore bloomes of setled mischiefes roote,
Come ech thing else, what furie can inuent,
Wreake all at once, infect the ayre with plagues,   20
Till badd to worse, till worse to worst be turnde.
Let mischiefes know no meane, nor plagues an end.
Let th'ofsprings sinne exceede the former stocke:
Let none haue time to hate his former fault,
But still with fresh supplie let punisht cryme   25
Increase, till tyme it make a complet sinne.
   Goe to: some fact, which no age shall allowe,
Nor yet conceale: some fact must needes be darde,

That for the horror great and outrage fell
Thereof, may well beseeme *Pendragons* broode.   30
And first, whiles *Arthurs* nauies homewards flott
Triumphantly bedeckt with *Romaine* spoyles :
Let *Guenouer* expresse what franticke moodes
Distract a wife, when wronging wedlockes rights,
Both fonde and fell, she loues and loathes at once.   35
Let deepe dispaire pursue, till loathing life
Her hatefull heade in cowle and cloister lurke.

Let traiterous *Mordred* keepe his sire from shoare.
Let *Bryttaine* rest a pray for forreine powers,
Let sworde and fire still fedde with mutuall strife   40
Tourne all the Kings to ghoastes, let ciuill warres
And discorde swell till all the realme be torne.

Euen in that soyle whereof my selfe was Duke,
Where first my spowse *Igerna* brake her vowe,
Where this vngracious ofspring was begotte,   45
In *Cornwell*, there, let *Mordreds* death declare,
Let *Arthurs* fatall wounde bewray the wrong,
The murther vile, the rape of wife and weale,
Wherewith their sire incenst both Gods and man :

Thus, thus *Pendragons* seede so sowne and reapte,   50
Thus cursed imps, ill borne, and worse consum'd,
Shall render iust reuenge for parents crimes,
And penance due t'asswadge my swelling wrath.

The whiles O *Cassiopæa* gembright signe,
Most sacred sight, and sweete *Cœlestiall* starre,   55
This *Clymat's* ioy, plac'd in imperiall throne
With fragrant Oliue branche portending peace :
And whosoe'r besides ye heauenly pow'rs
(Her stately trayne with influence diuine,
And milde aspect all prone to *Bryttaines* good)   60
Foresee what present plagues doe threate this Isle :

29 the] *So corrected in the Garrick copy by means of a little printed slip pasted over the last letter. The Kemble copy shows the original reading to have been* thy   54 gembright] gempright *Q*

Preuent not this my wreake. For you their rest's
A happier age a thousand yeares to come :
An age for peace, religion, wealth, and ease,
When all the world shall wonder at your blisse : 65
That, that is yours. Leaue this to *Gorlois* ghoast.
    And see where com's one engine of my hate.
With moods and manners fit for my reuenge. *Exit.*

The second scene.

Gueneuora. Fronia.

Guen. AND dares he after nine yeares space returne,
     And see her face, whom he so long disdain'de ?
Was I then chose and wedded for his stale,
To looke and gape for his retirclesse sayles,
Puft backe, and flittering spread to euery winde ? 5
    O wrong content with no reuenge : seeke out
Vndared plagues, teach *Mordred* how to rage.
Attempt some bloodie, dreadfull, irkesome fact,
And such as *Mordred* would were rather his.
    Why stayest ? it must be done : let bridle goe, 10
Frame out some trap beyonde all vulgar guile,
Beyonde *Medea's* wiles : attempt some fact,
That any wight vnwildie of her selfe,
That any spowse vnfaithfull to her phere,
Durst euer attempt in most dispaire of weale. 15
Spare no reuenge, b'it poyson, knyfe, or fire.
    Fron. Good Madame, temper these outragious moodes,
And let not will vsurpe, where wit should rule.
    Guen. The wrath, that breatheth bloode, doth loath to lurke.
What reason most with holdes, rage wringes perforce. 20
I am disdainde : so will I not be long :
That very houre, that he shall first arriue,
Shall be the last, that shall aforde him life.

I. ii. Gueneuora] Gneneuora *Q*

Though, neither seas, nor lands, nor varres abrode
Sufficed for thy foyle : yet shalt thou finde   25
Farre woorse at home : Thy deepe displeased spowse.
What e'r thou hast fubdude in all thy stay,
This hand shall nowe subdue : then stay thy fill.

What's this ? my mind recoyls, and yrkes these threats :
Anger delayes, my griefe gynnes to asswage,   30
My furie faintes, and sacred wedlockes faith
Presents it selfe.   Why shunst thou fearefull wrath ?
Add coales a freshe, preserue me to this venge.

At lest exyle thy selfe to realmes vnknowen,
And steale his wealth to helpe thy banisht state,   35
For flight is best.   O base and hartlesse feare.
Theft ? exyle ? flight ? all these may *Fortune* sende
Vnsought : but thee beseemes more high reuenge.

Come spitefull fiends, come heapes of furies fell,
Not one, by one, but all at once : my breast   40
Raues not inough : it likes me to be filde
With greater monsters yet.   My hart doth throbbe :
My liuer boyles : some what my minde portendes,
Vncertayne what : but whatsoeuer, it's huge.

So it exceede, be what it will : it's well.   45
Omit no plague, and none will be inough.
Wrong cannot be reueng'd, but by excesse.

  Fron. O spare this heate : you yeelde too much to rage,
Y'are too vniust : is there no meane in wrong ?

  Guen. Wrong claymes a meane, when first you offer wronge.
The meane is vaine, when wrong is in reuenge.   51
Great harmes cannot be hidde, the griefe is small,
That can receaue aduise, or rule it selfe.

  Fron. Hatred concealde doth often happe to hurte,
But once profest, it oftner failes reuenge.   55
How better tho, wert to represse your yre ?
A Ladies best reuenge is to forgiue.
What meane is in your hate ? how much soe'r
You can inuent, or dare : so much you hate.

Guen. And would you knowe what meane there is in hate?
Call loue to minde, and see what meane is there.   61
    My loue, redoubled loue, and constant faith
Engaged vnto *Mordred* workes so deepe :
That both my hart and marrow quite be burnt,
And synewes dried with force of woontlesse flames,   65
    Desire to ioy him still, torments my mynde :
Feare of his want doth add a double griefe.
Loe here the loue, that stirres this meanelesse hate.
    Fron. Eschew it farre : such loue impugnes the lawes.
    Guen. Vnlawfull loue doth like, when lawfull lothes.   70
    Fron. And is your loue of husbande quite extinct?
    Guen. The greater flame must needes delay the lesse.
Besides, his sore reuenge I greatly feare.
    Fron. How can you then attempt a fresh offence?
    Guen. Who can appoint a stint to her offence?   75
    Fron. But here the greatnesse of the fact should moue.
    Guen. The greater it, the fitter for my griefe :
    Fron. To kill your spowse?   *Guen.* A stranger, and a foe.
    Fron. Your liedge and king?   *Guen.* He wants both Realme
    and Crowne.
    Fron. Nature affordes not to your sexe such strength.   80
    Guen. Loue, anguish, wrath, will soone afforde inough.
    Fron. What rage is this?   *Guen.* Such as himselfe shall rue.
    Fron. Whom Gods doe presse inough, will you annoy?
    Guen. Whom Gods doe presse, they bende : whom man
    annoyes,
He breakes.   *Fron.* Your griefe is more then his desertes :   85
Ech fault requires an equall hate : be not seuere,
Where crimes be light : as you haue felt, so greeue.
    Guen. And seemes it light to want him nine yeare space?
Then to be spoild of one I hold more deare?
Thinke all to much, b'it ne'r so iust, that feedes   90
Continuall griefe : the lasting woe is worst.
    Fron. Yet let your highnesse shun these desperate moodes,
Cast of this rage, and fell disposed minde.

Put not shame quite to flight, haue some regard
Both of your sex, and future fame of life.   95
Vse no such cruell thoughts, as farre exceede
A manly minde, much more a womans hart.

   Guen. Well: shame is not so quite exilde, but that
I can, and will respect your sage aduise.
Your Counsell I accept, giue leaue a while,   100
Till fiery wrath may slake, and rage relent.   *Exit* FRON.

The third scene.

Gueneuora.   Angharat.

Guen. THE loue, that for his rage will not be rulde,
        Must be restrainde : fame shall receiue no foile.
Let *Arthur* liue, whereof to make him sure,
My selfe will dye, and so preuent his harmes.

   Why stayest thou thus amazde O slouthfull wrath?   5
Mischiefe is meant, dispatch it on thy selfe.

   Angh. Her breast not yet appeasde from former rage
Hath chaungde her wrath, which wanting meanes to worke
An others woe, (for such is furies woont,)
Seekes out his owne, and raues vpon it selfe.   10

   Asswage (alas) that ouer feruent ire,
Through to much anger, you offend too much :
Thereby the rather you deserue to liue,
For seeming worthy in your selfe to dye.

   Guen. Death is decreed : what kinde of death, I doubt :   15
Whether to dround, or stifill vp this breath.
Or forcing bloud, to dye with dint of knife.

   All hope of prosperous hap is gone, my fame,
My faith, my spouse : no good is left vnlost :
My selfe am left, ther's left both seas and lands,   20
And sword, and fire, and chaines, and choice of harmes.

   O gnawing easelesse griefe.   Who now can heale

    16 this] his *Q*   17 Or forcing] On sorcing *Q*

My maymed minde? it must be healde by death.

   Angh. No mischiefe must be done, whiles I be by,
Or if there must, there must be more then one.   25
If death it be you seeke, I seeke, it too :
Alone you may not die, with me you may.

   Guen. They, that will driue th'unwilling to their death,
Or frustrate death in those, that faine would die,
Offend alike.   They spoile, that bootelesse spare.   30

   Angh. But will my teares and mournings moue you nought?

   Guen. Then is it best to die, when friends doe mourne.

   Angh. Ech where is death : that, fates haue well ordainde,
That ech man may bereaue himselfe of life,
But none of death : death is so sure a doome :   35
A thousand wayes doe guide vs to our graues.

Who then can euer come too late to that,
Whence, when h'is come, he neuer can returne?
Or what auailes to hasten on our ends,
And long for that, which destenies haue sworne?   40

Looke backe in time, to late is to repent,
When furious rage hath once cut of the choice.

   Guen. Death is an ond of paine no paine it selfe.
Is't meete a plague, for such excessiue wrong,
Should be so short?   Should one stroke answere all?   45
And wouldst thou dye?   Well: that contents the lawes,
What then for *Arthurs* ire?   What for thy fame,
Which thou hast stainde?   What for thy stocke thou shamst?

Not death, nor life alone can giue a full
Reuenge : ioyne both in one.   Die : and yet liue.   50
Where paine may not be oft, let it be long.

Seeke out some lingring death, whereby, thy corse
May neither touch the dead, nor ioy the quicke.
Dye : but no common death : passe *Natures* boundes.

   Angh. Set plaintes aside, despaire yeelds no reliefe.   55
The more you search a wounde, the more it stings.

   Guen. When guiltie mindes torment them selues, they heale:

45 Should] Soould Q

Whiles woundes be cur'd, griefe is a salue for griefe.

    Angh. Griefe is no iust esteemer of our deedes :

What so hath yet beene done, proceedes from chaunce.   60

    Guen. The minde, and not the chaunce, doth make th'un-
    chast,

    Angh. Then is your fault from *Fate*, you rest excusde :

None can be deemed faultie for her *Fate*.

    Guen. No *Fate*, but manners fayle, when we offende.

Impute mishaps to *Fates*, to manners faultes.   65

    Angh. Loue is an error, that may blinde the best.

    Guen. A mightie error oft hath seemde a sinne.

My death is vowed, and death must needes take place.

    But such a death, as standes with iust remorse :

Death, to the worlde, and to her slipperie ioyes :   70

A full deuorce from all this Courtly pompe.

Where dayly pennance done for each offence,

May render due reuenge for euery wrong.

    Which to accomplish : pray my deerest friends,

That they forthwith attyrde in saddest guise,   75

Conduct me to the Cloister next hereby,

There to professe, and to renounce the world.

    Angh. Alas ! What chaunge were that, from Kingly rooffes

To Cloistered celles ? To liue, and die at once ?

To want your stately troupes, your friends and kinne ?   80

To shun the shewes and sights of stately Court.

To see in sort aliue, your Countries death ?

Yea, what so'er euen Death it selfe withdrawes

From any els, that life with drawes from you.

    Yet since your highnes is so fully bent,   85

I will obay, the whiles asswage your griefe.   *Exit.*

        86 *no period after* griefe *Q*

The fourth scene.

Mordred.   Gueneuora.   Conan.

Mord.   THE houre which earst I alwaies feared most,
           The certaine ruine of my desperate state,
Is happened now : why turnst thou (minde) thy back ?
Why at the first assault doest thou recoile ?

 Trust to't : the angry Heauens contriue some spight, 5
And dreadfull doome, t'augment thy cursed hap.
Oppose to ech reuenge thy guiltie heade,
And shun no paine nor plague fit for thy fact.

 What shouldst thou feare, that seest not what to hope ?
No danger's left before, all's at thy backe. 10
He safely stands, that stands beyond his harmoo.

 Thine (death) is all, that East, or West can see,
For thee we liue, our comming is not long,
Spare vs, but whiles we may prepare our graues,
Though thou wert slowe, we hasten of our sclues. 15

 The houre that gaue, did also take our liues :
No sooner men, then mortall were we borne.
I see mine end drawes on, I feele my plagues.

 Guen.   No plague for one ill borne, to dye as ill.

 Mord.   O Queene ! my sweete associate in this plunge, 20
And desperate plight, beholde, the time is come,
That either iustifies our former faults,
Or shortly sets vs free from euery feare.

 Guen.   My feare is past, and wedlock loue hath woonne.
Retire we thither yet, whence first we ought 25
Not to haue stird.   Call backe chast faith againe.

 The way, that leads to good, is ne'r to late :
Who so repents, is guiltlesse of his crimes.

 Mord.   What meanes this course ? Is *Arthurs* wedlocke safe ?
Or can he loue, that hath iust cause to hate ? 30

 That nothing else were to be feard :
Is most apparant, that he hates at home,

What e'r he be, whose fansie strayes abroad?

 Thinke then, our loue is not vnknowen to him:

Whereof what patience can be safely hopte?   35

Nor loue, nor soueraignetie can beare a peere.

 Guen. Why dost thou still stirre vp my flames delayde?

His strayes and errors must not moue my minde.

A law for priuate men bindes not the King.

 What, that I ought not to condemne my liedge, 40

Nor can, thus guiltie to myne owne offence?

Where both haue done amisse, both will relent.

He will forgiue, that needes must be forgiuen.

 Mord. A likely thing: your faults must make you friends:

What sets you both at odds, must ioine you both: 45

 Thinke well he casts already for reuenge,

And how to plague vs both. I know his law,

A Iudge seuere to vs, milde to himselfe.

 What then auailes you to returne to late,

When you haue past to farre? You feede vaine hopes. 50

 Guen. The further past, the more this fault is yours:

It seru'd your turne, t'usurpe your fathers Crowne.

His is the crime, whom crime stands most in steede.

 Mord. They, that conspire in faults offend a like:

Crime makes them equall, whom it iointly staines. 55

 If for my sake you then pertooke my guilt,

You cannot guiltlesse seeme, the crime was ioint.

 Guen. Well should she seeme most guiltlesse vnto thee,

Whate'r she be, that's guiltie for thy sake.

 The remnant of that sober minde, which thou 60

Hadst heretofore nere vanquisht, yet resists.

Suppresse for shame that impious mouth so taught,

And to much skild t'abuse the wedded bed.

 Looke backe to former *Fates*: *Troy* still had stoode,

Had not her Prince made light of wedlocks lore. 65

The vice, that threw downe *Troy*, doth threat thy Throne:

---

 58 should] should should *Q.* *The second* should *is crossed out with ink in the Garrick copy*

Take heede: there *Mordred* stands, whence *Paris* fell.   *Exit.*

  Cona. Since that your highnes knowes for certaine truth
What power your sire prepares to claime his right:
It neerely now concernes you to resolue   70
In humbliest sort to reconcile your selfe
Gainst his returne: *Mord.* will warre. *Cona.* that lies in
  chaunce.

  Mord. I haue as great a share in chaunce, as he.

  Cona. His waies be blinde, that maketh chaunce his guide.

  Mord. Whose refuge lies in *Chance*, what dares he not? 75

  Cona. Warres were a crime farre worse then all the rest.

  Mord. The safest passage is from bad to worse.

  Cona. That were to passe too farre, and put no meane.

  Mord. He is a foole, that puts a meane in crimes.

  Cona. But sword and fire would cause a common wound. 80

  Mord. So sword and fire will often seare the soare.

  Cona. Extremest cures must not be vsed first.

  Mord. In desperate times, the headlong way is best.

  Cona. Y'haue many foes. *Mord.* No more then faythfull
  friends.

  Cona. 'Trust to't, their faith will faint, where *Fortune* failes.
Where many men pretend a loue to one,   86
Whose power may doe what good, and harme he will:
T'is hard to say, which be his faithfull friends.
Dame Flatterie flitteth oft: she loues and hates
With time, a present friend an absent foe.   90

  ⟨*Mord.*⟩ But yet y'll hope the best: ⟨*Cona.*⟩ Euen then
  you feare
The worst. Feares follow hopes, as fumes doe flames.
Mischiefe is sometimes safe: but ne'r secure:
The wrongfull Scepter's held with trembling hand.

  Mord. Whose rule wants right, his safety's in his Sword. 95

---

75 *Chance*] *corrected in G Q from* chaunce *with a printed slip. Apparently the word was similarly corrected in the two lines above, but the slips have come off—as this one did as I was examining the copy in the British Museum*   91 *Mord., Cona.*] *Q omits: there are marks in G Q of slips which have become detached and lost.*

For Sword and Scepter comes to Kings at once.

   Cona. The Kingliest point is to affect but right,

   Mord. Weake is the Scepters hold, that seekes but right,

The care whereof hath danger'd many Crownes.

As much as water differeth from the fire,   100

So much man's profit iarres from what is iust.

   A free recourse to wrong doth oft secure

The doubtfull seate, and plucks downe many a foe.

The Sword must seldome cease : a Soueraignes hand

Is scantly safe, but whiles it smites.   Let him   105

Vsurpe no Crowne, that likes a guiltles life :

Aspiring power and Iustice sield agree.

He alwaies feares, that shames to offer wrong.

   Cona. What sonne would vse such wrong against his sire?

   Mord. Come sonne, come sire, I first preferre my selfe.   110

And since a wrong must be, then it excels,

When t'is to gaine a Crowne.   I hate a peere,

I loath, I yrke, I doe detest a head.

B'it *Nature*, be it *Reason*, be it *Pride*,

I loue to rule : my minde nor with, nor by,   115

Nor after any claimes, but chiefe and first.

   Cona. Yet thinke what fame and grieuous bruits would runne
      such disloyall and vniust attempts.

   Mord. Fame goe's not with our Ghosts, the senselesse soule

Once gone, neglects what vulgar bruite reports.   120

She is both light and vaine.   *Conan.* She noteth though.

   ⟨*Mord.*⟩ She feareth States.   *Conan.* She carpeth ne'r the
      lesse.

   Mord. She's soone supprest.   *Conan.* As soone she springs
      againe,

   Mord. Toungs are vntamde : and *Fame* is Enuies Dogge,

That absent barckes, and present fawnes as fast.   125

It fearing dares, and yet hath neuer done,

But dures : though Death redeeme vs from all foes

---

   122 *Mord.*] *Q omits* : *mark of detached slip G Q. Evidently this copy
was carefully revised by the printer at the author's request.*

Besides, yet Death redeemes vs not from Toungs.
E'r *Arthur* land, the Sea shall blush with blood.
And all the Stronds with smoaking slaughters reeke.   130
Now (*Mars*) protect me in my first attempt.
If *Mordred* scape, this Realme shall want no warres.   *Exeunt.*

CHORVS.

1 See here the drifts of *Gorlois* Cornish Duke,
   And deepe desire to shake his Soueraignes Throne :
   How foule his fall, how bitter his rebuke,
   Whiles wife, and weale, and life, and all be gone?
      He now in Hell tormented wants that good :   5
      Lo, lo the end of trayterous bones and blood.
2 *Pendragon* broylde with flames of filthy fires,
   By *Merlins* mists inioyde *Igerna's* bed,
   Next spoiled *Gorlois* doubting his desires,
   Then was himselfe through force of poyson sped.   10
      Who sowes in sinne, in sinne shall reape his paine :
      The Doome is sworne : Death guerdon's death againe.
3 Whiles *Arthur* warres abroade and reapes renowne,
   Gueneuora preferres his sonnes desire.
   And trayterous *Mordred* still vsurpes the Crowne,   15
   Affording fuell to her quenchlesse fire.
      But Death's too good, and life too sweete for thease,
      That wanting both, should tast of neithers ease.
4 In *Rome* the gaping gulfe would not decrease,
   Till *Curtius* corse had closde her yawning iawes :   20
   In *Theb's* the Rotte and Murreine would not cease,
   Till *Laius* broode had paide for breach of lawes :
      In *Brytain* warres and discord will not stent :
      Till *Vther's* line and offspring quite be spent.

The Argument of the second Act.

1 IN the first Scene a *Nuntio* declareth the successe of
   Arthur's warres in *France*, and *Mordred's* foile that
   resisted his landing.

2 In the second Scene *Mordred* enraged at the ouerthrow,
   voweth a second battaile, notwithstanding *Conan's* disswa-   5
   sion to the contrarie.

3 In the third Scene *Gawin* (brother to *Mordred* by the
   mother) with an Heralt from *Arthur* to imparle of peace,
   but after some debate thereof peace is reiected.

4 In the fourth Scene the King of *Ireland* & other forrein 10
   Princes assure *Mordred* of their assistance against *Arthur*.

¶ The Argument and manner of the
second dumbe shewe.

WHILES the Musicke sounded there came out of *Mordred's*
house a man stately attyred representing a King, who walking
once about the Stage.   Then out of the house appointed for *Arthur*,
there came three *Nymphes* apparailed accordingly, the first holding
a *Cornucopia* in her hand, the second a golden braunch of Oliue, the 5
third a sheaffe of *Corne*.   These orderly one after another offered
these presents to the King who scornefully refused.   After the which
there came a man bareheaded, with blacke long shagged haire
downe to his shoulders, apparailed with an Irish Iacket and shirt,
hauing an Irish dagger by his side and a dart in his hand.   Who 10
first with a threatning countenance looking about, and then spying
the King, did furiously chase and driue him into *Mordreds* house.
The King represented *Mordred*.   The three *Nymphes* with their
proffers the treatice of peace, for the which *Arthur* sent *Gawin*
with an Herault vnto *Mordred* who reiected it : The Irish man 15
signified Reuenge and Furie which *Mordred* conceiued after his
foile on the Shoares, whereunto *Mordred* headlong yeeldeth himselfe.

   II. Arg. 6 to], 9 after], 11 Princes] *have been clipped by the binder in
both copies.   So with* house a, the, three, the, orderly *below.*   11 assist-
ance] assistane *Q*

THE SECOND ACT
. and first Scene.

Nuntius.

Nunt. LO here at length the stately type of *Troy*,
    And *Brytain* land the promist seate of *Brute*,
Deckt with so many spoyles of conquered Kings.
Haile natiue soyle, these nine yeares space vnseene :
To thee hath long renowmed *Rome* at last   5
Held vp her hands, bereaft of former pompe.
But first inflamde with woonted valures heate,
Amidst our sorest siedge and thickest broyles,
She stoutly fought, and fiercely waged warres.

  Tiberius courage gaue, vpbraiding oft   10
The *Romane* force, their woonted lucke, and long
Retained rule, by warres throughout the world.
What shame it were, since such atchiued spoiles,
And conquests gaind both farre and wide, to want
Of courage then, when most it should be mou'd.   15
How *Brytaines* erst paide tribute for their peace,
But now rebell, and dare them at their doores :
For what was *Fraunce* but theirs? Herewith incenst
They fiercely rau'd, and bent their force a fresh.

  Which *Arthur* spying, cryed with thundring voyce,   20
Fye, (*Brytaines*) fye : what hath bewitcht you thus?
So many Nations foildc, must *Romans* foile?
What slouth is this? Haue you forgot to warre,
Which ne'r knew houre of peace? Turne to your foes,
Where you may bath in blood, and fight your fill.   25
Let courage worke : what can he not that dares?
Thus he puissant guide in doubtfull warres,
A shamde to shun his foes, inflamde his friends.

  Then yeelding to his stately Stead the raignes,
He furious driues the Romaine troupes about :   30

He plies each place, least *Fates* mought alter ought,
Pursuing hap, and vrging each successe.
He yeelds in nought, but instantly persists
In all attempts, wherein what so withstands
His wish, he ioyes to worke a way by wracke.   35
And matching death to death, no passage seekes,
But what destruction works, with blade or blood.
He scornes the yeelded way, he fiercely raues
To breake and bruse the rancks in thickest throngs,
All headlong bent, and prone to present spoile.   40

    The foes inforc't withstand : but much dismaide
They senselesse fight, whiles millions lose their liues.
At length *Tiberius*, pierst with point of speare,
Doth bleeding fall, engoard with deadly wound.
Hereat the rest recoile, and headlong flie,   45
Each man to saue himselfe. The battaile quailes
And *Brytaines* winne vnto their most renowne.

    Then *Arthur* tooke *Tiberius* breathlesse Corse,
And sent it to the Senators at *Rome*,
With charge to say : This is the tribute due   50
Which *Arthur* ought, as time hereafter serues,
He'il pay the like againe : the whiles he rests
Your debtor thus. But O ! this sweete successe
Pursu'd with greater harmes, turn'd soone to sowre.

    For lo : when forreine soiles and seas were past   55
With safe returne, and that the King should land :
Who, but his onely sonne (O outrage rare)
With hugie hoast withstoode him at the shoare ?
There were preparde the forreine aides from farre,
There were the borowed powers of diuers Kings,   60
There were our parents, brethren, sonnes and kinne,
Their wrath, their ire, there *Mordred* was thy rage.
Where erst we sought abroade for foes to foile,
Beholde, our *Fates* had sent vs foes vnsought.
When forreine Realmes supplanted want supplie :   65

    53 this] this this *Q   The second* this *is crossed out in GQ*

O blessed Home, that hath such boonne in store.
　But let this part of *Arthurs* prowesse lurke,
Nor let it e'r appeare by my report,
What monstrous mischiefes raue in ciuill warres.
O rather let due teares, and waylings want :　　　　70
Let all in silence sinke, what hence insu'd.
What best deserueth mention here, is this :
That *Mordred* vanquisht trusted to his flight,
That *Arthur* ech where victor is returnd.
　And lo : where *Mordred* comes with heauy head,　　75
He wields no slender waight that wields a Crowne.　*Exit.*

The second scene.

Mordred.　Conan.

Mord. ANd hath he wonne? Be Stronds & shoares possest ?
Is *Mordred* foilde ? the realme is yet vnwonne :
And *Mordred* liues reseru'd for *Arthurs* death :
Well : t'was my first conflict : I knew not yet
What warres requir'd : but now my sworde is flesht,　　5
And taught to goare and bath in houtest bloodo.
　Then thinke not *Arthur* that the Crowne is wonne :
Thy first successe may rue our next assault.
Euen at our next incounter (hap when 'twill)
I vowe by Heauen, by Earth, by Hell, by all,　　　　10
That either thou, or I, or both shall dye.
　Cona. Nought shoulde be rashly vowde against your sire.
　Mord. Whose breast is free from rage may soone b'aduisde.
　Cona. The best redresse for rage is to relent.
　Mord. Tis better for a King to kill his foes.　　　　15
　Cona. So that the Subiects also iudge them foes.
　Mord. The Subiects must not iudge their Kings decrees.
　Cona. The Subiects force is great.　*Mord.* Greater the Kings.
　Cona. The more you may, the more you ought to feare.

18 *Mord.*] *Arth.* Q

R 2

Mord. He is a foole, that feareth what he may.　20

Cona. Not what you may, but what you ought is iust.

Mord. He that amongst so many, so vniust,
Seekes to be iust, seekes perill to him selfe.

Cona. A greater perill comes by breach of lawes.

Mord. The Lawes doe licence as the Soueraigne lists.　25

Cona. Lest ought he list, whom lawes doe licence most.

Mord. Imperiall power abhorres to be restrainde.

Cona. As much doe meaner groomes to be compeld.

Mord. The *Fates* haue heau'de and raisde my force on high.

Cona. The gentler shoulde you presse those, that are low.　30

Mord. I would be feard :　*Cona.* The cause why Subiects
hate.

Mord. A Kingdom's kept by feare.　*Cona.* And lost by hate.
He feares as man himselfe, whom many feare.

Mord. The timerous Subiect dares attempt no chaundge.

Cona. What dares not desperate dread ?　*Mord.* What torture
threats.　35

Cona. O spare, tweare saffer to be lou'de.　*Mord.* As safe
To be obaide.　*Cona.* Whiles you command but well.

Mord. Where Rulers dare commaund but what is well :
Powre is but prayer, commaundment but request.

Cona. If powre be ioynde with right, men must obay.　40

Mord. My will must goe for right.　*Cona.* If they assent.

Mord. My sword shall force assent :　*Cona.* No, Gods
forbid.

Mord. What? shall I stande whiles *Arthur* sheads my bloode?
And must I yeelde my necke vnto the Axe ?
Whom *Fates* constrayne, let him forgoe his blisse :　45
But he that needlesse yeldes vnto his bane,
When he may shunne, doth well deserue to loose
The good he cannot vse : who woulde sustaine
A baser life, that may maintaine the best ?
We cannot part the Crowne : A regall Throne　50

21 *Q comma at end of line*　28 groomes] roomes *Q*　35 *Mord.*]
Cona. Q　42 *no comma after* No *Q*

Is not for two : The Scepter fittes but one.
But whether is the fitter of vs two,
That must our swordes decerne : and shortly shall.

Cona. How much were you to be renowmed more,
If casting off these ruinous attempts,   55
You woulde take care howe to supplie the losse,
Which former warres, and forraine broyles haue wrought.
Howe to deserue the peoples heartes with peace,
With quiet rest, and deepe desired ease.

Not to increase the rage that long hath raignde,   60
Nor to destroy the realme, you seeke to rule.
Your Father rearde it vp, you plucke it downe.
You loose your Countrey whiles you winne it thus :
To make it yours, you striue to make it none.
Where Kings Impose too much, the commons grudge :   65
Goodwill withdrawes, assent becomes but slowe.

Mord. Must I to gaine renowne, incurre my plague :
Or hoping prayse sustaine an exiles life ?
Must I for Countries ease disease my selfe,
Or for their loue dispise my owne estate?   70
No. Tis my happe that *Brytain* serues my tourne,
That feare of me doth make the Subiects crouch,
That what they grudge, they do constrayned yeeld.
If their assents be slowe, my wrath is swift,
Whom fauour failes to bende, let furie breake.   75
If they be yet to learne, let terrour teach,
What Kings may doe, what Subiects ought to beare.

Then is a Kingdome at a wished staye,
When whatsoeuer the Souereigne wills, or nilles,
Men be compelde as well to praise, as beare,   80

65 commons grudge] *corr. in G Q to* Realme enuies   67–70 Must I
... estate] *corr. in G Q to :*

> The first Art in a Kingdome is, to scorne
> The Enuie of the Realme. He cannot rule,
> That feares to be enuide. What can diuorce
> Enuie from Soueraigntie ? Must my deserts ?

In each case it is a printed slip attached at one end so that the words underneath can be read ; the backs of the slips are blank.

And Subiects willes inforc'd against their willes.

Cona. But who so seekes true praise, and iust renowme,
Would rather seeke their praysing heartes, then tongues.

Mord. True praise may happen to the basest groome,
A forced prayse to none, but to a Prince.   85
I wish that most, that Subiects most repine.

Cona. But yet where warres doe threaten your estate,
There needeth friendes to fortifie your Crowne.

Mord. Ech Crowne is made of that attractiue moulde,
That of it selfe it drawes a full defence.   90

Cona. That is a iust, and no vsurped Crowne.
And better were an exiles life, then thus
Disloyally to wronge your Sire and Liedge.
Thinke not that impious crimes can prosper long,
A time they scape, in time they be repaide.   95

Mord. The hugest crimes bring best successe to some.

Cona. Those some be rare.   *Mord.* Why may not I be rare?

Cona. It was their hap.   *Mord.* It is my hope.   *Cona.* But
    hope
May misse, where hap doth hurle.   *Mord.* So hap may hit,
Where hope doth aime.   *Conan.* But hap is last, and rules 100
The stearne.   *Mord.* So hope is first, and hoists the saile.

Cona. Yet feare: the first and last doe sielde agree.

Mord. Nay dare: the first and last haue many meanes.
But cease at length: your speach molests me much:
My minde is fixt.   Giue *Mordred* leaue to doe,   105
What *Conan* neither can allow, nor like.

Cona. But loe an Herault sent from *Arthurs* hoast:
Gods graunt his message may portend our good.

The third scene.

Herault.   Gawin.   Mordred.

Hera. YOVR Sire (O Prince) considering what distresse,
    The Realme sustaines by both your mutuall
waires,

Hath sent your brother *Gawin Albane* King
To treate of truce, and to imparle of peace.

    Mord. Speake brother: what commaundment sends my Sire?
What message doe you bring? My life, or death?   6

    Gawi. A message farre vnmeete, most needefull tho.
The Sire commaunds not, where the Sonne rebels:
His loue descends too deepe to wish your death.

    Mord. And mine ascends to high to wish his life.   10

    Gawi. Yet thus he offreth: though your faults be great,
And most disloyall to his deepe abuse:
Yet yeelde your selfe: he'il be as prone to grace,
As you to ruth: An Uncle, Sire, and Liedge.
And fitter were your due submission done,   15
Then wrongfull warres to reaue his right and Realme.

    Mord. It is my fault, that he doth want his right:
It is his owne, to vexe the Realme with warres.

    Gawi. It is his right, that he attempts to seeke:
It is your wrong, that driueth him thereto.   20

    Mord. T'is his insatiate minde, that is not so content,
Which hath so many Kingdomes more besides.

    Gawi. The more you ought to tremble at his powre.

    Mord. The greater is my conquest, if I winne.

    Gawi. The more your foile, if you should hap to loose.   25
For *Arthurs* fame, and vallure's such, as you
Should rather imitate, or at the least
Enuie, if hope of better fansies failde.
For whereas Enuie raignes, though it repines,
Yet doth it feare a greater then it selfe.   30

    Mord. He that enuies the valure of his foe,
Detects a want of valure in himselfe.
He fondly fights, that fights with such a foe,
Where t'were a shame to loose, no praise to winne:
But with a famous foe, succeede what will,   35
To winne is great renowne, to loose lesse foile.
His conquests, were they more, dismaie me not:
The oftner they haue beene, the more they threat

No danger can be thought both safe, and oft:
And who hath oftner waged warres then he?　　　　40
Escapes secure him not: he owes the price:
Whom *chaunce* hath often mist, *chaunce* hits at length
Or, if that *Chaunce* haue furthered his successe,
So may she mine: for *Chaunce* hath made me king.

　　Gawi. As *Chaunce* hath made you King, so *Chaunce* may
　　　change.　　　　45
Prouide for peace: that's it the highest piers,
No state except, euen Conquerours ought to seeke.

　　Remember *Arthurs* strength, his conquestes late,
His fierie mynde, his high aspiring heart.

　　Marke then the oddes: he expert, you vntried:　　　　50
He ripe, you greene: yeelde you, whiles yet you may,
He will not yeelde: he winnes his peace with warres.

　　Modr. If *Chaunce* may chaunge, his *Chaunce* was last to
　　　winne.
The likelier now to loose: his hautie heart
And minde I know: I feele mine owne no lesse.　　　　55
As for his strength, and skill, I leaue to happe:
Where many meete, it lies not all in one.

　　What though he vanquisht haue the Romaine troupes?
That bootes him not: him selfe is vanquisht here.
Then waigh your wordes againe: if Conquerours ought　　60
To seeke for peace: The Conquered must perforce.

　　But he'ill not yeelde, he'il purchase peace with warres.
Well: yeelde that will: I neither will, nor can:
Come peace, come warres, chuse him: my danger's his,
His saffetie mine, our states doe stande alike.　　　　65
If peace be good, as good for him, as me:
If warres be good, as good for me, as him.

　　Gawi. What Cursed warres (alas) were those, wherein
Both sonne and sire shoulde so oppose themselues?
Him, whom you nowe vnhappie man pursue,　　　　70
If you should winne, your selfe would first bewayle.
Giue him his Crowne, to keepe it perill breeds.

Mord. The Crowne Ile keepe my selfe : insue what will :
Death must be once : how soone, I lest respect.
He best prouides that can beware in time,   75
Not why, nor when : but whence, and where he fals.

   What foole, to liue a yeare or twaine in rest,
Woulde loose the state, and honour of a Crowne?

   Gawi. Consider then your Fathers griefe, and want :
Whom you bereaue of Kingdome, Realme, and Crowne.   80

   Mord. Trust me : a huge and mightie kingdome tis,
To beare the want of Kingdome, Realme, and Crowne.

   Gawi. A common want, which woorkes ech worldlings woe,
That many haue too much, but none inough.
It were his praise, could he be so content,   85
Which makes you guiltie of the greater wrong.

   Wherefore thinke on the doubtfull state of warres,
Where *Mars* hath sway, he keepes no certayne course.
Sometimes he lettes the weaker to preuaile,
Some times the stronger stoupes : hope, feare, and rage   90
With eylesse lott rules all, vncertayne good,
Most certaine harmes, be his assured happes.

   No lucke can last, nowe here, now their it lights :
No state alike, *Chaunce* blindly snatcheth all,
And *Fortune* maketh guiltie whom she listes.   95

   Mord. Since therefore feare, and hope, and happe in warres
Be all obscure, till their successe be seene :
Your speach doth rather driue me on to trie,
And trust them all, mine onely refuge now.

   Gawi. And feare you not so strange and vncouth warres? 100
   Mord. No, were they warres that grew from out the ground.
   Gawi. Nor yet your sire so huge, your selfe so small?
   Mord. The smallest axe may fell the hugest oake.
   Gawi. Nor that in felling him, your selfe may fall?
   Mord. He falleth well, that falling fells his foe.   105
   Gawi. Nor common *Chance* whereto each man is thrall?
   Mord. Small manhood were to turne my backe to *Chance.*
   Gawi. Nor that if *Chance* afflict, kings brooke it not?

Mord. I beare no breast so vnpreparde for harmes.
Euen that I holde the kingliest point of all,   110
To brooke afflictions well : And by how much
The more his state and tottering Empire sagges,
To fixe so much the faster foote on ground.

No feare but doth foreiudge, and many fall
Into their *Fate*, whiles they doe feare their *Fate*.   115
Where courage quailes, the feare exceeds the harme,
Yea worse than warre it selfe, is feare of warre.

Gawi. Warre seemeth sweete to such as haue not tried :
But wisedome wils we should forecast the worst.
The end allowes the act : that plot is wise,   120
That knowes his meanes, and least relies on *Chance*.
Eschue the course where errour lurkes, their growes
But griefe, where paine is spent, no hope to speed.

Striue not aboue your strength : for where your force
Is ouer matchte with your attempts, it faints,   125
And fruitlesse leaues, what bootlesse it began.

Mord. All things are rulde in constant course : No *Fate*
But is foreset, The first daie leades the last.
No wisedome then : but difference in conceit,
Which workes in many men, as many mindes.   130

You loue the meane, and follow vertues race :
I like the top, and aime at greater blisse.
You rest content, my minde aspires to more :
In briefe, you feare, I hope : you doubt, I dare.

Since then the sagest counsailes are but strifes,   135
Where equall wits may wreast each side alike,
Let counsaile go : my purpose must proceede :
Each likes his course, mine owne doth like me best.

Wherefore e'r *Arthur* breath, or gather strength,
Assault we him : least he assault vs first.   140
He either must destroie, or be destroide.
The mischiefe's in the midst : catch he that can.

Gawi. But will no reason rule that desperate minde?

Mord. A fickle minde that euerie reason rules.

I rest resolu'd : and to my Sire say thus :　　　　145
　　If here he stay but three daies to an end,
And not forthwith discharge his band and hoast,
Tis *Mordreds* oath : assure himselfe to die.
But if he finde his courage so to serue,
As for to stand to his defence with force :　　　　150
In *Cornewalle* if he dare, I'le trye it out.

　　Gawi. O strange contempt : like as the craggy rocke,
Resists the streames, and flings the waltering waues
A loofe, so he reiects and scornes my words.　　　*Exit.*

The fourth scene.

Gilla. Gillamor. Cheldrichus.
Dux Pictorum. Conan.

Mord. LO, where (as they decreed) my faithfull friends
　　　　　Haue kept their time, be all your powers repaird ?
　　Gilla. They be : and all with ardent mindes to *Mars*,
They cry for warres, and longing for th'allarme
Euen now they wish t'incounter with their foes.　　　5
　　Mord. What could be wisht for more ?　Puissant King.
For your great helpe and valiant *Irish* force,
If I obtaine the conquest in these warres,
Whereas my father claimes a tribute due
Out of your Realme, I here renounce it quite.　　　10
And if assistance neede in doubtfull times,
I will not faile to aide you with the like.
　　Gyll. It doth suffice me to discharge my Realme,
Or at the least to wreke me on my foes.
I rather like to liue your friend and piere,　　　15
Then rest in *Arthurs* homage and disgrace.
　　Mord. Right noble Duke, through whom the *Saxons* vowe
Their liues with mine, for my defence in warres :

If we preuaile and may subdue our foes:
I will in lieu of your so high deserts,   20
Geue you and yours all *Brytish* lands that lie
Betweene the floud of *Humber*, and the *Scottes*,
Besides as much in *Kent* as *Horsus* and
Hengistus had, when *Vortigern* was King.

    Chel. Your gracious proffers I accept with thankes,   25
Not for the gaine, but that the good desire
I haue henceforth to be your subiect here,
May thereby take effect: which I esteeme
More then the rule I beare in *Saxon* soile.

    Mord. (Renowmed Lord) for your right hardy *Picts*,   30
And chosen warriers to maintaine my cause,
If our attempts receiue a good successe,
The *Albane* Crowne I giue to you and yours.

    Pict. Your highnes bountie in so high degree,
Were cause inough to moue me to my best.   35
But sure your selfe, without regard of meede,
Should finde both me and mine at your commaund.

    Mord. Lord *Gilla*, if my hope may take successe,
And that I be thereby vndoubted King,
The *Cornish* Dukedome I allot to you.   40

    Gilla. My Liedge to further your desir'd attempts,
I ioyfully shall spend my dearest blood.
The rather, that I found the King your Sire
So heauy Lord to me, and all my stocke.

    Mord. Since then our rest is on't, and we agreed   45
To warre it out: what resteth now but blowes?
Driue Destnies on with swords, *Mars* frames the meanes,
Henceforth what *Mordred* may, now lies in you.
Ere long if *Mars* insue with good successe,
Looke whatsoe'r it be, that *Arthur* claimes,   50
By right, or wrong, or conquests gaind with blood,
In *Brytaine*, or abroade is mine to giue.

    To shewe I would haue said: I cannot giue,

      51 or wrong] *So corr. with printed slip in GQ*: a wrong *KQ*

What euery hand must giue vnto it selfe.
Whereof who lists to purchase any share,   55
Now let him seeke and winne it with his Sword:
The *Fates* haue laide it open in the field.

   What Starres (O Heauens) or Poles, or Powers diuine
Doe graunt so great rewards for those that winne?
Since then our common good, and ech mans care   60
Requires our ioint assistance in these toyles:
Shall we not hazard our extreamest hap,
And rather spend our *Fates*, then spare our foes?

  .The cause, I care for most, is chiefely yours:
This hand and hart shall make mine owne secure.   65
That man shall see me foiled by my selfe,
What e'r he be, that sees my foe vnfoilde.

   Feare not the feild because of *Mordreds* faults,
Nor shrinke one iotte the more for *Arthurs* right.
Full safely *Fortune* guideth many a guilt,   70
And *Fates* haue none but wretches whom they wrenche.

   Wherefore make speede to cheare your Souldiers harts,
That to their fires you yet may adde more flames.
The side that seekes to winne in ciuill warres,
Must not content it selfe with woonted heate.   75

Exeunt omnes preter Mordred & Conan.

Cona. WOuld God your highnes had beene more ad-
        uisde,
Ere too much will had drawen your wits too farre:
Then had no warres indangerd you, nor yours,
Nor *Mordreds* cause required forreine care.

   Mord. A troubled head: my minde reuolts to feare,   80
And beares my body backe: I inwards feele my fall.
My thoughts misgeue me much: downe terror: I
Perceiue mine ende: and desperate though I must
Despise Dispaire, and somewhat hopelesse hope.
The more I doubt, the more I dare: by feare   85
I finde the fact is fittest for my fame.

What though I be a ruine to the Realme,
And fall my selfe therewith? No better end.
His last mishaps doe make a man secure.
Such was King *Priams* ende, who, when he dyed,   90
Closde and wrapt vp his Kingdome in his death.
A solemne pompe, and fit for *Mordreds* minde,
To be a graue and tombe to all his Realme.   *Exeunt.*

CHORVS.

1   Ye Princely Peeres extold to seates of State,
     Seeke not the faire, that soone will turne to fowle:
         Oft is the fall of high and houering *Fate,*
     And rare the roome, which time doth not controwle.
             The safest seate is not on highest hill,   5
             Where windes, and stormes, and thunders thumpe their ill.
             Farre safer were to follow sound aduise,
             Then for such pride to pay so deare a price.

2   The mounting minde that climes the hauty cliftes,
     And soaring seekes the tip of lofty type,   10
         Intoxicats the braine with guiddy drifts,
     Then rowles, and reeles, and falles at length plum ripe.
             Loe: heauing hie is of so small forecast,
             To totter first, and tumble downe at last.
             Yet *Pægasus* still reares himselfe on hie,   15
             And coltishly doth kicke the cloudes in Skie.

3   Who sawe the griefe engrauen in a Crowne,
     Or knew the bad and bane whereto it's bound:
         Would neuer sticke to throwe and fling it downe,
     Nor once vouchsafe to heaue it from the ground.   20
             Such is the sweete of this ambitious powre,
             No sooner had, then turnde eftsoones to sowre:
             Atchieu'd with enuie, exercisde with hate,
             Garded with feare, supported with debate.

4   O restlesse race of high aspyring head,   25
   O worthlesse rule both pittyed and inuied :
   How many Millions to their losse you lead :
With loue and lure of Kingdomes blisse vntryed ?
   So things vntasted cause a quenchlesse thirst,
   Which, were they knowne, would be refused first,   30
   Yea, oft we see, yet seeing cannot shonne
   The fact, we finde as fondly dar'd, as donne.

The argument of the third Act.

1   IN the first Scene *Cador* and *Howell* incite and exhort
     Arthur vnto warre : Who mooued with Fatherly affection
     towards his sonne, notwithstanding their perswasions re-
     solueth vpon peace.

2   In the second Scene, an Herault is sent from *Mordred* to 5
     commaund *Arthur* to discharge his armies vnder paine of
     death, or otherwise if he dare, to trie it by Battaile.

3   In the third Scene *Arthur* calleth his Assistants and Souldiers
     together, whom he exhorteth to pursue their foes.

4   In the fourth Scene *Arthur* between griefe and despaire 10
     resolueth to warre.

¶ The Argument and manner of the
third dumbe shewe.

DVring the Musicke after the second Act. There came vppon
   the stage two gentlemen attyred in peaceable manner, which
brought with them a Table, Carpet, and Cloth : and then hauing
couered the Table they furnisht it with incense on the one ende, and
banqueting dishes on the other ende . Next there came two gentle- 5
men apparelled like Souldiers with two naked Swordes in their
handes, the which they laide a crosse vpon the Table.   Then there
came two sumptuously attyred and warrelike, who, spying this
preparation smelled the incense and tasted the banquet.   During

the which there came a Messenger and deliuered certaine letters to 10
those two that fedde on the daineties: who, after they had well
viewed and perused the letters, furiously flung the banquet vnder
feete: and violently snatching the Swordes vnto them, they hastily
went their way.   By the first two that brought in the banquet was
meant the seruaunts of Peace, by the second two were meant the 15
seruaunts of Warre: By the two last were meant *Arthur* and *Cador*.
By the Messenger and his Letters was meant the defiance from
Mordred.

THE THIRD ACT
and Fyrste scene.

Arthur. Cador. Howell.

Arth. IS this the welcome that my Realme prepares?
    Be these the thankes I winne for all my warres?
Thus to forbid me land? to slaie my friends?
To make their bloud distaine my Countrie shoares?

  My sonne (belike) least that our force should faint   5
For want of warres, preparde vs warres himselfe.
He thought (perhaps) it mought empaire our fame,
If none rebeld, whose foile might praise our power.

  Is this the fruit of *Mordreds* forward youth,
And tender age discreet beyond his yeres?   10
O false and guilfull life, O craftie world:
How cunningly conuaiest thou fraude vnseene?
Thambicious seemeth meeke, the wanton chast,
Disguised vice for vertue vants it selfe.

  Thus (*Arthur*) thus hath *Fortune* plaid her part,   15
Blinde for thy weale, cleare sighted for thy woe.
Thy kingdome's gone, thy phere affordes no faith,
Thy sonne rebels, of all thy wonted pompe
No iot is left, and *Fortune* hides her face.
No place is left for prosperous plight, mishaps   20

    16 *comma after* Cador Q
    III. i. Fyrste] *So corr. with printed slip in GQ*: second *KQ*

Haue roome and waies to runne and walke at will.
    Lo (*Cador*) both our states, your daughter's trust,
My sonn's respect, our hopes reposde in both.
    Cado. The time (puissant Prince) permits not now
To moane our wrongs, or search each seuerall sore.   25
Since *Arthur* thus hath ransackt all abroade,
What meruaile ist, if *Mordred* raue at home?
When farre and neere your warres had worne   word,
What warres were left for him, but ciuill wari
    All which requires reuenge with sword and fire,   30
And to pursue your foes with present force.
In iust attempts *Mars* giues a rightfull doome.
    Arth. Nay rather (*Cador*) let them runne their race,
And leaue the Heauens reuengers of my wrong.
Since *Brytaines* prosperous state is thus debasde   35
In seruile sort to *Mordreds* cursed pride,
Let me be thrall, and leade a priuate life:
None can refuse the yoake his Countrie beares.
But as for warres, insooth my flesh abhorres,
To bid the battayle to my proper bloud.   40
Great is the loue, which nature doth inforce
From kin to kin, but most from sire to sonne.
    Howe. The noble necke disdaines the seruile yoke,
Where rule hath pleasde, subiection seemeth strange.
A King ought alwaies to preferre his Realme,   45
Before the loue he beares to kin or sonne.
    Your Realme destroide is neere restord againe,
But time may send you kine and sonnes inough.
    Arth. How hard it is to rule th'aspiring minde,
And what a kingly point it seemes to those,   50
Whose Lordlie hands the stately Scepter swaies,
Still to pursue the drift they first decreed:
My wonted minde and kingdome lets me know.
    Thinke not, but if you driue this hazard on,
He desperate will resolue to winne or die: 55

        29 *Q comma at end of line*   31 present] presence *Q*

Whereof who knowes which were the greater guilt,
The sire to slaie the sonne, or sonne the sire.
  Cado. If bloudie *Mars* doe so extreamly swaie,
That either sonne or sire must needs be slaine,
Geue Lawe the choice: let him die that deserues.   60
Each impotent affection notes a want.
  No worse a vice then lenitie in Kings,
Remisse indulgence soone vndoes a Realme.
He teacheth how to sinne, that winkes at sinnes,
And bids offend, that suffereth an offence.   65
The onely hope of leaue increaseth crimes,
And he that pardoneth one, emboldneth all
To breake the Lawes.   Each patience fostereth wrongs.
  But vice seuerely punisht faints at foote,
And creepes no further off, then where it falls.   70
One sower example will preuent more vice,
Than all the best perswasions in the world.
Rough rigour lookes out right, and still preuailes :
Smooth mildnesse lookes too many waies to thriue.
  Wherefore since *Mordreds* crimes haue wrongd the Lawes 75
In so extreame a sort, as is too strange :
Let right and iustice rule with rigours aide,
And worke his wracke at length, although too late :
That damning Lawes, so damned by the Lawes,
Hee may receiue his deepe deserued doome.   80
  So let it fare with all, that dare the like :
Let sword, let fire, let torments be their end.
Seueritie vpholds both Realme and rule.
  Arth. Ah too seuere, farre from a Fathers minde.
Compassion is as fit for Kings as wrath.   85
Lawes must not lowre.   Rule oft admitteth ruthe.
So hate, as if there were yet cause to loue :
Take not their liues as foes, which may be friends.
To spoile my sonne were to dispoile my selfe :
Oft, whiles we seeke our foes, we seeke our foiles.   90
Let's rather seeke how to allure his minde

With good deserts : deserts may winne the worst.
    Howe. Where *Cato* first had saued a theefe from death,
And after was himselfe condemnd to die :
When else not one would execute the doome,   95
Who but the theefe did vndertake the taske ?
If too much bountie worke so bad effects
In thanklesse friends, what for a ruthlesse foe ?
Let Lawes haue still their course, the ill disposde
Grudge at their liues, to whom they owe too much.   100
    Arth. But yet where men with reconciled mindes
Renue their loue with recontinued grace,
Attonement frames them friends of former foes,
And makes the moodes of swelling wrath to swage.
No faster friendship, than that growes from griefe,   105
When melting mindes with mutuall ruth relent.
How close the seuered skinne vnites againe,
When salues haue smoothlie heald the former hurts ?
    Cado. I neuer yet sawe hurt so smoothly heald,
But that the skarre bewraid the former wound :   110
Yea, where the salue did soonest close the skinne,
The sore was oftner couered vp than cur'de.
Which festering deepe and hilde within, at last
With sodaine breach grew greater than at first.
    What then for mindes, which haue reuenging moodes,   115
And ne'r forget the crosse they forced beare ?
Whereto if reconcilement come, it makes
The t'one secure, whiles t'other workes his will
    Attonement sield defeates, but oft deferres
Reuenge : beware a reconciled foe.   120
    Arth. Well, what auailes to linger in this life,
Which *Fortune* but reserues for greater griefe ?
This breath drawes on but matter of mishap :
Death onely frees the guiltlesse from anoies.
Who so hath felt the force of greedie *Fates*,   125
And dur'de the last decree of grislie death,

        114 *comma at end of line Q*

Shall neuer yeeld his captiue armes to chaines,
Nor drawne in triumph decke the victors pompe.

Howe. What meane these wordes? Is *Arthur* forc'de to feare,
Is this the fruit of your continuall warres,   130
Euen from the first remembrance of your youth?

Arth. My youth (I graunt) and prime of budding yeares
Puft vp with pride and fond desire of praise,
Foreweening nought what perils might ensue,
Aduentured all, and raught to will the raignes.   135

But now this age requires a sager course,
And will aduisde by harmes to wisedome yeelds.
Those swelling spirits the selfe same cause which first
Set them on gog, euen *Fortunes* fauours quaild.

And now mine oftnest skapes doe skare me most,   140
I feare the trappe, whereat I oft haue tript:
Experience tels me plaine that *Chance* is fraile,
And oft, the better past, the worse to come.

Cado. Resist these doubts: tis ill to yeeld to harmes.
T'is safest then to dare when most you feare.   145

Arth. As safe sometimes to feare, when most we dare.
A causelesse courage giues repentance place.

Howe. If *Fortune* fawne. *Arth.* Each waie on me she frowns.
For winne I, loose I, both procure my griefe.

Cado. Put case you winne, what griefe? *Arth.* Admit I
doe,   150
What ioy? *Cador.* Then may you rule. *Arth.* When I may
die.

Cado. To rule is much. *Arth.* Small if we couet naught.

Cado. Who couets not a Crowne. *Arth.* He that discernes
The swoord aloft. *Cador.* That hangeth fast. *Arth.* But by
A haire. *Cador.* Right holdes it vp. *Arth.* Wrong puls it
downe.   155

Cado. The Commons helpe the King. *Arth.* They sometimes hurt.

Cado. At least the Peeres. *Arth.* Sield, if allegeance want

139 *Fortunes*] *Fortunes* Q

Cado. Yet Soueraigntie. *Arth.* Not, if allegeance faile.

Cado. Doubt not, the Realme is yours. *Arth.* T'was mine
   till now.

Cado. And shall be still. *Arth.* If *Mordred* list. *Cador.* T'were
   well   160

Your crowne were wonne. *Arth.* Perhaps tis better lost.

Howe. The name of rule should moue a princely minde.

Arth. Trust me, bad things haue often glorious names.

Howe. The greatest good that *Fortune* can affoord.

Arth. A dangerous good that wisedome would eschue.   165

Howe. Yet waigh the hearesaie of the olde renowme,

And *Fame* the Wonderer of the former age :

Which still extolls the facts of worthyest wights

Preferring no deserts before your deeds.

Euen the exhorts you to this new attempts,   170

Which left vntryde your winnings be but losse.

  Arth. Small credit will be giuen of matters past

To *Fame*, the Flatterer of the former age.

Were all beleeu'd which antique bruite imports,

Yet wisedome waighes the perill ioinde to praise :   175

Rare is the *Fame* (marke well all ages gone)

Which hath not hurt the house it most enhaun'st.

  Besides, *Fame's* but a blast that sounds a while,

And quickely stints, and then is quite forgot.

Looke whatsoe'r our vertues haue atchieu'd,   180

The *Chaos* vast and greedy time deuours.

  To day all *Europe* rings of *Arthurs* praise :

T'wilbe as husht, as if I ne'r had beene.

What bootes it then to venture life or limme,

For that, which needes e'r long we leaue, or loose ?   185

  Cado. Can blinde affection so much bleare the wise,

Or loue of gracelesse Sonne so witch the Sire ?

That what concernes the honour of a Prince

With Countries good and Subiects iust request,

158 allegeance] *corr. with printed slip in G Q to* subiection   159 Doubt
Doube *Q*   161 better] bettes *Q*   185 loose ?] loose, *Q*

Should lightly be contemned by a King?   190
   When *Lucius* sent but for his tribute due,
You went with thirteene Kings to roote him out :
Haue *Romaines,* for requiring but their owne,
Aboad your nine yeares brunts : Shall *Mordred* scape,
That wrong'd you thus in honour, Queene, and Realme?   195
   Were this no cause to stirre a King to wrath,
Yet should your Conquests late atchieu'd gainst *Rome*
Inflame your minde with thirst of full reuenge.
   Arth. Indeede, continuall warres haue chafte our mindes,
And good successe hath bred impatient moodes.   200
Rome puffes vs vp, and makes vs too too fierce :
There, *Brytaines,* there we stand, whence *Rome* did fall.
   Thou *Lucius* mak'st me proude, thou heau'st my minde :
But what? shall I esteeme a Crowne ought else,
Then as a gorgeous Crest of easelesse Helme,   205
Or as some brittel mould of glorious pompe,
Or glittering glasse, which, whiles it shines, it breakes?
All this a sodaine *Chaunce* may dash, and not
Perhaps with thirteene Kings, or in nine yeares :
All may not finde so slowe and lingring *Fates.*   210
   What, that my Country cryes for due remorse
And some reliefe for long sustained toyles?
By Seas and Lands I dayly wrought her wrecke,
And sparelesse spent her life on euery foe.
Eche where my Souldiers perisht, whilest I wonne :   215
Throughout the world my Conquest was their spoile.
   A faire reward for all their deaths, for all
Their warres abroad, to giue them ciuill warres.
What bootes it them reseru'd from forreine foiles
To die at home?   What ende of ruthelesse rage?   220
   At least let age, and *Nature* worne to nought,
Prouide at length their graues with wished groanes.
Pitty their hoary haires, their feeble fists,
Their withered lims, their strengths consumde in Campe.
Must they still ende their liues amongest the blades?   225

Rests there no other *Fate* whiles *Arthur* raignes?
   What deeme you me? a furie fedde with blood,
Or some *Ciclopian* borne and bred for braules?
Thinke on the minde, that *Arthur* beares to peace:
Can *Arthur* please you no where but in warres?   230
   Be witnesse Heauens how farre t'is from my minde,
Therewith to spoile or sacke my natiue soile:
I cannot yeelde, it brookes not in my breast,
To seeke her ruine, whom I erst haue rulde.
What reliques now so e'r both ciuill broyles,   235
And forreine warres haue left, let those remaine:
Th'are fewe inough, and *Brytaines* fall to fast.

The second scene.

An Herault from Mordred.

Howe. LO here an Herault sent from *Mordreds* Campe,
    A froward message, if I reede aright:
We mought not stirre his wrath: perhaps this may:
Perswasions cannot moue a *Brytaines* moode,
And yet none sooner stung with present wrong.   5
   Herau. Haile peerelesse Prince, whiles *Fortune* would, our
    King,
Though now bereft of Crowne and former rule.
Vouchsafe me leaue my message to impart,
No iotte inforst, but as your Sonne affords.
   If here you stay but three dayes to an ende,   10
And not forthwith discharge your bands and hoast,
Ti's *Mordreds* oath: Assure your selfe to die.
But if you finde your courage so to serue,
As for to stand to your defence with force,
In *Cornewell* (if you dare) he'il trye it out.   15
   Arth. Is this the choyce my Sonne doth send his Sire,
And must I die? Or trye it if I dare?
To die were ill, thus to be dar'd is worse.

Display my standart forth, let Trumpe and Drumme
Call Souldiers nere, to heare their Soueraignes heast.   20

The third scene.

Gawin King of Albanie.   Aschillus King of Denmarke.
King of Norway.   A number of Souldiers.

Arth. O Friends and fellowes of my weriest toyles,
          Which haue borne out with me so, many brunts,
And desperate stormes of wars and brainsicke *Mars*:
Loe now the hundreth month wherein we winne.

    Hath all the bloud we spent in forreine Coasts,   5
The wounds, and deaths, and winters boad abroade,
Deserued thus to be disgrac'd at home?

    All *Brytaine* rings of warres: No towne, nor fielde
But swarmes with armed troupes: the mustering traines
Stop vp the streetes: no lesse a tumult's raisde,   ,   10
Then when *Hengistus* fell and *Horsus* fierce
With treacherous truce did ouerrunne the Realme.

    Each corner threatneth Death: both farre and nere
Is *Arthur* vext.   What if my force had faild,
And standarde falne, and ensignes all beene torne,   15
And *Roman* troupes pursude me at the heeles,
With lucklesse warres assaid in forreine soiles?

    Now that our *Fortune* heaues vs vp thus hie,
And Heauens themselues renewe our olde renowme:
Must we be darde? Nay, let that Princocke come,   20
That knowes not yet himselfe, nor *Arthurs* force,
That n'er yet waged warres, that's yet to learne
To giue the charge: Yea let that Princocke come,
With sodayne Souldyers pampered vp in peace,
And gowned troupes, and wantons worne with ease: 25
With sluggish *Saxons* crewe, and *Irish* kernes,
And *Scottish* aide, and false redshanked *Picts*,
Whose slaughters yet must teach their former f ,.e.

They shall perceaue with sorrow e'r they part,
When all their toyles be tolde, that nothing workes   30
So great a wast and ruine in this age,
As doe my warres.   O *Mordred* blessed Sonne :
No doubt, these market mates so highly hier'd
Must be the stay of thy vsurped state.

And least my head inclining now to yeares,   35
Should ioy the rest, which yet it neuer reapt :
The Traytor *Gilla*, traind in treacherous iarres,
Is chiefe in armes, to reaue me of my Realme.

What corner (ah) for all my warres shall shrowde
My bloodlesse age : what seate for due deserts ?   40
What towne, or field for auncient Souldiers rest ?
What house ? What rooffe ? What walls for weried lims ?

Stretch out againe, stretch out your conquering hands,
Still must we vse the force so often vsde.
To those, that will pursue a wrong with wreke,   45
He giueth all, that once denies the right.

Thou soile which erst *Diana* did ordaine
The certaine seate and bowre of wandring *Brute* :
Thou Realme which ay I reuerence as my Saint,
Thou stately *Brytaine* th'auncient tipe of *Troy*,   50
Beare with my forced wrongs : I am not he,
That willing would impeach thy peace with warres.

Lo here both farre and wide I Conqueror stand,
Arthur each where thine owne, thy Liedge, thy King.
Condemne not mine attempts : he, onely he   55
Is sole in fault, that makes me thus thy foe.

Here I renounce all leagues and treats of truce,
Thou *Fortune* henceforth art my garde and guide.
Hence peace, on warres, runne *Fates*, let *Mars* be iudge,
I erst did trust to right, but now to rage.   60

Goe : tell the boy that *Arthur* feares no brags,
In vaine he seekes to braue it with his Sire.
I come (*Mordred*) I come, but to thy paine.

32 *Mordred*] *Morered* Q

Yea, tell the boy his angry father comes,
To teach a Nouist both to die, and dare.   *Herault Exit.*   65
    Howe. If we without offence (O greatest guide
Of *Brytish* name) may poure our iust complaints :
We most mislike that your too milde a moode
Hath thus withheld our hands and swords from strokes.
    For what ? were we behind in any helpe ?   70
Or without cause did you misdoubt our force,
Or truth so often tried with good successe ?
    Goe to : Conduct your army to the fielde,
Place man to man, oppose vs to our foes :
As much we neede to worke, as wish your weale.   75
    Cado. Seemes it so sowre to winne by ciuill warres ?
Were it to goare with Pike my fathers breast,
Were it to riue and cleaue my brothers head,
Were it to teare peecemeale my dearest childe,
I would inforce my grudging handes to helpe.   ,   80
    I cannot terme that place my natiue soyle,
Whereto your trumpets send their warrlike sounds.
If case requir'd to batter downe the Towres
Of any Towne, that *Arthur* would destroy :
Yea, wer't of *Brytaines* selfe, which most I rede :   85
Her bulwarkes, fortresse, rampiers, walles and fence,
These armes should reare the Rams to runne them downe.
    Wherefore ye Princes, and the rest my mates,
If what I haue auerd in all your names,
Be likewise such as stands to your content,   90
Let all your Yeas auow my promise true.
    Soul. Yea, yea, &c.
    Asch. Wherein renowmed King my selfe, or mine,
My life, my Kingdome, and all *Denmarke* powre
May serue your turne, account them all your owne.   95
    King of Norway. And whatsoe'r my force or *Norwaie* aide
May helpe in your attempts, I vow it here.
    Gawi. As heretofore I alwayes serude your heast,

        67 name)] name ? *Q*   77 breast] braest *Q*

So let this daie be iudge of *Gawins* trust.
Either my brother *Mordred* dies the death 100
By mine assault, or I at least by his.

 Arth. Since thus (my faithfull mates) with vowes alike,
And equall loue to *Arthurs* cause you ioyne
In common care, to wreake my priuate wrongs:
Lift vp your Ensignes efts, stretch out your strengths, 105
Pursue your *Fates*, performe your hopes to *Mars*,
Loe here the last and outmost worke for blades.

 This is the time that all our valour craues.
This time by due desert restores againe
Our goods, our lands, our liues, our weale and all. 110
This time declares by *Fates* whose cause is best,
This, this condemnes the vanquisht side of guilt.

 Wherefore if for my sake you scorne your selues,
And spare no sword nor fire in my defence:
Then whiles my censure iustifies your cause, 115
Fight, fight amaine: and cleare your blades from crime,
The Iudge once changde, no warres are free from guilt.

 The better cause giues vs the greater hope
Of prosperous warres, wherein if once I hap
To spie the wonted signes, that neuer failde 120
Their guide, your threatning lookes, your firie eies,
And bustling bodies prest to present spoile:
The field is wonne. Euen then me thinkes I see
The wonted wasts and scattered heads of foes,
The *Irish* carcas kickt, and *Pictes* opprest, 125
And *Saxons* slaine, to swim in streames of bloud.
I quake with hope. I can assure you all,
We neuer had a greater match in hand.

 March on: delaie no *Fates* whiles *Fortune* fawnes,
The greatest praise of warres consists in speed. 130
       Exeunt Reges et Cohors.

   130 S.D. *Reges*] *Regis Q*

The fourth scene.

Cador. Arthur.

Cado. Since thus (victorious King) your Peeres, allies,
　　　Your Lords, and all your powres be ready prest,
For good, for bad, for whatsoe'r shall hap,
To spend both limme and life in your defence :
Cast of all doubts, and rest your selfe on *Mars* :　　　　　5
A hopelesse feare forbids a happy *Fate*.

　Arth. In sooth (good *Cador*) so our *Fortune* fares,
As needes we must returne to woonted force.
To warres we must : but such vnhappy warres,
As yeeld no hope for right or wrong to scape.　　　　　10

　My selfe foresees the *Fate*, it cannot fall
Without our dearest blood : much may the mir:de
Of pensiue Sire presage, whose Sonne so sinnes.
All truth, all trust, all blood, all bands be broke,
The seedes are sowne that spring to future spoyle,　　' 15
My Sonne, my Nephew, yea each side my selfe,
Nerer then all (woe's me) too nere, my foe.

　Well : t'is my plague for life so lewdly ledde,
The price of guilt is still a heauier guilt.
For were it light, that eu'n by birth my selfe　　　　　20
Was bad, I made my sister bad : nay were
That also light, I haue begot as bad.
Yea worse, an heire assignde to all our sinnes.

　Such was his birth : what base, what vulgar vice
Could once be lookt for of so noble blood ?　　　　　25
The deeper guilt descends, the more it rootes :
The younger imps affect the huger crimes.　　　　　*Exeunt.*

CHORVS.

1　When many men assent to ciuill warres,
　And yeelde a suffradge to inforce the *Fates* :
　No man bethinkes him of his owne mishappe,
　But turnes that lucke vnto an other's share.

Whereas if feare did first forewarne ech foyle,   5
Such loue to fight would breed no *Brytains* bane.
    And better were still to preserue our peace,
Then thus to vent for peace through waging warres.
What follie to forgoe such certayne happes,
And in their steede to feede vncertayne hopes?   10
    Such hopes as oft haue puft vp many a Realme,
Till crosse successe hath prest it downe as deepe :
Whiles blind affection fetcht from priuate cause
Misguiding wit hath maskt in wisedom's vaile,
Pretending what in purpose it abhorr'd.   15

2   Peace hath three foes incamped in our breasts,
Ambition, *Wrath*, and *Enuie* : which subdude,
We should not faile to finde eternall peace.
    T'is in our powre to ioy it all at will,
And fewe there be, but if they will, they may :   20
But yet euen those, who like the name of peace,
Through fond desire repine at peace it selfe.
    Betweene the hope whereof, and it it selfe,
A thousand things may fall : that further warres.
The very speech sometimes and treats of truce,   25
Is slasht and cut a sunder with the sword.
    Nor sield the name of peace doth edge our mindes,
And sharpeneth on our furie till we fight :
So that the mention made of loue and rest
Is oft a whetstone to our hate and rage.   30

3   Lo here the end, that Kingly pompe imparts,
The quiet rest, that Princely pallace plights.
Care vpon care, and euery day a newe
Fresh rysing tempest tires the tossed mindes.
    Who striues to stand in pompe of Princely port,   35
On guiddy top and culme of slippery Court,
Findes oft a heauy *Fate*, whiles too much knowne
To all, he falles vnknowne vnto himselfe.

34 rysing] rysiyg Q

Let who so else that list, affect the name,
But let me seeme a Potentate to none: 40
My slender barke shall creepe anenst the shoare,
And shunne the windes, that sweepe the waltering waues.
   Prowde *Fortune* ouerskippes the saffest Roades,
And seekes amidst the surging Seas those Keeles,
Whose lofty tops and tacklings touch the Cloudes.   45

4   O base, yet happy Boores! O giftes of Gods
Scant yet perceau'd: when poudred Ermine roabes
With secrete sighes mistrusting their extreames,
In bailefull breast forecast their foultring *Fates*,
And stirre, and striue, and storme, and all in vaine: 50
   Behold, the Peasant poore with tattered coate,
Whose eyes a meaner *Fortune* feedes with sleepe,
How safe and sound the carelesse Snudge doth snore.
   Low rooffed lurkes the house of slender hap,
Costlesse, not gay without, scant cleane within: ' 55
Yet safe: and oftner shroudes the hoary haires,
Then haughty Turrets rearde with curious art,
To harbour heads that wield the golden Crest.
   With endlesse carke in glorious Courts and Townes,
The troubled hopes and trembling feares doe dwell.   60

The Argument of the fourth Act.

1   IN the first Scene *Gildas* and *Conan* conferre of the state
    of *Brytaine*.
2   In the Second Scene *Nuntius* maketh report of the whole
    battaile, with the death of *Mordred* and *Arthurs* and *Cadors*
    deadly wound.   5
3   In the third Scene *Gildas* and *Conan* lament the infortunate
    state of the Countrie.

41 creepe] ceeepe *Q*   43 ouerskippes] ouerhippes *Q*

⁋ *The Argument and manner of the*
fourth dumbe shewe.

DVring the Musicke appointed after the third act, there came a Lady Courtly attyred with a counterfaite Childe in her armes, who walked softly on the Stage. From an other place there came a King Crowned, who likewise walked on an other part of the Stage. From a third place there came foure Souldiers all armed, who 5 spying this Lady and King, vpon a sodaine pursued the Lady from whom they violently tooke her Childe and flung it against the walles ; She in mournefull sort wringing her hands passed her way. Then in like manner they sette on the King, tearing his Crowne from his head, and casting it in peeces vnder feete draue him by 10 force away ; And so passed themselues ouer the Stage. By this was meant the fruit of Warre, which spareth neither man woman nor childe, with the ende of *Mordreds* vsurped Crowne.

THE FOVRTH ACT
and first scene.

Gildas. Conan.

Gild.   LORD *Conan*, though I know how hard a thing
         It is, for mindes trainde vp in Princely Thrones,
To heare of ought against their humor's course :
Yet : sithence who forbiddeth not offence,
If well he may, is cause of such offence :   5
I could haue wisht (and blame me not my Lord)
Your place and countnance both with Sonne and Sire,
Had more preuailde on either side, then thus
T'haue left a Crowne in danger for a Crowne
Through ciuill warres, our Countries woonted woe.   10
Whereby the Kingdom's wound still festring deepe,
Sucks vp the mischiefe's humor to the hart.
     The staggering state of *Brytaines* troubled braines,
Headsicke, and sore incumbred in her Crowne,

---

10 peeces] peeeces *Q. The Argument is clipped, shortening* Courtly, likewise, Souldiers, Lady, She, they, vnder, childe, *and cutting off* on *and* By

With guiddy steps runnes on a headlong race.   15
Whereto this tempest tend's, or where this storme
Will breake, who knowes? But Gods auert the worst.

   Cona. Now surely (*Gildas*) as my duety stood,
Indifferent for the best to Sonne and Sire :
So (I protest) since these occasions grewe,   20
That in the depth of my desire to please,
I more esteemde what honest faith requir'd
In matters meete for their estates and place :
Than how to feede each fond affection prone
To bad effects, whence their disgrace mought growe.   25

   And as for *Mordreds* desperate and disloyall plots,
They had beene none, or fewer at the least,
Had I preuail'd : which *Arthur* knowes right well.

   But eu'n as Counters goe sometimes for one,
Sometimes for thousands more, sometimes for none :   30
So men in greatest countnance with their King,
Can worke by fit perswasion sometimes much :
But sometimes lesse : and sometimes nought at all.

   Gild. Well : wee that haue not spent our time in warres,
But bent our course at peace, and Countries weale,   35
May rather now expect what strange euent,
And *Chaunce* insues of these so rare attempts :
Then enter to discourse vpon their cause,
And erre as wide in wordes, as they in deedes.

   Cona. And Lo : to satisfie your wish therein,   40
Where comes a Souldier sweating from the Camps.

The second scene.

Nuncius.

Nunc. THOU *Eccho* shrill that hauntst the hollow hilles,
     Leaue off that woont to snatch the latter word :
Howle on a whole discourse of our distresse,
Clippe of no clause : sound out a perfect sense.

Gild. What fresh mishap (alas) what newe annoy,   5
Remoues our pensiue mindes from wonted woes,
And yet requires a newe lamenting moode?
Declare : we ioy to handle all our harmes :
Our many griefes haue taught vs still to mourne.

Nunc. But (ah) my toung denies my speech his aide :   10
Great force doth driue it forth : a greater keepes
It in.   I rue surprisde with woontlesse woes.

Cona. Speake on, what griefe so e'r our *Fates* af

Nunc. Small griefes can speake : the great astonisi.   and.

Gild. What greater sinnes could hap, then what be   ? 15
What mischiefes could be meant, more then were wro

Nunc. And thinke you these to be an end to sinnes ?
No.   Crime proceedes : those made but one degree.
What mischiefes carst were done, terme sacred deedes :
Call nothing sinne, but what hath since insu'd.   20
A greater griefe requires your teares : Behold
These fresh annoyes : your last mishaps be stale.

Cona. Tell on (my friend) suspend our mindes no more :
Hath *Arthur* lost?   Hath *Mordred* woonne the field?

Nunc. O : nothing lesse.   Would Gods it were but so.   25
Arthur hath woonne : but we haue lost the field.
The field?   Nay all the Realme, and *Brytaines* bounds.

Gild. How so?   If *Arthur* woonne, what could we loose?
You speake in cloudes, and cast perplexed wordes.
Vnfolde at large : and sort our sorrowes out.   30

Nunc. Then list a while : this instant shall vnwrappe
Those acts, those warres, those hard cuents, that all
The future age shall eu'r haue cause to curse.

Now that the time drewe on, when both the Camps
Should meet in *Cornwell* fieldes th'appointed place :   35
The reckelesse troupes, whom *Fates* forbad to liue,
Till noone, or night, did storme and raue for warres.
They swarmde about their Guydes, and clustring cald
For signes to fight, and fierce with vprores fell,

                    30 our] out *Q*

They onwards hayld the hastning howres of death. 40
A direfull frenzie rose : ech man his owne,
And publike *Fates* all heedlesse headlong flung.

    On *Mordreds* side were sixtie thousande men,
Some borowed powres, some *Brytans* bred at home.
The *Saxons, Irish, Normans, Pictes,* and *Scottes* 45
Were first in place, the *Brytanes* followed last.

    On *Arthurs* side there were as manie more.
Islandians, Gothes, Noruegians, Albanes, Danes,
Were forraine aides, which *Arthur* brought from *Fraunce,*
A trustie troupe, and tryed at many a trench. 50

    That nowe the day was come, wherein our State
For aye should fall, whenceforth men might inquire
What *Brytaine* was : these warres thus neere bewraide.
Nor could the Heauens no longer hide these harmes,
But by prodigious signes portende our plagues. 55

    For lo : er both the Campes encountering coapt,
The Skies and Poles opposed themselues with stormes. .
Both East, and West with tempestes darke were dim'd,
And showres of Hayle, and Rayne outragious powr'd.
The Heauens were rent, ech side the lightnings flasht, 60
And Clowdes with hideous clappes did thundering roare.

    The armies all agast did senselesse stand,
Mistrusting much, both Force, and Foes, and *Fates.*
T'was harde to say, which of the two appal'd
Them most, the monstrous ayre, or too much feare. 65

    When *Arthur* spide his Souldiers thus amaz'd,
And hope extinct, and deadly dreade drawne on :
My mates (quoth he) the Gods doe skowre the skies,
To see whose cause and courage craues their care.
The *Fates* contende to worke some straunge euent : 70
And *Fortune* seeks by stormes in Heauens and Earth,
What pagions she may play for my behoofe.
Of whom she knowes, she then deserues not well,
When lingring ought, she comes not at the first.

    Thus saide : reioycing at his dauntlesse minde, 75

They all reuiude, and former feare recoylde.

By that the light of *Titan's* troubled beames
Had pearceing scattered downe the drowping fogges,
And greeted both the Campes with mutuall viewe :
Their choller swelles, whiles fell disposed mindes   80
Bounce in their breastes, and stirre vncertayne stormes.
Then palenes wanne and sterne with chearelesse chaunge,
Possessing bleake their lippes and bloodlesse cheekes,
With troublous trembling shewes their death is nere.

When *Mordred* sawe the danger thus approacht,   85
And boystrous throngs of Warriers threatning blood :
His instant ruines gaue a nodde at *Fates*,
And minde though prone to *Mars*, yet daunted pausde.

The hart which promist earst a sure successe,
Now throbs in doubts : nor can his owne attempts,   90
Afforde him feare, nor *Arthurs* yeelde him hope.
This passion lasts not long, he soone recalls
His auncient guise, and wonted rage returnes.
He loathes delayes, and scorcht with Scepters lust,
The time and place, wherein he oft had wisht   95
To hazarde all vpon extreamest *Chaunce*,
He offred spies, and spide pursues with speede.

Then both the Armies mette with equall might,
This stird with wrath, that with desire to rule :
And equall prowesse was a spurre to both.   100
The *Irish* King whirlde out a poysned Dart,
That lighting pearced deepe in *Howels* braines,
A peerelesse Prince and nere of *Arthurs* bloud.

Hereat the Aire with vprore lowde resoundes,
Which efts on mountains rough rebounding reares.   105
The Trumpets hoarce their trembling tunes doe teare :
And thundring Drummes their dreadfull Larums ring.
The Standards broad are blowne, and Ensignes spread,
And euery Nation bends his woonted warres.

Some nere their foes, some further off doe wound,   110
With dart, or sword, or shaft, or pike, or speare,

The weapons hide the Heauens : a night composde
Of warrelike Engines ouershades the field.
From euery side these fatall signes are sent :
And boystrous bangs with thumping thwacks fall thicke.   115
   Had both these Camps beene of vsurping Kings,
Had euery man thereof a *Mordred* beene,
No fiercelier had they fought for all their Crownes.
The murthers meanelesse waxt, no art in fight,
Nor way to ward nor trie each others skill,   120
But thence the blade, and hence the bloud ensues.
   Cona. But what ?   Did *Mordreds* eyes indure this sight ?
   Nunc. They did.   And he himselfe the spurre of fiends
And *Gorgons* all, least any part of his
Scapt free from guilt, enflamde their mindes to wrath.   125
And, with a valure more, then Vertue yeelds,
He chearde them all, and at their backe with long
Outreached speare, stirde vp each lingring hand.
All furie like frounst vp with frantick frets.
   He bids them leaue and shunne the meaner sort,   130
He shewes the Kings, and *Brytaines* noblest peeres.
   Gild. He was not now to seeke what bloud to drawe :
He knewe what iuice refresht his fainting Crowne.
Too much of *Arthurs* hart.   O had he wist
How great a vice such vertue was as then.   135
In Ciuill warres, in rooting vp his Realme ?
O frantike fury, farre from Valures praise.
   Nunc. There fell *Aschillus* stout of *Denmarke* King,
There valiant *Gawin Arthurs* Nephew deare,
And late by *Augels* death made *Albane* King,   140
By *Mordreds* hand hath lost both life and Crowne.
   There *Gilla* wounded *Cador Cornish* Duke,
In hope to winne the Dukedome for his meede.
The *Norway* King, the *Saxons* Duke, and *Picts*,
In wofull sort fell groueling to the ground.   145
   There Prince and Peasant both lay hurlde on heapes :
Mars frownde on *Arthurs* mates : the *Fates* waxt fierce,

And iointly ranne their race with *Mordreds* rage.

   Cona. But with what ioy (alas) shall he returne,
That thus returnes, the happier for this fielde ?   150

   Nunc. These odds indure not long, for *Mars* retires,
And *Fortune* pleasde with *Arthurs* moderate feare,
Returnes more full, and friendlyer then her woont.

   For when he saw the powers of *Fates* opposde,
And that the dreadfull houre thus hastened on :   155
Perplexed much in minde, at length resolues,
That feare is couered best by daring most.

   Then forth he pitcht : the *Saxon* Duke withstoode,
Whom with one stroke he headlesse sent to Hell.
Not farre from thence he spide the *Irish* King,   160
Whose life he tooke as price of broken truce.

   Then *Cador* foreward prest, and haplie mette
The Traytor *Gilla*, worker of these warres,
Of whom by death he tooke his due reuenge.

   The remnant then of both the Camps concurre,   165
They *Brytaines* all, or most : few Forreines left.
These wage the warres, and hence the deaths insue.
Nor t'one, nor t'other side, that can destroy
His foes so fast, as tis it selfe destroyed.

   The brethren broach their bloud : the Sire his Sonnes,   170
The Sonne againe would proue by too much Wrath,
That he, whom thus he slew, was not his Sire.
No blood nor kinne can swage their irefull moodes.
No forreine foe they seeke, nor care to finde :
The *Brytaines* bloud is sought on euery side.   175

   A vaine discourse it were to paint at large
The seuerall *Fates*, and toiles of either side.
To tell what grones and sighes the parting Ghosts
Sent forth : who dying bare the fellest breast :
Who chaunged cheare at any *Brytaines* fall :   180
Who oftnest strooke : who best bestowde his blade :
Who ventred most : who stoode : who fell : who failde :
Th'effect declares it all : thus far'd the field.

Of both these Hoasts so huge and maine at first,
There were not left on either side a score,   185
For Sonne, and Sire to winne, and loose the Realme.

    The which when *Mordred* saw, and that his Sire
Gainst foes, and *Fates* themselues would winne the field,
He sigh'd, and twixt despaire and rage he cryed,
Here (*Arthur*) here, and hence the Conquest comes :   190
Whiles *Mordred* liues, the Crowne is yet vnwoonne.

    Hereat the prince of prowesse much amaz'd,
With thrilling teares, and countnance cast on ground.
Did groaning fetch a deepe and earnefull sigh.

    Anone they fierce encountering both concur'd,   195
With griesly lookes, and faces like their *Fates* :
But dispar mindes, and inward moodes vnlike.

    The Sire with minde to safegard both, or t'one :
The Sonne to spoile the t'one, or hazard both.
No feare, nor fellnes failde on either side :   200
The wager lay on both their liues and bloods.

    At length when *Mordred* spyde his force to faint,
And felt him selfe opprest with *Arthurs* strength,
(O haplesse lad, a match vnmeete for him)
He loathes to liue in that afflicted state,   205
And valiant with a forced Vertue, longs
To die the death : in which perplexed minde,
With grenning teeth, and crabbed lookes he cryes,
I cannot winne : yet will I not be wonne.

    What should we shun our *Fates*, or play with *Mars*,   210
Or thus defraude the warres of both our blouds?
Whereto doe we reserue our selues? Or why
Be we not sought ere this, amongst the dead ?
So many thousands murthred in our cause,
Must we suruiue, and neither winne nor loose ?   215

    The *Fates* that will not smile on either side,
May frowne on both : So saying forth he flings,
And desperate runs on point of *Arthurs* Sword,
(A Sword (alas) prepar'd for no such vse)

Whereon engoarde he glides, till nere approcht, 220
With dying hand he hewes his fathers head.
So through his owne annoy, he noyes his Liedge :
And gaines by death accesse to daunt his Sire.

There *Mordred* fell, but like a Prince he fell.
And as a braunch of great *Pendragons* grafte 225
His life breaths out, his eyes forsake the Sunne,
And fatall Cloudes inferre a lasting Clips.
There *Arthur* staggering scant sustaind him selfe,
There *Cador* found a deepe and deadly wound,
There ceast the warres, and there was *Brytaine* lost. 230

There lay the chosen youths of *Mars*, there lay
The peerelesse Knights, *Bellona's* brauest traine.
There lay the Mirrours rare of Martiall praise,
There lay the hope and braunch of *Brute* supprest.
There *Fortune* laid the prime of *Brytaines pride*, 235
There laide her pompe, all topsie turuie turnde.   *Exit.*

The third scene.

Gildas. Conan.

Gild. Come cruell griefes, spare not to stretch our
            strengths,
Whiles bailefull breastes inuite our thumping fists.
Let euery signe, that mournefull passions worke,
Expresse what piteous plightes our mindes amaze.

This day supplants what no day can supply, 5
These handes haue wrought those wastes, that neuer age,
Nor all the broode of *Brute* shall e'er repaire.
That future men may ioy the surer rest,
These warres preuent their birth, and nip their spring.

What Nations earst the former age subdude 10
With hourelie toyles to *Brytaines* yoke, this day
Hath set at large, and backwardes turnde the *Fates*.
Hencefoorth the *Kernes* may safely tread their bogges :

The *Scots* may now their inrodes olde renewe,
The *Saxons* well may vow their former claimes,   15
And *Danes* without their danger driue vs out.

    These warres found not the'ffect of woonted warres,
Nor doth their waight the like impression woorke:
There seuerall *Fates* annoyde but seuerall men,
Heere all the Realme and people finde one *Fate*.   20
What there did reache but to a Souldiers death,
Containes the death of all a Nation here.

    These blades haue giuen this *Isle* a greater wounde,
Then tyme can heale.   The fruite of ciuill warres:
A Kingdom's hand hath goard a Kingdom's heart,   25
   Cona. When Fame shall blaze these acts in latter yeares,
And time to come so many ages hence
Shall efts report our toyles and *Brytish* paynes:
Or when perhaps our Childrens Children reade,
Our woefull warres displaid with skilfull penne: 30
They'l thinke they heere some sounds of future facts,   '
And not the ruines olde of pompe long past.
Twill mooue their mindes to ruth, and frame a fresh
New hopes, and feares, and vowes, and many a wish,
And *Arthurs* cause shall still be fauour'd most.   35

    He was the ioy, and hope, and hap of all,
The Realmes defence, the sole delay of *Fates*,
He was our wall and forte, twice thirteene yeares
His shoulders did the *Brytaine* state support.

    Whiles yet he raignd, no forren foes preuailde,   40
Nor once could hope to binde the *Brytaine* boundes:
But still both farre and nere were forc'd to flie,
They thrall to vs, we to our selues were free.

    But now, and hencefoorth aye, adue that hope,
Adue that pompe, that freedome, rule and all: 45
Let *Saxons* now, let *Normans*, *Danes*, and *Scottes*,
Enioye our medowes, fieldes, and pleasant plaines:
Come, let vs flye to Mountaines, Cliffes and Rockes,
A Nation hurt, and ne'r in case to heale.

Hencefoorth the waight of *Fates* thus falne aside,   50
We rest secure from feare of gréater foile :
Our leasure serues to thinke on former times,
And know what earst we were, who now are thus.   *Exeunt.*

CHORVS.

1   O *Brytaines* prosperous state were Heauenlye powers
      But halfe so willing to preserue thy peace,
    As they are prone to plague thee for thy warres.
    But thus (O Gods) yea, thus it likes you still,
    When you decree to turne, and touse the worlde,   5
    To make our errors cause of your decrees.
      We fretting fume, and burning wax right wood,
    We crye for swordes, and harmefull harnesse craue,
    We rashly raue, whiles from our present rage,
    You frame a cause of long foredeemed doome.   10

2   When *Brytaine* so desir'd her owne decaie,
    That eu'n her natiue broode would roote her vp :
    Seamde it so huge a woorke, (O Heauens) for you
    To tumble downe, and quite subuert her state,
    Vnlesse so many Nations came in aide ?   15
    What thirst of spoile (O *Fates* ?) In ciuil warres
    Were you afraide to faint for want of blood ?
      But yet, O wretched state in *Brytaines* fond,
    What needed they to stoope to *Mordreds* yoke,
    Or feare the man themselues so fearefull made ?   20
    Had they, but lynckt like friendes in *Arthurs* bandes,
    And ioynde their force against the forren foes :
    These warres and ciuill sinncs had soone surceast,
    And *Mordred* reft of rule had feard his Sire.

3   Would Gods these warres had drawne no other blood,   25
    Then such as sproong from breasts of forreine foes :
    So that the fountaine, fedde with chaungelesse course,
    Had found no neerer vents for dearer iuyce.

Ch. 1 were] *So corr. with ink in GQ from* wert   4 *Q period at end
of line*

Or if the *Fates* so thirst for *Brytish* blood,
And long so deepely for our last decaie :   30
O that the rest were sparde and safe reseru'd,
Both *Saxons*, *Danes*, and *Normans* most of all.
    Heereof when ciuill warres haue worne vs out,
Must *Brytaine* stand, a borrowed blood for *Brute*.

4   When prosperous haps, and long continuing blisse,   35
Haue past the ripenesse of their budding grouth,
They fall and foulter like the mellow fruite,
Surcharg'd with burden of their owne excesse.
So *Fortune* wearyed with our often warres,
Is forc'd to faint, and leaue vs to our fates.   40
    If men haue mindes presaging ought their harmes,
If euer heauie heart foreweene her woe :
What *Brytaine* liues, so far remou'd from home,
In any Ayre, or Pole, or Coast abroade :
But that euen now through *Natures* sole instinct,   45
He feeles the fatall sword imbrue his breast,
Wherewith his natiue soyle for aye is slaine ?
What hopes, and happes lye wasted in these warres ?
Who knowes the foyles he suffered in these fieldes ?

The argument of the fift Act.

1   IN the first scene *Arthur* and *Cador* returned deadlie
     wounded and bewaild the misfortune of themselues and
     their Countrie, and are likewise bewailed of the *Chorus*.

2   In the seconde scene the Ghoast of *Gorlois* returneth
     reioycing at his reuendge, and wishing euer after a happier 5
     Fate vnto *Brytaine*, which done, he descendeth where he
     first rose.

❡ *The Argument and manner of the*
fift and last dumbe shewe.

SOunding the Musicke, foure gentlemen all in blacke halfe armed, halfe vnarmed with blacke skarffes ouerthwart their shoulders should come vppon the stage. The first bearing alofte in the one hand on the trunchion of a speare an Helmet, an arming sworde, a Gauntlet, &c. representing the Trophea: in the other hand 5 a Target depicted with a mans hart sore wounded & the blood gushing out, crowned with a Crowne imperiall and a Lawrell garland, thus written in the toppe. *En totum quod superest*, signi-fying the King of *Norway* which spent himselfe and all his power for *Arthur*, and of whom there was left nothing but his heart to 10 inioy the conquest that insued. The seconde bearing in the one hand a siluer vessell full of golde, pearles, and other iewels repre-senting the *Spolia* : in the other hande a Target with an Olephant and Dragon thereon fiercely combating, the Dragon vnder the Olephant and sucking by his extreme heate the blood from him is 15 crushed in peeces with the fall of the Olephant, so as both die at last, this written aboue, *Victor, an Victus*? representing the King of *Denmarke*, who fell through *Mordreds* wound, hauing first with his souldiers destroyed the most of *Mordreds* armie. The third bearing in the one hand a *Pyramis* with a Lawrell wreath about it repre- 20 senting victorie. In the other hand a Target with this deuise : a man sleeping, a snake drawing neere to sting him, a Leazard preuenting the Snake by fight, the Leazard being deadlie wounded awaketh the man, who seeing the Leazard dying, pursues the Snake, and kils it, this written aboue, *Tibi morimur*. Signifying *Gawin* 25 King of *Albanye* slaine in *Arthurs* defence by *Mordred*, whom *Arthur* afterwardes slewe. The fourth bearing in the one hande a broken piller, at the toppe thereof the Crowne and Scepter of the vanquisht King, both broken asunder, representing the conquest ouer vsurpation : in the other hand a Target with two Cockes 30 painted thereon, the one lying dead, the other with his winges broken, his eyes pecked out, and the bloode euerye where gushing foorth to the grounde, he standing vppon the dead Cocke and crowing ouer him, with this embleme in the toppe, *Qua vici, perdidi*,

14 combating] combacting *Q*

signifying *Cador* deadly wounded by *Gilla* whom he slewe.   After 35
these followed a King languishing in complet Harnesse blacke,
brused & battered vnto him, besprinkled with blood.   On his head
a Lawrell garland, leaning on the shoulders of two Heraults in
mourning gownes & hoods, th'on in *Mars* his coate of arms, the
other in *Arthurs*, presenting *Arthur* victoriously but yet deadly 40
wounded. there followed a page with a Target whereon was por-
traited a Pellican pecking her blood out of her brest to feede her
young ones, through which wound she dieth, this writen in the
toppe, *Qua foui, perii*, signifying *Arthurs* too much indulgencie of
Mordred, the cause of his death.   All this represented the dismayed 45
and vnfortunate victorie of *Arthur*, which is the matter of the Act
insuing.

THE FIFT ACT
and first Scene.

Arthur.   Cador.   Chorus.

Arth.   COme *Cador*, as our frendship was most firme   ,
            Throughout our age, so now let's linke as fast.
Thus did we liue in warres, thus let vs dye
In peace, and arme in arme pertake our *Fates*.
Our woundes, our greefe, our wish, our hap alike,   5
Our end so neere, all craue eche others helpe.

   Cado.   O King, beholde the fruite of all our *Fame* :
Lo here our Pompe consumed with our selues,
What all our age with all our warres had woonne,
Loe here one day hath lost it all at once.   10

   Welk: so it likes the Heauens : thus *Fortune* gibes :
She hoyseth vp to hurle the deeper downe.

   Chor. 1.   O sacred Prince : what sight is this we see ?
Why haue the *Fates* reseru'd vs to these woes
Our onely hope : the stay of all our Realme :   15
The piller of our state : thus sore opprest ?

   O would the Gods had fauour'd vs so much :
That, as we liu'd partakers of your paines,
And likewise ioyde the fruit of your exploytes :

So hauing thus bereft our Soueraignes blisse,   20
They had with more indifferent doome conioynd
The Subiects both, and Soueraignes bane in one.
  It now (alas) ingendereth double greefe,
To rue your want, and to bewaile our woes.
  Arth. Rue not my *Brytaines* what my rage hath wrought, 25
But blame your King, that thus hath rent your Realme.
My meanelesse moodes haue made the *Fates* thus fell,
And too much anger wrought in me too much.
  For had impatient ire indu'rde abuse,
And yeelded where resistance threatned spoyle :   30
I mought haue liu'd in forreine coastes vnfoilde,
And six score thousand men had bene vnmoande.
  But wrong incensing wrath to take reuenge
Preferred *Chaunce* before a better choyse.
  Chor. 2. T'was *Mordreds* wrong and to vniust desertes   35
That iustly mooude your Highnesse to such wrath :
Your claime requir'd no lesse then those attempts :
Your cause right good was prais'd, and praide for most.
  Arth. I claimd my Crowne, the cause of claime was good,
The meanes to clame it in such sorte was bad.   40
  Yea : rather then my Realme and natiue soile
Should wounded fall, thus brused with these warres :
I should haue left both Realme, and right, and all :
Or dur'd the death ordaind by *Mordreds* oath.
  Cado. And yet so farre as *Mars* coulde bide a meane,   45
You hatelesse sought the safegard of them all.
  Whereto the better cause, or badder *Chaunce*
Did drawe, you still inclinde : preferring oft
The weaker side, sometimes for loue, sometimes
For right, (as *Fortune* swaide) your Sonne, your selfe.   50
  So pittie spar'd, what reason sought to spoyle :
Till all at length, with equall spoyle was spent.
  Chor. 3. Would Gods your minde had felt no such remorse,
And that your foes had no such fauour founde.
So mought your friends haue had far frendlier *Fates*,   55

If Rebels for their due deserts had dyde.
　The wickeds death is safety to the iust.
To spare the Traitors, was to spoile the true.
Of force he hurtes the good, that helpes the bad.
　In that you sought your Countries gaine, t'was well :　60
In that you shunned not her losse, t'was hard.
Good is the frend, that seekes to do vs good :
A mighty frend, that doth preuent our harmes.
　Arth. Well : so it was : it cannot be redrest :
The greater is my greefe, that sees it so.　65
　My lyfe (I feele) doth fade, and sorrowes flowe,
The rather that my name is thus extinct.
In this respect, so *Mordred* did succeede,
O, that my selfe had falne, and *Mordred* liu'd :
That hauing conquer'd all my foes but him,　70
I mought haue left you him, that conquer'd me.
　O heauie wretched lotte : to be the last
That falles, to viewe the buriall of my Realme.
Where each man else hath fealt his seuerall *Fate*,
I onely pine opprest with all their *Fates*.　75
　Chor. 4. Although your Highnesse do susteine such greefe,
As needes enforceth all your Realme to rue :
Yet since such ruth affordeth no releefe,
Let due discretion swage each curelesse sore,
And beare the harmes, that run without redresse.　80
The breath-　The losse is ours, that loose so rare a Prince,
lesse body　You onely win, that see your foe here foilde.
of Mordred
in Armour　*Arth.* A causelesse foe. When warres did call me hence
as he fell is　He was in yeares but young, in wit too olde.
brought
vpon the　As vertue shineth most in comliest wightes,　85
Stadge.　When inward gifts are deckt with outward grace :
So did his witte and feature feede that hope,
Which falsely trainde me to this wofull hap.
　His minde transformed thus, I cannot chuse
But long to see what change his face sustaines.　90
My blood and kinred doubled in his birth,

Inspires a mixt, and twice descending loue,
Which driues my dying vaines to wish his view.
Vnhealme his luckelesse head, set bare his face :
That face which earst pleas'd me and mine to much.   95

   Chor. 1. See (worthest King) the hope of all your Realme,
Had not his lust to rule preuented all.

   Arth. I see (alas) I see (hide, hide againe :
O spare mine eyes) a witnesse of my crimes :
A fearefull vision of my former guilte :   100
A dreadfull horror of a future doome :
A present gaule of minde.   O happie they,
Whose spotlesse liues attaine a dreadlesse death.

   And thou, O haplesse boye, O spight of *Fates*,
(What mought I terme thee, Nephew, Sonne, or both ?)   105
Alas, how happie should we both haue bene,
If no ambitious thought had vext thy head.
Nor thou thus striu'de to reaue thy Fathers rule,
But staide thy tyme, and not forstalde vs both ?

   Cado. The hoat spurde youth that forste the forward steedes,
Whiles needes he would his Fathers Chariot guide,   111
Neglecting what his Sire had said in charge,
The fires, which first he flung about the poles,
Himselfe at last most wofull wretch inflamde.
So to much loue to houer in the Heauens   115
Made him to paie the price of rash attemptes.

   Arth. What ruth, (ah,) rent the wofull Fathers hart,
That sawe himselfe thus made a Sonnelesse Sire ?
Well : since both Heauens and Hell conspir'd in one,
To make our endes a mirror to the worlde,   120
Both of incestious life, and wicked birth :
Would Gods the *Fates* that linckt our faultes alike,
Had also fram'de our minds of frendlier mouldes :
That, as our linage had approcht too neere,
So our affections had not swaru'd to farre.   125

   Then mought I liu'd t'inlarge the *Brytaines* praise,
In rearing efts the first triumphant *Troy*

And after thou succeeding mine attempts,
Haue spent thy courage in a iuster cause.

    But t'would not be: Ambition grew to greate: 130
We could not ioyne our mindes: our *Fates* we ioynde:
And through thy blood, a way was made to mine.

    Chor. 2. And must we needes (O worthiest Peeres) forgoe,
By this vntimely *Fate* our greatest hope?
That in your ripest yeares and likelyest time,   135
Your chiefest force should on this sodaine fall?

    Chor. 3. Haue you throughout your youth made *Brytaines*
        pompe
A Soueraigne of so many Nations stout,
To th'end ere halfe your age vntimely death
Should leaue vs Subiect to our woonted foiles?   140

    Chor. 4. See, see, our idle hopes, our brittle trust,
Our vaine desires, our ouer fickle state,
Which, though a while they sayle on quiet seas,
Yet sinke in surge, ere they ariue to Rode.
O wofull warres, O *Mordreds* cursed pride,   145
That thus hath wrought both King, and Kingdomes woe.

    Cado. Let plaints and mournings passe, set moanes a part.
They made much of themselues: Yea too too much
They lou'd to liue, that seeing all their Realme
Thus topsie turuey turnd, would grudge to dye.   150

    Arth. Yea sure: since thus (O *Fates*) your censure seemes,
That free from force of forreine foes, there rests,
That *Mordred* reape the glory of our deaths:
B'it so: driue on your doome, worke your decree:
We fearelesse hide what bane so e'r you bidde.   155

    And though our ends thus hastened through your heasts,
Abruptly breake the course of great attempts:
Yet goe we not inglorious to the ground:
Set wish a part: we haue perfourmd inough.

    The *Irish* King and Nation wilde we tamde: 160
The *Scots* and *Picts*, and *Orcade* Isles we wanne:

    144 Rode] *So corr. with small printed slip in GQ*: hode *KQ*

The *Danes* and *Gothes* and *Friseland* men, with all
The Isles inserted nere those Seas, And next
The *Germaine* King, and *Saxons* we subdude.
   Not *Fraunce*, that could preuaile against our force,   165
Nor lastly *Rome*, that rues her pride supprest.
Ech forreine power is parcell of our praise,
No titles want to make our foes affraide.
   This onely now I craue (O *Fortune* erst
My faithfull friend) let it be soone forgot,   170
Nor long in minde, nor mouth, where *Arthur* fell.
Yea : though I Conquerour die, and full of *Fame* :
Yet let my death and parture rest obscure.
No graue I neede (O *Fates*) nor buriall rights,
Nor stately hearce, nor tombe with haughty toppe :   175
But let my Carkasse lurke : yea, let my death
Be ay vnknowen, so that in euery Coast
I still be feard, and lookt for euery houre.

         Exeunt.   Arthur & Cador.

  Chor. 1. Lo here the end that *Fortune* sends at last
To him, whom first she heau'd to highest happe.   180
The flattering looke wherewith he long was led :
The smiling *Fates*, that oft had fedde his *Fame* :
The many warres and Conquests, which he gaind,
Are dasht at once : one day inferres that foile,
Whereof so many yeares of yore were free.   185
  Chor. 2. O willing world to magnifie man's state :
O most vnwilling to maintaine the same.
Of all misfortunes and vnhappy *Fates*,
Th'unhappiest seemes, to haue beene hapie once.
T'was *Arthur* sole, that neuer found his ioyes   190
Disturb'd with woe, nor woes relieu'd with ioye.
In prosperous state all Heauenly powres aspir'd :
Now made a wretch, not one, that spares his spoile.
  Chor. 3. Yea *Fortunes* selfe in this afflicted case,
Exacts a paine for long continued pompe.   195
She vrgeth now the blisse of woonted weale,

And beares him downe with waight of former *Fame*,
His prayses past be present shame : O tickle trust :
Whiles *Fortune* chops and chaungeth euery *Chaunce*,
What certaine blisse can we enioy a liue,   200
Vnlesse, whiles yet our blisse endures, we die ?

   Chor. 4. Yea : since before his last and outmost gaspe,
None can be deemde a happy man or blest,
Who dares commit him selfe to prosperous *Fates*,
Whose death preparde attends not hard at hand ?   205
That sithence death must once determine all,
His life may sooner flie, then *Fortune* flitte.

The second scene.

Gorlois.

Gorl. NOW *Gorlois* swage thy selfe.   Pride hath his pay :
Murther his price : Adult'rie his desert :
Treason his meede : Disloyaltie his doome :
Wrong hath his wreake : and Guilt his guerdon beares.
Not one abuse erst offered by thy foes   5
But since most sternely punisht, is now purg'd.
Where thou didst fall, eu'n on the selfe same soile
Pendragon, Arthur, Mordred, and their stocke,
Found all their foiles : not one hath scapte reuenge :
Their line from first to last quite razed out.   10

   Now rest content, and worke no further plagues :
Let future age be free from *Gorlois* Ghost.
Let *Brytaine* henceforth bath in endlesse weale.
Let *Virgo* come from Heauen, the glorious Starre :
The Zodiac's ioy : the Planets chiefe delight :   15
The hope of all the yeare : the ease of Skies :
The Aires reliefe, the comfort of the Earth.

   That vertuous *Virgo* borne for *Brytaines* blisse :
That pierelesse braunch of *Brute* : that sweete remaine
Of *Priam's* state : that hope of springing *Troy* :   20
Which time to come, and many ages hence
Shall of all warres compound eternall peace.

Let her reduce the golden age againe,
Religion, ease, and wealth of former world.
Yea, let that *Virgo* come and *Saturnes* raigne,   25
And yeares oft ten times tolde expirde in peace.
A Rule, that else no Realme shall euer finde,
A Rule most rare, vnheard, vnseene, vnread,
The sole example that the world affordes.

That (*Brytaine*) that Renowme, yea that is thine.   30
B'it so: my wrath is wrought. Ye furies blacke
And vglie shapes, that houle in holes beneath:
Thou *Orcus* darke, and deepe *Auernas* nooke,
With duskish dennes out gnawne in gulfes belowe,
Receaue your ghastly charge, Duke *Gorlois* Ghoast: 35
Make roome: I gladly thus reuengde returne.
And though your paine surpasse, I greete them tho:
He hates each other Heauen, that haunteth Hell.

Descendit.

EPILOGVS.

See heere by this the tickle trust of tyme:
The false affiance of each mortall force,
The wauering waight of *Fates*: the fickell trace,
That *Fortune* trips: the many mockes of life:
The cheerelesse change: the easelesse brunts and broyles,   5
That man abides: the restlesse race he runnes.

But most of all, see heere the peerelesse paines:
The lasting panges: the stintlesse greefes: the teares:
The sighes: the grones: the feares: the hopes: the hates:
The thoughts and cares, that Kingly pompe impartes.   10

What follies then bewitch thambicious mindes,
That thirst for Scepters pompe the well of woes?
Whereof (alas) should wretched man be proude,
Whose first conception is but Sinne, whose birth
But paine, whose life but toyle, and needes must dye?   15

See heere the store of great *Pendragons* broode,
The to'ne quite dead, the to'ther hastening on,
As men, the Sonne but greene, the Sire but ripe:

U 2

Yet both forestalde ere halfe their race were run.
As Kinges, the mightiest Monarches in this age,   20
Yet both supprest and vanquisht by themselues.
   Such is the brittle breath of mortall man,
Whiles humane *Nature* workes her dayly wrackes:
Such be the crazed crests of glorious Crownes,
Whiles worldly powers like sudden puffes do passe.   25
And yet for one that goes, another comes,
Some borne, some dead: So still the store indures.
So that both *Fates* and common care prouide
That men must needes be borne, and some must rule.
   Wherefore ye Peeres, and Lordings lift aloft,   30
And whosoe'r in Thrones that iudge your thralls:
Let not your Soueraingty heaue you to hye,
Nor their subiection presse them downe too lowe.
It is not pride, that can augment your power,
Nor lowlie lookes, that long can keepe them safe: ,   35
   The *Fates* haue found a way, whereby ere long
The proude must leaue their hope, the meeke their feare.
Who ere receau'd such fauor from aboue,
That could assure one day vnto himselfe?
Him, whom the Morning found both stout and strong,   40
The Euening left all groueling on the ground.
   This breath and heate wherewith mans life is fedde
Is but a flash, or flame, that shines a while,
And once extinct, is as it ne'r had bene.
Corruption hourely frets the bodies frame,   45
Youth tends to age, and age to death by kinde.
Short is the race, prefixed is the end,
Swift is the tyme, wherein mans life doth run.
But by his deedes t'extend renowme and fame,
That onely vertue workes, which neuer fades.   50

FINIS.

Thomas Hughes.

Sat cytò, si sat benè: vtcunȝ:
Quod non dat spes, dat optio.

¶ Heere after followe such

speeches as were penned by others, and pro-
nounced in stead of some of the former spee-
ches penned by Thomas Hughes.

A speach penned by William

Fulbecke gentleman, one of the societie of Grayes-
Inne, and pronounced in stead of *Gorlois*
his first speeche penned by Thomas
Hughes, and set downe in the first
Scene of the first Acte.

A*Lecto* : thou that hast excluded mee
From feeldes *Elysyan*, where the guiltlesse soules
Avoide the scourge of *Radamanthus* Ire :
Let it be lawfull, (sith I am remou'd
From blessed Ilands, to this cursed shoare,   5
This loathed earth where *Arthurs* table standes,
With Ordure foule of *Harpies* fierce disteind,)
The fates and hidden secrets to disclose
Of blacke *Cocytus* and of *Acheron*,
The floudes of death the lakes of burning soules.   10
Where Hellish frogges doe prophecie reuenge :
Where *Tartars* sprights with carefull heede attende
The dismall summons of *Alectoes* mouth.
My selfe by precept of *Proserpina*,
Commaunded was in presence to appeare,   15
Before the Synode of the damned sprightes.
In fearefull moode I did performe their hest,
And at my entrance in th'inchaunted snakes,
Which wrap themselus about the furies neckes,

Did hisse for ioy : and from the dreadfull benche   20
The supreme furie thus assignde her charge.
Gorlois quoth she thou thither must ascend.
Whence through the rancour of malicious foes
Wearyed with woundes thou didst descend to vs.
Make *Brytaine* now the marke of thy reuenge   25
On ruthlesse *Brytaines* and *Pendragons* race,
Disbursse the treasure of thy Hellish plagues.
Let blood contend with blood, Father with Sonne,
Subiect with Prince, and let confusion raigne.
She therewithall enioynde the duskie cloudes   30
Which with their darkenesse turnde the earth to Hell,
Conuert to blood and poure downe streames of blood.
Cornewell shall groane, and *Arthurs* soule shall sigh,
Before the conscience of *Gueneuora*
The map of hell shall hang and fiendes shall rage :   35
And *Gorlois* ghost exacting punishment,
With dreames, with horrors and with deadly traunce
Shall gripe their hearts : the vision of his corse
Shalbe to them, as was the terror vile
Of flaming whippes to *Agamemnons* sonne.   40
And when the Trumpet calles them from their rest
Aurora shall with watry cheekes behold
Their slaughtered bodies prostrate to her beames.
And on the banckes of *Cambala* shall lye
The bones of *Arthur* and of *Arthurs* knightes :   45
Whose fleete is now tryumphing on the seas.
But shall bee welcom'd with a Tragedie.
Thy natiue soyle shalbe thy fatall gulfe
Arthur : thy place of birth thy place of death.
Mordred shalbe the hammer of my hate   50
To beate the bones of Cornish Lordes to dust.
Ye rauening birdes vnder *Celenoes* power,
I doe adiure you in *Alectoes* name.
Follow the sworde of *Mordred* where he goes.

20 benche] benthe Q

Follow the sworde of *Mordred* for your foode.   55
Aspyring *Mordred*, thou must also dye.
And on the Altar of *Proserpina*
Thy vitall blood vnto my Ghost shall fume.
Heauen, Earth, and hell, concurre to plague the man
That is the plague of Heauen, Earth, and hell.   60
Thou bids *Alecto* : I pursue my charge.
Let thy *Cerastæ* whistle in mine eares,
And let the belles of *Pluto* ring reuenge.

¶One other speeche penned

by the same gentleman, and pronounced in steade
of *Gorlois* his last speache penned by *Tho-*
mas Hughes, and set downe in the second Scene of the fift and last Act.

DEath hath his conquest : hell hath had his wish.
Gorlois his vow : *Alecto* her desire.
Sinne hath his pay : and blood is quit with blood,
Reuenge in Tryumphe beares the strugling hearts.
Now *Gorlois* pearce the craggie Rockes of hell,   5
Through chinckes wherof infernall sprites do glaunce,
Returne this answere to the furies courte.
That Cornewell trembles with the thought of warre :
And *Tamers* flood with drooping pace doth flowe,
For feare of touching *Camballs* bloodie streame.   10
Brytaine remember, write it on thy walles,
Which neyther tyme nor tyrannie may race,
That Rebelles, Traytors and conspirators,
The semenarye of lewde *Cateline*,
The Bastard Coouie of Italian birdes,   15
Shall feele the flames of euer flaming fire,
Which are not quenched with a sea of teares.

59, 11, 12, 15, 16 *Q period at end of line*

And since in thee some glorious starre must shine,
When many yeares and ages are expirde
Whose beames shall cleare the mist of miscontent   20
And make the dampe of *Plutoes* pit retire,
Gorlois will neuer fray the *Brytans* more.
For *Brytaine* then becomes an Angels land,
Both Diuels and sprites must yeelde to Angels power,
Vnto the goddesse of the Angels land.   25
Vaunt *Brytaine* vaunt, of her renowmed raigne,
Whose face deterres the hagges of hell from thee :
Whose vertues holde the plagues of heauen from thee,
Whose presence makes the earth fruitfull to thee :
And with foresight of her thrice happie daies,   30
Brytaine I leaue thee to an endlesse praise.

Besides these speaches there was also penned a *Chorus* for
the first act, and an other for the second act, by Maister
Frauncis Flower, which were pronounced accordingly.
The dumbe showes were partly deuised by Maister
Christopher Yeluerton, Maister *Frauncis Bacon*,
Maister *Iohn Lancaster* and others, partly
by the saide Maister *Flower*, who with
Maister *Penroodocke* and the said
Maister *Lancaster* directed
these proceedings
at Court.
(·.·)

18, 21 *Q period at end of line*

NOTES

Act numbers or book numbers in these notes are printed in Roman capitals, scenes and chapter numbers in small letters, line numbers in Arabic : *Macbeth* III. i. 77 means Act III, scene i, line 77, and *Historia Britonum* IV. iii means Book IV, chapter or section iii.   Arg. = Argument, Ch. = Chorus, D.S. = Dumb Show, Ep. = Epilogue, Pr. = Prologue, S.D. = Stage Direction.   The line numbers in the Seneca references are those of the Teubner edition (Peiper and Richter, 1867) ; the readings are those of the Aldine edition of 1517, of which Peiper and Richter say : 'si uniuersum spectamus, nullum librum uel manu scriptum uel inpressum fatendum est tam prope ad genuinam recensionis uolgaris condicionem accedere quam Aldinam.'

GORBODUC

(NOTES BY DR. H. A. WATT)

The argument of the Tragedie : the ultimate source of the story of King Gorboduc and his two sons is the Latin chronicle of Geoffrey of Monmouth, the *Historia Regum Britanniae*.   Here the account is as follows :

'Post hunc [i. e. Rivallo, son of Cunedagius] uero successit Gurgustius filius eius ; cui Sisillius ; cui Lago Gurgustii nepos ; cui Kinmarcus Sisillii filius ; post hunc Gorbogud.   Huic nati fuerunt duo filii : quorum unus Ferrex, alter Porrex nuncupabatur.   Cum autem in senium uergeret pater, orta est contentio inter eos, uter eorum in regno succederet.   At Porrex maiori cupiditate subductus, paratis insidiis Ferrecem fratrem interficere parat ; quod cum illi compertum fuisset, fratre uitato, in Gallias transfretauit.   Sed Suardi regis Francorum auxilio usus, reuersus est et cum fratre dimicauit.   Illis autem pugnantibus, Ferrex est interfectus et tota multitudo quae eum comitabatur.   Porro eorum mater, cui nomen Widen, cum de filii nece certior facta esset, ultra modum commota, in alterius odium uersa est.   Diligebat enim defunctum magis altero ; unde tanta ira ob ipsius mortem ignescebat, ut ipsum in fratrem uindicare affectaret.   Nacta ergo tentorium, quo ille sopitus fuerat, aggreditur eum cum suis ancillis et in plurimas sectiones dilacerauit.   Exin ciuilis discordia multo tempore populum afflixit, et regnum quinque regibus submissum est, qui sese mutuis cladibus infestabant ' (II. xvi, ed. San-Marte).

It will be seen that the authors follow the Latin chronicle closely,

the only marked changes being that in the play no mention is made
of the flight of Ferrex into France, and Porrex, instead of Ferrex,
is made the aggressor.   The authors may have found an immediate
source in Grafton's chronicle, 1556, which follows Geoffrey's version
closely.   In the tragedy many of the details of the story are brought
out, it should be noted, not in the action, but in the dumb shows
which precede each of the acts.

Arg. 7–9. *for want of issue* ... *became vncertaine* : the earliest
indication in the play of its political purpose, obvious throughout
from numerous allusions.   In fact, the entire tragedy, and especially
the last act, is very largely an argument for the limitation of the
succession, and but one of the means which English statesman were
taking, in Parliament and out, to suggest to Queen Elizabeth that
she either marry and bear children, or definitely appoint her successor and thereby decide at once the claims to the succession of
Mary Stuart, Lady Katharine Grey, and others.

The P. to the Reader : i. e. the Printer (John Daye) to the
Reader.

6. *W. G.*: William Griffith, the printer of the first (unauthorized)
edition, Sept. 22, 1565.

8–9. *the said Lord was out of England* : from 1563 to 1566
Sackville was travelling in France and Italy, where he was engaged
for part of the time on a diplomatic mission.   See F. W. Maitland's
article entitled *Thomas Sackville's Message from Rome* in the
English Historical Review for Oct., 1900, pp. 757-60.

10–11. *excedingly corrupted* : this is not true ; the pirated edition
of 1565 contained very few mistakes.

30. *the house from whense she is descended* : the Inner Temple.

The names of the Speakers : the first five names are taken
from the Latin chronicle.   The names of the four 'dukes' are,
according to Geoffrey, Cloten rex Cornubiae, Staterius rex Albaniae,
Ymner rex Loegriae, and Rudaucus rex Kambriae (II. xvii).   The
other proper names are classical ; concerning the significance of
those of the counsellors and of the parasites see note on II. i.

The domme shew : the dumb shows of *Gorboduc* are the most
striking native element in the tragedy.   Nowhere in Seneca do we
have any hint of such performances.   Their purpose was to supply
the action which the drama itself lacked and to point out in the
form of an allegorical pantomime the moral lessons which the
audience was to derive from the play.   Although a species of enter-
tainment, allegorical in character, had long been employed between
the acts in Italian comedy and tragedy, it is likely that the authors
of *Gorboduc* obtained their suggestion for the dumb shows from the
allegorical tableaux or 'stands' which were a regular accompaniment of city pageants and court masques, and which were usually
political in character.   This view of their origin is borne out by the
appearance in the dumb shows of certain characteristics of the
civic entertainments, notably the 'six wilde men'—the familiar
Elizabethan processional police—in the first dumb show, and the
firearms in the fifth.

I. D.S. 1. *Musicke of Violenze* : each of the dumb shows begins with music, and in each instance there has been an attempt to make the music harmonize with the nature of the pantomime presented. This is, of course, most noticeable in the fifth dumb show, where 'drommes and fluites' introduce 'a company of Hargabusiers and of Armed men ', but it is sufficiently apparent in the fourth, where the three Furies appear ' as though out of hell ' to the weird squealing of ' Howboies '.

Actus primus. Scena prima : it will be noted that no stage directions of any kind are given. These will be inserted, whenever necessary, in the notes. The opening scene of the tragedy takes place in a room of Gorboduc's palace.

I. i. 1–6. *The silent . . . griefull plaint* : this speech of Videna's is distinctly Senecan in style and should be compared with *Hercules Furens* 125–40, *Oedipus* 1–5, *Agamemnon* 53–6, and *Octavia* 1–6. The dialogue which follows between Videna and Ferrex, with its speeches of equal length, its play upon words, and its general rhetorical quality, is almost certainly an attempt by Norton, the author of the first three acts, at Senecan *stichomythia*. The passage should be compared with such a stichomythic series of verses in Seneca as, for example, *Medea* 192–200.

3–4. *makes me . . . or shame* : the half dozen instances of rhyming couplets which occur in the body of the tragedy Miss L. Toulmin Smith suggests (in her reprint of the tragedy in *Englische Sprach- und Literaturdenkmale des 16., 17., und 18. Jahrhts.*, Heil bronn, 1883, p. xv), may have been ' slips of the pen, relics of the old habit of rhyming '. They are used for no apparent effect and occur only once at the end of a speech (II. ii. 27–8). The other instances all occur within the speech (I. i. 3–4, 73–4 ; II. i. 103–4 ; III. i. 106–7 ; III. i. 164–5). These instances occur mainly in the acts written by Norton. There is one instance of alternate end-rhyme—probably accidental (I. i. 16–18). The two or three internal rhymes which occur (I. i. 36 ; IV. ii. 190 ; V. ii. 9) are evidently unintentional ; the first of the rhyming words does not, in the first two instances at least, appear after the internal caesura, and the rhyme in each case roughens and spoils the verse.

25. *To spoile thee of my sight* : probably a printer's error for ' to spoile me of thy sight '.

59–61. *When lordes, . . . of gouernance*. possibly an allusion to Northumberland's attempt at the accession of Mary Tudor in 1553 to put upon the throne his daughter-in-law Lady Jane Grey, basing his action on the nomination of the boy king, Edward VI.

Actus primus. Scena secunda : the following debate evidently takes place in the council-chamber of King Gorboduc.

I. ii. 47–8. *the Gods . . . For kings* : an expression of the attitude of right-thinking Englishmen toward their queen, the belief that she was divinely appointed to rule. Similar expressions occur in II. i. 144–5 and V. ii. 55.

74. *Shew forth . . . of circumstance* : a verse of only four feet—probably accidental.

105. *To draw . . . swifter pace* : to cause death, who is slow when a man is young, to quicken his pace.

131. *tempred youthe with* : youth tempered with, &c.

161–3. *bloudie ciuill . . . in Camberland* : Morgan, or Marganus, was the son of Gonorilla, eldest daughter of King Leir, and Maglaunus, duke of Albany. With the help of his cousin Cunedagius, son of Regan, Leir's second daughter, he deposed his aunt, Cordeilla, Leir's youngest daughter, who had become queen at her father's death. The cousins divided the kingdom, Morgan taking the section north of the Humber, Cunedagius, the part south. Later Morgan permitted flatterers to persuade him that he should rule the entire island ; accordingly he invaded the provinces of Cunedagius, but after a bloody civil war he was defeated and slain by the latter ' in pago Kambriae '. (See *Historia Regum Britanniae* II. xv.) There are so many details in this story of the two cousins which correspond with those in the story of Ferrex and Porrex as Norton and Sackville have retold it, but which are not in Geoffrey's account of the civil war between the brothers, that there can be no doubt but that the authors of *Gorboduc* borrowed from the chronicler's account of the first civil war details for their own version of the second. The frequent references to Morgan in the earlier part of *Gorboduc* and the fact that in all the chronicles the history of the two cousins immediately precedes that of the two brothers seem to establish this borrowing beyond question.

165. *Three noble . . . forefather Brute* : Brute, or Brutus, the natural son of Sylvius, grandson of Aeneas, had three sons, Locrinus, Kamber, and Albanactus, who divided the kingdom at his death. (*Historia Regum Britanniae* I. iii ; II. i.)

197. *With hatefull slaughter he preuentes the fates* : he anticipates the fate which would naturally be his brother's by murdering him. The classical phrasing of this and of other lines throughout the tragedy (e. g. III. i. 11 ; IV. ii. 225–6) is at once apparent. Some of this phrasing may have come from Surrey's translation of the second and fourth books of Vergil's *Aeneid*, since the metre of *Gorboduc* was undoubtedly suggested by this translation ; but the authors of the tragedy were university men, and would fall, naturally enough, into classical usages.

293. *the head to stoupe beneth them bothe* : for the king to make his own rank lower than that of his sons.

232. *But longe . . . to rule* : a hypermetrical verse which there is no need to reduce to the pentameter. One editor, R. W. Sackville-West, omits the *but*, but this omission of the adversative conjunction spoils the force of the sentence.

251. *other here my lordes* : an inversion for ' other lords who are here '.

262–8. *Suche is . . . wold attaine* : an example of the sententious moralizing which has been imitated from Seneca. Other examples occur in II. i. 143–55 ; III. Ch. 1–3; and elsewhere in the tragedy.

273. *For his three sonnes three kingdoms* : see note on I. ii. 165.

277–82. *princes slaine . . . chaunce againe* : at the time when

Gorboduc was written, the War of the Roses, that great civil strife which cost England so much royal blood, was yet ' rawe in minde '. The last line expresses at once the fear of serious-minded Englishmen that, if Elizabeth at her death were to leave the succession disputed, the bloody scenes of the War of the Roses would be re-enacted, and their hope that such a civil war might be averted.

330–1. *To soone ... on fire* : Phaeton, in Greek mythology the son of the Sun-god Phoebus, in a rash attempt to drive his father's chariot through the heavens, set the earth on fire and was himself destroyed. The story is again alluded to in the third stanza of the Chorus at the end of this act and is but one of the numerous borrowings from classical myth which appear in the tragedy. Seneca makes frequent use of the Phaeton story (see *Medea* 602–5, 834; *Hercules Oetaeus* 681–6; *Hippolytus* 1090–1104).

364. *fensed eares* : see note on I. ii. 131.

Chorus : The council has, of course, broken up, and the king and the councillors have departed. It is probable that the Chorus remains on the stage during the entire performance of the tragedy. The Chorus in *Gorboduc* is, of course, borrowed directly from Seneca. As far as its proper function as chorus goes, it is purely formal. In fact, it is much more detached from the action than in any of the Senecan plays. In the latter it occasionally takes the part of an actor, engaging in conversation with some one of the regular characters ; in *Gorboduc* its expression is confined to the utterance of moral platitudes suggested by the misfortunes of the characters in the main action. In Seneca the Chorus is made up of persons whose fortunes we may suppose to be connected more or less directly with those of the leading actors ; in *Gorboduc* the Chorus consists simply of ' foure auncient and sage men of Brittaine '. In *Gorboduc*, however, it should be noted, the Chorus has the new function of expounding to the audience at the end of the act the significance of the pantomime presented at the beginning of the act.

I. Ch. 16. *the proude sonne of Apollo* : Phaeton ; see note on I. ii. 330–1.

23. *A myrrour ... Princes all* : the figurative use of the word *mirror*, though a common literary affectation which occurs repeatedly in Elizabethan literature, recalls Sackville's contributions to the famous *Mirror for Magistrates*. Although these contributions, the powerful *Induction* and the *Legend of Buckingham*, did not appear until 1563, there is evidence that they were composed at about the same time as the tragedy, and many ideas and phrases in the poems are strikingly similar to those in the play.

Actus secundus. Scena prima : the action takes place at the Court of Ferrex.

II. i. *Ferrex. Hermon. Dordan* : the arrangement of the characters in this scene and in the closely parallel scene following is an evidence of the influence of the moral plays on the structure of *Gorboduc*. Just as in moral plays of the *Everyman* type we have a central figure accompanied by personified evil on the one hand and personified good on the other hand, and a contest between good and evil for the soul of the central figure, so in *Gorboduc* we have in the old king and each of his two sons central figures accompanied by good and evil counsellors. From this point of view the chief actors with their good and their evil angels may be divided as follows :

Good Counsellor.	Central Figure.	Evil Counsellor.
Eubulus.	Gorboduc.	Arostus.
Dordan.	Ferrex.	Hermon.
Philander.	Porrex.	Tyndar.

The counsellors are, of course, mere colourless lay figures. It should be noted further that just as in the moral plays the personified virtues and vices are given tag-names—Riches, Good Deedes, Vice, &c.—to indicate their characters, so here some attempt has been made to indicate the characters of the counsellors by the names given them ; Eubulus means *The Good Counsellor*, and Philander, the *Friend of Man*, while Tyndar, an abbreviation of Tyndarus, is suspiciously like *Tinder*, a name which fits the parasite's character exactly.

II. i. 16. *The hellish prince* : Pluto or Dis, in Greek mythology the ruler of the under-world.

36-44. *Yea and ... his reigne* : on these lines Warton has the following note : ' The chaste elegance of the following description of a region abounding in every convenience, will gratify the lover of classical purity.' The description is, of course, a glorification of England.

126-9. ,,*Wise men ... to come* : the quotation marks are used here and elsewhere in the tragedy, as often in Elizabethan literature, to mark a particular bit of sententious moralizing. It seems curiously inconsistent thus to mark the words of the traitorous Hermon, but the device is employed again toward the end of this harangue. The particular lines here have a general reference to contemporary political conditions.

143-5. *Know ye ... in rascail routes* : see *Jocasta* II. i. 390-3 and notes thereon.

194. *I feare ... draweth on* : Dordan here, like Philander in the closely parallel scene following and Eubulus at the end of the tragedy, acts as a detached chorus leader or expositor, who remains alone at the end of the scene to croak his fears of the outcome of the policies determined upon in the debate immediately preceding.

198. *Secretaries wise aduise* : the secretary was Eubulus ; see the Names of the Speakers.

Actus secundus. Scena secunda : at the Court of Porrex.

II. Ch. 10. *lawes kinde* : the laws of kindred.

25-6. *Loe, thus ... cuppe forsake* : the couplet at the end serves to explain the significance of the dumb show at the beginning of the act. *Poyson in golde to take* is Seneca's ' *uenenum in auro bibitur* ' (*Thyestes* 453).

Actus tertius. Scena prima : the Court of the old king. Gorboduc, Eubulus, and Arostus are present at the opening of the scene; Philander and the Nuntius enter later (l. 58 and l. 154 respectively).

III. i. 2–3. *Simois stayned . . . with bloud*: the Senecan '*fluc-tusque Simois caede purpureos agens*' (*Agamemnon* 215). On this passage Warton has the following note : 'It must be remembered that the ancient Britons were supposed to be immediately descended from the Trojan Brutus, and that consequently they were acquainted with the pagan history and mythology.' This explanation, however, is hardly necessary to account for so many allusions to Greek mythology in the work of writers who were so steeped in Seneca as were Norton and Sackville.

15. *lyued to make a myrrour of* : see note on I. Ch. 23.

57–8. *Loe yonder . . . hast Philander* : a characteristically Senecan method of introducing a new actor upon the stage. With these lines compare, for example, *Troas* 526–7 :

> 'cohibe parumper ora, questusque opprime :
> gressus nefandos dux Cephallenum admouet.'

122. *And adde . . . latter age* : this line and line 155 in the speech of the Nuntius at the end of the scene are the only Alexandrines in the tragedy. As they are used for no apparent purpose, they were probably accidental.

132. *Loe here the perill* : Eubulus appears here, as elsewhere in the tragedy, as the expositor of the moral.

155. *O king the greatest griefe*. here as in Act v the Nuntius performs the regular Senecan part of reporting the events which do not occur on the stage and of thereby, in this instance at least, keeping bloodshed decently from the sight of the audience.

161. *his owne most bloudy hand* : a familiar Senecan figure; cf

| 'rudem cruore regio dextram inbuit.' | (*Troas* 226.) |
| 'hominum cruenta caede pollutas manus.' | (*Octavia* 435.) |
| '. . . in patrios toros |
| tuli paterno sanguine adspersas manus.' | (*Thebais* 267–8.) |

III. Ch. 12. *Morgan his . . . cosyns hand* : see note on I. ii. 161–3.

13. *plagues pursue the giltie race* : the idea expressed here and elsewhere in the tragedy is the classical one of the family curse that cannot be escaped. In Seneca it appears, for example, in those tragedies which set forth the fate overhanging the house of Cadmus or of Oedipus (see *Hercules Furens* 386–94; *Thebais* 276–8; *Hippolytus* 698–700).

21–2. *hence doth . . . & woe* : the usual explanation by the Chorus of the meaning of the dumb show at the beginning of the act.

IV. D.S. 2. *from vnder the stage, as though out of hell* : one may assume from this the presence of a trap-door in the stage, similar, no doubt, to those implied in *Jocasta* II. D.S. 6–7, III. D.S. 3; *The Misfortunes of Arthur* I. D.S. 1–2, and V. ii. 38. S.D.; *Gismond of Salerne*, IV. i. 1. S.D. Plays at the Inns of Court and court masques were usually performed on simple platforms sufficiently elevated to allow the audience a free view of the performance and to allow for the occasional presence, as here, of actors under the stage.

9–10. *Tantalus, Medea, Athamas, Ino, Cambises, Althea*: Tantalus was the grandfather of Atreus, who killed the sons of his brother Thyestes. Medea killed her children by Jason when he planned to desert her. Athamas, the son of Aeolus, King of Thessaly, was made mad by Hera and slew his son Learchus. Ino, the wife of Athamas, threw herself into the sea with her remaining son after the murder of Learchus. Cambises, son of Cyrus, a mad king of the Medes and Persians, killed both his brother and his sister. Althea, wife of Aeneus, King of Calydon, caused the death of her son Meleager.

Actus quartus. Scena prima: a room in the palace of Gorboduc.

IV. i. 1. *Why should I lyue*: with Act IV begins the work of Sackville. The last two acts of the tragedy are distinctly fresher and more dramatic than the first three; the opening impassioned speech of Videna is, for example, much superior in power and in language to anything which Norton has produced in the first three acts. It and other passages in the last two acts should be compared with Sackville's contributions to the *Mirror for Magistrates*, his powerful *Induction* and the *Legend of Buckingham*. This speech of Videna should be also compared with Seneca's *Medea* 1–55.

30–1. *Thou Porrex, . . . and me*: inversion of the iamb in the first foot occurs occasionally in the first three acts; much more frequently in the last two. The inversion is usually for rhetorical emphasis. Cf. ll. 65–73 of this scene. The repetition of words in '*Thou* Porrex, *thou*' seems to be a mannerism of Sackville, since it occurs only once in the three acts written by Norton (III. i. 27) but several times in the last two acts (e. g. IV. i. 9, 29, 53, 65; IV. ii. 106, 120; V. i. 56).

53–7. *Or if . . . reward therefore*: *Thebais* 443–7:

' in me arma et ignes uertite. in me omnis ruat
unam iuuentus; . . .
                    . . . ciuis atque hostis simul
hunc petite uentrem qui dedit fratres uiro.'

71–6. *Ruthelesse, vnkinde . . . to life*: *Hercules Oetaeus* 143–6:

' quae cautes Scythiae, quis genuit lapis?
num Titana ferum te Rhodope tulit,
te praeruptus Athos, te fera Caspia,
quae uirgata tibi praebuit ubera?'

and *Aeneid* IV. 365–7:

'nec tibi diua parens, generis nec Dardanus auctor,
perfide; sed duris genuit te cautibus horrens
Caucasus, Hyrcanaeque admorunt ubera tigres.'

Actus quartus. Scena secunda: the Court of Gorboduc again. Gorboduc and Arostus hold the stage at the beginning of the scene; Eubulus, Porrex, and Marcella enter later at points clearly indicated by the dialogue.

IV. ii. 70–1. *the minde . . . be fraile*: a possible reminiscence of

Mark xiv. 38, which reads in Tyndale's translation, 'the sprete is redy, but the flessh is weeke.'

166. *Marcella*: one of the queen's ladies-in-waiting performs here the function of the Nuntius in reporting the murder of Porrex. For the touch of colour and romance which she adds, however, to the part of the messenger see *Introduction*, p. lxxxiii.

225-6. *And straight . . . corpes forsooke*: the classical phraseology of these and of many other lines in the tragedy is unmistakable.

IV. Ch. 5-6. *Beholde how . . . brother slayes*: the didactic function of the Chorus is especially marked here.

11. *The dreadfull furies*: the customary reference to the dumb show at the beginning of the act.

V. D.S. 3-4. *after their peeces discharged*: the use of fire: ns and of fireworks on the Elizabethan stage was very frequent. The first Globe theatre, it will be remembered, was destroyed in 1   by a fire resulting from such a discharge of firearms as is mentio   here. Jonson ridicules the use of fireworks on the stage in the Prologue to *Every Man in his Humour* (acted 1598):

> 'Nor nimble squib is seen, to make afeard
>   The gentlewomen.'

8. *by the space of fiftie yeares*: the Latin chronicle reads simply *multo tempore*. (See note, p. 297.)

11. *Dunwallo Molmutius*: the son of Cloten, King of Cornwall, who, according to the Latin chronicle, conquered the petty kings and reduced Great Britain again to a single monarchy (*Historia Regum Britanniae* II. xvii).

Actus quintus. Scena prima: the last act takes place at what had been the Court of Gorboduc. It consists of a specific argument for the limitation of the succession to the English throne. Elizabeth's first Parliament had petitioned her through a committee headed by Thomas Gargrave, Speaker of the House of Commons, that she 'by marriage bring forth children, heires both of their mothers vertue and Empire'. (See Camden, William. *Historie of the most renowned and victorious Princesse Elizabeth, Late Queene of England.* Lond., 1630. I. 25-37.) A year after the performance of *Gorboduc* another petition was addressed to the queen, the record of which, taken from the Commons' Journal (I. 62-5) is as follows:

'Friday,	15 Janry, 1562-3.	Speaker.	
Saturday 16	„	„	A motion made by a Burgess at length for the Succession.
Monday 18	„	„	Divers members spoke on the same subject.
Tuesday 19	„	„	A Committee was appointed, and on
Tuesday 26	„	„	A petition devised by the Committees, to be made to the Queen's Maj^y by Mr Speaker, for Limitation of Succession read by Mr Norton, one of the Committees.'

From these entries it is evident that Norton took an active part in the discussion regarding the succession. Concerning Sackville's interest in the question there is less positive evidence.

v. i. 41-2. *Eke fully . . . they ought*: the reasons for the omission between these verses in the edition of 1571 of eight lines which appeared in the surreptitious edition of 1565 (see footnote) have been variously stated. Miss Smith believes the omission a mere inadvertence on the part of the printer. Cooper, following Warton, remarks that 'the eight omitted lines are in an act especially ascribed to Sackville and were opposed to the more lax opinions of Norton, who in revising the tragedy probably left them out from his dislike of the sentiment they conveyed.' In support of this latter view it should be added that John Daye was Norton's printer. The lines, it will be noted, are an expression of the Elizabethan idea of complete and unresisting submission to royal authority, the doctrine of passive non-resistance.

64-5. *So giddy . . . the sea*: *Hercules Furens* 171 'fluctuque magis mobile uulgus'.

92-4. *the rascall . . . neuer trustie*: Sackville has expressed the same idea in the *Legend of Buckingham* (Stanza 61):

> ' O, let no prince put trust in commontie,
> Nor hope in fayth of giddy people's mynde.'

124. *Fergus*: all the other lords have, of course, departed.

137. *Discended from . . . noble bloud*: the Duke of Albany (Staterius he is named in the *Historia Regum Britanniae*) was the direct descendant of Albanactus, son of Brute and Duke of Albany or Scotland (see note on I. ii. 165). In the Latin chronicle he is represented as the last of the petty kings to hold out against Dunwallo Molmutius.

Actus quintus. Scena secunda: Eubulus is, of course, alone when the scene begins; the other lords and the Nuntius enter later.

v. ii. 26-41. *One sort . . . enraged sort*: this pedantic division of the rebels into groups is a striking example of the formal preciseness which characterizes Seneca's style.

120. *From forreine . . . a prince*: while Elizabeth was dallying with foreign suitors for her hand, her subjects were dreading a foreign king and especially Philip of Spain. It is not clear why the Duke of Albany should be here referred to as a foreign prince.

155. *by colour of pretended right*: a reference to the claims of the Duke of Albany to the throne, and an allusion in contemporary politics to false claims to the succession.

165-8. *Right meane . . . to aduaunce*: an argument, as L. H. Courtney has pointed out (*Notes and Queries*, ser. 2, v. 10, p. 262), for the justice of the claim of Lady Katharine Grey to the succession. Her name rested both upon 'natiue line' and on the 'vertue of some former lawe', that, namely, of Henry VIII, whereas Mary Stuart had no such warrant and was foreign born. The use of the pronoun *hers* in the text is significant.

234–52. *Hereto it . . . to rest*: a summary by the 'Good Counsellor' of the action of the play, and a final expounding of the moral with particular reference, it will be seen, to the allegory of the dumb shows. Eubulus here takes the place of the Chorus, which does not appear after the last act.

264–71. *Parliament should . . . quiet stay*: a statesman's advice as to the action the English Parliament should take to determine the succession to the throne.

278–9. *For right . . . to last*: a healthy English moral, which Courthope characterizes as 'a noble conclusion, and quite unlike the moral of Seneca's plays'.

JOCASTA

The opening scene is taken directly from Dolce, who in this part of the play dealt very freely with his original. But he kept closely to the main lines of the action as laid down by Euripides and only departed occasionally from the original arrangement of the episodes, as the following abstract of the *Phoenissae* will show:

	lines
Prologue by Jocasta	1– 87
Paedagogus and Antigone	88– 201
Parode by Chorus	202– 260
Polynices and Chorus	261– 300
Jocasta, Polynices	301– 415
Jocasta, Polynices, Eteocles	416– 637
First stasimon	638– 689
Creon, Eteocles	690– 783
Second stasimon	784– 833
Teiresias, Menoeceus, Creon	834– 985
(Dolce interpolates the Priest's part and extends the dialogue between Menoeceus and Creon.)	
Soliloquy of Menoeceus (omitted by Dolce)	985–1018
Third stasimon	1019–1066
Messenger, Jocasta	1067–1283
Chorus	1284–1309
Creon, Messenger	1310–1484
Monody of Antigone	1485–1537
Oedipus, Antigone, Creon	1538–1766

I. i. 1: as is usual in texts of this period, the name first given in the scene heading is understood to be that of the first speaker.

35. *Thebs*: here, and in line 183, obviously a monosyllable; but apparently used as a dissyllable in lines 113, 203, and 255 of this scene. Gascoigne adopts the same licence as Kinwelmersh. Usually he pronounces the word as one syllable (II. i. 45, 61, 383, 468, 516, 559, 578, 597, and 627; II. ii. 79); but in II. ii. 107 it is two syllables.

70–1. „*Experience proues*, &c.: 'The lines marked with initial commas are so distinguished to call the attention to some notable sentiment or reflection.'—F. J. C. (Francis James Child) in *Four Old Plays*.

89. *Phocides lande*: 'Phocis. The early poets are in the habit of using the genitive of classical proper names, or the genitive slightly altered, for the nominative. Thus Skelton writes *Zenophontes* for Xenophon, *Eneidos* for Eneis, &c.'—F. J. C. *u. s.*

221–40. *The simple . . . to lawe*: this speech is considerably enlarged by Kinwelmersh, the corresponding Italian text being as follows:

> 'Color che i seggi e le reali altezze
> Ammiran tanto veggono con l' occhio
> L' adombrato splendor ch' appar di fuori,
> Scettri, gemme, corone, aurati panni;
> Ma non veggon dappoi con l' intelletto
> Le penose fatiche, e i gravi affanni,
> Le cure, e le molestie, a mille a mille,
> Che di dentro celate e ascose stanno.'

263. At the top of the page of Gabriel Harvey's copy of *The Posies*, now in the Bodleian Library, he has written above the stage direction giving the names: 'Seneca saepe, the state of princes.' He evidently refers to the commonplaces of the preceding speech.

I. ii. 4–5. *To whom . . . gouenour*: these lines are, of course, inconsistent with the change made by Kinwelmersh in the stage-direction just above, in which he speaks of ' hir gouenour', although the Italian text says plainly ' Bailo di Polinice'. The phrase, 'hir gouenour,' is repeated in the stage-direction at the end of this scene. The change may have been made deliberately, for it is supported by the text of the *Phoenissae*, from which Dolce has departed more in the opening than in any other part of the play.

71. *To trappe him in*: this broken line was perhaps suggested by the irregular metre of this speech in the Italian text. In Euripides all Antigone's speeches in this scene are in strophic measures, which Dolce apparently attempted to present, in part at least, by varying the length of his lines. The English translators reduced all except the choruses to blank verse.

173. *It standes not*, &c.: cf. Laertes' speech to Ophelia (*Hamlet* I. iii): 'Then weigh what loss your honour may sustain, &c.'— F. J. C. *u. s.*

181–90. *You cannot be . . . fade away*: here again, as will be seen by a comparison with the original, which is given below, the Italian has been extended by the translator:

> ' E 'l grido d' onestà che di voi s' ode
> E qual tenero fior, ch' ad ogni fiato
> Di picciol' aura s' ammarcisce e muore.'

I. Ch. 1–63: the choruses, especially those of Kinwelmersh, are more loosely translated than the dialogue. The original of this one is here given, for purposes of comparison:

'Se, come ambiziosa e ingorda mente
Noi miseri mortali
Diverse cose a desiar accende,
Così sapesse antiveder i mali,
E quel che parimente
Giova all' umana vita, e quel ch' offende :
Tal piange oggi, e riprende
Fortuna chi gioioso e lieto fora :
Perocchè con prudente accorto ciglio
S' armeria di consiglio,
Di quanto porge il Ciel contento ogn' ora ;
Laddove avvien che con non poco affanno
Quel più si cerca ch' è più nostro danno.
Alcun di questo umil fugace bene,
Che si chiama bellezza,
Superbo andò, che sospirò dappoi :
Altri bramò dominio, altri richezza,
E n' ebbe angoscie e pene,
O vide acerbo fine ai giorni suoi :
Perchè non è fra noi   •
Stato di cui fidar possa alcuno.
Quinci l' instabil Diva in un momento
Volge ogni uman contento,
E n' invola i diletti ad uno ad uno :
Talchè tutto 'l gioir che 'l cor n' ingombra
A par delle miserie è fumo et ombra.
Da grave error fu circondato e cinto
Quei che tranquilla vita
Fose nella volgar più bassa gente.
Quando la luce a chi regge è sparita,
A noi si asconde il giorno,
E sdegna il Sol mostrarsi in Oriente :
Nè può sì leggermente
Il Principe patir ruina, o scempio,
Che 'l suddito meschin non senta il danno :
E di ciò d' anno in anno
Scopre il viver uman più d' uno esempio.
Così delle pazzie de' Real petti
Ne portano il flagel sempre i soggetti.
Ecco siccome voglia empia, e perversa
D' esser soli nel Regno
L' uno e l' altro fratello all' arme ha spinto :
Ma Polinice con più onesto sdegno
Move gente diversa
Contra la patria : onde ne giace estinto
Nel cor di velen tinto
Il debito, l' amor, e la pietate :
E, vinca chi si vuol de' due fratelli,
Noi Donne, e tutti quelli
Di Tebe, sentirem la crudeltate

Di Marte, che l' aspetto ad ambi ha mostro,
Per tinger la sua man nel sangue nostro.
  Ma tu, figlio di Semele, e di Giove,
Che l' orgogliose prove
Vincesti de' Giganti empi e superbi,
Difendi il popol tuo supplice pio,
Che te sol cole, e te conosce Dio.'

II. i. 40. *My feebled . . . and agonie*: my feet enfeebled with age
and suffering.

73–9. *Thou this . . . mothers due*: it is curious to note how from
translation to translation this passage has lost the beauty and force
of the original. Readers of Greek should look up the text of *Phoenissae* 339–57, thus translated by Mr. A. S. Way:

'But thou, my son, men say, hast made affiance
  With strangers: children gotten in thine halls
Gladden thee, yea, thou soughtest strange alliance !
  Son, on thy mother falls

Thine alien bridal's curse to haunt her ever.
  Thee shall a voice from Laïus' grave accuse.
The spousal torch for thee I kindled never,
  As happy mothers use ;

Nor for thy bridal did Ismenus bring thee
  Joy of the bath ; nor at the entering-in
Of this thy bride did Theban maidens sing thee.
  A curse be on that sin,

Whether of steel's spell, strife-lust, or thy father
  It sprang, or whether revel of demons rose
In halls of Oedipus !—on mine head gather
  All tortures of these woes.'

Dolce renders this as follows :

'Tu in tanto, figliuol mio, fatt' hai dimora
In lontani paesi, e preso moglie,
Onde di pellegrine nozze attendi,
Quando piacerà al Ciel, figliuolo e prole :
Il che m' è grave, e molto più, figliuolo,
Che potuto non m' ho trovar presente,
E fornir quell' officio che conviene
A buona madre.'

391–3. *If lawe . . . buckler best*: the Greek (*Phoenissae* 524–5),
Latin, and Italian versions underlying this passage are given below:

εἴπερ γὰρ ἀδικεῖν χρή, τυραννίδος πέρι
κάλλιστον ἀδικεῖν

'Nam si uiolandum est ius, imperii gratia
Violandum est : aliis rebus pietatem colas.'

'Che s' egli si convien per altro effetto,
Si convien molto più (se l' uomo è saggio)
Per cagiòn di regnar romper la legge.'

392–3. (*margin*). *Tullyes opinyon*: Cicero, *De officiis* I. viii. 'Declarauit id modo temeritas C. Caesaris, qui omnia iura diuina atque humana peruertit, propter eum, quem sibi ipse opinionis errore finxerat, principatum.' Gascoigne's marginal note is a little astray, in that Cicero does not give this maxim as his own view, but merely ascribes it to Caesar.

393. *beare the buckler best*: offer the best defence or justification.

410. *hir*: ambition's.

415. *Equalitie*: the translation here indicates that Gascoigne used the edition of *Giocasta* published by Aldus in octavo in 1549, in which we have the reading *egualità*; in the duodecimo edition of 1560 the word *equità* is substituted. Kinwelmersh evidently used the same edition, for line 116 of IV. i, which is found in the duodecimo but is omitted in the original octavo edition, is also omitted from the English translation, which in Act IV is done by Kinwelmersh.

419. *that other*: ambition.

441. *That compts ... to command*: that takes pride in absolute rule.

534–6. *For wall ... be callde*: these three lines are a misunderstanding of the original Italian, which reads:

> 'Il cauto Capitan sempre è migliore
> Del temerario; e tu, più che ciascuno,
> Vile, ignorante, e temerario sei.'

545–6. *Good Gods ... to flight*. another mistranslation. The Italian merely says: 'Oimè, chi vide mai cosa piu fiera?'

II. ii. 56. *Cammassado*: camisado. 'It is a sudden assault, wherein the souldiers doe were shirts over their armours, to know their owne company from the enemy, least they should in the darke kill of their owne company in stead of the enemy; or when they take their enemies in their beds and their shirts, for it commeth of the Spanish *Camiça*, i. e. a shirt.' Minsheu, *Dict. Etym.*, quoted by F. J. C. *u. s.*

65. *As who ... defence*: do you expect them to make no defence?

76. *to done*: to do. Dative of verbal noun.

81. *Well with the rest*: well with the help of the other citizens.

III. i. 1. *Thou trustie guide*: 'The reader with remember Milton's imitation of this passage at the beginning of *Samson Agonistes* and Wordsworth's beautiful reminiscence of both poets.'—F. J. C. *u. s.*

86. *Venus*: the 'angrie Queene' was, of course, Hera. The mistake in the margin is corrected in a contemporary handwriting in the copy of Q 3 at the British Museum.

118-20. *I see ... be greene*: Dolce seems to have taken some details of this sacrificial scene from Seneca. Cf. these lines with *Oedipus* 318 24:

> 'non una facies mobilis flammae fuit.
> imbrifera qualis inplicat uarios sibi
> iris colores parte quae magna poli
> curuata picto nuntiat nimbos sinu:
> quis desit illi quisue sit dubites color.

caerulea fuluis mixta oberrauit notis,
sanguinea rursus, ultimum in tenebras abit.'

150-1. *Why fleest ... fell*: a very natural misunderstanding of the Italian text, which reads:

'*Cre.*   Perchè mi fuggi ?
Tire.   Io certo
Non ti fuggo, o Signor, ma la fortuna.'

It suggests, however, that Gascoigne did not even consult the original Greek, *Phoenissae* 898 :

KPE. Μεῖνον· τί φεύγεις μ᾽; Τ. ἡ τύχη σ᾽, ἀλλ᾽ οὐκ ἐγώ.

III. ii. 72-3. *A beast ... life*: the second line is an addition by Gascoigne. The Italian says merely:

'È pazzo l' uom che sè medesmo uccide.'

103. *Thesbeoita*: as to the significance of the MS. and Q1 reading *Thesbrotia*, see *Introduction*, p. xxxvii.

IV. i. 57. *Whose names ye haue alreadie vnderstoode*: the names of the captains, although given in Euripides, were as a matter of fact suppressed by Dolce. They are given in the Latin translation of the *Phoenissae*, together with the names of the seven gates, including the *portas Homoloidas* and *Electrae portas* so often referred to in the stage-directions of the English play.

123. *die the death*: it is at this point that there is an omission from the second edition of the Italian version, as pointed out in the note on II. i. 415 ; the Italian edition of 1560 adds :

'O che forse periscano ambedue.'

179-81. *Antigone ... daunce*: a singularly inept rendering, both in the Italian and the English, of the original Greek. *Phoenissae* 1264-6:

᾽Ω τέκνον, ἔξελθ᾽, ᾽Αντιγόνη δόμων πάρος·
οὐκ ἐν χορείαις οὐδὲ παρθενεύμασι
νῦν σοι προχωρεῖ δαιμόνων κατάστασις.

'Antigone, figliuola, esci di fuora
Di questa casa di mestizia e pianto:
Esci, non per cagion di canti o balli.'

IV. ii. 40-2. *In mourning weede ... despoyle my selfe*: a ludicrous mistranslation of the Italian, which reads :

'Qui pria vestei, Signor, la mortal gonna,
E qui onesto fia ben ch' io me ne spogli.'

v. ii. 164. *With staggring ... Stigian reigne*: the alliteration of this line is characteristic of Gascoigne. Cf. v. iii. 5 and v. iv. 11. See Schelling, *Life and Writings of George Gascoigne*, pp. 31-42.

200. *we haue wonne*: at this point Gascoigne has omitted two lines, which close the speech in the Italian version :

'Poichè miseramente in questa guerra
I tre nostri Signor perduto abbiamo.'

Scena 3, Scena 4: as to the metre of these lines see note on I. ii. 71.

v. iii. 22. *O Polinice*: at the beginning of this speech of Antigone's, two lines which occur in the Italian version have been omitted:

> 'Madre, perduto io v' ho, perduto insieme
> Ho i miei cari fratelli.'

v. v. 128. *I will ensue ... steppes*: another instance of growing weakness as the translations recede from the original. In the *Phoenissae* (1669) Antigone says:

> Νὺξ ἆρ' ἐκείνη Δαναΐδων μ' ἔξει μίαν.

The allusion is, of course, to the daughters of Danaus, who were forced to marry the sons of Aegyptus, and killed them on their wedding night. The mistake was made by Dolce, who has:

> 'Io seguirò lo stil d' alcune accorte.'

135. *What others ... not thee*: another mistranslation, for which Dolce was mainly responsible. The Greek reads (*Phoenissae* 1674):

> Γενναιότης σοι, μωρία δ' ἔνεστί τις.

In the Latin version the original is prosaically but correctly translated:

> 'Generositas tibi inest, sed tamen stultitia quaedam inest.'

Dolce changes this to:

> 'Quel ch' in altri è grandezza è in te pazzia.'

Gascoigne submissively follows Dolce, and makes it clear that he did not consult either the original text or the Latin translation.

v. Ch. 1–15: this is Dolce's, though the thought is taken from Seneca. The Greek play ends with a 'tag' purporting to be spoken by the Chorus, not in their assumed character as persons in the drama, but in their true character as Athenians contending in a dramatic competition. The tag takes the form of a prayer to Victory, 'O mighty lady, Victory, pervade my life, and cease not to give me crowns.' Alluding to the fact that the *Phoenissae* gained the second prize, it signifies a hope that the play may please readers as well as it pleased the judges, and that other successes may follow.—See A. W. Verrall, *Euripides the Rationalist*, pp. 169–70. Dolce probably omitted the tag because he did not understand its significance, and having to substitute something for it, he turned to his favourite author, Seneca.

GISMOND OF SALERNE

As to the general relation of this play to its sources—the First Novel of the Fourth Day of Boccaccio's *Decamerone*, Dolce's *Didone* (1547), and Seneca—see *Introduction*.

Arg. 10. *a clouen cane*: we have here the first indication that the authors of the tragedy did not use the translation of Boccaccio's novel published just before in Painter's *Palace of Pleasure*. The cane sent by Ghismonda is described by Boccaccio as *fessa*, *i. e.* 'split', or, as the author of the argument says, 'cloven'; Painter mistranslates *fessa* by the word *hollowe*. This, together with much other evidence, given in detail below, entitles us to reject the conclusion arrived at by Sherwood (*Die Neu-Englischen Bearbeitungen der Erzählung Boccaccios von Ghismonda und Guiscardo*) and adopted by Brandl (*Quellen des weltlichen Dramas*) that Painter was most probably used: it is manifest that Painter was not followed: if used at all, his translation was carefully checked and corrected by comparison with the original.

Of the characters not found or implied in Boccaccio's novel, Cupid is taken from Dolce, Renuchio, Megaera, and the Chorus from Seneca, Lucrece and Claudia are the conventional confidantes of classical tragedy.

I. i: in this act (written by 'Rod. Staf.') little use is made of the novel, the purpose of the dramatist being to present Gismond's grief at the loss of her husband, which Boccaccio does not even refer to, contenting himself with the statement that after a short married life she became a widow, and returned home to her father.

S.D. There was evidently a machine to let Cupid down, as well as a trap door for Megaera (IV. i).

1–12. *Loe I . . . his brest*: Dolce in the prologue to *Didone* introduced Cupid as the evil influence which worked the Queen's ruin. The original suggestion came perhaps from Vergil (for in Dolce's prologue Cupid appears in the form of Ascanius), perhaps from a Latin translation of the *Hippolytus* of Euripides, where Aphrodite speaks the prologue, but so far as the English dramatists are concerned, it is obvious that not only the idea, but the words, were taken directly from Dolce:

> ' Io, che dimostro in viso,
>   A la statura, e a i panni,
>   D' esser picciol fanciullo,
>   Si come voi mortale:
>   Son quel gran Dio, che 'l mondo chiama Amore.
> · Quel, che pò in cielo, e in terra,
>   Ét nel bollente Averno;
>   Contra di cui non vale
>   Forza, ne human consiglio:
>   Ne d' ambrosia mi pasco,

Si come gli altri Dei,
Ma di sangue, e di pianto.
Ne l' una mano io porto
Dubbia speme, fallace, e breve gioia;
Ne l' altra affanno, e noia,
Pene, sospiri, e morti.'   (*Didone* 1–16.)

The indebtedness of the English to the Italian tragedy, however, goes much further than the borrowing of a single passage or a single character or device. Not only is the supernatural machinery taken from Dolce's play, but the whole conception of Gismond, the grief-stricken widow a second time the victim of Love, is due to the Italian tragedy, and not to the novel, for Boccaccio's heroine is presented in a very different light. The forces to which his Ghismonda yields are natural forces. Speaking on his own behalf in the Introduction to the Fourth Day, Boccaccio says : ' Carissime donne . . . io conosco, che altra cosa dir non potrà alcun con ragione, se non che gli altri, ed io, che v' amiamo, naturalmente operiamo. Alle cui leggi, cioè della natura, voler contrastare, troppo gran forze bisognano, e spesse volte, non solamente in vano, ma con gran-dissimo danno del faticante s' adoperann.' The obedience of his heroine to this law of nature is conscious and deliberate : ' si pensò di volere avere, se esser potesse, occultamente un valoroso amante.' Her plea to her father in her own defence is to the same effect—that she is made of flesh, and not of rock or iron—a plea which the English dramatist has weakened by placing it not in her mouth, but in that of the Aunt, Lucrece, and putting it before, not after, the event. At the end of the novel, the lovers' fate is lamented, but they are felt to be objects of envy as well as compassion. ' Il Re con rigido viso disse. Poco prezzo mi parebbe la vita mia a dover dare per la metà diletto di quello, che con Guiscardo ebbe Ghis-monda.' The writers of the English tragedy took a very different view. R. Wilmot, in his preface to *Tancred and Gismunda*, protests that his purpose 'tendeth only to the exaltation of virtue and suppression of vice', and compares the tragedy with Beza's *Abraham* and Buchanan's *Jephtha*, apologizing for any defects on account of the youth of his coadjutors. ' Nevertheless herein they all agree, commending virtue, detesting vice, and lively deciphering their overthrow that suppress not their unruly affections.' Accordingly the Chorus in *Gismond of Salerne* hold up ' worthy dames' such as Lucrece and Penelope as ' a mirrour and a glasse to womankinde ', and exhort their hearers to resist Cupid's assaults and be content with a moderate and virtuous affection (Choruses II, III, IV). The Epilogue assures the ladies in the audience that such disordered passions are unknown ' in Britain land '.

13–16. *Well hath . . . forthblowen*: these lines might be sug-gested by *Didone* II. i. 27–9 :

' Dio più ch' altro possente ;
Dio, che disprezzi le saette horrende
Del gran padre d' i Dei';

but are more probably taken direct from Seneca, with whom this thought is a commonplace. See *Phaedra* 191-2 and *Octavia* 566-8, and compare the references to Mars and Troy in the following lines with *Phaedra* 193 and *Octavia* 832-3.

25. *The bloody . . . my might*: *Phaedra* 193:

> 'Gradiuus istas belliger sensit faces.'

29-32. *In earth . . . the soile*: *Octavia* 831-3:

> 'fregit Danaos, fregit Atridem.
> regna euertit Priami, claras
> diruit urbes.'

Hercules Oetaeus 476:

> 'uicit et superos amor.'

45-8. *What Natures . . . for ruthe*: cf. Ovid, *Metamorphoses* x. 311-14:

> 'ipse negat nocuisse tibi sua tela Cupido,
> Myrrha, facesque suas a crimine uindicat isto.
> stipite te Stygio, tumidisque adflauit Echidnis
> e tribus una Soror.'

Hercules Oetaeus 197:

> 'Cyprias lacrimas Myrrha tuetur.'

See also Chaucer, *Troilus and Criseyde* IV. st. 163 (l. 1139).

61-4. *This royall . . . and woe*: these lines resemble a passage in Dolce's prologue (27-34):

> 'Con quella face ardente,
> C' hò nel mio petto ascosa,
> Il che subito i' fei
> Ch' ella mi strinse al seno
> Sotto imagine falsa
> Del pargoletto mio nipote caro:
> Et d' occulto veneno
> L' hebbi il misero cuor colmo e ripieno.'

But the resemblance may be due to a common origin in Seneca's *Medea* 823-4:

> 'imas
> urat serpens flamma medullas.'

I. ii. 1-8. *Oh vaine . . . states vnrest*: cf. *Didone* v. i. 37-43:

> 'Et tu volubil Dea, che 'l mondo giri
> Calcando i buoni, e sollevando i rei:
> Che t' hò fatto io? che invidia ohime t' ha mosso
> A ridurmi a lo stato, in ch' io mi trovo?
> Quanto mutata m' hai da quel ch' io fui,
> Che in un sol punto m' hai levato, e tolto
> Tutto quel, che mi fea viver contenta.'

30-1. *Thy sprite . . . after come*: though 'Rod. Staf.' did not obtain much help from Boccaccio in his part of the play, he found

that a line or two which Ghismonda uses in the novel about her
lover might be transferred in application to her husband. She
says of the soul (*anima*) of Guiscardo : ' Io son certa, che ella
è ancora quicentro, e riguarda i luoghi de' suoi diletti, e de' miei :
e come colei, che ancor son certa, che m' ama, aspetta la mia, dalla
quale sommamente è amata.' Like his fellows, ' Rod. Staf.' used
the novel in the original, and not in the English translation. The
evidence here is slight, but the two lines of the text bear a closer
resemblance to the Italian than to Painter's : ' Truly I am well
assured, that it is yet here within, that hath respecte to the place,
aswell of his owne pleasures, as of mine, being assured (as she who
is certaine, that yet he looveth me) that he attendeth for myne, of
whom he is greatly beloved.'

33–6. *But yet ... a wife*: Didone v. i. 55–6:

> Però è ben tempo di prouar s' io posso
> Finir le pene mie con questa mano.'

I. iii. 19–20. *His lamp ... longer bide*: cf. Oedipus 1001–11.

53–9. *Oh sir ... neuer none*: Senecan stichomythia.

I. Ch. This Chorus is identical in thought with that which closes
Act II in Dolce, but as both are mere tissues of Senecan commonplaces, this similarity does not necessarily prove indebtedness. One
or two resemblances in phraseology are, however, noted below.
There appear to be also reminiscences of *Thyestes* 596–622, *Octavia*
933–5, *Oedipus* 1010–11, *Agamemnon* 57–70, *Hercules Furens*
376–82, *Phaedra* 1132–52, *Octavia* 915–18, in the order given ; but
the resemblance is in no case very close.

9–10. *No raùsom ... worthy dedes*: Didone u. s. 16–17 :

> ' In van contra di lor nostro intelletto
> Opra l' alta virtù d' i doni suoi.'

11. *twelue labors*: of Hercules.

13. *king*: Alexander.

23. *he*: Hector.

29–30. *Loke what ... not remoue*: Oedipus 1010–11 :

> ' non illa deo uertisse licet
> quae nexa suis currunt causis.'

33–6. *But happy ... and miserie*: Didone u. s. 25–7 :

> ' Beato chi più tosto s' avicina
> Al fine, a cui camina
> Chi prima è nato, ò nascera giamai.'

The last three lines were probably taken by Dolce from *Hercules
Oetaeus* 104–11 :

> ' par ille est superis cui pariter dies
> et fortuna fuit. mortis habet uices
> lente cum trahitur uita gementibus.
> quisquis sub pedibus fata rapacia
> et puppem posuit liminis ultimi,
> non captiua dabit bracchia uinculis

nec pompae ueniet nobile ferculum.
numquam est ille miser cui facile est mori.'

But they might have been suggested by a Latin translation of
Sophocles :

μὴ φῦναι τὸν ἄπαντα νικᾳ λόγον· τὸ δ᾽, ἐπεὶ φανῇ,
βῆναι κεῖθεν ὅθεν περ ἥκει πολὺ δεύτερον ὡς τάχιστα.

(*Oedipus Colonaeus* 1225-8.)

or by Cicero's ' Non nasci homini longe optimum esse, proximum
autem quam primum mori ' (*Tusc.* I. xlviii). The thought was taken
by Sophocles from Theognis, but with the latter writer Dolce, who
knew no Greek, was probably unacquainted.

41-4. *Not Euripus . . . mortall woe* : cf. *Agamemnon* 57-70 ;
Hercules Furens 376-82.

45-52. *Whoes case . . . of all* : cf. *Hippolytus* 1132-52 ; *Octavia*
915-8.

Act II : we have again a tedious dialoguizing of considerations
which Boccaccio expresses in a few lines, and again borrowings
from another part of the novel, in themselves of no great moment, but
pointing to the Italian text rather than to Painter as the authority
on which they rest. The passages in question are given below.

II. i. 26-9. *For if . . . semely shape* : the parallels with the *Didone*
in this act are fewer and less striking. In this passage Gismond expresses herself in much the same terms as Dido (I. i. 32-4) :

' Et ch' a l' incontro era sciochezza grande
A consumar il fior de' miei verd' anni
Senza gustar alcun soave frutto.'

The comparison of a wave-beaten ship with which Gismond closes
this speech (53-8) is used by Aeneas in *Didone* (II. ii. 87-94), but
this is a favourite Senecan metaphor (see *Medea* 945-51 and *Agamemnon* 139-44).

38-40. *No, no . . . pleasure past* : cf. Boccaccio :

' Sono adunque, sicome da te generata, di carne, e sì poco vivuta,
che ancor son giovane : e per l' una cosa, e per l' altra piena di con-
cupiscibile desiderio : al quale maravigliosissime forze hanno date
l' aver già, per essere stata maritata, conosciuto qual piacer sia a così
fatto desiderio dar compimento.'

Painter translates the passage thus :

' I am then as you be, begotten of fleshe, and my yeres so few, as
yet but yonge, and thereby full of lust and delight. Wherunto the
knowledge which I have had alredy in mariage, forceth me to accomplishe that desire.'

59-63. *Suffiseth this . . . yor blisse* : the author of Act II (probably
Henry Noel) either had not learn. the lesson one admirer of Seneca's
tragedies used to teach his pupils—' how and wherein they may
imitate them, and borrow somet}ing out of them '—or he preferred
to rely on his own efforts. His imitations of Seneca are as few and
faint as of the *Didone*. The chorus was, no doubt, suggested by

Octavia 298–312 and 689–95. The only other parallel I have thought worth noting is this passage, which may be compared with *Agamemnon* 126–9 :

> ' Regina Danaum et inclitum Ledae genus
> quid tacita uersas quidue consilii inpotens
> tumido feroces impetus animo geris?
> licet ipsa sileas, totus in uultu est dolor.'

II. ii. 19–28. *such passions . . . that age* : Boccaccio and Painter :

' Esser ti dovè, Tancredi, manifesto, essendo tu di carne, aver generata figliuola di carne, e non di pietra, o di ferro : e ricordar ti dovevi, e dei, quantunque tu ora sii vecchio, chenti, e quali, e con che forza vengano le leggi della giovanezza.'

' You ought deare father to knowe, that your selfe is of fleshe, and of fleshe you have engendred me your doughter, and not of Stone or Iron. In likewyse you ought, and must remember (although now you be arrived to olde yeares) what yonge folkes bee, and of what great power the lawe of youth is.'

III. i. 1. *Now shall . . . can do* : cf. the beginning of Euripides *Hippolytus* :

APHRODITE. Πολλὴ μὲν ἐν βροτοῖσι κοὐκ ἀνώνυμος
θεὰ κέκλημαι Κύπρις οὐρανοῦ τ' ἔσω·

δείξω δὲ μύθων τῶνδ' ἀλήθειαν τάχα·

This act (by ' G. Al.') contains no parallels with Dolce worth noting ; but the imitations of Seneca are more numerous.

11. *Iuno . . . forclosed* : marriage prevented.

III. ii. 1. *Pitie, that . . . gentle hart* : borrowed, of course, from Chaucer. This whole speech is modelled upon Seneca, *Phaedra* 368–94 ; cf. especially 18–20 of the text with *Phaedra* 389–91.

21–31. *Whoes sharp . . . for day* : *Phaedra* 105–6 :

> ' non me quies nocturna non altus sopor
> soluere curis : alitur et crescit malum.'

The presaging or disturbing dream is, of course, a stock device of classical Renascence tragedy. Dido has such a dream in Dolce ; so had Sophonisba in Trissino, and Orbecche in Giraldi.

III. iii. 6–8. *that doeth . . . of rest* : *Phaedra* 106–8, 649–51.

41–8. *Assuredly it . . . some thing enclosed* ; the dramatist's direct reference to Boccaccio is here obvious :

' Guiscardo il prese ; ed avvisando costei non senza cagione dovergliele aver donato, e così detto, partitosi, con esso sene tornò alla sua casa. E guardando la canna, e quella trovando fessa, l' aperse.'

' Guiscardo toke it, and thought that shee did not geve it unto him without some special purpose, went to his chamber, and loking upon the Cane perceived it to be hollowe, and openyng it founde the letter within whiche shee had written.'

For the significance of Painter's mistranslation of *fessa*, see above.

57–70. *Mine owne . . . owne.* G.: cf. the letter from Troilus to Criseyde signed *Le vostre T.*', v. st. 189–203.

86–8. *Not only . . . to thee*: *Phaedra* 621–4.

III. Ch. 1–4. *Full mighty . . . earth belowe*:

> 'quid fera frustra bella mouetis?
> inuicta gerit tela Cupido.
> flammis uestros obruet ignes,
> quibus extinxit fulmina saepe
> captumque Iouem caelo traxit.'   (*Octavia* 820–4.)

> 'et iubet caelo superos relicto
> uultibus falsis habitare terras.'   (*Phaedra* 299–300.)

5–8. *Then how . . . and sire*:

> 'sacer est ignis, credite laesis,
> nimiumque potens.
> qua terra mari cingitur alto
> quaque ethereo
> candida mundo sidera currunt.'   (*Phaedra* 336–40.)

9–12. *But why . . . their floure*: Minerva and Diana were virgin goddesses.

17–19. *For Loue . . . into smart*:

> 'uis magna mentis blandus atque animi calor
> amor est. iuuentae gignitur luxu otio,
> nutritur inter laeta fortunae bona.'   (*Octavia* 573–5.)

33–8. *Whoe yeldeth . . . is cold*:

> 'extingue flammas neue te dirae spei
> praebe obsequentem. quisquis in primo obstitit
> pepulitque amorem tutus ac uictor fuit,
> qui blandiendo dulce nutriuit malum
> sero recusat ferre quod subiit iugum.'   (*Phaedra* 136–40.)

> 'quem si fouere atque alere desistas, cadit
> breuique uires perdit extinctus suas.'   (*Octavia* 576–7.)

41. *But he . . . in gold*:

> 'uenenum in auro bibitur.'   (*Thyestes* 453.)

Act IV: the writer of this act (undoubtedly Christopher Hatton, who was Master of the Game at the Grand Christmas of 1561–2, when *Gorboduc* was performed) evidently kept an eye on the *Didone*. Megaera, who opens the act, is no doubt derived ultimately from Seneca's *Thyestes*, where she drives the ghost of Tantalus to curse his own descendants. He comes unwillingly:

> 'quid ora terres uerbere et tortos ferox
> minaris angues? quid famem infixam intimis
> agitas medullis? flagrat incensum siti
> cor et perustis flamma uisceribus micat.
> sequor.'

In *Didone* the ghost introduced is that of Sichaeus; the serpents and other torments are applied, not to the bearer, but to the victim of the curse. Cupid says in the Prologue :

> ' Però discendo al fondo
> De l' empia styge, e del suo cerchio fuora
> Vò trar la pallid' ombra
> Del misero Sicheo
> (Che ben impetrerò de Pluto questa
> Gratia degna, et honesta)
> Et vò, ch' a Dido ella si mostri inanzi :
> Tolto prima d' Abysso
> Una de le ceraste ;
> Che in vece di capei, torte e sanguigne
> A le tempie d' intorno
> Ondeggiano di quelle
> Furie spietate e felle,
> Che sogliono voltar sossopra il mondo.
> Et questa i' vò, che tutto l' empi il core
> Di sdegno, e di furore,
> Fin ch' à morte trabocchi, .
> Et turbar vegga gli occhi
> De la sirocchia altera
> Di quei, che move il sole, e ogni sphera.'

In *Didone* II. i Cupid brings the snake on to the stage :

> ' Che in tanto io le porrò su '1 bianco petto
> Questo serpe sanguigno, horrido, e fiero,
> C' hò divelto pur' hora
> Dal capo di Megera,
> Il quale il cor di lei roda e consumi.'

We learn later (III. i. 79–83) that the serpent was actually seen on Dido's neck :

> ' Fu posto a lei da non veduta mano
> Un serpe al collo, che con molti nodi
> Lo cinse errando, e sibillando pose
> La testa in seno ; e la vibrante lingua
> Quinci e quindi lecò le poppe e '1 petto.'

Hatton spared the English audience some of the details, but he gave them two snakes instead of one, and added a characteristic moral turn at the end of Megaera's speech (37–44).

The Gentlemen of the Inner Temple were apparently fond of these grisly sights ; see *Gorboduc* IV. D.S. and IV. Ch. 12–15.

IV. i. 1–14. *Vengeance and . . . do fele* : these lines are doubtless imitated from the opening of the *Thyestes*, but the same examples of the pains of hell occur in *Octavia* 631–5 and *Didone* IV. i. 126–33.

IV. ii. 1–16. *O great . . . pitt remaine* : the invocation of Jove's thunder came originally from Sophocles, *Electra* 823–6 :

> ποῦ ποτε κεραυνοὶ Διός, ἢ ποῦ φαέθων
> "Αλιος, εἰ ταῦτ' ἐφορῶντες κρύπτουσιν ἕκηλοι ;

But it was probably suggested to Hatton by *Phaedra* 679–90 or *Thyestes* 1081–1100; this stock device of Seneca was to become no less familiar in Elizabethan tragedy. It had already been used in *Gorboduc* (end of III. i) :

> ' O heauens, send down the flames of your reuenge ;
> Destroy, I say with flash of wrekeful fier
> The traitour sonne, and then the wretched sire.'

The original passage in the *Phaedra* was quoted—or rather misquoted—in *Titus Andronicus* IV. i. 81–2 :

> ' Magni Dominator poli,
> Tam lentus audis scelera ? tam lentus vides ?'

Shakespeare possibly had it in mind when he made Lear say (II. iv. 230–1) :

> ' I do not bid the thunder bearer shoot,
> Nor tell tales of thee to high-judging Jove.'

122. *Iulio, this is the case* : the rhymed Alexandrines, with strongly marked alliteration, here break off, and the usual measure of the tragedy (iambic pentameter, rhymed alternately) is resumed. The alliteration continues.

IV. iii : in Boccaccio and Painter Tancred sees Guiscardo before Ghismonda.

17–28. *No, no . . . and myne*: this is taken from Boccaccio, apparently directly, and not through Painter's translation :

' Ghismonda, parendomi conoscere la tua virtù, e la tua onestà, mai non mi sarebbe potuto cader nell' animo (quantunque mi fosse stato detto) se io co' miei occhi non l'avessi veduto, che tu di sotto-porti ad alcuno huomo, se tuo marito stato non fosse, avessi, non che fatto, ma pur pensato.'

' Gismonda, I had so much affiaunce and truste in thy vertue and honestie, that it coulde never have entred into my mynde (althoughe it had bene tolde me, if I had not sene it with mine owne propre eyes) but that thou haddest not onely in deede, but also in thought, abandoned the companie of all men, except it had bene thy husbande.'

55–82. *Father . . . to stay* : Gismond's speech is much shorter and weaker than in the novel; some parts of this famous passage in Boccaccio had been already used by the dramatists, and some were unusable on account of their conception of the character and situation.

IV. iv. **36–9.** *But greater . . . my self* : taken, not from Painter, but from the original :

' Al quale Guiscardo niuna altra cosa disse, se non questo. Amor può troppo più, che nè voi, nè io possiamo.'

' To whom Guiscardo gave no other aunswere, but that Love was of greater force, than either any Prince or hym selfe.'

v. i : it is in this scene that the imitation of Seneca is most extensive and most obvious. Renuchio is the regular Senecan messenger, the detailed horror of his story is quite after Seneca's manner, and there are many lines translated, with slight alterations, from the narratives of the *Thyestes* and other plays, as will be seen from the parallel passages given below.

1-2. *O cruel . . . be told*:

'O sors acerba.'   (*Phaedra* 1000.)

'O dira fata saeua miseranda horrida.'   (*Troades* 1066.)

The imitations of Seneca were made, so far as one is able to judge, from the original, and not from the English translation of 1581. The latter reveals occasional similarities of phrase, as in this instance, where the translators render Seneca's lines :

'O heavy happe.' . . .

'O dyre, fierce, wretched, horrible,
O cruell fates accurste.'

But these might well be mere coincidences ; and such instances of the use of the same words are rare. In most cases the version of the Gentlemen of the Inner Temple gives every evidence of independence of the English translation. A fair idea of the relation of the two to the original text is given by comparing the longer passages given below with Heywood's rendering of the same lines in his translation of the *Thyestes*, which is also reproduced.

21-38. *What newes . . . yow bring*: *Thyestes* 626-40 :

'*Chor.*   quid portas noui ?
Nunt. Quaenam ista regio est ?   Argos et Sparte inpios
        sortita fratres et maris gemini premens
        fauces Corinthos, an feris Hister fugam
        praebens Alanis, an sub aeterna niue
        Hyrcana tellus, an uagi passim Scythae ?
Chor. quis hic nefandi est conscius monstri locus ?
        effare et istud pande quodcumque est malum.
Nunt. Si steterit animus, si metu corpus rigens
        remittet artus. haeret in uultu trucis
        imago facti. ferte me insanae procul
        illo procellae ferte, quo fertur dies
        hinc raptus.
Chor.   animos grauius incertos tenes.
        quid sit quod horres effer, autorem indica.
        non quaero quis sed uter. effare ocius.'

40-2. *although my . . . haue seen*: *Phaedra* 1004 :

'uocem dolori lingua luctifica negat.'

45-68. *Fast by . . . is found*: this description is modelled upon *Thyestes* 641-79, with a possible reminiscence of the tower in the *Troas* (630-1), from which Astyanax leaps 'intrepidus animo'. The passage from the *Thyestes* is copied also in Giraldi's *Orbecche*. IV. i. 59-62 :

> 'Giace nel fondo di quest' alta torre,
> In parte sì solinga, e sì riposta,
> Che non vi giunge mai raggio di Sole,
> Un luoco dedicato a' sacrificii.'

149–67. *Cho. O cruel . . . and all*: *Thyestes* 743–52:

> ' *Chor.*   o saeuum scelus.
> *Nunt.* exhorruistis? hactenus non stat nefas,
>   plus est.
> *Chor.*   An ultra maius aut atrocius
>   natura recipit?
> *Nunt.*   sceleris hunc finem putas?
>   gradus est.
> *Chor.*   quid ultra potuit? obiecit feris
>   lanianda forsan corpora atque igne arcuit.
> *Nunt.* utinam arcuisset. ne tegat functos humus,
>   ne soluat ignis, auibus epulandos licet
>   ferisque triste pabulum saeuis trahat.
>   Votum est sub hoc, quod esse supplicium solet.'

182–8. *The warme . . . they tore*: *Thyestes* 755–6:

> ' erepta uiuis exta pectoribus tremunt
> spirantque uenae corque adhuc pauidum salit.'

201–4. *Thy father . . . of all*: this passage makes it clear that R. W[ilmot], the writer of Act v, translated independently from Boccaccio, and was not content to rely upon Painter:

> ' Il tuo padre ti manda questo, per consolarti di quella cosa, che tu più ami, come tu hai lui consolato di ciò, che egli più amava.'

> ' Thy father hath sent thee this presente, to comforte thy selfe with the thing, which thou doest chieflie love, as thou haste comforted him of that which he loved most.'

The *di* of the last line, which the dramatist translated 'with' and Painter 'of', seems to mean 'concerning, with respect to, for'; and here Painter comes nearer the original than R. W.; but the divergence is none the less significant.

207–8. *O haynous . . . ones beleue*: *Thyestes* 753–4:

> ' O nullo scelus
> credibile in aeuo quodque posteritas neget.'

It will be seen that in ll. 149–67, 182–8, 207–8 Wilmot has appropriated the whole of *Thyestes* 743–56, which is accordingly given below in Heywood's translation for purposes of comparison:

> ' *Chor.*   O heynous hateful act.
> *Mess.* Abhorre ye this? ye heare not yet the end of all the fact,
>   There follows more.
> *Chor.*   A fiercer thing, or worse then this to see
>   Could Nature beare?
> *Mess.*   why thinke ye this of gylt the end to be?

        It is but part.

Chor.   what could be more ? to cruel beastes he cast
        Perhappes their bodyes to be torne, and kept from fyres at
           last.

Mess.   Would God he had : that neuer tombe the dead might ouer
           hyde,
        Nor flames dissolue, though them for food to foules in
           pastures wyde
        He had out throwen, or them for pray to cruell beastes
           would flinge.
        That which the worst was wont to be, were here a wished
           thing.
        That them their father saw untombd : but oh more cursed
           crime
        Uncredible, the which denye will men of after tyme :
        From bosomes yet alive out drawne the trembling bowels
           shake,
        The vaynes yet breath, the feareful hart doth yet both pant
           and quake.'

v. ii. 25–50. *Ah pleasant . . . derely loue :* it is worth while to
compare this soliloquy with the passage in Boccaccio on which it is
founded and with Painter's translation :

'Ahi dolcissimo albergo di tutti i miei piaceri, maladetta sia la
crudeltà di colui, che con gli occhi della fronte or mi ti fa vedere.
Assai m' era con quegli della mente riguardarti a ciascuna ora. Tu
hai il tuo corso fornito, e di tale, chente la fortuna tel concedette, ti
se' spacciato. Venuto se' alla fine, alla qual ciascun corre. Lasciate
hai le miserie del mondo, e le fatiche, e dal tuo nemico medesimo
quella sepoltura hai, chè il tuo valore ha meritata. Niuna cosa ti
mancava ad aver compiute esequie, se non le lagrime di colei, la
qual tu, vivendo, cotanto amasti : le quali, acciocchè tu l' avessi,
pose Iddio nell' animo al mio dispietato padre, che a me ti man-
dasse : ed io le ti darò (comechè di morire con gli occhi asciutti,
e con viso da niuna cosa spaventato proposto avessi) e dateleti,
senza alcuno indugio farò, che la mia anima si congiugnerà con
quella, adoperandol tu, che tu già cotanto cara guardasti.'

'Oh sweete harboroughe of my pleasures, cursed be the crueltye
of him that hath caused mee at this time to loke uppon thee with
the eyes of my face : it was pleasure ynoughe, to see thee every
hower, amonges people of knowledge and understanding. Thou
hast finished thy course, and by that ende, which fortune vouchsafed
to give thee, thou art dispatched, and arrived to the ende wherunto all men have recourse : thou hast forsaken the miseries and
traveyles of this world, and haste had by the enemy himselfe such
a sepulture as thy worthinesse deserveth. There needeth nothing
els to accomplishe thy funerall, but onely the teares of her whom
thou diddest hartelye love all the dayes of thy lyfe. For having
wherof, our Lord did put into the head of my unmercifull father to
send thee unto me, and truly I will bestow some teares uppon thee,

although I was determined to die, without sheading any teares at all, stoutlie, not fearefull of any thinge. And when I have powred them out for thee, I will cause my soule, which thou hast heretofore so carefully kepte, to be joyned wyth thine.'

R. W., in line 32, correctly translates 'con quegli della mente', which Painter woefully misunderstands; and in the last line quoted, the sense of 'che tu già cotanto cara guardasti' is more closely rendered by the dramatist than by the professed translator.

THE MISFORTUNES OF ARTHUR

Pr. 131-3. *Thus ... to stadge*: a somewhat daring piece of flattery in face of the execution of Mary Queen of Scots on Feb. 8, 1587, and the preparations already made on both sides for the final conflict between England and Spain.

Arg. 1. *Vther Pendragon*: 'The cause why he was surnamed Pendragon, was, for that Merline the great prophet likened him to a dragons head, that at the time of his natiuitie maruelouslie appeared in the firmament at the corner of a blasing star, as is reported. But others supposed that he was so called of his wisedome and serpentine subtilitie, or for that he gaue the dragons head in his banner.'—Holinshed, *Historie of England* V. x.

11-12. *the Saxons ... poysoned*: H. C. Grumbine in his edition of the play published in *Litterarhistorische Forschungen* (Berlin, 1900) has shown that Geoffrey of Monmouth's *Historia Regum Britanniae* was the main source of the tragedy. This particular incident of the poisoning of Uther by the Saxons is given by Geoffrey, and omitted by Malory from *Le Morte Darthur*: 'Erat namque prope aulam fons nitidissimae aquae, quam rex solitus fuerat potare, cum caeteros liquores propter infirmitatem abhorreret. Fontem namque aggressi sunt nefandi proditores, ipsumque undique ueneno infecerunt, ita ut manans aqua tota corrumperetur. Ut ergo potauit rex ex ea, festinae morti succubuit' (VIII. xxiv).

13. *Mordred*: so far the names and incidents are taken from Geoffrey; this name and the fact of Mordred's incestuous birth are taken from Malory: 'kynge Arthur begate vpon her Mordred and she was his syster on the moder syde Igrayne ... But al this tyme kyng Arthur knewe not that kyng Lots wyf was his syster' (I. xix). In Geoffrey, Modredius is the son of Lot.

16. *Gueneuora*: in Geoffrey, Guanhumara ; in Malory, Guenever. The story, however, is taken in the main from Geoffrey : 'Arturus, Modredo nepoti suo ad conseruandum Britanniam, atque Ganhumarae reginae committens, cum exercitu suo portum Hamonis adiuit' (X. ii). 'Hostes quoque suos miseratus. praecepit indigenis sepelire eos : corpusque Lucii ad senatum deferre, mandans non debere aliud tributum ex Britannia reddi. Deinde post subsequentem hyemem, in partibus illis moratus est : et ciuitates Allobrogum subiugare uacauit. Adueniente uero aestate, cum

Romam petere affectaret, et montes transcendere incoepisset, nunciatur ei Modredum nepotem suum, cuius tutelae commiserat Britanniam, eiusdem diademate per tyrannidem et proditionem insignitum esse; reginamque Ganhumaram, uiolato iure priorum nuptiarum, eidem nefanda Venere copulatam esse' (X. xiii). 'Postquam tandem, etsi magno labore, littora adepti fuerunt, mutuam reddendo cladem, Modredum et exercitum eius pepulerunt in fugam . . . Quod ut Ganhumarae reginae annunciatum est, confestim desperans, ab Eboraco ad urbem Legionum diffugit, atque in templo Iulii martyris, inter monachas eiusdem caste uiuere proposuit, et uitam monachalem suscepit' (XI. i). In Malory the Queen's retirement to a nunnery takes place after Arthur's death : 'and whan quene Gueneuer vnderstood that kyng Arthur was slayn & al the noble kny3tes syr Mordred & al the remenaunte / Than the quene stale aweye & v ladyes wyth hyr / & soo she wente to almesburye / & there she let make hir self a Nonne' (XXI. vii). Up to Arthur's landing she defends herself in 'the toure of london'.

The . . . first dumbe shewe: with this compare the dumb show before Act I of *Gorboduc u. s.*

The names of the speakers. Cador rex Cornubiae, Guillamurius rex Hyberniae, Aschillius rex Dacorum, Hoelus rex Armoricanorum Britonum, Cheldricus Saxonum dux are found in Geoffrey as well as the names Conan and Angarad; Gawayn is in Malory. Gildas is mentioned by Geoffrey as a previous historian (I. i).

I. i. I. *Gorlois*: this ghost is, of course, a reproduction of the familiar figure of Tantalus in the *Thyestes*. Particular passages borrowed or imitated are shown below.

22–6. *Let mischiefes . . . complet sinne : Thyestes* 26–32 :

> 'nec sit irarum modus
> pudorue : mentes caecus instiget furor,
> rabies parentum duret et longum nefas
> eat in nepotes. nec uacet cuiquam uetus
> odisse crimen : semper oriatur nouum
> nec unum in uno, dumque punitur scelus,
> crescat.

The renderings of Hughes surpass in exactitude and elegance those of the translation of 1581 : this instance will suffice as an example :

'Let them contend with all offence, by turnes and one by one
Let swordes be drawne : and meane of ire procure there may
    be none,
Nor shame : let fury blynd enflame theyr myndes and wrathful
    will,
Let yet the parentes rage endure and longer lasting yll
Through childrens children spreade : nor yet let any leysure
    be
The former fawte to hate, but still more mischiefe newe to see,
Nor one in one : but ere the gylt with vengeance be acquit,
Encrease the cryme.'

27–8. *Goe to . . . yet conceale*: *Thyestes* 192–3:
'age anime fac quod nulla posteritas probet,
sed nulla taceat.'

54. *Cassiopæa*: a brilliant new star appeared in this constellation
in 1572. This compliment to Queen Elizabeth, together with that
noted just below, must be commended for ingenuity.

63. *a thousand yeares to come*: Geoffrey dates Arthur's death
A. D. 542.

I. ii. 2. A curious punctuation mark (:') is used by the printer
at the end of this line, in lines 29, 37, *et passim*; but as it simply
means that he was short of the ordinary interrogation marks, the
colon and apostrophe have not been reproduced.

8–9. *Attempt some . . . rather his*: *Thyestes* 193–5:
'aliquod audendum est nefas
atrox cruentum tale quod frater meus
suum esse malit.'

11–16. *Frame out . . . or fire*: *Agamemnon* 117–22:
'tecum ipsa nunc euolue femineos dolos,
quod ulla coniunx perfida atque impos sui
amore caeco, quod nouercales manus
ausae, quod ardens impia uirgo face
Phasiaca fugiens regna Thessalica trabe:
ferrum, uenena.'

19. *The wrath . . . to lurke*: *Thyestes* 504:
'cum spirat ira sanguinem nescit tegi.'

21–3. *I am . . . him life*: *Hercules Oetaeus* 307–9:
'iam displicemus, capta praelata est mihi.
non praeferetur: qui dies thalami ultimus
nostri est futurus, hic erit uitae tuae.'

24–8. *Though, neither . . . nowe subdue*: *Hercules Oetaeus* 285–
90: 'gesseris caelum licet
totusque pacem debeat mundus tibi:
est aliquid hydra peius iratae dolor
nuptae. quis ignis tantus in coelum furit
ardentis Aetnae? quicquid est uictum tibi
hic uincet animus.'

29–33. *What's this . . . this venge*: *Hercules Oetaeus* 310–14:
'quid hoc? recedit animus et ponit minas,
iam cessit ira. quid miser langues dolor?
perdis furorem, coniugis sanctae fidem
mihi reddis iterum. quid uetas flammas ali?
quid frangis ignes? hunc mihi serua impetum.'

34–8. *At lest . . . high reuenge*: *Agamemnon* 122–5:
'uel Mycenaea domo
coniuncta socio profuge furtiua rate.
quid timida loqueris furta et exilium et fugas?
sors ista fecit. te decet maius nefas.'

39-42. *Come spitefull . . . monsters yet*: *Thyestes* 250-4:
'dira furiarum cohors
discorsque Erinnys ueniat et geminas faces
Megaera quatiens. non satis magno meum
ardet furore pectus, impleri iuuat
maiore monstro.'

42-4. *My hart . . . it's huge*: *Thyestes* 267-70:
'nescio quid animus maius et solito amplius
supraque fines moris humani tumet
instatque pigris manibus. haud quid sit scio,
sed grande quiddam est.'

46. *Omit no . . . be inough*: *Thyestes* 256:
'nullum relinquam facinus et nullum est satis.'

47. *Wrong cannot . . . by excesse*: *Thyestes* 195-6:
'scelera non ulcisceris
nisi uincis.'

It will be seen that the borrowing from Seneca in this speech is
continuous: there is really nothing of the author's own.

49-51. *is there . . . in reuenge*: *Thyestes* 1055-7:
'*Thy.*   sceleris est aliquis modus?
Atr. sceleri modus debetur, ubi facias scelus,
non ubi reponas.'

52-3. *Great harmes . . . it selfe*: *Medea* 155-6:
'leuis est dolor, qui capere consilium potest
et clepere sese, magna non latitant mala.'

54-5. *Hatred concealde . . . failes reuenge*: *Medea* 153-4:
'ira quae tegitur nocet,
professa perdunt odia uindictae locum.'

70. *Vnlawfull loue . . . lawfull lothes*: *Hercules Oetaeus* 360:
'inlicita amantur, excidit quicquid licet.'

74-5. *How can . . . her offence*: *Agamemnon* 150-1:
'*Nutr.* piget prioris et nouum crimen struis?
Clyt. res est profecto stulta nequitiae modus.'

84-5. *Whom Gods . . . He breakes*: *Hercules Oetaeus* 444-5:
'caelestis ira quos premit, miseros facit,
humana nullos.'

85-7. *Your griefe . . . so greeue*: *Hercules Oetaeus* 447-9:
'maior admisso tuus
alumna, dolor est: culpa par odium exigat.
cur saeva modice statuis? ut passa es, dole.'

98-9. *Well: shame . . . sage aduise*: *Hippolytus* 255-6:
'non omnis animo cessit ingenuo pudor:
paremus altrix.'

I. iii. 1–2. *The loue . . . no foile*: *Hippolytus* 256–7:

          'qui regi non uult amor
uincatur. haud te fama maculari sinam.'

7–10. *Her breast . . . it selfe*: *Hercules Furens* 1226–8:

'nondum tumultu pectus attonitum caret:
mutauit iras quodque habet proprium furor,
in se ipse saeuit.'

13–14. *Thereby the . . . to dye*: *Hippolytus* 261–2:

         'dignam ob hoc uita reor
quod esse temet autumas dignam nece.'

15–17. *Death is . . . of knife*: *Hippolytus* 263–4:

'decreta mors est: quaeritur fati genus.
laqueone uitam finiam an ferro incubem?'

18–19. *All hope . . . left vnlost*: *Hercules Furens* 266–7:

'cuncta iam amisi bona:
mentem arma famam coniugem.'

Cf. *Macbeth* V. iii. 22–9.

20–1. *My selfe . . . of harmes*: *Medea* 166–7:

'Medea superest, hic mare et terras uides,
ferrumque et ignes et deos et fulmina.'

22–3. *Who now . . . by death*: *Hercules Furens* 1268–9:

          'nemo polluto queat
animo mederi. morte sanandum est scelus.'

Cf. *Macbeth* V. iii. 40–6.

27. *Alone you . . . you may*: *Thebais* 66:

'perire sine me non potes, mecum potes.'

28–30. *They, that . . . Offend alike*: *Thebais* 98–9:

            'qui cogit mori
nolentem in aequo est quique properantem inpedit.'

31–2. *But will . . . doe mourne*: *Hippolytus* 888–9:

'*Thes.*   lacrimae nonne te nostrae mouent?
Phaed. mors optima est perire lacrimant dum sui.'

33–6. *Ech where . . . our graues*: *Thebais* 151–3:

'ubique mors est. optume hoc cauit deus.
eripere uitam nemo non homini potest,
at nemo mortem: mille ad hanc aditus patent.'

Cf. *Julius Caesar* I. iii. 91–7. The same idea is expressed by
Marston (1 *Antonio and Mellida* III. ii), Beaumont and Fletcher,
Massinger (*The Duke of Milan* I. iii), and Shirley (*Love's Cruelty*
V. i).

37–40. *Who then . . . haue sworne*: *Hercules Furens* 869–71:

'nemo ad id sero uenit unde numquam,
cum semel uenit, potuit reuerti.
quid iuvat dirum properare fatum?'

Cf. *Hamlet* III. i. 78–80.

43. *Death is . . . it selfe*: *Thyestes* 246:
'de fine poenae loqueris, ego poenam uolo.'

44–54. *Is't meete . . . Natures boundes*: *Oedipus* 957–72:
'itane? tam magnis breues
poenas sceleribus soluis atque uno omnia
pensabis ictu? moreris: hoc patri sat est.
quid deinde matri, quid male in lucem editis
gnatis, quid ipsi quae tuum magna luit
scelus ruina flebilis patriae dabis?
soluenda non est illa quae leges ratas
natura in uno uertit Oedipode, nouos
commenta partus, supplicis eadem meis
nouetur. iterum uiuere atque iterum mori
liceat renasci semper, ut totiens noua
supplicia pendas. utere ingenio· minor.
quod saepe fieri non potest fiat diu.
mors eligatur longa. quaeratur uia
qua nec sepultis mixtus et uiuis tamen
exemptus erres. morere sed citra patrem.'

61. *The minde . . . th' unchast*: *Hippolytus* 743:
'mens inpudicam facere non casus solet.'

62–3. *Then is . . . her Fate*: *Oedipus* 1041:
'fati iota culpa est nemo fit fato nocens.'

65. *Impute mishaps . . . manners faultes*: *Hippolytus* 149
'nam monstra fato, moribus scelera inputes.'

67. *A mightie . . . a sinne*: *Hercules Furens* 1245:
'saepe error ingens sceleris optinuit locum.'

I. iv. 1 7. *The houre . . . guiltie heade*: *Agamemnon* 227–32:
'quod tempus animo semper ac mente horrui,
adest profecto rebus extremum meis.
quid terga uertis anime? quid primo impetu
deponis arma? crede perniciem tibi
et dira saeuos fata moliri deos.
oppone cunctis uile suppliciis caput.'

9. *What shouldst . . . to hope*: *Medea* 163:
'qui nil potest sperare, desperet nihil.'

Agamemnon 147:
'cui ultima est fortuna, quid dubium timet?'

11. *He safely . . . his harmes*: *Thebais* 198–9:
'cuius haud ultra mala
exire possunt in loco tuto est situs.'

12–16. *Thine (death)* . . . *our liues*: Hercules Furens 874–8:

'tibi crescit omne,
et quod occasus uidet et quod ortus.
parce uenturis. tibi mors paramur.
sis licet segnis, properamus ipsi.
prima quae uitam dedit hora, carpit.'

24–8. *My feare* . . . *his crimes*: Agamemnon 240–4:

'amor iugalis uincit ac flectit retro.
remeemus illuc, unde non decuit prius
abire. sed nunc casta repetatur fides.
nam sera numquam est ad bonos mores uia.
quem poenitet peccasse, poenae est innocens.

36. *Nor loue* . . . *a peere*: Agamemnon 260:

'nec regna socium ferre nec taedae sciunt.'

37–43. *Why dost* . . . *be forgiuen*: Agamemnon 261–8:

'Aegisthe quid me rursus in praeceps rapis
iramque flammis iam residentem excitas?
permisit aliquid uictor in captas sibi:
nec coniugem hoc respicere nec dominam decet.
lex alia solio est alia priuato toro.
quid quod seueras ferre me leges uiro
non patitur animus turpis admissi memor.
det ille ueniam facile cui uenia est opus.'

48. *A Iudge* . . . *to himselfe*: Agamemnon 271:

'nobis maligni iudices aequi sibi.'

53. *His is* . . . *in steede*: Medea 503–4:

'cui prodest scelus,
is fecit.'

58–9. *Well should* . . . *thy sake*: Medea 506:

'tibi innocens sibi quisquis est pro te nocens.'

74. *His waies* . . . *his guide*: Agamemnon 146:

'caeca est temeritas quae petit casum ducem.'

77. *The safest* . . . *to worse*: Agamemnon 116:

'per scelera semper sceleribus tutum est iter.'

Cf. *Macbeth* III. ii :

'Things bad begun make strong themselves by ill.'

Marston, *The Malcontent* V. ii :

'Black deed only through black deed safely flies.'

Jonson, *Catiline* I. ii :

'The ills that I have done cannot be safe
But by attempting greater.'

Webster, *The White Devil* II. i :

   'Small mischiefs are by greater made secure.'

Massinger, *Duke of Milan* II. i :

   'One deadly sin, then, help to cure another.'

79. *He is . . . in crimes* : *Agamemnon* 151 :

   'res est profecto stulta nequitiae modus.'

81. *So sword . . . the soare* : *Agamemnon* 153 :

   'et ferrum et ignis saepe medicinae loco est.'

82. *Extremest cures . . . vsed first* : *Agamemnon* 154 :

   'extrema primo nemo temptauit loco.'

83. *In desperate . . . is best* : *Agamemnon* 155 :

   'capienda rebus in malis praeceps uia est.'

93. *Mischiefe is . . . ne'r secure* : *Hippolytus* 169 :

   'scelus aliqua tutum, nulla securum tulit.'

94–5. *The wrongfull . . . his Sword* : *Hercules Furens* 345–6 :

       'rapta sed trepida manu
sceptra optinentur. omnis in ferro est salus.'

Cf. *King John* III. iv :

   'A sceptre snatch'd with an unruly hand
   Must be as boisterously maintain'd as gain'd.'

97–8. *The Kingliest . . . but right* : *Thyestes* 213–15 :

   '*Sat.* rex uelit honesta : nemo non eadem uolet.
   Atr. ubicumque tantum honesta dominanti licent,
      precario regnatur.'

121–3. *She is . . . soone supprest* : *Octavia* 596–8 :

   '*Sen.* leuis atque uana. *Nero.* sit licet, multos notat.
   Sen. excelsa metuit. *Nero.* non minus carpit tamen.
   Sen. facile opprimetur.'

II. i : 'The entire scene is a dramatization of Geoffrey of Monmouth' (Grumbine). '[Arturus] ipse etenim audita suorum strage, quae paulo ante eisdem dabatur, cum legione irruerat, et abstracto Caliburno gladio optimo excelsa uoce atque uerbis commilitones suos inanimabat, inquiens : 'Quid facitis, uiri ? ut quid muliebres permittitis illaesos abire ? ne abscedat illorum ullus uiuus. Mementote dextrarum uestrarum, quae tot praeliis exercitatae, terdena regna potestati meae subdiderunt. ... Mementote libertatis uestrae, quam semiuiri isti et uobis debiliores demere affectant. Ne abeat ullus uiuus, ne abeat. Quid facitis ?'—Haec et plura alia uociferando, irruebat in hostes, prosternabat, caedebat et cuicunque obuiabat, aut ipsum aut ipsius equum uno ictu interficiebat ... Viso igitur rege suo in hunc modum decertante, Britones maiorem audaciam capessunt : Romanos unanimiter inuadunt : densata caterua incedunt :

et dum ex una parte pedestres hoc modo infestarent, equestres ex
alia prosternere et penetrare conantur. Resistunt tamen acriter
Romani: et monitu Lucii, illustris regis uicem illatae cladis Brito-
nibus reddere elaborabant. Tanta igitur ui in utraque parte pu-
gnatur, ac si tunc primum recenter conuenirent. Hinc autem Arturus
saepius ac saepius ut praedictus est hostes percutiens, Britones ad
perstandum hortabatur. Fiebat itaque in utraque parte caedes
abhorrenda . . . Tunc multa milia Romanorum conciderunt. Tunc
etiam Lucius imperator intra turmas occupatus, cuiusdam lancea
confossus interiit. At Britones usque insequentes, uictoriam, licet
maximo labore, habuerunt ' (X. xi).

' Hostes quoque suos miseratus, praecepit indigenis sepelire eos:
corpusque Lucii ad senatum deferre, mandans non debere aliud
tributum ex Britannia reddi ' (X. xiii).

'Ut igitur infamia praenunciati sceleris aures ipsius attigit continuo
dilata inquietatione, quam Leoni regi Romanorum ingerere affec-
tauerat: dimisso Hoelo duce Armoricanorum cum exercitu
Galliarum, ut partes illas pacificaret: confestim cum Insulanis
tantummodo regibus, eorumque exercitibus in Britanniam remea-
uit. . . . [Modredus] Arturo in Rutupi portum applicanti obuiam
uenit: et commisso praelio maximam stragem dedit applicantibus. . . .
Postquam tandem, etsi magno labore, littora adepti fuerunt, mutuam
reddendo cladem, Modredum et exercitum eius pepulerunt in
fugam ' (XI. i).

II. i. 1-2. *Lo here . . . of Brute*: Geoffrey: ' Erat tunc nomen
insulae Albion, quae a nemine, exceptis paucis gygantibus, inhabita-
batur. . . . Denique Brutus de nomine suo insulam Britanniam,
sociosque suos Britones appellat ' (I. xvi).

II. ii. 12-15. *Nought shoulde . . . his foes*: *Octavia* 452-5:

> ' *Sen.* in nihil propinquos temere constitui decet.
> *Nero.* iustum esse facile est cui uacat pectus metu.
> *Sen.* magnum timoris remedium clementia est.
> *Nero.* extinguere hostem maxima est uirtus ducis.'

18. *The Subiects . . . the Kings*: *Octavia* 190:

> ' *Nutr.* uis magna populi est.   *Oct.* principis maior tamen.'

19. *The more . . . to feare*: *Octavia* 462:

> 'hoc plus uerere quod licet tantum tibi.'

20-1. *He is . . . is iust*: *Octavia* 465-6:

> ' *Nero.* inertis est nescire quid liceat sibi.'
> *Sen.* id facere laus est quod decet, non quod licet.'

25-6. *The Lawes . . . licence most*: *Troas* 344-5:

> ' *Pyrrh.* quodcumque libuit facere uictori, licet.
> *Agam.* minimum decet libere cui multum licet.'

29-30. *The Fates . . . are low*: *Troas* 704-5:

> ' quoque te celsum altius
> superi leuarunt, mitius lapsos preme.'

41-2. *My will ... Gods forbid*: *Octavia* 472-3:

'*Nero*. statuam ipse. *Sen*. quae consensus efficiat rata.
Nero. despectus ensis faciet. *Sen*. hoc absit nefas.'

45-8. *Whom Fates ... cannot vse*: *Hippolytus* 448-51:

'quem fata cogunt hic quidem uiuat miser,
at si quis ultro se malis offert uolens
seque ipse torquet, perdere est dignus bona
quis nescit uti.'

61-4. *Nor to ... it none*: *Thebais* 555-9:

'ne precor ferro erue
patriam ac penates neue, quas regere expetis,
euerte Thebas. quis tenet mentem furor?
petendo patriam perdis? ut fiat tua,
uis esse nullam?'

67-8. *Must I ... exiles life*: *Thebais* 586-7:

'ut profugus errem semper? ut patria arcear
opemque gentis hospes externae sequar?'

footnote. The first ... the Realme: *Hercules Furens* 357:

'ars prima regni est posse te inuidiam pati.'

footnote. He cannot ... from Soueraigntie: *Thebais* 654-6:

'regnare non uult esse qui inuisus timet.
simul ista mundi conditor posuit deus
odium atque regnum.'

71-3. *No. Tis ... constrayned yeeld*: *Octavia* 504-6:

'munus deorum est ipsa quod seruit mihi
Roma et senatus quodque ab inuitis preces
humilesque uoces exprimit nostri metus.'

78-80. *Then is ... as beare*: *Thyestes* 205-7:

'maximum hoc regni bonum est,
quod facta domini cogitur populus sui
tam ferre quam laudare.'

82-6. *But who ... most repine*: *Thyestes* 209-12:

'*Sat*. at qui fauoris gloriam ueri petit,
animo magis quam uoce laudari uolet.
Atr. laus uera et humili saepe contingit uiro,
non nisi potenti falsa. quod nolunt, uelint.'

92-3. *And better ... and Liedge*: *Thebais* 617-18:

'melius exilium est tibi
quam reditus iste.'

104-6. *But cease ... nor like*: *Octavia* 600-1:

'Desiste tandem iam grauis nimium mihi
instare. liceat facere quod Seneca improbat.'

II. iii. 39. *No danger . . . and oft*: Hercules Furens 330–1:

> 'nemo se tuto diu
> periculis offerre tam crebris potest.'

42. *Whom chaunce . . . at length*: Hercules Furens 332:

quem saepe transit casus aliquando inuenit.

60–1. *if Conquerours . . . must perforce*: Hercules Furens 372–3:

> 'pacem reduci uelle uictori expedit,
> uicto necesse est.'

64. *chuse him*: let him choose.

68–71. *What Cursed . . . first bewayle*: Thebais 638–41:

> 'quale tu hoc bellum putas,
> in quo execrandum uictor admittit nefas
> si gaudet? hunc quem uincere infelix cupis
> cum uiceris, lugebis.'

81–2. *Trust me . . . and Crowne*: Thyestes 470:

> 'immane regnum est posse sine regno pati.'

87–92. *Wherefore thinke . . . assured happes*: Thebais 629–33:

> 'fortuna belli semper ancipiti in loco est.
> quodcumque Mars decernit: exaequat duos,
> licet inpares sint gladius et spes et metus,
> sors caeca uersat. praemium incertum petit,
> certum scelus.'

100–1. *And feare . . . the ground*: Medea 169:

> '*Nutr.* non metuis arma? *Med.* sint licet terra edita.'

105. *He falleth . . . his foe*: Hercules Oetaeus 353:

> 'felix iacet, quicumque, quos odit, premit.'

107. *Small manhood . . . to Chance*: Oedipus 86:

> 'haud est uirile terga fortunae dare.'

109. *I beare . . . for harmes*: Hippolytus 1003:

> 'non inparatum pectus aerumnis gero.'

110–13. *Euen that . . . on ground*: Oedipus 82–5:

> 'regium hoc ipsum reor
> aduersa capere quoque sit dubius magis
> status et cadentis imperi moles labat,
> hoc stare certo pressius fortem gradu.'

114–15. *No feare . . . their Fate*: Oedipus 1014–16:

> 'multis ipsum timuisse nocet.
> multi ad fatum uenere suum
> dum fata timent.'

117. *Yea worse . . . of warre*: Thyestes 572:

> 'peior est bello timor ipse belli.'

118. *Warre seemeth . . . not tried*: 'Dulce bellum inexpertis' is one of the *Adages* of Erasmus and the title of one of Gascoigne's longer poems (Cambridge edition, v. I, p. 141).

127–8. *All things . . . the last*: *Oedipus* 1008–9:

'omnia certo tramite uadunt:
primusque dies dedit extremum.'

The same fatalistic note had been already struck in *Gorboduc* and *Gismond of Salerne*, and is continued throughout Elizabethan tragedy.

141–2. *He either . . . that can*: *Thyestes* 203–4:

'aut perdet, aut peribit: in medio est scelus
positum occupanti.'

152–4. *like as . . . my words*: *Hippolytus* 588–90:

'ut dura cautes undique intractabilis
resistit undis et lacessentes aquas
longe remittit, uerba sic spernit mea.'

ii. iv. 80 1. *A troubled . . . body backe*: *Thyestes* 418–20:

'nunc contra in metûs
reuoluor, animus haeret ac retro cupit
corpus referre.'

iii. i. 11–14. *O false . . . it selfe*: *Hippolytus* 926–9:

'o uita fallax. obditos sensus geris
animisque pulcram turbidis faciem induis.
pudor inpudentem celat audacem quies,
pietas nefandum.'

20–1. *No place . . . at will*: *Troas* 432–3:

'prosperis rebus locus
ereptus omnis, dira qua ueniant habent.'

22. *daughter's*: Geoffrey describes Guanhamara as 'ex nobili genere Romanorum editam: quae in thalamo Cadoris ducis educata, totius insulae mulieres pulchritudine superabat' (IX. ix).

124. *Death onely . . . from anoies*: *Oedipus* 955:

'mors innocentem sola fortunae eripit.'

125–8. *Who so . . . victors pompe*: *Hercules Oetaeus* 107–10:

'quisquis sub pedibus fata rapacia
et puppem posuit fluminis ultimi,
non captiua dabit bracchia uinculis
nec pompae ueniet nobile ferculum.'

132–9. *My youth . . . fauours quaild*: *Troas* 275–8:

'fateor, aliquando inpotens
regno ac superbus altius memet tuli,
sed fregit illos spiritus haec quae dare
potuisset alii causa fortunae fauor.'

145. *T'is safest . . . you feare*: Hippolytus 730:
'tutissimum est inferre cum timeas gradum.'

148–61. Senecan hemistichomythia.

151–2. *Then may . . . couet naught*: Thyestes 442–3:
' *Tant.* pater, potes regnare.   *Thy.* cum possim mori.
Tant. summa est potestas.   *Thy.* nulla si cupias nihil.'

154–5. *But by A haire*: the sword of Damocles.

163. *Trust me . . . glorious names*: Thyestes 446:
'mihi crede, falsis magna nominibus placent.'

192. *thirteene Kings*: the names are given in Geoffrey IX. xii.

201–2. *Rome puffes . . . did fall*: Troas 273–5:
'Troia nos tumidos facit
nimium ac feroces? stamus hoc Danai loco
unde illa cecidit.'

203–16. *Thou Lucius . . . lingring Fates*: Troas 279–84:
'tu me superbum Priame tu timidum facis.
ego esse quicquam sceptra nisi uano putem
fulgore tectum nomen et falso comam
uinclo decentem? casus haec rapiet breuis
nec mille forsan ratibus aut annis decem.
non omnibus fortuna tam lenta imminet.'

III. iii. 1–65. *O Friends . . . and dare.* The hint for this impressive speech was probably given by Geoffrey: 'Arturus quoque suum exercitum in aduersa parte statuit, quem per nouem diuisit agmina pedestria cum dextro ac sinistro cornu quadrata: et unicuique praesidibus commissis, hortatur ut periuros et latrones interimant, qui monitu proditoris sui de externis regionibus in insulam aduecti, suos eis honores demere affectabant. Dicit etiam diuersos diuersorum regnorum Barbaros imbelles atque belli usus ignaros esse, et nullatenus ipsis uirtuosis uiris et pluribus debellationibus usis resistere posse, si audacter inuadere et uiriliter decertare affectarent' (XI. ii).

11–12. The story of *Hengistus* and *Horsus* is given in Geoffrey VI. x–xv.

47–8. *Diana . . . Brute*: Brutus, having landed on the island of Leogecia, found there a deserted city, in which there was a temple of Diana. The image of the goddess, addressed by Brutus, gave the following oracular response (Geoffrey I. xi):
'Brute, sub occasu solis trans Gallica regna,
    insula in Oceano est undique clausa mari:
insula in Oceano est habitata Gygantibus olim,
    nunc deserta quidem: gentibus apta tuis.
hanc pete; namque tibi sedes erit illa perennis:
    hic fiet natis altera Troia tuis:
hic de prole tua reges nascentur: et ipsis
    totius terrae subditus orbis erit.'

100. *brother Mordred*: Malory I. xix: 'kynge Arthur rode vnto Carlyon / And thyder cam to hym kyng Lots wyf of Orkeney in maner of a message / but she was sente thyder to aspye the Courte of kynge Arthur / and she cam rychely bisene with her four sones / gawayn Gaherys / Agrauaynes / and Gareth...for she was a possynge fayr lady / wherfore / the kynge cast grete loue vnto her / and desyred to lye by her / so they were agreed / and he begate vpon her Mordred / and she was his syster on the moder syde Igrayne.'

In Geoffrey, Modred is the son of Lot, and Arthur's nephew ; ' Lot autem, qui tempore Aurelii Ambrosii sororem ipsius duxerat : ex qua Walgannum et Modedrium genuerat ' (IX. ix).

III. iv. 6. *A hopelesse . . . happy Fate* : *Troas* 434 :

'miserrimum est timere cum speres nihil.'

14. *All truth . . . be broke* : *Thyestes* 47–8 :

'fratris et fas et fides
iusque omne pereat.'

20–2. *For were . . . as bad* : *Thebais* 367–9 :

'hoc leue est quod sum nocens :
feci nocentes. hoc quoque etiamnunc leue est,
peperi nocentes.'

III. Ch. 33–4. *Care vpon . . . tossed mindes* : *Agamemnon* 62 3 :

'alia ex aliis cura fatigat
uexatque animos noua tempestas.'

35–8. *Who striues . . . vnto himselfe* : *Thyestes* 391–2, 401–3 :

'stet quicumque uolet potens
aulae culmine lubrico :
. . . . . .
illi mors grauis incubat,
qui notus nimis omnibus,
ignotus moritur sibi.'

41–5. *My slender . . . the Cloudes* : *Hercules Oetaeus* 698–703 :

'stringat tenuis litora puppis
nec magna meos aura phaselos
iubeat medium scindere pontum.
transit tutos fortuna sinus,
medioque rates quaerit in alto
quarum feriunt suppara nubes.'

59–60. *With endlesse . . . doe dwell* : *Hercules Furens* 163–4 :

'turbine magno spes sollicitae
urbibus errant trepidique metus.'

IV. D.S. 3–5. *an other place . . . a third place* : there are evidently three entrances. The second dumbe shewe also appears to require three entrances, the first ' out of Mordred's house ', the second ' out of the house appointed for Arthur ', and the third for ' a man bareheaded '.

IV. i. 4–5. *who forbiddeth . . . such offence*: *Troas* 300:
'qui non uetat peccare, cum possit, iubet.'

IV. ii. 8. *Declare . . . our harmes*: *Troas* 1076–7:
'prosequere: gaudet aerumnas meus dolor
tractare totas.'

14. *Small griefes . . . astonisht stand*: *Hippolytus* 615:
'curae leues loquuntur, ingentes stupent.'

Cf. *Macbeth* IV. iii:
'Give sorrow words: the grief that does not speak
Whispers the o'erfraught heart, and bids it break.'

15–18. *What greater . . . one degree*: *Thyestes* 745–7:
'*Chor.* an ultra maius aut atrocius
natura recipit? *Nunt.* sceleris hunc finem putas?
gradus est.'

202–4. *At length . . . for him*: Grumbine suggests that Hughes
had in mind the following lines of the *Aeneid* (I. 474–6):
'parte alia fugiens amissis Troilus armis,
infelix puer atque impar congressus Achilli,
fertur equis.'

217–23. *So saying . . . his Sire*: these particulars of the death
of father and son are taken from Malory: 'Thenne the kyng gate hys
spere in bothe his handes & ranne toward syr Mordred cryeng
tratour now is thy deth day come / And whan syr Mordred herde
syr Arthur he ranne vntyl hym with his swerde drawen in his hande
And there kyng Arthur smote syr mordred vnder the shelde wyth
a foyne of his spere thorughoute the body more than a fadom / And
whan syr Mordred felte that he had hys dethes wounde / He thryst
hym self wyth the myght that he had vp to the bur of kynge Arthurs
spere / And right so he smote his fader Arthur wyth his swerde
holden in bothe his handes on the syde of the heed that the swerde
persyd the helmet and the brayne panne / and therwythall syr
Mordred fyl starke deed to the erthe / And the nobyl Arthur fyl in
a swoune to the erthe' (XXI. iv).

Geoffrey's account of the final battle is as follows:
'Postquam autem multum diei in hunc modum duxerunt, irruit
tandem Arturus cum agmine uno, quo sex milia sexcentos et sexaginta
sex posuerat, in turmam illam ubi Modredum sciebat esse, et uiam
gladiis aperiendo, eam penetrauit, atque tristissimam caedem inges-
sit. Concidit namque proditor ille nefandus, et multa milia cum eo.
Nec tamen ob casum eius diffugiunt caeteri: sed ex omni campo
confluentes, quantum audaciae dabatur, resistere conantur. Com-
mittitur ergo dirissima pugna inter eos, qua omnes fere duces qui
in ambabus partibus affuerant, cum suis cateruis corruerunt. Corruerunt etenim in parte Modredi: Cheldricus, Elafius, Egbrictus,
Bunignus, Saxones: Gillapatriae, Gillamor, Gislafel, Gillarium, Hy-

bernenses. Scoti etiam et Picti cum omnibus fere quibus dominabantur. In parte autem Arturi Olbrictus rex Norwegiae, Aschillius rex
Daciae, Cador Limenic, Cassibellanus, cum multis milibus suorum
tam Britonum quam caeterarum gentium quas secum adduxerat. Sed
et inclytus ille Arturus rex letaliter uulneratus est, qui illinc ad sananda uulnera sua in insulam Auallonis aduectus, cognato suo Constantino, filio Cadoris ducis Cornubiae, diadema Britanniae concessit, anno ab incarnatione dominica quingentesimo quadragesimo
secundo ' (XI. ii).

IV. iii. 36–9. *He was . . . state support* : *Troas* 128–31 :

> ' columen patriae mora fatorum
> tu praesidium Phrygibus fessis
> tu murus eras umerisque tuis
> stetit illa decem fulta per annos.'

V. D.S. 25. *Tibi morimur* : we die for thee.

34. *Qua vici, perdidi* : as I won, I lost.

44. *Qua foui, perii* : as I cherished, I perished.

V. i. 32. *six score thousand* : in Geoffrey, ' sexies uiginti milia
(IX. xix).

74–5. *Where each . . . their Fates* : *Troas* 1071 :

> ' sua quemque tantum, me omnium clades premit.'

110–14. *The hoat . . . wretch inflamde* : *Medea* 602–5 :

> ' ausus aeternos agitare currus
> immemor metae iuuenis paternae
> quos polo sparsit furiosus ignes
> ipse recepit.'

127. *the first triumphant Troy* : Brutus, after his arrival in
Britain, ' condidit itaque ciuitatem ibidem, eamque Troiam nouam
uocauit ' (Geoffrey I. xvii). Cf. II. i. 1–2 and III. iii. 47–51 of this
play.

131. *We could . . . we ioynde* : *Hippolytus* 1192–3 :

> ' non licuit animos iungere, at certe licet
> iunxisse fata.'

149–50: *They lou'd . . . to dye* : *Thyestes* 886–7 :

> ' uitae est auidus quisquis non uult
> mundo secum pereunte mori.'

188–9. *Of all . . . hapie once* ; Boethius, *Consolatio* II, Prose iv :
' Nam in omni aduersitate fortunae infelicissimum genus est infortunii, fuisse felicem.' Translated by Chaucer ; ' For in alle adversitee of fortune, the most unsely kinde of contrarious fortune is to
han ben weleful.' Cf. *Troilus and Criseyde* III, st. 233 ; *Inferno* v.
121–3 ; *Locksley Hall* 76.

V. ii. 7–8. *Where thou . . . their stocke* : Uther pursued Gorlois
into Cornwall, where the latter was slain in battle (Geoffrey VIII.
xix–xx).

14–29. *Let Virgo . . . world affordes* : the loyal compliment to
the Queen usual on these occasions. Cf. I. i. 54–61 and note thereon.

25. *Virgo come and Saturnes raigne* : Vergil, *Eclogue* IV. 6 :
'iam redit et Virgo, redeunt Saturnia regna.'

Ep. 38-9. *Who ere . . . vnto himselfe*: *Thyestes* 619-20 :
' nemo tam diuos habuit fauentes,
crastinum ut possit sibi polliceri.'

40-1. *Him, whom . . . the ground*: *Thyestes* 613-14 :
' quem dies uidit ueniens superbum,
hunc dies uidit fugiens iacentem.'

53-4. *Sat cytò, si sat benè* : this part of Hughes's motto is quoted
by St. Jerome as a saying of M. Porcius Cato's. Epist. LXVI :
' Scitum est illud Catonis, *sat cito, si sat bene.*' See Heinrich
Jordan's edition of Cato, *Dicta memorabilia* 80. The whole motto
seems to mean : Quickly enough, if well enough ; in any case, what
my own hope does not afford, your approval does.

I. i. (Fulbecke) 20. *benthe* is probably a misprint for *benche*,
though Grumbine suggests a derivation from Gk. βένθος : ' the depth
of the sea, hence, perhaps, Pluto's pit.'

44. *Cambala* : Geoffrey XI. ii : ' Arturus autem interna anxietate
cruciatus, quoniam totiens euasisset confestim prosecutus est eum
[Modredum] in praedictam patriam usque ad flumen Cambula, ubi
ille aduentum eius expectabat.'

52. *Celenoes* : Celeno was one of the Harpies. Grumbine
compares *Aeneid* III. 209-13 :

' seruatum ex undis Strophadum me littora primum
accipiunt : Strophades Graio stant nomine dictae,
insulae Ionio in magno, quas dira Celaeno
Harpyiaeque colunt aliae, Phineia postquam
clausa domus, mensasque metu liquere priores.'

62. *Cerastæ* : a genus of venomous serpents found in Africa and
some parts of Asia, having a projecting scale or ' horn ' above each
eye ; the horned viper. Early and poetic uses are drawn vaguely
from Pliny and other ancient writers, who probably meant a species
of the same genus.—N. E. D.

v. ii. (Fulbecke) 23-31. *For Brytaine . . . endlesse praise* : The
play fitly ends with Fulbecke's adulation of the Queen, carried to its
customary point of extravagance. The ' Angels land ' is, of course,
an allusion to the famous quip of Pope Gregory in the slave market
at Rome : ' Rursum interrogauit quod esset uocabulum gentis illius.
Mercator respondit : Angli uocantur. At ille : Bene, inquit, Angli,
quasi angeli, quia et angelicos uultus habent ' (*S. Gregorii Magni
Vita Auctore Joanne Diacono* I. xxi).

GLOSSARY.

G. = *Gorboduc*.
J. = *Jocasta*.
S. = *Gismond of Salerne*.
A. = *The Misfortunes of Arthur*.

Arg. = Argument.
Ch. = Chorus.
D.S. = Dumb Show.
Ep. = Epilogue.
Pr. = Prologue.

abusde, deceived. *G.* V. ii. 1.

abye, pay for. *S.* IV. ii. 94, *et passim*.

accompt, recount. *J.* V. ii. 8.

accursing, cursing. *J.* I. i. 150.

acquiet, alleviate. *J.* V. i. 14, *where the Italian text has* acqueti

acquite, fulfil. *J.* III. i. 22. Relieve. *J.* II. ii. 7.

adrad, terrified. *G.* V. i. 112.

aduertise, inform. *J.* III. i. 115.

affectes, affections. *J.* I. Ch. 11. Passions. *J.* II. i. 270.

affray, terrify. *J.* II. ii. 61.

allarme! to arms! *J.* V. ii. 184.

allowe, approve. *G.* I. ii. 69, *et passim*.

all to, altogether, completely, entirely. *G. The P. to the Reader* 13.

amased, dismayed. *J.* IV. i. 75; *S.* Arg. 24.

ameruailed, astonished. *S.* V. i. 115.

anenst, along. *A.* III. Ch. 41.

anoye, distress, torment. *S. An other &c.* 3, *et passim*.

apay, appease, satisfy. *J.* II. i. 450; *S.* V. i. 94.

astonnied, astonished. *S.* V. i. 123.

atached, arrested. *S.* Arg. 29.

auaile, profit, advantage. *J.* I. i. 192.

auowe, vow. *G.* II. i. 112, *et passim*. Prove. *A.* Pr. 8.

ayenst, against. *S.* I. ii. 22.

bandurion, bandores. The bandore (modern corruption *banjo*) was a musical instrument resembling a guitar or lute, with three, four, or six wire strings, used as a bass to the cittern. *J.* I. D.S. 3.

battailes, battalions. *J.* I. ii. 148. Cf. *Henry V*, IV. iii. 69.

bayne, bathe. *S.* V. iv. 28.

baynes, baths. *J.* V. i. 18.

beates, abates, impairs. *J.* II. i. 408.

become, go, gone. *J.* III. ii. 100; IV. i. Ch. 13.

behest, promise, duty. *S.* II Ch 23.

behight, promise. *G.* I. ii. 97, *et passim*. Command. *S.* V. i. 75.

behofe, advantage. *G.* I. ii. 153, *et passim*.

behouefull, advantageous. *G.* I. ii. 141.

belike, probably. *A.* III. i. 5.

berayed, besmirched. *G. The P. to the Reader* 13.

bereft, bereued, taken away. *G.* II. i. 172, *et passim*.

beseeme, become. *J.* II. i. 349, 609.

bestad, beset. *J.* II. i. 170; II. ii. 76.

betroutht, pledged. *J.* IV. i. 121.

bewray, betray, reveal. *G.* IV. ii. 115, *et passim*.

blased, blazoned. *J.* II. i. 492.

boad, endured. *A.* III. iii. 6.

bolne, swollen. *J.* IV. ii. 65.

bootes, benefits. *A.* II. iii. 59, *et passim*.

bootelesse, without remedy. *G.* II. ii. 65, *et passim*.

braide, sudden movement, start. *G.* IV. ii. 222.

broach, shed. *A.* IV. ii. 170.
bronde, brand, sword. *J.* II. i. 10.
brooke, endure. *A.* II. iii. 108, 111.
brust, burst. *J.* V. ii. 14.
brute, bruit, rumour. *J.* I. ii. 176,
et passim.
bye, pay for. *G.* IV. i. 30.

cammassado, a night attack. See
note on *J.* II. ii. 56.
cankred, venomous, malicious. *J.*
V. ii. 67, 88.
caitife, caytif, cowardly, wretched
(L. *captiuus*). *G.* IV. i. 35; *J.* V.
v. 200; *S.* IV. ii. 27.
carefull, full of care; anxious. *G.*
I. i. 3, *et passim.*
carke, load, burden. *A.* III. Ch. 59.
Cassiopæa, see note on *A.* I. i. 54.
censure, judgement. *A.* III. iii. 115.
certes, assuredly. *S.* V. ii. 13.
cesse, cease. *S.* IV. iv. 15.
chere, countenance. *G.* IV. ii. 165,
et passim.
chiualrie, cavalry. *J.* IV. i. 81,
where the Italian text reads la
cavalleria.
cleane, completely. *J.* II. i. 63, *et
passim.*
clepe, call. *G.* IV. ii. 61.
cliftes, cliffs. *A.* II. Ch. 9.
clips, eclipse. *A.* IV. ii. 227.
cliue, cliff. *S.* IV. Ch. 33.
coate, cot, humble dwelling. *S.* I.
Ch. 45.
commoditie, advantage. *J.* II. i.
257, *et passim.*
companie, comrades. *J.* IV. D.S. 15.
conceit, what is conceived in the
mind. *J.* II. i. 358; *A.* II. iii. 129.
conge, leave. *J.* III. ii. 113.
consent, common agreement. *G.* V.
ii. 255, 256.
contentation, contentment. *J.* II. i.
447.
contentations, causes of content.
J. II. i. 95.
coouie, covey. *A. One other speeche
&c.* 15.
coroziue, destroyer. *J.* II. i. 402.
cortine, curtain. *S.* Arg. 19, *et
passim.*

couer, conceal. *J.* II. i. 179, 358.
crosse, adverse. *A.* III. Ch. 12.
culme, top. *A.* III. Ch. 36.
cyndring, reducing to ashes. *J.* II.
i. 387.
cythren, citterns—instruments similar to guitars, but played with a
plectrum or quill. *J.* I. D.S. 2.

Dan, dominus, lord. *J.* IV. Ch. 20.
darke, darken. *G.* III. i. 138.
danger, endanger. *A.* I. iv. 99.
daunting, stunning. *J.* V. ii. 86.
debowelled, disembowelled. *S.*
Arg. 30; V. i. 210.
decerne, decide, decree. *A.* II. ii.
53.
defend, ward off. *G.* II. i. 197.
degree, rank. *S.* Ep. 3.
denouncing, proclaiming. *A.* I.
Arg. 4.
deprauing, dispraising. *A.* Pr. 67.
despoyle, see *dispoyle.*
determe, determine. *S.* V. i. 221;
V. ii. 45.
deuote, vowed, devoted. *A.* Pr. 74.
deuoyer, sense of duty. *A.* Pr. 124.
disclosed, opened. *S.* III. iii. 47.
disease, annoy, displease. *J.* II. i.
142.
dishonested, dishonoured. *G. The
P. to the Reader* 14.
dispar, unlike. *A.* IV. ii. 197.
disporte, recreation, amusement.
S. Arg. 17; IV. ii. 49.
dispoyle, uncover. *G.* IV. ii. 216.
Deprive. *A.* I. i. 7. Deprive of
life. *J.* IV. ii. 42; *A.* III. i. 89.
distaine, stain, pollute. *G.* V. ii. 12,
et passim.
distraine, distress. *S.* II. i. 55;
V. i. 6.
divine, divining. *J. The names of
the Interloquutors* 10. Diviner.
J. I. i. 39, *et passim.*
dolour, sorrow. *J.* IV. i. 232, *et
passim.*
doluen, delved, digged. *S.* IV. ii.
150.
drere, misfortune, sorrow. *S.* I. iii.
25, *et passim.*
drift, purpose. *A.* I. Ch. i, *et passim.*
dround, drown. *A.* I. iii. 16.

dure, endure. *A.* I. iv. 127.

earnefull, yearning, grievous. *A.* IV. ii. 194.

efts, again. *A.* III. iii. 105, *et passim.*

eftsoones, forthwith. *J.* I. ii. 59; *A.* II. Ch. 22. Again. *J.* III. ii. 109.

egall, equal. *G.* I. ii. 42, *et passim.*

egalnesse, equality. *G.* I. ii. 181, 186.

eke, also. *G.* I. i. 53, *et passim.*

elde, old age. *J.* III. i. 18.

ells, else. *S.* IV. Ch. 29.

embowed, arched. *J.* I. i. 230.

emplied, employed. *S.* II. ii. 1.

emprise, enterprise. *J.* II. ii. 72.

engoard, pierced. *A.* II. i. 44; IV. ii. 220.

enpalde, surrounded. *J.* I. ii. 158.

entend, give attention. *S.* III. ii. 41.

entreat, treat. *S. An other &c.* 15.

erst, first, before. *G.* I. ii. 89, *et passim.*

exul, exile. *J.* I. i. 165.

fact, act, deed. *G.* Arg. 5, *et passim.*

faile, deceive (L. *fallere*). *G.* II. i. 116.

fall, happen. *J.* II. i. 466, *et passim.* Belong. *S.* II. ii. 28.

feere, see *pheere.*

fell, fierce. *A.* I. ii. 93, *et passim.*

fet, fetched. *G.* IV. ii. 223.

filde, defiled. *A.* III. i. 113.

fine, end. *G.* V. ii. 22.

flittering, fluttering. *A.* I. ii. 5.

flowr, flourish. *J.* IV. i. 13, *et passim.*

foile, see *foyle.*

fonde, foolish. *G.* I. i. 50, *et passim.*

force, struggle, resist. *S.* II. i. 41.

fordoe, prevent. *J.* V. v. 114.

foredone, destroyed. *S.* I. ii. 12, *footnote.* Anticipated. *S.* V. ii. 33.

foredrad, dreaded beforehand. *J.* Arg. 6.

foreiudge, prejudice. *A.* II. iii. 114.

foresott, predestined. *S.* I. iii. 20, 21; *A.* II. iii. 128.

foreweening, realizing beforehand. *A.* III. i. 134.

forlore, utterly destroy. *S.* V. i. 59.

forwast, entirely waste. *J.* II. i. 517, *et passim.*

forworne, worn out. *J.* IV. i. 215.

foulter, falter. *A.* III. Ch. 49; IV. Ch. 37.

foyle, defeat. *J.* I. Ch. 21, *et passim.*

fraight, fraught. *J.* I. i. 95.

fraught, laden, filled. *J.* IV. i. 65. Burden. *S.* I. ii. 23.

frounst, wrinkled; with knit brows or pursed lips. *A.* IV. ii. 129.

fumbling, faltering. *J.* V. ii. 154.

furniture, provision. *G. The P. to the Reader* 1.

fyle, make smooth. *J.* II. i. 247.

gashfull, ghastly. *S.* IV. ii. 110.

gaulde, gall, torment. *J.* III. Ch. 4.

goared, pierced. *A.* IV. iii. 25.

gorget, a piece of armour for the throat. *J.* II. D.S. 17.

graffe, engraft, create. *J.* IV. Ch. 37.

graft, grafted. *G.* I. ii. 219.

gramercy, thanks. *J.* II. i. 24, *et passim.*

graued, buried. *G.* IV. i. 20; *S.* V. iii. 39.

gree, agree. *G.* I. ii. 167, *et passim.*

gree, pleasure. *J.* III. i. 101.

griesly, grisly, fearful, terrible. *J.* I. i. 139, *et passim.*

gripe, vulture. *G.* II. i. 18; *S.* IV. i. 11. The allusion in the former case is to Prometheus, in the latter to Tytius.

grudge, murmur. *A.* II. ii. 65, *et passim.*

gyves, shackles, especially for the legs. *S.* V. i. 79.

hap, happen. *J.* II. ii. 131, *et passim.*

hap, happe, fortune, chance. *J.* I. ii. 58, *et passim.*

harborrow, harbrough, refuge. *J.* II. i. 200; V. v. 149; *S.* V. ii. 25.

hargabusiers, arquebusiers. *G.* V. D.S. 2.

hateful, full of hatred. *G.* III. i. 167; IV. i. 27; *S.* V. i. 205.

headie, headstrong. *J.* II. Ch. 3; V. v. 14.

hearce, *see* herse.

hearclothes, haircloth. *J.* II. D.S. 3.

hearesaie, hearsay, report. *A.* III. i. 166.

heaue, uplift. *A.* III. i. 203; Ep. 32.

hent, taken. *J.* v. ii. 26.

herse, coffin. *S.* v. ii. 14; *A.* v. i. 175.

hest, command. *G.* III. i. 51, *et passim.*

hight, was called. *J.* IV. Ch. 17.

hoyse, hoist, uplift. *J.* v. Ch. 6; *A.* v. i. 12.

hugie, huge. *G.* IV. i. 9; v. i. 67; v. ii. 61, 109. Apparently a characteristic word with Sackville, who uses it also in the *Induction* to the *Mirror for Magistrates. A.* II. i. 58.

iarres, differs. *A.* I. iv. 101.

iarres, quarrels. *A.* III. iii. 37.

iarring, quarrelsome. *J.* I. ii. 58.

ielous, fearful, suspicious. *G.* I. i. 39; *J.* IV. i. 106; *S.* IV. Ch. 22.

ielousie, suspicion. *J.* I. ii. 117, 121.

imparle, treat. *A.* II. Arg. 8; II. iii. 4.

impe, offspring, child. *J.* I. i. 54, *et passim.*

impeach, hinder, break in upon. *A.* III. iii. 52.

inferre, bring on. *A.* IV. ii. 227; v. i. 184.

in post, hastily. *G.* v. i. 158.

instant, of the present day. *A.* Pr. 71.

inuade, attack. *G.* II. i. 159.

ioy, enjoy. *A.* I. ii. 66.

ioyning, adjoining. *J.* IV. i. 129.

irked, wearied. *J.* II. i. 200.

kernes, Irish foot-soldiers. *A.* IV. iii. 13.

kinde, nature. *G.* I. i. 11, *et passim.*

lefull, lawful. *S.* IV. iii. 21.

length, lengthen. *G.* I. ii. 134.

lese, lose. *J.* II. i. 26, *et passim.*

lest, least. *A.* II. iii. 74.

let, hinder. *S.* IV. ii. 52, *et passim.*

leuer, dearer, preferable. *S.* IV. iv. 51.

lief, leaf. *S.* I. ii. 12 *foot-note.*

like, please. *G.* v. i. 123, *et passim.*

list, like, please. *G.* III. i. 128, *et passim.*

lot, allot. *G.* I. ii. 151, *et passim.*

lowre, look black and threatening. *A.* III. i. 86.

lumpishe, unwieldy, dull. *J.* III. ii. 43.

lurke, lie hid. *A.* I. i. 37, *et passim.*

lustlesse, joyless, feeble. *J.* II. i. 65.

makelesse, without mate. *S.* II. i. 37.

manaceth, menaces, threatens. *A.* I. Arg. 6.

marches, borders. *G.* I. ii. 345.

masking, dancing with gestures similar to those of masquers. *A.* I. D.S. 7.

maskt, disguised itself. *A.* III. Ch. 14.

meanelesse, unmeasured, limitless. *A.* I. ii. 68, *et passim.*

message, messenger. *A.* III. ii. 2.

mindes, intends. *G.* v. ii. 79.

misdeme, fear, suspect. *G.* I. i. 39, *et passim.*

moe, more. *G.* I. ii. 167, *et passim.*

molt, melted. *S.* v. i. 126.

moote, a discussion of a hypothetical case by students at the Inns of Court for the sake of practice; now in use only at Gray's Inn. *A.* Pr. 26, 83.

murreine, murrain, cattle-disease. *A.* I. Ch. 21.

mustie, damp, gloomy. *J.* II. i. 569.

mutin, mutinous. *A.* Pr. 90.

ne, not. *G.* I. ii. 321, *et passim.*

nill, will not. *J.* II. ii. 52.

notes, denotes. *A.* III. i. 61.

nouist, novice. *A.* III. iii. 65.

noysome, harmful. *G.* II. Ch. 15.

olephant, elephant. *A.* v. D.S. 13.

oppress, overpower (L. *opprimere*). *G.* II. ii. 53, *et passim.*

ouerpining, distressing. *J.* v. i. 17.

ouerthwart, across. *A.* v. D.S. 2.

pagions, pageants. *A.* IV. ii. 72.

paire, impair. *S.* I. iii. 52.

paisse, balancing, leverage. *J.* IV. i. 46.

paled, pallid. *J.* V. v. 167.

parle, parley. *J.* II. D.S. 19. Cf. *Hamlet* I. i. 62.

part, depart. *J.* II. i. 612, *et passim.*

pawnes, pledges. *J.* II. i. 453.

peaze, appease. *G.* III. i. 103, *et passim.*

percase, perchance. *J.* III. i. 145, *et passim.*

perusing, examining. *J.* III. D.S. 11.

pheere, companion, consort. *J.* I. i. 75, *et passim.*

plage, plague. *G. The P. to the Reader* 8, *et passim.*

plague, torment. *A.* II. ii. 67, *et passim.*

plaine, complain, lament. *S.* III. ii. 40, *et passim.*

plat, flat. *S.* II. iii. 23.

plights, promises. *A.* III. Ch. 32.

politiquely, craftily. *J.* IV. D.S. 13.

posting, hastening. *J.* Ep. 30.

practicke, treacherous. *A.* Pr. 90.

practise, plot. *G.* II. i. 106, *et passim.*

preasse, company. *S.* III. ii. 37.

prefe, proof. *S.* III. iii. 28 ; IV. iv. 47.

presently, at once. *C.* V. i. 122, *et passim.*

presse, oppress. *A.* I. ii. 83, 84 ; II. ii. 30.

prest, ready. *J.* V. v. 183, *et passim.*

pretended, intended, offered. *G.* III. i. 38.

prickt, decorated. *J.* II. i. 302.

princocke, upstart, coxcomb. *A.* III. iii. 20, 23.

priuie, acquainted, informed. *G. The P. to the Reader* 10.

proper, peculiar, belonging exclusively to. *J.* II. i. 452.

protract, delay. *G.* IV. ii. 130.

proue, try. *S.* II. i. 81 ; V. ii. 52.

purchase, obtain. *J.* III. ii. 9 ; IV. ii. 8.

pyne, grieve, torment. *G.* IV. i. 17, *et passim.*

purueyed, provided, predestined. *J.* V. ii. 27.

pyramis, pyramid. *A.* V. D.S. 20.

quent, strange, far-fetched. *J.* II. i. 257.

quailed, languished. *S.* II. Ch. 6.

quit, relieve, release. *J.* IV. i. 15.

race, erase. *A. One other speeche &c.* 12.

rampiers, ramparts. *A.* III. iii. 86.

randon, rashness. *G.* II. i. 206 ; II. Ch. 2.

rased, utterly destroyed. *G.* I. ii. 190.

raught, reached. *S.* III. iii. 78. Gave. *A.* III. i. 135.

reacquite, reward. *S. An other &c.* 4, *et passim.*

recked, heeded, cared. *G.* I. ii. 321.

recklesse, free from care. *S.* I. iii. 30.

record, remember, recall (L. *recordari*). *G.* III. Ch. 9, *et passim.*

recourse, return. *S.* II. i. 12.

recure, remedy. *S. An other &c.* 4, *et passim.*

recurelesse, without remedy, mortal. *J.* I. i. 3 ; V. iv. 29 ; *S.* IV. i. 40.

rede, saying, counsel. *G.* II. Ch. 13, *et passim.*

rede, say. *A.* III. iii. 85.

reduce, bring back. *A.* V. ii. 23.

reede, guess. *A.* III. ii. 2.

reignes, reins and realms (play upon double sense). *G.* I. ii. 326.

reknowledge, recognize, acknowledge. *S.* IV. ii. 131.

religion, religious orders. *A.* Arg. 26.

remorse, pity. *A.* III. i. 211.

renome, renown. *S.* I. i. 54, *et passim.*

renomed, **renowmed**, renowned. *S.* IV. iii. 58, *et passim.*

repine, begrudge. *A.* II. ii. 86.

require, ask. *S.* IV. iv. 72, *et passim.*

rest, reliance. *A.* II. iii. 45.

resteth, remains for. *S.* V. iv. 2.

retirelesse, not returning. *A.* I. ii. 4

reue, take away from, deprive of *G.* II. i. 3, *et passim.*

reuolue, meditate upon, turn over in the mind. *A*. Pr. 76.

ridde, got rid of. *J*. II. ii. 1.

right, straight. *A*. III. i. 73.

rode, roadstead, harbour. *A*. v. i. 144.

rotte, a disease affecting sheep. *A*. I. Ch. 21.

ruthe, pity. *G*. IV. i. 13, *et passim*.

sagges, falls, gives way. *A*. II. iii. 112.

scant, hardly. *G*. *The P. to the Reader* 16, *et passim*.

scantly, hardly. *A*. I. iv. 105.

scout, outlook. *J*. II. i. 8.

seld, sield, sielde, seldom. *S*. v. i. 133, *et passim*.

selder, seldomer. *S*. II. iii. 20.

selfe, same. *G*. I. ii. 342, *et passim*.

set, esteem. *J*. II. i. 104.

sharpe, sharpen. *G*. I. ii. 179.

shene, bright. *S*. III. Ch. 10.

shrine, enshrine. *S*. v. iii. 40.

sield, see *seld*.

sillie, simple. *G*. IV. ii. 239, *et passim*.

sithe, sithens, since. *G*. I. ii. 338, *et passim*.

sittes, becomes. *S*. Ep. 3.

skapes, escapes. *A*. III. i. 140.

skilful, reasonable, rational. *S*. II. i. 66.

skilesse, unreasoning. *G*. II. Ch. 5; v. i. 104.

skils, kinds of knowledge. *A*. Pr. 14.

skride, descried. *J*. IV. ii. 7.

slack, delay. *S*. v. i. 117, 142.

slake, slacken. *A*. I. ii. 101.

snudge, one who lies snug. *A*. III. Ch. 53.

sole, lonely. *S*. II. i. 30, 52, 65.

sooth'd, established, confirmed. *A*. Pr. 79.

sort, company. *G*. v. ii. 26, 34, 41.

sorted, allotted. *G*. IV. ii. 143.

sowsse, flood. *J*. v. iii. 20.

spede, success. *S*. II. iii. 7.

speed, succeed. *A*. II. iii. 123.

spill, destroy. *S*. II. iii. 27.

spited, cherished spite. *S*. I. iii. 16.

splayde, displayed. *J*. II. i. 386.

spoile, deprive. *G*. I. i. 25; *A*. I. ii. 89. Destroy. *A*. I. iii. 30, *et passim*.

spolia, spoils of war. *A*. v. D.S. 13.

spred, noised abroad. *J*. I. i. 12.

sprent, scattered. *S*. v. i. 187.

stale, a laughing-stock. *A*. I. ii. 3.

startling, starting, startled. *J*. v. ii. 104.

stay, support. *G*. I. ii. 100, *et passim*. Restraint. *G*. I. ii. 117, *et passim*.

stayde, steadfast, assured. *J*. II. i. 459.

stayednesse, restraint, firmness. *G*. I. ii. 132.

stead, steed. *A*. II. i. 29.

stearne, see *sterne*.

steede, stead, place. *A*. Pr. 21, *et passim*.

stent, see *stint*.

stere, move. *S*. II. iii. 24.

sterne, rudder. *G*. v. ii. 85; *A*. II. ii. 101.

sterue, die. *S*. IV. Ch. 15.

stifeleth, is brought to nothing. *A*. I. i. 14.

still-pipes, pipes for playing soft music. *J*. v. D.S. 1.

stint, limit. *S*. I. iii. 18; *A*. I. ii. 75.

stint, make cease. *J*. I. i. 200, *et passim*. Cease. *S*. II. ii. 35; *A*. I. Ch. 23.

stocke, progeny, race. *A*. I. i. 14, *et passim*.

stoupen, stoop. *S*. I. Ch. 52.

streight, passage. *S*. v. i. 64.

streights, limits. *A*. Pr. 128.

sturres, commotions, disturbances. *J*. Ep. 21.

succede, follow, happen. *G*. I. i. 38; I. ii. 31. Succeed to. *G*. III. i. 73.

successe, consequence. *G*. I. i. 55, *et passim*.

sugred, sweet. *J*. IV. Ch. 10.

supernall, supernatural. *J*. I. i. 38.

surcease, cease. *J*. IV. i. 5; *A*. IV. Ch. 23.

sure, surely. *A*. II. iv. 36.

surpresse, suppress. *J*. Ep. 22.

suspect, suspicion. *J*. II. i. 6, *et passim*.

swaruynge, swerving. This old

pronunciation of 'er' is retained in 'clerk' and some names. *G.* I. ii. 20.

target, shield. *J.* II. D.S. 16.
teinte, touch. *J.* V. ii. 76.
tender, yielding. *G.* II. i. 138.
tene, sorrow. *S.* IV. iii. 31.
therwhile, in the meantime. *J.* I. ii. 124.
tho, then. *A.* I. ii. 56.
thoughtfull, anxious. *G.* IV. ii. 259.
throwes, throes. *G.* IV. i. 68.
tickle, inconstant, uncertain. *A.* V. i. 198; Ep. 1.
tofore, before. *S. A sonet &c.* 1.
touse, tear to pieces. *A.* IV. Ch. 5.
trade, occupation. *G.* I. ii. 55.
trauaile, labour. *G.* I. i. 2, *et passim.*
trophea, arms won from a defeated enemy. *A.* V. D.S. 5.
trothlesse, treacherous. *J.* I. ii. 91.
trustlosse, not to be trusted. *J.* II. i. 98, *et passim.*
tuition, protection. *A.* Arg. 16.
twinke, moment. *G.* IV. ii. 202.

vaile, veil. *A.* III. Ch. 14.
vallure, valour. *A.* II. iii. 26.
vauntage, advantage. *G.* II. i. 157, *et passim.*
vaut, vault. *S.* Arg. 12, *et passim.*
vent, smell, snuff up (hunting term). *A.* III. Ch. 8.
ver, spring. *J.* IV. Ch. 22.
violles, ancient musical instruments of much the same form as violins. *J.* I. D.S. 2.
vnhap, *S.* Arg. 28, *et passim.*
vnhealme, remove the helmet from. *A.* V. i. 94.
vnkindly, unnatural. *G.* I. ii. 183, *et passim.*
vnweldy, feeble. *S.* II. ii. 56.
   vnwildie of herselfe, lacking self-control. *A.* I. ii. 13.

vnweting, without knowing. *S.* IV. ii. 64.
venge, revenge. *A.* I. ii. 33.
vouch, call. *S.* I. i. 46.
vre, use, practice. *G.* I. ii. 132, *et passim.*

wade, go. *G.* V. i. 44; *S.* I. Ch. 57; II. ii. 35.
wakefull, watchfull. *G.* I. ii. 39.
waltering, weltering. *A.* II. iii. 153; III. Ch. 42.
want, lack. *G.* V. ii. 198, *et passim.*
wealfull, happy. *S. An other &c.* 7; IV. ii. 57.
weedes, garments. *J.* V. v. 243.
weenes, thinks. *J.* I. i. 239, *et passim.*
well, in elegant language. *A.* Pr. 67.
wemlesse, spotless. *S.* IV. iii. 10.
werry, weary. *S.* Arg. 7.
wete, know. *S.* Ep. 14.
whelme, overwhelm. *J.* II. i. 584.
whilome, formerly. *G.* I. ii. 164, *et passim.*
wight, man. *G.* I. i. 41, *et passim.*
wood, mad. *A.* IV. Ch. 7.
woontlesse, unaccustomed. *A.* I. ii. 65.
worthyed, made worthy. *S.* III. iii. 63.
wrapt, rapt, transported. *G.* IV. ii. 239.
wreke, avenge. *G.* I. ii. 358, *et passim.*
wrekeful, avenging. *G.* II. i. 14, *et passim.*
wrie, indirect, deceitful. *G.* I. ii. 29.

yelden, resigned. *S.* II. iii. 41.
yfrought, *see fraught.*
ymeint, mingled. *S.* III. ii. 34.
yrke, find irksome. *A.* I. iv. 113.
yrkes, becomes weary of. *A.* I. ii. 29.

INDEX TO INTRODUCTION